Studies in Natural Language Processing

Inheritance, Defaults and the Lexicon

Studies in Natural Language Processing

Inheritance, Defaults and the Lexicon

Edited by
TED BRISCOE
ANN COPESTAKE
VALERIA DE PAIVA

CAMBRIDGE
UNIVERSITY PRESS

Published by the Press Syndicate of the University of Cambridge
The Pitt Building, Trumpington Street, Cambridge CB2 1RP
40 West 20th Street, New York, NY 10011-4211, USA
10 Stamford Road, Oakleigh, Melbourne 3166, Australia

© Cambridge University Press 1993

First published 1993

Typeset from Latex in Times by Hodgson Associates, Turnbridge Wells, UK.

Printed in the United States of America

Library of Congress Cataloging-in-Publication Data
Inheritance, defaults and the lexicon / edited by Ted Briscoe, Ann
    Copestake and Valeria de Paiva.
        p. cm.
    Includes bibliographical references and index.
    ISBN 0-521-43027-5
    1. Lexicology – Data processing.   2. Lexical grammar – Data
processing.   I. Briscoe, E. J., 1959–   . II. Copestake, Ann.
III. Paiva, Valeria de.
P326.I54   1993
413'.0285 – dc20   93-15210
                                                         CIP

A catalog record for this book is available from the British Library.

ISBN 0-521-43027-5 hardback

Contents

Contributors

Afzal Ballim   ISSCO, 54 route des Acacias, 1227 Geneva, Switzerland
Ted Briscoe   University of Cambridge Computer Laboratory,
New Museums Site, Pembroke Street, Cambridge, CB2 3QG, UK
Lynne J. Cahill   School of Cognitive and Computing Sciences,
University of Sussex, Brighton, BN1 9QN, Sussex, UK
Bob Carpenter   Philosophy Department,
Carnegie Mellon University, Pittsburgh, PA 15213, USA
John Carroll   University of Cambridge Computer Laboratory,
New Museums Site, Pembroke Street, Cambridge, CB2 3QG, UK
Ann Copestake   University of Cambridge Computer Laboratory,
New Museums Site, Pembroke Street, Cambridge, CB2 3QG, UK
Roger Evans   School of Cognitive and Computing Sciences,
University of Sussex, Brighton, BN1 9QN, Sussex, UK
Gerald Gazdar   School of Cognitive and Computing Sciences,
University of Sussex, Brighton, BN1 9QN, Sussex, UK
Hans-Ulrich Krieger   Deutsches Forschungszentrum für Künstliche Intelligenz, Stuhlsatzenhausweg 3, D-6600 Saarbrücken 11, Germany
Michael Morreau   IMS, University of Stuttgart, Keplerstrasse 17, D-7OOO Stuttgart 1, Germany
Lionel Moser   School of Cognitive and Computing Sciences,
University of Sussex, Brighton, BN1 9QN, Sussex, UK
John Nerbonne   Deutsches Forschungszentrum für Künstliche Intelligenz, Stuhlsatzenhausweg 3, D-6600 Saarbrücken 11, Germany
Valeria de Paiva   University of Cambridge Computer Laboratory,
New Museums Site, Pembroke Street, Cambridge, CB2 3QG, UK
Graham Russell   ISSCO, 54 route des Acacias, 1227 Geneva, Switzerland
Antonio Sanfilippo   University of Cambridge Computer Laboratory,
New Museums Site, Pembroke Street, Cambridge, CB2 3QG, UK
Susan Warwick-Armstrong   ISSCO, 54 route des Acacias, 1227 Geneva, Switzerland
Piek Vossen   Deptartment of English, University of Amsterdam,
Spuistraat 210, 1012 VT Amsterdam, Netherlands
Rémi Zajac   Project Polygloss, IMS-CL/IfI-AIS, University of Stuttgart, Keplerstrasse 17, D-7OOO Stuttgart 1, Germany

1   Introduction

TED BRISCOE

In recent years, the lexicon has become the focus of considerable research in (computational) linguistic theory and natural language processing (NLP) research; the reasons for this trend are both theoretical and practical. Within linguistics, the role of the lexicon has become increasingly central as more and more linguistic generalisations have been seen to have a lexical dimension, whilst for NLP systems, the lexicon has increasingly become the chief 'bottleneck' in the production of habitable applications offering an adequate vocabulary for the intended task. This edited collection of essays derives from a workshop held in Cambridge in April 1991 to bring together researchers from both Europe and America and from both fields working on formal and computational accounts of the lexicon. The workshop was funded under the European Strategic Programme in Information Technology (ESPRIT) Basic Research Action (BRA) through the ACQUILEX project ('Acquisition of Lexical Information for Natural Language Processing') and was hosted by the Computer Laboratory, Cambridge University.

The ACQUILEX project is concerned with the exploitation of machine-readable versions of conventional dictionaries in an attempt to develop substantial lexicons for NLP in a resource efficient fashion. However, the focus of the workshop was on the representation and organisation of information in the lexicon, regardless of the mode of acquisition. Nevertheless, several contributions present substantial lexical fragments, in keeping with this broader goal of unjamming the lexical 'bottleneck'; whilst the central issue of the workshop — the use of typing and (default) inheritance to impose more structure on lexical organisation — directly addresses the issue of keeping the lexicon tractable through effective expression and exploitation of lexical generalisations. All the contributions to this volume derive from presentations and subsequent discussion at the workshop, and all address pertinent issues in the design and development of lexicons within the context of contemporary unification-based grammatical theories, such as Head(-driven) Phrase Structure Grammar (HPSG, Pollard and Sag, 1987) or Unification Categorial Grammar (UCG, Zeevat *et al.*, 1987). This introduction is intended to place the research reported in the various contributions in the appropriate context: section 1.1 briefly describes the changing conception of the lexicon within (generative) linguistic theory, section 1.2 reviews relevant work on knowledge representation within the field of artificial intelligence and

1

goes on to outline some of the formal issues for a (unification-based) theory of lexical knowledge representation, providing the reader with a brief guide to the way in which each contribution addresses these issues. Section 1.3 suggests directions for further research.

1.1   The Lexicon in Linguistic Theory

The lexicon has usually been viewed as the repository of idiosyncratic and unpredictable facts about lexical items organised as an (alphabetic) list; for example, that *kill* in English means 'x cause y to die' and is a transitive verb with regular morphology. On the other hand, the fact that the subject of *kill* appears to the left of it in typical English sentences, or that its past participle is *killed*, were taken to be predictable and quite general statements about English syntax and morphophonology which should be stated independently of the lexicon. However, within generative linguistic theory since the 1970s there has been a consistent increase in the role of the lexicon in capturing linguistic generalisations, both in the sense that more and more of the rules of grammar are coming to be seen as formal devices which manipulate (aspects of) lexical entries, and in the sense that many of these rules are lexically governed and must, therefore, be restricted to more finely specified classes of lexical items than can be obtained from traditional part-of-speech classifications. As the importance of the lexicon has increased, so the role of other components of the overall theory of grammar has declined; thus in some contemporary theories, the syntactic component is reduced to one or two general principles for the combination of constituents, whilst all the information concerning the categorial identity and mode of combination of these constituents is projected from individual lexical entries. This makes it increasingly difficult to view the lexicon as an unrelated list of lexical entries (like a conventional dictionary) because such an organisation does not easily support flexible generalisation across classes of lexical items.

1.1.1   Lexical Grammar

Chomsky (1970) discussed the problems raised by nominalisation for generative (transformational) grammar and proposed a new theory of grammar in which lexical redundancy rules rather than transformations were used to express the relationship between a verb and a morphologically derived nominal. Chomsky's arguments for this modification were, in part, concerned with the restriction of transformational operations, but also with the idiosyncratic properties of many derived nominals; that is, the rules which relate derived nominals to their corresponding verbs are often semi-productive because, for example, although the morphological operation involved in the derivation of the nominal is regular, its primary meaning is specialised and unpredictable (*revolve, revolution*). Work following this influential paper has tended to emphasise the semi-productive or lexically governed nature of many other phenomena and to make greater use of formal devices, such as lexical redundancy rules, which serve to relate lexical entries and enrich the structure of the lexicon. The introduction to Moortgat *et al.* (1980) provides a detailed account of these developments.

One landmark in the development of lexical grammar is the account of sub-categorisation and coordination developed within Generalized Phrase Structure Grammar (GPSG, Gazdar *et al.*, 1985). Simplifying somewhat, lexical items are subcategorised via a feature which effectively indexes them to specific Phrase Structure (PS) rules which introduce their appropriate syntactic arguments as phrasal sisters; for example, the PS rules in (1a,b) are appropriate expansions for transitive verbs which take a noun phrase (NP) object and for verbs taking infinitival verb phrase (VP) objects, respectively.

(1)   a   VP → V[Subcat 2] NP[Acc]

        b   VP → V[Subcat 6] VP[Infin]

        c   X → X X[Conj and]

Verbs of each type will be listed in the lexicon with appropriate values for the Subcat feature, so *kill* would have the value 2, whilst *try* would be 6. GPSG also posited very general PS rule schemata for coordination of which a simplified example is given in (1c), for binary conjunction where X ranges over syntactic categories. These rules interact together to predict the (un)grammaticality of the examples in (2) in a simple and intuitive way.

(2)   a   Kim [$_{VP}$ [$_{VP}$ killed Sandy] [$_{VP}$ and tried to leave]]

        b   Kim killed [$_{NP}$ [$_{NP}$ Sandy] [$_{NP}$ and her friend]]

        c   Kim tried [$_{VP}$ [$_{VP}$ to pay] [$_{VP}$ and to leave]]

        d   *Kim killed [$_?$ [$_{NP}$ Sandy] [$_{VP}$ and to leave]]

Thus, coordination is constrained by lexical complementation in the form of PS rules indexed to lexical (sub)classes via the Subcat feature. However, the search for a unified account of local grammatical agreement led Pollard (1984) to propose a framework in which the Subcat feature takes as value an ordered list of syntactic categories and PS rules are replaced by a very general PS schema which combines a lexical item with the topmost category of its Subcat list and creates a new phrasal category with a 'popped' Subcat list. In this framework, the (simplified) lexical entry for a transitive verb would be (3a) and the PS schema would construct the analysis outlined in (3b) (where the Subcat feature is abbreviated to its value).

(3)   a   kill : V[Subcat <NP[Acc] NP[Nom]>]

        b   [$_{V[<>]}$ Kim [$_{V[<NP[Nom]>]}$ killed him]]

Agreement of features such as person, number or case (illustrated here) can be straightforwardly and uniformly enforced by encoding such features on categories specified on the Subcat list of lexical items. Within this framework, the syntactic component has been drastically reduced, since individual PS rules have been replaced by a single schema which builds constituents according to the specifications of Subcat lists projected from lexical entries. This schema will, however, interact with that for coordination in (1c) to cover the examples illustrated in (2).

One apparent disadvantage of this radically lexical approach to grammar is that it appears to involve considerable redundancy and loss of generalisation if the lexicon is organised as an unrelated list of entries; for example, (3a) encodes the information that the subject of *kill* combines with it after its object and that the subject must be nominative. However, these facts generalise to all verbs of English whilst the fact the *kill* takes only one object generalises to all transitive verbs. Further developments of syntactic theory have reinforced the trend to relocate information in the lexicon (e.g. Pollard and Sag, 1987; Steedman, 1985; Zeevat *et al.*, 1987). The contributions in this volume all address, directly or indirectly, issues of lexical organisation designed to eradicate this redundancy.

1.1.2   Lexical Semantics

Most formal semantic theories have concentrated on the problems of compositional rather than lexical semantics; that is, the construction of sentence meaning from the meaning of constituent words and phrases. Many lexical theories of grammar are monostratal, admitting only one level of syntactic representation (e.g. Gazdar *et al.*, 1985). These theories associate semantic representations with each syntactic constituent in some fashion; for instance, early versions of GPSG paired a semantic rule with each syntactic PS rule, which built the semantics of the left-hand mother category out of the semantics of each right-hand daughter category. Within the more radically lexical theories, the compositional semantics of (at least) lexical items and their syntactic arguments is also relocated in the lexicon. Such theories are often called sign-based because they formally instantiate Saussure's concept of a linguistic sign as the (arbitrary) association of sound, form and meaning (e.g. Pollard and Sag, 1987). In a sign-based theory, the lexical entry for a transitive verb will include the information that its syntactic subject and object function semantically as the (ordered) arguments of the predicate associated with the verb. This information too generalises to all transitive verbs, but locating it in the lexicon allows the same very general schema which is used to construct the syntactic representation of phrases and clauses to also build up the semantic representation in tandem. (An example of a lexical entry of this type is given in the next section.)

Recently, there has been renewed interest and research on the meaning of words themselves and, in particular, work on how lexical semantic properties affect both syntactic behaviour and compositional semantic interpretation. To take just two examples: Levin (1988, 1992) has argued that it is not adequate to simply list alternative syntactic realisations of verbs in terms of separate lexical entries with distinct values for the Subcat feature or its equivalent, because such alternate realisations are partly predictable on a semantic basis and may have semantic consequences. For instance, change of possession verbs such as *give* often undergo the dative alternation illustrated in (4a,b).

(4)   a   Kim gave the beer to Sandy
      b   Kim gave Sandy the beer
      c   Kim slid the beer to Sandy / the table edge
      d   Kim slid Sandy / *the table edge a beer

Change of position verbs such as *slide*, however, can only undergo the dative alternation if they can be interpreted as conveying a change of possession, as (4d) illustrates. Pustejovsky (1991) discusses examples such as (5a,b,c) in which *enjoy* conveys an identical relationship of pleasurable experience between the experiencer subject and an event denoted by the verb's object of which the experiencer is agent.

(5)   a   Kim enjoys making films
      b   Kim enjoys film-making
      c   Kim / Coppola enjoyed that film

Positing separate lexical entries on the basis of the differential syntactic realisations of *enjoy* with either an NP or progressive VP object fails to capture the semantic relatedness of these examples; thus, in (5b) we need to account for the manner in which the implicit agent of the event-denoting NP *film-making* is associated with Kim, whilst in (5c) we must explain the mechanism which allows *that film* to denote an event of Kim watching (or Coppola making) a film. Pustejovsky refers to this latter process as logical metonymy, since he argues that *enjoy* coerces its artifact-denoting NP object into an event of some type, whilst the lexical semantic representation of the NP itself determines the broad nature of the understood event — compare *Kim enjoyed a beer*.

Work of this type on lexical semantics, as well as much other research on, for example, aksionsart (Zaenen, 1993; Sanfilippo, 1990), the argument structure of derived nominals (Grimshaw, 1990), or regular polysemy (Copestake and Briscoe, 1991; Nunberg and Zaenen, 1992) poses a considerable challenge to lexical grammar and theories of lexical organisation. Such theories must demonstrate how lexical semantic information affects patterns of syntactic realisation and also the process of compositional interpretation. However, the uncovering of regularities and generalisations concerning lexical semantic properties also creates the need for further structure in the lexicon.

1.2   Knowledge Representation

The representation and intelligent manipulation of knowledge is a major area of research in Artificial Intelligence (AI). Knowledge representation languages

(KRLs) have been developed from 'network-like' representations of information organised around the principle of (default) inheritance between nodes of the network organised in terms of ISA hierarchies (see e.g. Brachman and Schmolze, 1985). The formal specification and development of KRLs remains an active area of research within AI, as does the wider study of default (nonmonotonic) logic (e.g. Reiter, 1980; Moore, 1985) as well as their interrelationships (Morreau, this volume). A theory of grammar must also provide a formal language with an appropriate syntax and semantics in which grammatical knowledge can be elegantly expressed and manipulated. As linguistic theories have become more lexical, the focus of such metatheoretical work has also shifted to the lexicon. I will refer to the language in which the lexicon is expressed as the lexical representation language (LRL). It is not clear that an adequate LRL should have all the properties of a general purpose KRL system. However, several researchers have suggested 'network-like' LRL schemes for lexical organisation based around the notion of default inheritance (de Smedt, 1984; Flickinger *et al.*, 1985), whilst Gazdar (1987) argued that nonmonotonic reasoning was applicable to both lexical and non-lexical linguistic phenomena. In what follows, I will restrict discussion to the application of these ideas within the lexical components of unification-based approaches to grammar. (Daelemans *et al.* (1992) provide a comprehensive overview of the use of default inheritance mechanisms within linguistic theory in general.)

1.2.1   The Lexical Representation Language

Most monostratal and lexical theories of grammar, such as LFG (Kaplan and Bresnan, 1982), GPSG (Gazdar *et al.*, 1985), HPSG (Pollard and Sag, 1987) or UCG (Zeevat *et al.*, 1987), treat syntactic categories as feature structures (FSs) with unification as the mode of combination of information in FSs. Unification is a form of bi-directional pattern matching used extensively in theorem proving and logic programming, which owes its introduction into linguistic theory as much to work in NLP (Kay, 1984; Shieber *et al.*, 1983) as to work on theories of lexical grammar. An FS for the transitive verb *kill* is given in Fig. 1.1 which could constitute (the syntactic and semantic part of) its lexical entry in a theory of the type outlined in §1.1.1. This FS is displayed in attribute-value matrix notation in which coindexing indicates token identity of subparts of the FS and bold face expressions give the type of each (sub)-FS (see below). Unification of two FSs, if defined, produces a new FS in which the information from both is monotonically combined. Shieber (1986) and Kasper and Rounds (1990) provide detailed introductions to unification-based approaches to grammar and to the syntax and semantics of the formalism.

The FS in Figure 1.1 is simple by comparison to that which would be required in a realistic, wide-coverage grammar, yet already it encodes a large amount of information much of which is true of other transitive verbs. The LRL should

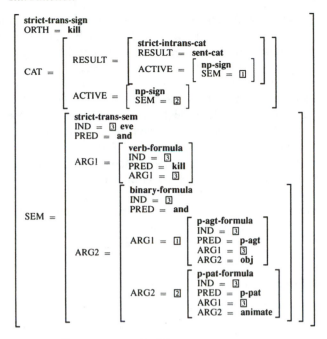

Figure 1.1: Feature structure for *kill*

allow the aspects of this FS common to all transitive verbs to be expressed just once rather than repeated in each individual lexical entry. Shieber *et al.* (1983) describe the use of lexical templates to name and define subparts of FSs common to classes of lexical items and to abbreviate entries themselves to lists of template names which would be expanded to full FSs on demand. This approach compacts lexical entries and allows the expression of many generalisations, particularly as templates can be embedded within other template definitions. However, templates are abbreviatory devices which do not enforce any specific organisation of the lexicon and which do not strongly constrain the featural content of FSs. Flickinger *et al.* (1985) and Pollard and Sag (1987) propose that the lexicon be represented as an inheritance hierarchy in which information common to a class of lexical items is inherited by all its subclasses; thus, the information that verbs take nominative subjects is associated with the verb class node and inherited by all subclasses, such as transitive verbs. These proposals enrich the structure of the lexicon in a fashion which allows generalisations about lexical (sub)classes to be expressed economically.

Following Aït-Kaci (1984), Moens *et al.* (1989) present a typed FS system and Carpenter (1990, 1992) develops a scheme in which FSs are typed and structured via a partial order on types. Thus, a type places appropriateness conditions on a class of FSs and these conditions must also be satisfied by FSs which are subtypes of that type. The type system can be used to define an inheritance hierarchy in which FSs 'lower' in the type hierarchy are monotonically enriched with information derived from appropriateness conditions. Carpenter's (1992) framework can be used to define an LRL in which commonalities between lexical entries can be captured succinctly in terms of the type system, whilst the operations that generate fully specified entries via the inheritance system are defined in terms of standard, declarative unification-based operations. These proposals constitute a considerable strengthening of the theory of lexical organisation, and Carpenter's framework is capable of expressing the hierarchical, inheritance based theory of lexical organisation outlined in Pollard and Sag (1987). Zajac (this volume), Copestake *et al.* (this volume) and de Paiva (this volume) all describe what are basically variants of this general approach. However, unfortunately much of the elegance of the approach is gained at the cost of the expressivity of the resulting system, in that no account of default inheritance has been developed within this framework.

1.2.2   *Default Inheritance*

Though inheritance based on typing is formally attractive, the inheritance system defined is monotonic and absolute, and there appear to be linguistic phenomena which require a notion of default inheritance if the pattern of regularities and sub-regularities which occur in the lexicon is to be characterised insightfully. For example, regular past participle formation in English involves the 'addition' of the *+ed* morpheme to the verb stem (e.g. *walk, walked; touch, touched*). However, there are verbs for which past participle formation is irregular (e.g. *sleep, slept; write, wrote*) and within these irregular verbs there are subregular classes (as well as purely lexical exceptions, such as *go, went*). We can express the relationship between the regular and subregular classes and lexical exceptions in terms of default inheritance, as indicated schematically in Figure 1.2, where material in brackets abbreviates the morphosyntactic and morphophonological properties of the past participle, and the names preceding the bracketed material designate classes or instances of classes.

Construed informally as a default inheritance hierarchy, Figure 1.2 states that all the verbs mentioned are members of the class 'Verb', and may, therefore, be expected to (default) inherit verbal properties associated with this class. One such property is that of forming a past participle through addition of *+ed*. However, this property is overruled by the two irregular subclasses and the irregular item *go* by the explicit introduction of a subregular rule or instance of past participle formation (though in other respects these subclasses will, by default, behave as predicted by the class 'Verb'). This approach allows us to capture the intuition that, say, *sleep* is a verb which is just abnormal with respect to past participle formation. Furthermore, since the *+t* specification 'contradicts' the regular one, the majority of formalisations of default inheritance override the

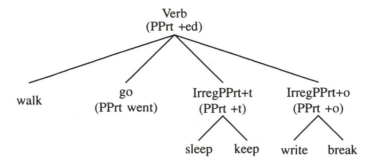

Figure 1.2: Schematic default inheritance hierarchy

regular specification, and thus predict the ungrammaticality of *sleeped* (but see Fraser and Hudson (1992) for an exception). Within typed inheritance frameworks, such as that of Carpenter (1992), it is not possible to describe these facts in this manner. Instead it would be necessary to treat the classes of irregular and regular past participle formation verbs as distinct and unrelated subtypes of a type that did not specify any details of this process, thus missing the intuition that the irregular cases are subregularities which block or preempt the regular one (e.g. Aronoff, 1976).

Several of the contributions to this volume consider the issue of augmenting a unification-based system with default inheritance using the mechanisms of default unification; Carpenter (this volume) provides an overview of the problems of providing a satisfactory definition of default unification, ordering of inheritance in the case of inheritance of non-orthogonal (inconsistent) information from multiple sources, and so forth. Copestake (this volume) describes the particular approach taken to these problems in the use of default unification in a typed FSs system incorporating orthogonal default inheritance; the ACQUILEX LKB. Russell *et al.* (this volume) present a unification-based system (ELU) which incorporates default multiple inheritance and prioritisation by canonical ordering, in the case of non-orthogonality. Krieger and Nerbonne (this volume) also describe a typed FS system which employs default unification to induce default multiple inheritance for the specification of inflectional rules. Evans *et al.* (this volume) present a different lexical theory of default inheritance (DATR) based on operations on path specifications of the type employed in PATR (Shieber, 1986). This approach is compatible with any linguistic theory employing attribute-value structures, including unification-based ones. Evans *et al.* show that prioritised multiple default inheritance, as well as orthogonal inheritance, can be expressed within this theory. Each of these approaches can, in principle, express the pattern of regularity and subregularity found in past participle formation and schematised in Figure 1.2, and indeed much else (see section 1.2.3 below).

1.2.3   Lexical Rules

One feature of the sketch of past participle formation outlined above is that it fails to capture the creative aspect of such processes in terms of 'rules' that license alternative lexical entries on the basis of the prior existence of a 'base' morphologically simple entry of the appropriate class. The extent to which it is possible to dispense with lexical rules through the use of more expressive theories of lexical inheritance and organisation is considered explicitly by Krieger and Nerbonne (this volume) and is implicit in most of the approaches represented. For instance, DATR incorporates no such notion, whilst ELU restricts itself to (disjunctive) specification of variant entries within a class. Krieger and Nerbonne argue that lexical rules are not required for inflectional morphological processes and propose a more syntagmatic and structuralist morpheme-based view of processes of derivation and conversion.

Most formulations of lexical rules are unattractively powerful and not unification-based. Shieber *et al.*'s (1983) lexical rules encode arbitrary (non-monotonic) mappings between two FSs as sets of 'input' and 'output' path equations. Pollard and Sag (1987) treat lexical rules as conditional implications between typed lexical signs (i.e. FSs). Flickinger and Nerbonne (1992) propose an even more flexible and powerful mechanism in which lexical rules map between word classes in a default inheritance hierarchy which do not necessarily stand in an inheritance relationship, imposing additional constraints and creating derived entries. Copestake and Briscoe (1991) generalise Carpenter's (1992) framework to incorporate a lexical rule default inheritance hierarchy whose rules map typed FSs into other typed FSs (whose types are not in a subsumption relation) imposing arbitrary (nonmonotonic) constraints. Carpenter (1991) demonstrates that all these approaches are potentially too powerful in that, when combined with categorial or HPSG-style approaches to subcategorisation, they allow the associated theories to generate all the recursively enumerable languages.

Bresnan and Kanerva (1989) make use of a more restrictive notion of lexical rule which only allows monotonic enrichment of underspecified FSs for capturing certain types of grammatical relation changing rules. However, it is not clear how this more restrictive type of lexical rule (which basically reduces lexical rules to a type of inheritance relation) would be capable of expressing derivational morphological rules or rules of conversion. For example, it is difficult to see how the rules which relate verbs to their derived nominal counterparts (e.g. *teach* → *teacher, teaching, purchase* → *purchaser, purchase* etc.) can be reduced to monotonic enrichments of underspecified lexical entries, since it is part of the conventional wisdom concerning such rules that they relate basic verbs to derived nouns. The approach taken by Krieger and Nerbonne (this volume) circumvents this problem at the cost of requiring the introduction of zero-morphemes to characterise processes of conversion. In addition, Russell *et al.* (this volume) make crucial use of the variant mechanism in ELU in their characterisation of the class of 'dual-past' verbs (e.g. *dream, dreamt, dreamed*), suggesting that, in cases where blocking is not absolute, we will require more complex mechanisms than default inheritance (as defined in all the approaches represented here).

1.2.4 Lexical Fragments

Despite its novelty, the more structured approach to lexical specification based on (default) inheritance has prompted development of a considerable number of lexical fragments, such as Andry *et al.* (1992), Flickinger (1987), Sanfilippo and Poznanski (1992) and Copestake (1992b) (see Daelemans *et al.* (1992) for a comprehensive overview). Cahill (this volume) reports the re-representation of a substantial lexicon for traffic report processing in DATR and discusses the consequent advantages of reformulation. Krieger and Nerbonne (this volume) consider in detail a small fragment of German inflectional and derivational morphology. Sanfilippo (this volume) and Copestake and Vossen (this volume) discuss the use of the ACQUILEX LKB in a substantial treatment of English verb complementation and in the construction of a lexical semantic inheritance hierarchy for English nouns from a machine-readable dictionary, respectively.

1.3 Future Research

Several researchers have proposed to augment or replace the lexical theories discussed above with more powerful and expressive mechanisms. Quite apart from the issue of lexical rules discussed above, Carpenter (1992) and others have proposed disjunctive constraint languages, Flickinger and Nerbonne (1992) advocate the use of an unrestricted network-based, default inheritance formalism of the type familiar from artificial intelligence and object-oriented programming, and so forth. Unconstrained addition of such operations considerably complicates either the computational tractability or the semantic interpretation of the formalism, or both, and there is still debate over which such extensions are linguistically and formally desirable. In a wider context, it is not clear that a restriction to unification-based formalisms is either tenable or desirable; Pustejovsky (1991), for example, makes use of mechanisms drawn from general purpose knowledge representation languages developed within artificial intelligence to characterise certain lexical semantic processes. Hobbs *et al.* (1987) argue that capturing the semantics of lexical items requires a first-order logical representation and mechanisms which support abductive as well as deductive inference. Undoubtedly the inferential processes involved in language comprehension extend beyond the limited mechanisms provided within unification-based formalisms; however, it is not clear yet whether lexical operations *per se* require them.

There are many challenging theoretical issues, particularly in the area of lexical semantics, which must be addressed before anything like an adequate theory of the lexicon can be developed. However, the research environment made possible by the availability of a variety of (implemented) prototypes should make exploration and development of lexical theories considerably easier — ideas which until recently had to be tested introspectively or by laboriously searching through printed dictionaries can now often be explored in a matter of seconds using available databases based on machine-readable dictionaries in conjunction with such prototypes (see, e.g. Boguraev and Briscoe, 1989). As it becomes easier to develop substantial lexical fragments from existing resources, problems such as the reusability, maintainability and modifiability of lexical systems become pressing (e.g. Briscoe, 1991). However, there seems little doubt that the highly structured approaches to lexicon organisation proposed in this book will provide a sound basis for solving such problems.

Acknowledgements

I would like to thank Ann Copestake and Valeria de Paiva for undertaking much of the work involved in organising the workshop and editing this collection, as well as the ESPRIT programme for making the workshop possible.

2   Skeptical and Credulous Default Unification with Applications to Templates and Inheritance

BOB CARPENTER

Abstract

We present a definition of skeptical and credulous variants of default unification, the purpose of which is to add default information from one feature structure to the strict information given in another. Under the credulous definition, the default feature structure contributes as much information to the result as is consistent with the information in the strict feature structure.[1] Credulous default unification turns out to be non-deterministic due to the fact that there may be distinct maximal subsets of the default information which may be consistently combined with the strict information. Skeptical default unification is obtained by restricting the default information to that which is contained in every credulous result. Both definitions are fully abstract in that they depend only on the information ordering of feature structures being combined and not on their internal structure, thus allowing them to be applied to just about any notion of feature structure and information ordering. We then consider the utility of default unification for constructing templates with default information and for defining how information is inherited in an inheritance-based grammar. In particular, we see how templates in the style of PATR-II can be defined, but conclude that such mechanisms are overly sensitive to order of presentation. Unfortunately, we only obtain limited success in applying default unification to simple systems of default inheritance. We follow the Common Lisp Object System-based approach of Russell *et al.* (1990, this volume), in which information is always inherited from more specific sources before being inherited from more general sources. But in the case of orthogonal (multiple) inheritance in which information is inherited from distinct sources of incomparable specificity, a depth-first ordering is imposed based on the linear specification of the inheritance hierarchy.

2.1   Introduction

In many approaches to knowledge representation, some flavor of attribute-value logic is used to characterize objects in the empirical domain. In particular, the most well-known non-transformational linguistic formalisms such as LFG,

---

[1] Jo Calder (1991) independently proposed a definition of 'priority union' which is equivalent to our definition of credulous default unification.

GPSG and HPSG are (or can be) expressed in terms of attribute-value logics with fairly straightforward semantics. From the point of view of natural language processing, the attribute-value logics employed in these formalisms can be effectively characterized in terms of feature structures, where logical conjunction can be efficiently computed by unification. Our presentation in this chapter is based on feature structures, but it naturally generalizes to alternative treatments of attribute-value logics such as those proposed by Aït-Kaci (1986), Pereira and Shieber (1984), Johnson (1988) and Smolka (1988).

Most current linguistic theories such as LFG, HPSG, GPSG, CG, GB, along with many others, partition grammatical information into syntactic and lexical components. The distinction between the two components usually comes down to the fact that syntax involves some notion of recursive structure, while the lexicon is where information about the linguistic categories assigned to surface expressions is used to ground out the structural recursion. These linguistic theories employ syntactic components which are highly streamlined, with the burden of the representational work being placed on the lexicon. It is not unusual to see grammars with lexical categories represented by feature structures with more than one hundred nodes. Thus there is a strong demand for expressive methods of lexical knowledge representation and in particular, methods for expressing generalizations. But most useful lexical generalizations have exceptions and it is laborious to constantly introduce new concepts into an inheritance hierarchy to cover exceptional cases. Our focus in this paper is the extension of lexical inheritance to defaults. Of course, when grammar rules are stated in the same language as the lexicon, as in HPSG (Pollard and Sag, 1987), FUG (Kay, 1984) and PATR-II (Shieber *et al.*, 1983), then the techniques presented here can be applied to syntactic information organization as well.

In unification-based grammar processing systems such as PATR-II and its descendents, a collection of hierarchically dependent templates may be defined and then incorporated into the definition of lexical entries and grammar rules. Using an example from HPSG (Pollard and Sag 1987), one template can be used for information about subcategorization, while another can contain information about agreement. Such templates are orthogonal, while a template for a transitive verb with a sentential object is more specific than a template for a transitive verb, which is in turn more specific than the template for an arbitrary lexical verb, which is itself more specific than the template for an arbitrary verbal category. By making use of such templates, lexical entries and grammar rules can be expressed much more succinctly than if the lexical entry for each word had to be independently specified.

It is widely believed that the organization of practical knowledge representation systems should allow for some notion of information that can be obtained by default. But as soon as the term 'default' is introduced, a number of possible interpretations immediately present themselves. Thus we try to make clear up front which particular kind of default reasoning we try to capture. We follow the intuition that defaults provide a method for allowing information to be deduced about an object if it is consistent with what is already known about the object. We also follow a number of other motivations, which include the restriction that more specific information should overrule information gained from more general sources. Such intuitions are guided by the (in)famous Tweety Triangle in which Tweety is a penguin, penguins are birds, birds are fliers, but penguins are non-fliers.[2] Here the intuition is that Tweety is not a flier, as the information that Tweety is a penguin is more specific than the information that Tweety is a bird. But other intuitions are tested when we consider the pacifism of Nixon in the Nixon Diamond example in which Nixon is both a quaker and a republican, while quakers are pacifists and republicans are non-pacifists. We consider ways to resolve information conflicts related to that found in the Nixon Diamond. There are two sources in which such conflicts can arise. The first is when we are unifying one feature structure by default into another and there are two pieces of information in the default feature structure which are consistent with the strict information, but are inconsistent with the strict information when taken together. The second is when we are resolving conflicts across levels of an inheritance hierarchy as in the Nixon Diamon example itself.

We consider two distinct approaches to default unification. Both approaches are non-symmetric in that they are designed to take one feature structure representing strict information and add in the information in a second feature structure representing default information. The methods vary in terms of how much inconsistency they are willing to tolerate before concluding that a piece of default information should be discarded. Credulous unification gets its name from the fact that it tries to add as much of the default information as is possible to the strict information without creating an inconsistency. As there may in general be distinct maximal subsets of the default information which can be consistently added to the strict information, credulous default unification may return more than one result. For instance, in the Nixon Diamond case, a credulous reasoner would conclude non-deterministically that either Nixon is a pacificist or that Nixon is not a pacificist. On the other hand, skeptical unification is deterministic in that it keeps all and only the default information that is contained in every credulous result. Thus in a skeptical approach to reasoning, we would not be able to conclude that Nixon is either a pacificist or that he is not a pacifist.

Even with what we take to be a sensible definition of default unification, we see that our problems are far from over when it comes to designing a lexical template or inheritance system that is defined in terms of default unification. We present a standard definition of templatic inheritance with defaults which suffers

---

[2] While the Tweety Triangle usually arises with ISA and ISNOTA links, it can just as easily arise with feature inheritance. Consider a case where the bird concept provides a value **yes** to a feature such as FLIER while the penguin concept provides the contradictory value **no** for the FLIER feature.

from a sensitivity to order that overrides even the specificity ordering induced on the templates. Templates are also not very satisfying in that constraints from a single template are incorporated piecemeal and interleaved with information from inherited templates rather than being taken as a unified whole. In particular, the standard approach to templates emphasizes user presentation order by employing a completely depth-first strategy to unfold template definitions. For instance, a default feature value which was specified to hold in a template definition before a strict value would cause a conflict in that the default is added if it is consistent with the information already inherited up to the point at which the default is found without considering what strict information might come later that might override it.

After considering templatic inheritance, we consider an approach to default inheritance which inherits information from more specific sources before information from more general sources. We allow information attached to a concept in an inheritance hierarchy to be marked as either strict or default. Strict information is all inherited and taken to override any default information. In particular, strict information on a superconcept overrides default information on a subconcept. After carrying out strict inheritance, default information is inherited by default unification. The order in which default structures are unified is based on the resolution strategy of the Common Lisp Object System, an idea first considered by Russell *et al.* (1990, this volume). But even with this approach, there is residual order-sensitivity when inconsistencies arise from a combination of information from sources neither of which is more specific than the other. In these cases, user presentation order is used to resolve conflicts with results that may be surprising.

2.2   Feature Structures

In this section we review the basics of feature structures, including subsumption (information entailment) and unification (information conjunction). We only consider the most straightforward PATR-style feature structures. The definition of defaults that we present later is sufficiently abstract that it can be applied to more sophisticated notions of feature structure such as those presented by Aït-Kaci (1986), Moshier (1988), Moshier and Rounds (1987) and Carpenter (1990).

Feature structures are a means of representing information about the value of an object's attributes or features. To get off the ground, we assume a finite set Feat of *basic features* and a finite set Atom of *atomic values*. We display features such as NUM, VFORM, SUBCAT in small capitals and atoms such as **sing**, **present-participle** and **noun** in bold face. A feature structure is either basic, in which case it must be one of the atomic values, or it is complex, in which case it provides values for a number of features. These values in turn are themselves taken to be either atomic or complex feature structures.

2.2.1 Feature Structures

Following Kasper and Rounds (1986, 1990), we define feature structures as a kind of labeled finite-state automata. The standard graph of such an automata brings out the relationship between feature structures and other frame-based knowledge representation systems. The only complications in the definition stems from the standard treatment of atomic values which must be such that there are no features defined for an atomic feature structure. We thus allow atomic values to label some (but not necessarily all) of the nodes in the graph from which there are no outgoing arcs.

Definition 1 (Feature Structure) *A feature structures is a tuple* $F = \langle Q, q_0, \delta, \alpha \rangle$ *where:*

- *Q: a finite set of* nodes
- *$q_0 \in Q$: the* root node
- *δ : Feat $\times Q \to Q$: the partial* feature value *function*
- *$\alpha : Q \to$ Atom : the partial* atomic value *function*

subject to the following constraints:[3]

- (Connectedness)
  every node must be reachable from the root (see below)
- (Atomic Values)
  only nodes without features can be atomic values so that if $\alpha(q)$ is defined then $\delta(f, q)$ is undefined for every $f \in$ Feat
- (Acyclic)
  the resulting graph is acyclic in that there is no path π and non-empty path π' such that $\delta(\pi, q_0) = \delta(\pi \cdot \pi', q_0)$ (see below).

We provide two graphical depictions of the same feature structure in Figure 2.1 and Figure 2.2. The diagram in Figure 2.1 shows the graphical representation of feature structures in a standard finite-state transition diagram. This graphical notation soon becomes unwieldy, and so it is standardized in a record- and frame-like attribute-value matrix notation displayed in Figure 2.2. In the attribute-value matrix notation, each bracketed grouping corresponds to a node in the graphical representation. The tag [4] in Figure 2.2 is taken to indicate structure sharing for subgraphs. Using this notation, substructures that are reachable by different sequences of features are displayed only once.

---

[3] Sometimes the atomic value function α is required to be one to one, as in Pereira and Shieber (1984) and Rounds and Kasper (1986, 1990). Everything we say is compatible with such an assumption as with the more general notions of extensionality discussed in Carpenter (1990).

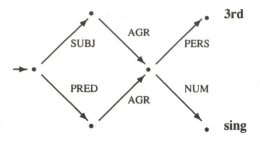

Figure 2.1: Feature structure: graph notation

$$\begin{bmatrix} \text{subj} : \begin{bmatrix} \text{AGR} : \boxed{4} \begin{bmatrix} \text{PERS} : \textbf{3rd} \\ \text{NUM} : \textbf{sing} \end{bmatrix} \end{bmatrix} \\ \text{PRED} : \begin{bmatrix} \text{AGR} : \boxed{4} \end{bmatrix} \end{bmatrix}$$

Figure 2.2: Feature structure: AVM notation

It is important to be able to represent sequences of features, which are called *paths*, so we take Path = Feat*. We let ϵ be the empty path. We extend the definition of the transition function to paths by taking $\delta(\epsilon, q) = q$ and $\delta(f \cdot \pi, q) = \delta(\pi, \delta(f, q))$. We say that q' is *reachable* from q if there is a path π such that $q' = \delta(\pi, q)$. Thus it can be seen that the connectedness requirement amounts to requiring there to be a path of features from the root node to every other node in the feature structure.

It should also be noted that we have explicitly ruled out cyclic feature structures. Acyclicity is easily enforced by requiring that no path has a proper extension that leads to the same node as it does. Acyclic feature structures needlessly complicate results that are most easily presented in terms of acyclic feature structures. Our definitions below could be extended to allow cycles, but we do not do so here.

2.2.2   Subsumption

In this section we see how two feature structures can be compared to determine when one contains more information than the other. Our approach to subsumption is due to Moshier (1988) and Moshier and Rounds (1987). In particular, for each feature structure, we associate a pair of sets which determine the path equivalences that hold and the atomic values assigned to paths by a feature structure. In particular, we let $\equiv_F$ be the equivalence relation induced between paths by the structure sharing in F and let $\mathcal{P}_F$ be the partial function induced by F which maps paths in F to atomic values.

Definition 2 (Abstract Feature Structure) *If* $F = \langle Q, q_0, \delta, \alpha \rangle$ *is a feature structure, we let* $\equiv_F \subseteq$ Path $\times$ Path *and* $\mathcal{P}_F$: Path $\rightarrow$ Atom *be such that:*

- *(Path Equivalence)*
  $\pi \equiv_F \pi'$ *if and only if* $\delta(\pi, q_0) = \delta(\pi', q_0)$
- *(Path Value)*
  $\mathcal{P}_F(\pi) = \sigma$ *if and only if* $\alpha(\delta(\pi, q_0)) = \sigma$

The pair $\langle \mathcal{P}, \equiv_F \rangle$ is called the abstract feature structure *corresponding to F.*

We see below that both the path equivalence relation and path value function are in fact finite for any feature structure, a useful consequence of eliminating cyclic feature structures which are always defined for infinitely many paths.

We say that a feature structure F subsumes another feature structure F' if and only if the information in F is contained in the information in F'; that is, if F' provides at least as much information about path values and structure sharing as F. Thus the abstract feature structure corresponding to F is sufficient to determine its information content and thus subsumption.

Definition 3 (Subsumption) *F subsumes F', written $F \sqsubseteq F'$, if and only if:*

- $\pi \equiv_F \pi'$ *implies* $\pi \equiv_{F'} \pi'$
- $\mathcal{P}_F(\pi) = \sigma$ *implies* $\mathcal{P}_{F'}(\pi) = \sigma$

Thus F subsumes F' if and only if every piece of information in F is contained in F'. Some examples of subsumption are as follows, where each left-hand side properly subsumes the right-hand side in that the converse subsumptions do not hold.

(1) $\quad \begin{bmatrix} \text{F} : \mathbf{a} \end{bmatrix} \sqsubseteq \begin{bmatrix} \text{G} : \mathbf{a} \\ \text{G} : \mathbf{b} \end{bmatrix}$

(2) $\quad \begin{bmatrix} \text{H} : \begin{bmatrix} \text{F} : \mathbf{a} \end{bmatrix} \end{bmatrix} \sqsubseteq \begin{bmatrix} \text{H} : \begin{bmatrix} \text{F} : \mathbf{a} \\ \text{G} : \mathbf{b} \end{bmatrix} \\ \text{J} : \mathbf{c} \end{bmatrix}$

(3) $\quad \begin{bmatrix} \text{F} : \begin{bmatrix} \text{G} : \mathbf{a} \end{bmatrix} \\ \text{G} : \begin{bmatrix} \text{G} : \mathbf{a} \end{bmatrix} \end{bmatrix} \sqsubseteq \begin{bmatrix} \text{F} : \boxed{1} \begin{bmatrix} \text{G} : \mathbf{a} \end{bmatrix} \\ \text{G} : \boxed{1} \end{bmatrix}$

We let $\bot$ be the single node feature structure with no atomic value assigned. Thus $\pi \equiv_\bot \pi'$ if and only if $\pi = \pi' = \epsilon$ and $\mathcal{P}(F)$ is undefined everywhere. Note that $\bot \sqsubseteq F$ for every feature structure F. We sometimes include $\bot$ in our attribute-value matrices to denote the lack of any known value.

We are not interested in the difference between feature structures which only vary in the identity of their nodes and if $F \sqsubseteq F'$ and $F' \sqsubseteq F$ then we say that F and F' are *alphabetic variants*. None of our definitions are sensitive to the difference between feature structures which are alphabetic variants.

2.2.3   Unification

Unification is an operation of information conjunction, and as such, can be naturally defined in terms of subsumption, a relation of information containment.

The unification of two feature structures is defined to be the most general feature structure which contains all the information in both of the feature structures. In particular, we have the following standard definition.

Definition 4 (Unification)   *The unification $F \sqcup F'$ of two feature structures F and F' is taken to be the least upper bound of F and F' in the collection of feature structures ordered by subsumption.*

Unpacking the definition, $F \sqcup F' = F''$ if and only if $F \sqsubseteq F''$, $F' \sqsubseteq F''$ and for every F''' such that $F \sqsubseteq F'''$ and $F' \sqsubseteq F'''$ we have $F'' \sqsubseteq F'''$. Moshier (1988) shows how to define unification directly in terms of abstract feature structures and also proves that the operation is well-defined up to alphabetic variance.   Consistency is defined in terms of unification, where two feature structures F and F' are said to be *consistent* if their unification $F \sqcup F'$ is defined. Similarly, a finite set $\{F_1, \ldots, F_n\}$ is said to be consistent if $F_1 \sqcup \cdots \sqcup F_n$ is well-defined. Some examples of unification are given below.

(4) $\left[\text{F} : \mathbf{a} \right] \sqcup \left[\text{G} : \mathbf{b} \right] = \begin{bmatrix} \text{F} : \mathbf{a} \\ \text{G} : \mathbf{b} \end{bmatrix}$

(5) $\begin{bmatrix} \text{F} : \boxed{1} \\ \text{G} : \boxed{1} \end{bmatrix} \sqcup \begin{bmatrix} \text{F} : \begin{bmatrix} \text{H} : \mathbf{a} \end{bmatrix} \\ \text{G} : \begin{bmatrix} \text{J} : \mathbf{b} \end{bmatrix} \end{bmatrix} = \begin{bmatrix} \text{F} : \boxed{1} \begin{bmatrix} \text{H} : \mathbf{a} \\ \text{J} : \mathbf{b} \end{bmatrix} \\ \text{G} : \boxed{1} \end{bmatrix}$

(6) $\begin{bmatrix} \text{F} : \begin{bmatrix} \text{G} : \mathbf{a} \\ \text{H} : \mathbf{b} \end{bmatrix} \\ \text{J} : \begin{bmatrix} \text{G} : \mathbf{a} \\ \text{H} : \mathbf{c} \end{bmatrix} \end{bmatrix} \sqcup \begin{bmatrix} \text{F} : \boxed{1} \\ \text{J} : \boxed{1} \end{bmatrix}$ undefined

(7) $\begin{bmatrix} \text{F} : \boxed{1} \begin{bmatrix} \text{G} : \bot \end{bmatrix} \\ \text{H} : \begin{bmatrix} \text{J} : \boxed{1} \end{bmatrix} \end{bmatrix} \sqcup \begin{bmatrix} \text{F} : \begin{bmatrix} \text{G} : \boxed{2} \end{bmatrix} \\ \text{H} : \boxed{2} \begin{bmatrix} \text{J} : \bot \end{bmatrix} \end{bmatrix}$ undefined

(8) $\left[\text{F} : \mathbf{a} \right] \sqcup \left[\text{F} : \begin{bmatrix} \text{G} : \mathbf{b} \end{bmatrix} \right]$ undefined

The notion of abstract feature structure yields a number of pleasant technical results. The most important of these results for our purposes is that every feature structure can be decomposed into a unification of atomic feature structures, where atomic feature structures are defined as follows:

Definition 5 (Atomic Feature Structure)   *A feature structure is* atomic *if it is of one of the following two forms:*

- (Path Value)
  the feature structure contains a single path assigned to an atomic value.
- (Path Sharing)
  the feature structure contains only a pair of (possibly identical) paths which are shared.

Thus an atomic feature structure consists of either a single path being assigned an atomic value or the structure sharing between two (possibly identical) paths. The case where two identical paths are shared yields the information that the path is defined but its value is not known. Of course, these are just the components that make up our definition of $\equiv_F$ and $\mathcal{P}(F)$. We define a notation for extracting the atomic feature structures from a given feature structure:

(9) $At(F) = \{F' \sqsubseteq F \mid F' \text{ atomic}\}$

In general, we have the following results concerning the atomic decomposition of a feature structure.

Proposition 1

- $At(F)$ *is finite*
- $F = \bigsqcup At(F)$
- *if* $A \in At(F)$ *then if* $A = G \sqcup G'$ *then* $A = G$ *or* $A = G'$
- $F \sqsubseteq F'$ *if and only if* $At(F) \subseteq At(F')$

Proof: The fact that $At(F)$ is finite stems from the fact that there are only finitely many paths defined in any given feature structure.

The fact that $F = \bigsqcup At(F)$ arises from the fact that every piece of information in F is captured by some atomic feature structure in $At(F)$, so that $F \sqsubseteq \bigsqcup At(F)$. But since $G \sqsubseteq F$ for every $G \in At(F)$, we have $\bigsqcup At(F) \sqsubseteq F$ and hence $\bigsqcup At(F) = F$.

Neither information about a single path sharing or an atomic value can come from a feature structure which is not subsumed by an atomic one so that if $G \sqcup G' = F$ then either $F \sqsubseteq G$ or $F \sqsubseteq G'$, in which case the conditions that $G \neq F$ and $G' \neq F$ and $G \sqcup G' = F$ cannot be simultaneously satisfied.

The fact that subsumption reduces to inclusion of atomic constraints follows from the definition of subsumption. □

Of course this gives us a set-theoretic characterization of the information in feature structures as sets of atomic feature structures, a technique exploited originally by Pereira and Shieber (1984) and later by Moshier (1988). Taking this view of feature structures makes many of the following definitions easier to digest, particularly as we keep in mind the last of the above results which allows us to reduce subsumption to set inclusion between atomic feature structures.

2.2.4   *Generalization*

For our purposes, the order-theoretic dual to unification in which the greatest lower bound of two feature structures is computed is useful when it comes to define the skeptical form of default unification. The generalization of two feature structures is defined to be the most specific feature structure which contains only information found in both feature structures.

Definition 6 (Generalization)   *The generalization $F \sqcap F'$ of two feature structures is defined to be their greatest lower bound in the subsumption ordering.*

Some examples of generalization are as follows:

(10) $$\begin{bmatrix} \text{F} : \mathbf{a} \\ \text{G} : \mathbf{b} \end{bmatrix} \sqcap \begin{bmatrix} \text{G} : \mathbf{b} \\ \text{H} : \mathbf{c} \end{bmatrix} = \begin{bmatrix} \text{G} : \mathbf{b} \end{bmatrix}$$

(11) $$\begin{bmatrix} \text{F} : \boxed{1}\,\mathbf{a} \\ \text{G} : \boxed{1} \end{bmatrix} \sqcap \begin{bmatrix} \text{F} : \mathbf{c} \\ \text{G} : \mathbf{b} \end{bmatrix} = \begin{bmatrix} \text{F} : \bot \\ \text{G} : \mathbf{b} \end{bmatrix}$$

(12) $$\begin{bmatrix} \text{F} : \boxed{1}\begin{bmatrix} \text{G} : \mathbf{a} \\ \text{H} : \mathbf{b} \end{bmatrix} \\ \text{J} : \boxed{1} \end{bmatrix} \sqcap \begin{bmatrix} \text{F} : \boxed{2}\begin{bmatrix} \text{G} : \mathbf{a} \\ \text{H} : \mathbf{c} \end{bmatrix} \\ \text{G} : \boxed{2} \end{bmatrix} = \begin{bmatrix} \text{F} : \boxed{3}\begin{bmatrix} \text{G} : \mathbf{a} \\ \text{H} : \bot \end{bmatrix} \\ \text{G} : \boxed{3} \end{bmatrix}$$

It is important to note that while unification corresponds to conjunction, generalization does not correspond to disjunction (a detailed discussion of this point may be found in Pollard and Moshier, 1990). In particular, the distributive law fails so that for instance:

(13) $(\begin{bmatrix} \text{F} : \mathbf{a} \end{bmatrix} \sqcap \begin{bmatrix} \text{F} : \mathbf{b} \end{bmatrix}) \sqcup \begin{bmatrix} \text{F} : \mathbf{c} \end{bmatrix} = \begin{bmatrix} \text{F} : \mathbf{c} \end{bmatrix} \neq (\begin{bmatrix} \text{F} : \mathbf{a} \end{bmatrix} \sqcup \begin{bmatrix} \text{F} : \mathbf{c} \end{bmatrix}) \sqcap (\begin{bmatrix} \text{F} : \mathbf{b} \end{bmatrix} \sqcup \begin{bmatrix} \text{F} : \mathbf{c} \end{bmatrix})$

Thus it can be seen that generalization is more like information intersection than disjunction. In fact, Moshier (1988) showed that generalization could be defined by means of intersecting atomic values, so that we have the following.

Proposition 2 $At(F \sqcap G) = At(F) \cap At(G)$

In particular, the generalization of a finite set of feature structures is always well defined.

Other linguistic applications for generalization have been proposed by Karttunen (1984) and Pereira and Shieber (1984).

2.3   Default Unification

In this section, we present two alternative definitions of an operation of default unification, the purpose of which is to take a feature structure F, whose information is taken to be strict, and combine it with a feature structure G, whose information is taken to be defeasible.

2.3.1   *Credulous Default Unification*

In the credulous approach to default reasoning, the idea is to maintain as much of the default information as is possible, as long as it does not conflict with the strict information. We base our definition of credulous default unification directly on this intuition. We should also note that an equivalent definition was independently proposed in slightly different terms by Calder (1991).

Definition 7 (Credulous Default Unification) *The result of credulous-ly adding the default information in G to the strict information in F is given by:*

$$F \stackrel{<}{\sqcup}_c G = \{F \sqcup G' \mid G' \sqsubseteq G \text{ is maximal such that } F \sqcup G' \text{ is defined}\}$$

First off, it should be noted that the definition returns a set of feature structures rather than a unique value. This is because there may be more than one G' which is maximal such that it subsumes G and is consistent with F. For instance, consider the following example (taken out of context from Bouma, 1990a).

$$(14) \quad \begin{bmatrix} F : \mathbf{a} \end{bmatrix} \stackrel{<}{\sqcup}_c \begin{bmatrix} F : \boxed{1}\,\mathbf{b} \\ G : \boxed{1}\,\mathbf{b} \end{bmatrix} = \left\{ \begin{bmatrix} F : \mathbf{a} \\ G : \mathbf{b} \end{bmatrix}, \begin{bmatrix} F : \boxed{1}\,\mathbf{a} \\ G : \boxed{1} \end{bmatrix} \right\}$$

The non-determinism in (14) arises with the following choices of G' according to the definition of credulous default unification:

$$(15) \quad F = \begin{bmatrix} F : \mathbf{a} \end{bmatrix} \qquad G = \begin{bmatrix} F : \boxed{1}\,\mathbf{b} \\ G : \boxed{1} \end{bmatrix}$$

$$G' = \begin{bmatrix} F : \bot \\ G : \mathbf{b} \end{bmatrix} \qquad G' = \begin{bmatrix} F : \boxed{1} \\ F : \boxed{1} \end{bmatrix}$$

The credulous default unification operation is greedy in that it tries to maximize the amount of information it retains from the default structure. As a consequence, there may be more than one answer. This situation is common in other credulous default logics. Evans (1987) allowed such a credulous definition in his reconstruction of the feature specification default component of GPSG (Gazdar *et al.*, 1985). In general, there may be more than one result in $F \stackrel{<}{\sqcup}_c G$ if there are two pieces of information in G which are each compatible with F independently, but not when taken together. If the logic of feature structures were closed under disjunction, as in the logic presupposed by Calder (1991), then such a non-deterministic result could be expressed as the disjunction of the set of values in $(F \stackrel{<}{\sqcup}_c G)$.

Now that we have a definition of default unification, albeit a credulous one, we can see that it satisfies a number of desiderata which have been previously put forward for notions of default unification. In particular, we have the following.

Proposition 3

- Credulous default unification is always well-defined.
  That is, $(F \stackrel{<}{\sqcup}_c G)$ is always non-empty.
- All strict information is preserved.
  If $H \in (F \stackrel{<}{\sqcup}_c G)$ then $F \sqsubseteq H$.
- It reduces to standard unification in case F and G are consistent.
  That is, $(F \stackrel{<}{\sqcup}_c G) = \{F \sqcup G\}$ if $F \sqcup G$ is well-defined.

- It is always finite.

  That is, $(F \stackrel{<}{\sqcup}_c G)$ is a finite set.

Proof: The fact that $(F \stackrel{<}{\sqcup}_c G)$ is always non-empty arises from the fact that $\perp \sqsubseteq G$ is such that $F \sqcup \perp = F$ is defined.

All strict information is preserved as every result is expressed as a unification of the strict information with some additional information contained in G.

If $F \sqcup G$ is well-defined then $G' = G$ is the unique maximal feature structure such that $G' \sqsubseteq G$ and $F \sqcup G'$ is well-defined.

Finiteness derives from the fact that we can break down any feature structure into the join of a finite set of atoms in the information ordering. In computing $F \stackrel{<}{\sqcup}_c G$, any maximal $G' \sqsubseteq G$ that we keep to unify in with F is composed of the join of a finite subset of the atoms which make up G.   □

It is significant to note that our definition of credulous default unification is not in any way based on the internal structure of feature structures, but is derived entirely from the information containment ordering among them. Such a definition would be applicable in any partial order where least upper bounds are defined for pairs of bounded elements.

While it is not immediately obvious how to define nested applications, if we were to treat the set of results returned by credulous default unification as disjunctions in the standard way (that is, by taking the unification of a set of feature structures to distribute over the members of the set), then we could see that the operation is not associative. That is, we could find F, G and H such that $F \stackrel{<}{\sqcup}_c (G \stackrel{<}{\sqcup}_c H) \neq (F \stackrel{<}{\sqcup}_c G) \stackrel{<}{\sqcup}_c H$. We take up this lack of associativity when we consider the skeptical notion of default unification and consider how default unification can be integrated into a lexical knowledge representation system with inheritance.

It is rather difficult to compare our notion of credulous default unification to other proposals for default unification as our operation returns multiple answers, while previous definitions have assumed a unique result (with the notable exception of Evans, 1987).

2.3.2   *Skeptical Default Unification*

Now that we have a notion of credulous default unification which tries to maintain as much information from the default feature structure as possible, we turn our attention to a more skeptical definition which attempts to only maintain default information which is not in any way conflicted. To do this, it suffices to simply generalize the set of feature structures which results from credulous unification.

Definition 8 (Skeptical Default Unification) $F \stackrel{<}{\sqcup}_s G = \sqcap (F \stackrel{<}{\sqcup}_c G)$

In particular, the definition of skeptical default unification leads to a unique result. The only default information that remains is that which is found in every credulous result. Consider the following example of skeptical unification:

$$
(16) \quad \begin{bmatrix} F : \mathbf{a} \end{bmatrix} \stackrel{<}{\sqcup}_s \begin{bmatrix} F : \boxed{1}\,\mathbf{b} \\ G : \boxed{1} \\ H : \mathbf{c} \end{bmatrix} = \sqcap \left(\begin{bmatrix} F : \mathbf{a} \end{bmatrix} \stackrel{<}{\sqcup}_c \begin{bmatrix} F : \boxed{1}\,\mathbf{b} \\ G : \boxed{1} \\ H : \mathbf{c} \end{bmatrix} \right)
$$

$$
= \sqcap \left\{ \begin{bmatrix} F : \mathbf{a} \\ G : \mathbf{b} \\ H : \mathbf{c} \end{bmatrix}, \begin{bmatrix} F : \boxed{1}\,\mathbf{a} \\ G : \boxed{1} \\ H : \mathbf{c} \end{bmatrix} \right\} = \begin{bmatrix} F : \mathbf{a} \\ G : \bot \\ H : \mathbf{c} \end{bmatrix}
$$

Thus we can see that all of the information that is contained in both of the credulous extensions is maintained in the skeptical result. In particular, since both credulous results are defined for the path G, the result is defined for the path G, but since they provide conflicting atomic values, no value is retained in the result. On the other hand, the fact that the H feature has value **c** is maintained in the result, as it is found in every credulous extension.

This example shows how in general atomic information from the default feature structure is only maintained in the result of skeptical unification if it does not cause a conflict when combined with any other information drawn from either the strict or default feature structure. In fact, skeptical unification could be defined in these terms without going through the definition of credulous default unification.

Note that our notion of default unification is distinct from that proposed by Copestake *et al.* (Copestake, this volume), as their unification strategy gives preference to path sharing over path values during default unification. Thus the fact that F and G were shared would be kept in the result, while the information that their values were **b** would be discarded. Also note that our method of default unification cannot be compared to the PATR-II notion of overwriting (Shieber, 1986), as overwriting only applies to single atomic descriptions and not to entire feature structures. We come back to a notion of overwriting when we consider templates below. Our notion of default unification reduces to Kaplan's (1987) sketch of an operation of priority union, under the strong assumption that both feature structures contain no structure sharing. Priority union was simply not defined in the case where either the default or strict feature structure contained structure sharing. Bouma's (1990a,b) approach to structure sharing was the most difficult aspect of his rather intricate definition of default unification. We compare our notion of skeptical default unification with Bouma's operation below.

Not surprisingly, the skeptical notion of default unification maintains the desiderata satisfied by credulous unification.

Proposition 4

* $F \stackrel{<}{\sqcup}_s G$ is always well defined (and produces a unique result).

- Strict information is preserved.
  That is, $F \sqsubseteq (F \mathbin{\overset{<}{\sqcup}}_s G)$
- It reduces to standard unification if F and G are consistent.
  That is, $(F \mathbin{\overset{<}{\sqcup}}_s G) = (F \sqcup G)$ if $F \sqcup G$ is well defined.

Proof: That $F \mathbin{\overset{<}{\sqcup}}_s G$ is always well-defined follows from the fact that $F \mathbin{\overset{<}{\sqcup}}_c G$ is always non-empty and finite non-empty meets are always well-defined.

The fact that $F \sqsubseteq (F \mathbin{\overset{<}{\sqcup}}_s G) = \sqcap(F \mathbin{\overset{<}{\sqcup}}_c G)$ follows from the fact that $F \sqsubseteq H$ for every $H \in (F \mathbin{\overset{<}{\sqcup}}_c G)$.

If F and G are consistent then $F \mathbin{\overset{<}{\sqcup}}_c G = \{F \sqcup G\}$ and hence $F \mathbin{\overset{<}{\sqcup}}_s G = \sqcap(F \mathbin{\overset{<}{\sqcup}}_c G) = \sqcap\{F \sqcup G\} = F \sqcup G$. □

We now consider some additional examples of skeptical unification. In each case, we have shown the credulous feature structures that would be defined on the way to computing the result of skeptical default unification. First consider the case where there is a three-way sharing in the default structure which is incompatible with two values in the original structure.

$$(17) \quad \begin{bmatrix} F : \mathbf{a} \\ H : \mathbf{b} \end{bmatrix} \mathbin{\overset{<}{\sqcup}}_s \begin{bmatrix} F : \boxed{1} \\ G : \boxed{1} \\ H : \boxed{1} \end{bmatrix}$$

$$= \sqcap \left\{ \begin{bmatrix} F : \mathbf{a} \\ H : \mathbf{b} \end{bmatrix} \sqcup \begin{bmatrix} F : \boxed{1} \\ G : \boxed{1} \\ H : \bot \end{bmatrix}, \begin{bmatrix} F : \mathbf{a} \\ H : \mathbf{b} \end{bmatrix} \sqcup \begin{bmatrix} F : \bot \\ G : \boxed{1} \\ H : \boxed{1} \end{bmatrix} \right\}$$

$$= \sqcap \left\{ \begin{bmatrix} F : \boxed{1}\,\mathbf{a} \\ G : \boxed{1} \\ H : \mathbf{b} \end{bmatrix}, \begin{bmatrix} F : \mathbf{a} \\ G : \boxed{1}\,\mathbf{b} \\ H : \boxed{1} \end{bmatrix} \right\} = \begin{bmatrix} F : \mathbf{a} \\ G : \bot \\ H : \mathbf{b} \end{bmatrix}$$

Adding the fact that all of the path values are **b** in the default structure does not change the result.

$$(18) \quad \begin{bmatrix} F : \mathbf{a} \\ H : \mathbf{b} \end{bmatrix} \mathbin{\overset{<}{\sqcup}}_s \begin{bmatrix} F : \boxed{1}\,\mathbf{b} \\ G : \boxed{1} \\ H : \boxed{1} \end{bmatrix} = \begin{bmatrix} F : \mathbf{a} \\ G : \bot \\ H : \mathbf{b} \end{bmatrix}$$

It is interesting to compare the previous examples to the following one.

$$(19) \quad \begin{bmatrix} F : \mathbf{a} \\ H : \mathbf{b} \end{bmatrix} \mathbin{\overset{<}{\sqcup}}_s \begin{bmatrix} F : \boxed{1} \\ G : \boxed{1} \\ H : \boxed{1} \\ J : \boxed{1} \end{bmatrix} = \begin{bmatrix} F : \mathbf{a} \\ G : \bot \\ H : \mathbf{b} \\ J : \bot \end{bmatrix}$$

This last example is interesting in that it provides a result which is distinctly different from the result given by Bouma's (1990a,b) definition of default unification in which the sharing between G and J would be maintained in the result after the paths F and H were removed from the sharing in the default feature structure due to the fact that they might cause conflicts. In this case, Bouma's default unification returns a more specific value than our skeptical notion (though of course, some of the credulous results are as specific as Bouma's result, as Bouma correctly never takes more than a maximally consistent subset of the default information). But consider the following case, for which our notion of skeptical default unification returns a result more specific than Bouma's notion:

$$(20) \qquad \begin{bmatrix} F : \boxed{1} \\ G : \boxed{1} \end{bmatrix} \mathbin{\stackrel{\leq}{\sqcup}}_s \begin{bmatrix} F : \mathbf{a} \end{bmatrix} = \begin{bmatrix} F : \boxed{1}\,\mathbf{a} \\ G : \boxed{1} \end{bmatrix}$$

This example illustrates how Bouma's definition does not meet the desideratum that default unification reduce to standard unification if the default information is wholly consistent with the strict information. Bouma simply discards the information that F's value is **a**, as this value is a *potential* conflict according to Bouma's definition because the strict feature structure provides information about F's value, namely that it is shared with G's value. Now consider the following two examples, which demonstrate an interesting contrast.

$$(21) \qquad \begin{bmatrix} F : \begin{bmatrix} H : \mathbf{c} \end{bmatrix} \end{bmatrix} \mathbin{\stackrel{\leq}{\sqcup}}_s \begin{bmatrix} F : \boxed{1} \begin{bmatrix} H : \mathbf{a} \\ J : \mathbf{b} \end{bmatrix} \\ G : \boxed{1} \end{bmatrix}$$

$$= \sqcap \left\{ \begin{bmatrix} F : \begin{bmatrix} H : \mathbf{c} \end{bmatrix} \end{bmatrix} \sqcup \begin{bmatrix} F : \begin{bmatrix} H : \bot \\ J : \boxed{2}\,\mathbf{b} \end{bmatrix} \\ G : \begin{bmatrix} H : \mathbf{a} \\ J : \boxed{2} \end{bmatrix} \end{bmatrix} \right\}$$

$$= \begin{bmatrix} F : \begin{bmatrix} H : \mathbf{c} \\ J : \boxed{2}\,\mathbf{b} \end{bmatrix} \\ G : \begin{bmatrix} H : \mathbf{a} \\ J : \boxed{2} \end{bmatrix} \end{bmatrix}$$

$$(22) \qquad \begin{bmatrix} F : \begin{bmatrix} H : \mathbf{c} \end{bmatrix} \end{bmatrix} \mathbin{\stackrel{\leq}{\sqcup}}_s \begin{bmatrix} F : \boxed{1} \begin{bmatrix} H : \mathbf{a} \\ J : \mathbf{b} \\ K : \bot \end{bmatrix} \\ G : \boxed{1} \end{bmatrix}$$

$$= \sqcap \left\{ \begin{bmatrix} F : \begin{bmatrix} H : \mathbf{c} \end{bmatrix} \end{bmatrix} \sqcup \begin{bmatrix} F : \begin{bmatrix} H : \bot \\ J : \boxed{2}\,\mathbf{b} \\ K : \boxed{3}\,\bot \end{bmatrix} \\ G : \begin{bmatrix} H : \mathbf{a} \\ J : \boxed{2} \\ K : \boxed{3} \end{bmatrix} \end{bmatrix} \right\} = \begin{bmatrix} F : \begin{bmatrix} H : \mathbf{c} \\ J : \boxed{2}\,\mathbf{b} \\ K : \boxed{3}\,\bot \end{bmatrix} \\ G : \begin{bmatrix} H : \mathbf{a} \\ J : \boxed{2} \\ K : \boxed{3} \end{bmatrix} \end{bmatrix}$$

In these two examples we see that whether or not a feature is specified as being defined in the default information has a strong bearing on whether it comes out shared in the result. This is because as much of the sharing from the default structure as is consistent with the strict structure is kept in the result. In particular, the fact that the path F · K is defined in the second example above means that the sharing between it and G · K which is induced by the sharing between F and K is kept in the result. It is interesting to note that Bouma's definition of default unification first relaxes the constraints in the default feature structure in part by replacing every path sharing which is internal to a feature structure with a collection of structure sharing constraints which hold only between terminal nodes in the feature structure. This leads to structures much like those found in Prolog terms, where the only sharing allowed is between variables. To accomplish such a relaxation, Bouma recursively replaces every internal path sharing such as that between F and G above with the collection of sharings between F · L and G · L for every feature L (as long as the strict feature structure is not defined for any of the new paths). It is surprising and probably undesirable for the two examples above to provide different results. This unwanted behavior could be eliminated by enforcing a type discipline on feature structures so that they are closed like first-order terms in that they provide values for every feature for which they are appropriate (such systems have been studied by Calder, 1987, Moens *et al.*, 1989 and Carpenter, 1990). The default feature structure in the first example above is not closed in this sense and would thus never arise.

2.4   Templatic Inheritance

In this section we discuss a notion of templates which can be thought of as abbreviatory conventions for lexical entries. Our definitions closely follow those of PATR-II (Shieber *et al.*, 1983). We begin by defining a specification language for templates and lexical entries. After this, we show how feature structures are associated with basic expressions according to such a specification.

We present the syntax of the specification language in BNF in Figure 2.3. The * in the definitions is taken to be of the Kleene variety and denotes arbitrarily many occurrences of the pattern it is attached to, while | is taken to indicate disjunction and parentheses are used for grouping. We take the types <expr> of basic expressions, <path> of paths (sequences of features), <template-name> of template names and <atom> of atomic values to be given. Typologically, we use N for template names, **a** for atoms, Φ for descriptions, ϕ for atomic descriptions and π for paths.

There are a number significant points to note about this definition. First, the operators ? and ! are used to mark the fact that information is to be interpreted by overwriting and by default respectively. But note that these operators can only apply to atomic descriptions. Secondly, note that templates can be included in descriptions, so that in general, one template may be defined in terms of others. It is this facility that allows such a system to be useful. The templates can be arranged hierarchically according to which are defined in terms of the

```
<lexicon> ::=  (<lex-entry>)* (<template-def>)*

<lex-entry> ::= <expr> lex <desc>

<template-def> ::= <template-name> template <desc>

<desc> ::= ( <template-name> | <at-desc>
             | (? <at-desc>) | (! <at-desc>) )*

<at-desc> ::= <path> : <atom>
            | <path> == <path>
```

Figure 2.3: Templatic lexical specification language

others. Note that a lexicon is itself simply a sequence of lexical entries where the category of an expression is described and of template definitions which associate template names with descriptions. For this kind of definition to get off the ground, the templates cannot be recursive in such a way that expanding a template T involves expanding T' and vice-versa (in other words, the induced hierarchy must be a partial ordering).

We can now use a highly simplified case of default unification to provide a definition of the feature structures that are associated with any given lexical entry. In computing this feature structure, we follow the definition given by the user depth-first in the linear order in which it is presented. The order that we include atomic constraints depends on the order in which they are encountered in a depth-first expansion of template definitions. In order to make our definition functional, we adopt the skeptical form of default unification. It would not be difficult to change it to a relational definition in which credulous unification was used. Similarly, disjunction could be incorporated into the description language in the same way. In the following definition, we take $MGSat(\phi)$ to be the minimal feature structure which satisfies the description ϕ, a result which was proved to exist (in a much more general setting) by Kasper and Rounds (1986, 1990).

Definition 9 (Templatic Inheritance) *The lexical entry F associated with an expression e where there is a lexical entry e* lex *Φ is given by the result of the function $F = Add(\bot, \Phi)$ where Add is defined according to the following clauses:*

- $Add(F, ()) = F$
- $Add(F, \phi \cdot \Phi) = Add(Add(F, \phi), \Phi)$
- $Add(F, !\phi) = MGSat(\phi) \stackrel{<}{\sqcup}_s F$
- $Add(F, ?\phi) = F \stackrel{<}{\sqcup}_s MGSat(\phi)$
- $Add(F, \phi) = F \sqcup MGSat(\phi)$

```
A template (B,C)
B template (E)
C template (D)
D template (E)
E template ().
```

Figure 2.4: Path length sensitivity example

- $Add(F,N) = add(F,\Phi)$ *if (N* template Φ*) is a template definition*

The immediate thing to note about this definition is that everything is evaluated depth-first according to how it is specified in the lexicon description. When it comes to adding in a default $?\phi$, we simply take the most general satisfier of the atomic description ϕ and skeptically unify it into what we have so far. Similarly, if we add an overwriting description $!\phi$ we unify what we have so far by default into the most general satisfier of ϕ, which we treat as providing strict information. Information that is neither overwriting nor default information is simply unified into the result. Note that this is the only way that conflicts might arise from such a specification, as default unification always succeeds.

It is important to note that since we only ever take the most general satisfiers of atomic descriptions when computing Add, the definition $F \stackrel{<}{\sqcup}_s MGSat(\phi)$ for adding the default information ϕ reduces to simply adding the information in ϕ if it is consistent with F. That is, defaults come all or nothing and are evaluated one at a time in this system. Of course, for overwriting, even though the overwriting feature structure will be atomic, it might lead to interesting behavior in evaluating $MGSat(\phi) \stackrel{<}{\sqcup}_s F$, as F is not restricted to being atomic. For instance, the kind of behavior we saw in (16) would result from evaluating a description such as the following:

(23)   (f:b, f==g, h:c, !(f:a))

With default and strict information, the Add is increasing so that $F \sqsubseteq Add(F,?\phi)$ and $F \sqsubseteq Add(F,\phi)$, but we do not in general have $F \sqsubseteq Add(F,!\phi)$ in the overwriting case, as information in ϕ can override information in F.

The most significant aspect of our definition of templatic inheritance is that descriptions are evaluated depth-first and left-to-right, including template expansions. Simply consider the template specifications in Figure 2.4 (it is not important what other information they contain). In the case of the specification in Figure 2.4, the information from template E is inherited by A before information from either C or D due to the implicit depth-first evaluation order. While it would be easy to change the definition to make it breadth-first rather than depth-first, we would still get odd results that are sensitive to path length rather than the specificity ordering. Consider evaluating the template specifications in Figure 2.4 in a breadth-first manner. In this case, we would evaluate the template E before or at the same time as the template D because we get to E after two steps from A through B but only after three steps when inherited through C and D. D itself is at a depth of two from A. Ideally, we would want to get the information from D before the information in E as D is defined in terms of E. We see how to get around some of these problems in the next section on default inheritance which uses a mixed breadth-first and depth-first approach to ordering default information. Other kinds of order-sensitivity in these definitions stem from the fact that a template may sandwich a call to another template in between some basic descriptions. In this case as well as in others like it, the template is evaluated in the position in which it is found, thus allowing it to override the default information which comes after it and be overridden by any information which might have been included before it. Of course, templates could always be placed before or after other information as a matter of style or by syntactic restriction on the description language. But one possible benefit to this kind of ordering system is that it is rather flexible in the opportunities it affords to the lexical designer and is at the same time straightforward to debug as the evaluation function is itself simple to follow.

Uses of this kind of templatic inheritance have been discussed in the PATR-II literature (see Shieber, 1986) and in the case of defaults, by Bouma (1990b). Our presentation extends the PATR-II specification somewhat by allowing default u-nification, while PATR-II itself contains overwriting which is broadly similar to what we have defined here. Bouma (1990b) extends the PATR-II template system by generalizing the description logic so that it is similar to the conjunctive portion of the Rounds/Kasper logic and allowing templates to apply at arbitrary levels of description, a move similar to that made in Carpenter's (1989) implementation of a PATR-II system with Rounds/Kasper-style syntax (including embedded templates, but not overwriting). In particular, if we allowed arbitrary conjunctions of descriptions such as $\Phi \wedge \Psi$ then we would simply take:

$$(24) \qquad Add(F, \Phi \wedge \Psi) = Add(Add(F, \Phi), \Psi)$$

Similarly, if we allowed descriptions of the form $\pi : \Phi$ where Φ is now an arbitrary description (possibly incorporating a template) then the most sensible choice for evaluating the defaults seems to be to take:

$$(25) \qquad Add(F, \pi : \Phi) = F[\pi := Add(F@\pi, \Phi)]$$

where $F@\pi$ is the value of F for the path π and where we take $F[\pi := G]$ to be the result of replacing F's π value with G. Such a brutal operation is necessary to account for the effects of overwriting. Without overwriting, the definition could simply add the information in $Add(F@\pi, \Phi)$ to F's π value by unification. In particular, this example recursively adds the constraint Φ from $\pi : \Phi$ to the value of F at π rather than computing the most general satisfier of Φ all on its own and unifying that value into F.

What is not apparent in trying to extend default templates to the full Rounds/Kasper-style logical language is how to apply the default or over-writing operators themselves to entire descriptions. That is, what to do with something like $?(\Phi \wedge \Psi)$ is rather open. It could be taken to evaluate $\Phi \wedge \Psi$ and then treat the result as a default, as in:

(26) $Add(F, ?(\Phi \wedge \Psi)) = F \stackrel{<}{\sqcup}_s Add(\bot, \Phi \wedge \Psi)$

Of course this would provide a different result than assuming that default specifications distribute as in:

(27) $Add(F, ?(\Phi \wedge \Psi)) = Add(F, ?\Phi \wedge ?\Psi)$

Of course, the same sorts of differences would be found with allowing the overwriting operator to apply to complex descriptions. A description language which applies default and overwriting operators to complex descriptions but is evaluated left to right would be misleading in cases such as $?\Phi \wedge !\Psi$ which would give priority to information in Φ over information in Ψ. As things stand in our PATR-II-like system, only fully distributed defaults or overwritings are allowed simply because the default and overwriting operators can only apply to atomic descriptions.

If we were willing to allow disjunctions of the form $\Phi \vee \Psi$, then we could make *Add* non-deterministic by allowing $Add(F, \Phi \vee \Psi)$ to return either $Add(F, \Phi)$ or $Add(F, \Psi)$. Of course, if we make *Add* non-deterministic, then we could employ credulous unification in the obvious way.

2.5   Default Inheritance

In this section, we turn our attention to the specification of a lexical inheritance system based explicitly on a notion of inheritance hierarchy which uses default unification to add more specific default information before more general default information. Unfortunately, as we have already mentioned, we are not able to excise all of the remaining order-sensitivity employing this method. Following Russell *et al.* (1990, this volume), we rely on the Common Lisp Object System method of resolving conflicts between inconsistent information inherited from orthogonal sources by visiting the sources in a depth-first order (see Steele, 1990, for details concerning the Common Lisp Object System).

As with the definition of templatic inheritance, the definition of default inheritance is based on a lexical specification. We present the language in which such specifications are expressed in BNF in Figure 2.5. Note the differences between the default inheritance specification language and the templatic inheritance specification language. Most significantly, the default inheritance system specifies a set of concept definitions rather than template definitions. A concept definition supplies three pieces of information: the superconcepts from which this concept inherits, the strict information attached to the concept and

```
<lexicon> ::= (<lex_entry>)* (<conc-def>)*

<conc-def> ::=  (<conc> isa (<conc>*)
                        strict <desc> default <desc>)

<lex-entry> ::= <expr> lex (<conc>)*

<desc> ::= (<atomic-desc>)*

<at-desc> ::= <path> : <atom>
            | <path> == <path>
```

Figure 2.5: Default inheritance specification language

the default information about the concept. Both strict and default information is presented as a simple description, thus making the distinction between default and strict information on a concept by concept rather than an atomic description by atomic description basis. One benefit of this approach, which we have not exploited here, is that a more general description logic could be provided; we use the simple PATR-II language, while a language such as that provided by Rounds and Kasper (1986, 1990) is slightly nicer to work with. Another thing to notice about the definition is that we allow both strict and default information to be attached to a given concept. According to our inheritance scheme, strict information is always inherited, while default information may be overridden.

We turn our attention now to specifying the categories associated with basic expressions by the lexicon. As we have said before, we are not able to totally eliminate the order dependence in inheritance and are thus sensitive to the way in which the inheritance between concepts is ordered in the description as well as the partial ordering it induces. But we do follow a specificity-based approach in taking default information in more specific concepts to override default information attached to more general concepts. But in cases where default information from orthogonal concepts is in conflict, we choose to maintain the information that comes from the first concept visited in a depth-first traversal of all of the concepts which are inherited by a lexical entry. To make matters more precise, we define for any sequence $(C_1, \ldots, C_n)$ of concepts, the depth-first ordering $(D_1, \ldots, D_m)$ of concepts from which they inherit information according to the inheritance hierarchy specification. This depth-first ordering is then used to induce the final inheritance ordering.

Definition 10 (Depth-first Ordering)
The depth first ordering $DF((C_1, \ldots, C_n))$ of the concepts inherited by an ordered sequence $(C_1, \ldots, C_n)$ of concepts is given by:

- $DF(C) = C \cdot DF(C_1) \cdots \cdot DF(C_n)$

```
A isa (B, F)    E isa (D)
B isa (C, E)    F isa (E,G)
C isa (D)       G isa ()
D isa ()


df(A) = A df(B) df(F)
      = A B df(C,E) F df(E,G)
      = A B df(C) df(E) F df(E) df(G)
      = A B C df(D) E df(D) F E df(D) G
      = A B C D E D F E D G
```

Figure 2.6: Depth-first ordering

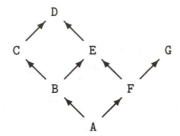

Figure 2.7: Inheritance hierarchy diagram

if C isa *$(C_1, \ldots, C_n)$ is part of the lexical specification*

- $DF((C_1, C_2, ..., C_n)) = DF(C_1) \cdot DF(C_2) \cdots \cdots DF(C_n)$

We provide a simple example in Figure 2.6, which illustrates many of the properties of the depth-first ordering. A graphical depiction of the hierarchy in Figure 2.6 is given in Figure 2.7.

As can be seen in Figure 2.6, in the case of multiple inheritance, the depth-first ordering contains more than one occurrence of some concepts. For instance, D appears three times in the final depth-first ordering in Figure 2.6, as there are three paths from A to D specified in the inheritance hierarchy. Multiple occurrences in the depth-first ordering, while easily eliminable with a more sophisticated definition, do not pose any problems, as our final ordering is only sensitive to the first occurrence of a concept in the depth-first ordering.

Note that we can use the depth-first ordering to define the specificity ordering.

Definition 11 (Specificity) *A concept C is equal or more* specific *than C' if and only if C' is an element of the sequence DF(C).*

The reason this definition makes sense is that $DF(C)$ is a list which is closed under superconcepts given in the lexical specification; that is, if a concept C appears in $DF((C_1, \ldots, C_n))$ and C' is specified as a superconcept of C, then

```
TS(A B C D E D F E D G)
= A TS(B C D E D F E D G)
= A B TS(C D E D F E D G)
= A B C TS(D E D F E D G)
= A B C F TS(D E D E D G)
= A B C F E TS(D D D G)
= A B C F E D TS(G)
= A B C F E D G
```

Figure 2.8: Topological ordering of concepts

C' appears in $DF((C_1, \ldots, C_n))$.

We use the depth-first sequence of subconcepts to perform a topological sort of the concepts inherited by any given sequence of concepts. More specifically, we form the final inheritance ordering by ordering elements from the front of the depth-first ordering as soon as all of their subconcepts are included.

Definition 12 (Topological Ordering)
$TS(C_1, \ldots, C_n) = TS_2(DF(C_1, \ldots, C_n))$ *where:*

- $TS_2(()) = ()$
- $TS_2(D_1, \ldots, D_m) = D_k \cdot TS_2((D_1, \ldots, D_m) - D_k)$ *if k is minimal such that there is no $D_j \neq D_k$ such that $1 \leq j \leq m$ and D_j is more specific than D_k.*

This definition is actually simpler than it appears as we are really doing nothing more than taking the depth-first ordering of concepts inherited by $(C_1, \ldots, C_n)$ and then successively choosing the first element in the depth-first order such that all of its subconcepts have already been chosen. We continue the example from Figure 2.6 in Figure 2.8. It can be seen in Figure 2.8 that the topological ordering respects the specificity ordering in that every concept occurs on the list before any of its superconcepts. On the other hand, it can also be seen that the depth-first ordering is used to order concepts neither of which is more specific than the other. For instance, the fact that F is more general than D means that D is ordered before F. But considering B and F, neither of which is more specific than the other, we take B before F, as B shows up before F in the depth-first ordering. C shows up before G for the same reason.

Note that we only consider subconcepts induced along the path from the concepts being inherited from and do not perform a global depth-first ordering of the entire graph, which provides different results in some cases. In particular, it may turn out that a concept C is inherited before an orthogonal concept C' in some cases and after C' in others if the specification is not uniform as to the order in which subconcepts are introduced. For instance, a specification that puts A isa (C,D) and B isa (D,C) would have the concept C inherited before D for A, but after D for B.

Now that we have defined the order in which concepts are visited for inheritance, it is a straightforward matter to characterize the linguistic categories (represented by feature structures) which are assigned by the lexicon. We first inherit all of the strict information and then inherit default information one concept at a time following the topological ordering of concepts.

Definition 13 (Default Inheritance)
A lexical entry (e lex $C_1, \ldots, C_n$*) assigns the category*

$$(\cdots (((F_1 \sqcup \cdots \sqcup F_m) \stackrel{<}{\sqcup}_s G_1) \stackrel{<}{\sqcup}_s G_2) \stackrel{<}{\sqcup}_s \cdots \stackrel{<}{\sqcup}_s G_{m-1}) \stackrel{<}{\sqcup}_s G_m$$

to e, where $TS(C_1, \ldots, C_n) = D_1, \ldots, D_m$ *and where* F_i *is the feature structure containing strict information and* G_i *is the feature structure holding default information attached to the concept* D_i.

For instance, in the hierarchy in Figure 2.6, we first combine all of the strict information and then successively skeptically unify in the default information from the inherited concepts in the order that they appear in the topological ordering. In particular, strict information from D overrides default information, even if it appears directly on A. Since we take the topological ordering, default information on C would override default information either on its superconcept D or on orthogonal concepts visited later in the topological ordering such as F or G. Obviously under this definition, information from more specific sources overrides information from more general sources.

We finally take up a point we promised to come back to concerning the (lack of) associativity of default unification. In particular, we have the following result:

(28) $\left(\begin{bmatrix} \text{F} : \mathbf{a} \end{bmatrix} \stackrel{<}{\sqcup}_s \begin{bmatrix} \text{F} : \boxed{1} \\ \text{G} : \boxed{1} \end{bmatrix} \right) \stackrel{<}{\sqcup}_s \begin{bmatrix} \text{G} : \mathbf{b} \end{bmatrix} =$

$* \begin{bmatrix} \text{F} : \boxed{1}\,\mathbf{a} \\ \text{G} : \boxed{1} \end{bmatrix} \stackrel{<}{\sqcup}_s \begin{bmatrix} \text{G} : \mathbf{b} \end{bmatrix} = \begin{bmatrix} \text{F} : \boxed{1}\,\mathbf{a} \\ \text{G} : \boxed{1} \end{bmatrix}$

$\neq \begin{bmatrix} \text{F} : \mathbf{a} \end{bmatrix} \stackrel{<}{\sqcup}_s \left(\begin{bmatrix} \text{F} : \boxed{1} \\ \text{G} : \boxed{1} \end{bmatrix} \stackrel{<}{\sqcup}_s \begin{bmatrix} \text{G} : \mathbf{b} \end{bmatrix} \right) =$

$* \begin{bmatrix} \text{F} : \mathbf{a} \end{bmatrix} \stackrel{<}{\sqcup}_s \begin{bmatrix} \text{F} : \boxed{1}\,\mathbf{b} \\ \text{G} : \boxed{1} \end{bmatrix} = \begin{bmatrix} \text{F} : \mathbf{a} \\ \text{G} : \bot \end{bmatrix}$

This kind of contrast is well-known in the inheritance literature and corresponds to the distinction between performing inheritance top-down and bottom-up. Such contrasts arise because default inheritance is rarely transitive. In particular, consider the following specification:

(29)   A isa (B) default f:a
        B isa (C) default f == g
        C isa () default g:b

The feature structure inherited by A according to our definitions maintains the sharing because our definition proceeds bottom-up. If we had been proceeding top-down instead, we would first inherit all of the information relevant to B before adding the information from B to the information attached to A. In the top-down case, no sharing would be inherited by A. It seems intuitively, at least, that the bottom-up definition is preferable, as the fact that f is shared with g is presented at a more specific node than the fact that g's value is b. In fact, it is generally much more straightforward to define a sensible notion of default inheritance bottom-up than it is to define inheritance in a top-down fashion.

2.6   Future Directions

While we have gone some distance in achieving a lexical organization that employs default information, we are still left with a distasteful degree of order sensitivity in the result. It remains to be seen whether a reasonable definition can be made that achieves complete order-neutrality and finds a sensible way to resolve orthogonal conflicts. Ideally, we would remain skeptical in the light of such conflicts, not choosing to favor information from one orthogonal source over another. On the other hand, working out such a definition is far from trivial. Of course, if no default information from orthogonal concepts ever arises, this is not a problem. Many systems such as Copestake *et al.* (this volume) and in the DATR system of Evans and Gazdar (1989a, 1989b) require orthogonal information to be always compatible.

One subject we have not even broached, which also presents a significant challenge for future research, is the characterization of recursive default constraints. In particular, we might want to state that the value of a path satisfies some concept definition. While such a system can be worked out even in the face of recursion in the case of purely strict information, the result being an interpreter for an HPSG-like grammar (see Franz, 1990; Carpenter, Pollard and Franz, 1991), no one has put forward a sensible definition for the default case. Immediate problems arise when considering such a system, even without recursion, such as whether to inherit a specification on a path before inheriting specifications on superconcepts, which may affect the same path's value.

Acknowledgements

I would like to thank Ted Briscoe, Jo Calder, Ann Copestake, Roger Evans and Graham Russell for getting me interested in default unification in the first place and discussing the basics of their own approaches with me. I would also like to thank Gosse Bouma for providing specific comments on comparisons between his definition and the one found here. I should also say that almost everything I know about defaults that I didn't learn from those mentioned above was gained in conversations with Rich Thomason.

3   Prioritised Multiple Inheritance in DATR

ROGER EVANS, GERALD GAZDAR AND LIONEL MOSER

Abstract

We characterise a notion of prioritised multiple inheritance (PMI) and contrast it with the more familiar orthogonal multiple inheritance (OMI). DATR is a knowledge representation language that was designed to facilitate OMI analyses of natural language lexicons: it contains no special purpose facility for PMI and this has led some researchers to conclude that PMI analyses are beyond the expressive capacity of DATR. Here, we present three different techniques for implementing PMI entirely within DATR's existing syntactic and semantic resources. In presenting them, we draw attention to their respective advantages and disadvantages.

3.1   Introduction

'Multiple inheritance', in inheritance network terminology, describes any situation where a node in an inheritance network inherits information from more than one other node in the network. Wherever this phenomenon occurs there is the potential for conflicting inheritance, i.e. when the information inherited from one node is inconsistent with that inherited from another. Because of this, the handling of multiple inheritance is an issue which is central to the design of any formalism for representing inheritance networks. For the formalism to be sound, it must provide a way of avoiding or resolving any conflict which might arise. This might be by banning multiple inheritance altogether, restricting it so that conflicts are avoided, providing some mechanism for conflict resolution as part of the formalism itself, or providing the user of the formalism with the means to specify how the conflict should be resolved.

Touretzky (1986, p. 70ff) provides a formal description of a number of properties that an inheritance network may have, and discusses their significance with respect to the problem of multiple inheritance. Tree-structured networks, as their name suggests, allow any node to inherit from at most one other node, so multiple inheritance conflict cannot arise. Orthogonal networks allow a node to inherit from more than one other node, but the properties it inherits from each must be disjoint, so that again, no conflict can possibly arise. In Touretzky's framework all inheritance links are essentially simple specifications of truth values (true, false or unknown) for predicates, and in this situation the orthogonality constraint is the only sure way to guarantee network consistency. However, more general inheritance patterns can be achieved by using more powerful inheritance mechanisms. One approach is to forego orthogonality and provide mechanisms for resolving among conflicting values inherited at a node (Touretzky's 'inferential distance' is an example of this). The examples in this paper indicate an alternative approach is also possible.

DATR (Evans and Gazdar, 1989a,b; 1990) is an inheritance network formalism designed for the representation of natural language lexical information. The basic descriptive features of DATR allow the specification of simple orthogonal networks similar to Touretzky's. For example, if we write:

```
A:   <a> == true.

B:   <b> == false.

C:   <a> == A
     <b> == B.
```

then we are specifying a network of three nodes (A B, and C), and two 'predicates' (DATR paths <a> and <b>), with C inheriting a value for <a> from A, and for <b> from B. The network is orthogonal, since <a> and <b> represent disjoint (sets of) predicates.

This case provides an example of a *functional* DATR theory: a DATR theory is functional if and only if the set of equations defines a (partial) function from node/path pairs to value or inheritance descriptors. Since functionality is defined extensionally, it is trivial (for user or implementation) to check that a DATR theory is functional. Every functional DATR theory is orthogonal. Of course, there is more to DATR than is illustrated by the tiny example above, but the longest-defined-subpath-wins principle ensures that basic inheritance is always orthogonal in functional DATR theories.

Orthogonal multiple inheritance (OMI) is a very desirable property of lexical representation systems. Consider an analysis in which we put the common properties of verbs at a V node and the (completely disjoint) common properties of words that take noun phrase complements at an NPC node. A transitive verb (VTR) is both a verb and a word that takes an NP complement, thus it should inherit from both V and NPC in this analysis. In DATR, this might be expressed as follows:

```
V:   <cat> == verb.

NPC:<comp cat> == np
    <comp case> == acc.

VTR:<cat> == V
    <comp> == NPC.
```

However, a number of recent lexical theories have invoked a form of inheritance in which multiple parents with *overlapping* domains are specified, and a priority ordering imposed to resolve potential inheritance conflicts (e.g. Flickinger, 1987; Russell *et al.*, 1991). In this prioritised multiple inheritance (PMI), precedence is given to nodes that come earlier in the ordering, so that the inherited value for a property comes from the first parent node in the ordering that defines that property, regardless of whether other later nodes also define it (possibly differently).

Here is an abstract example of PMI written in a DATR-like pseudoformalism:

```
A:   <a> == one.

B:   <a> == two
     <b> == two.

C:   <a> == three
     <b> == three
     <c> == three.

ABC:<> == A, B, C.
```

Under the intended interpretation of the example, ABC inherits from nodes A, B and C prioritised in that order, so that the following set of inferences could be drawn:

```
ABC:<a> = one
    <b> = two
    <c> = three.
```

while the following could not be drawn:

```
ABC:<a> = two
    <b> = three.
```

But, as the Mad Hatter once explained to Alice, pseudoformalisms have the great advantage of meaning whatever it is that one wants them to mean.

The question we address in this paper is whether DATR's style of OMI can be used to reconstruct PMI without making syntactic and semantic additions to the language. In fact, we shall describe no fewer than three different techniques for characterising PMI in DATR. For each technique, we consider the following simple scenario. We have nodes A and B defining values for paths <x> and <y> as follows:

```
A:   <x> == yes.

B:   <x> == no
     <y> == yes.
```

Our goal is to define a node C that will inherit values from node A where they are defined at A, but otherwise inherit them from node B. Thus we will want to be able to derive the following as theorems:

```
C:   <x> = yes
     <y> = yes.
```

A fundamental property of all three approaches is that node A cannot actually leave *any* value undefined, since failure at any point during query evaluation would cause failure of the entire query. Instead, at the point where querying A 'ought' to fail, some mechanism for transferring attention to B must be provided.

3.2   Prioritising Using Explicit Failure Paths

In the first approach, we use a global path inheritance specification as the 'failure-value' for A:

```
A:   <> == "<not from_A>"
     <x> == yes.
```

Here, the value for <x> is defined in the normal way, but the empty path case uses a global descriptor to allow inheritance at that point to be conditioned by the queried node. In effect, we allow the queried node to specify the inheritance default for A. In our example, the querying node is C, and the inheritance required is inheritance from B:

```
C:   <> == A:<>
     <not from_A> == B:<>.
```

B itself need have no special properties:

```
B:   <x> == no
     <y> == yes.
```

To see how this works out in practice, consider our two queries C:<x> and C:<y>. The derivation of C:<x> is a straightforward inheritance from A:[1]

```
C:<x>
A:<x>                    (using C:<> == A:<>)
yes                      (using A:<x> == yes)
```

The derivation of C:<y> looks like this:

---

[1] By derivation here we mean the sequence of inheritance evaluations leading to the definition of a value. The DATR sentence justifying the inheritance is shown in parentheses on the right where applicable.

```
C:<y>
A:<y>                      (using C:<> == A:<>)
C:<not from_A y>           (using A:<> == "<not from_A>")
B:<y>                      (using C:<not from_A> == B:<>)
yes                        (using B:<y> == yes)
```

In the first case, A supplies the value, and the conflicting value from B is not considered at all, while in the second, A fails to supply the value, and so the value at B is inherited by C.

It is easy to see that this technique can be extended to an arbitrary sequence of nodes to try in turn — by adding B:<> == "<not from_B>", C can specify a further inheritance for values not defined at either A or B. It is also possible to extend this approach to more complex inheritance patterns, including cases where A or B itself inherits from a further node.

The explicit failure path approach is minimalist in the DATR resources it employs, and offers a clean, understandable, low level solution to the problem. However, (adopting a procedural metaphor) this approach to PMI in DATR effectively chains evaluation of the query at B after evaluation at A. This means that if the attempted evaluation at A changes the evaluation context, the mechanism will not function correctly: the inheritance specification "<not from_A>" exploits both the global node (through which it inherits) and the local path (to which it prefixes). If either of these have been changed during evaluation at A, the inheritance may not be as expected.

3.3   Prioritising Using Evaluable Paths

One way to overcome the problem just described is to evaluate the inheritance possibilities separately using evaluable paths. Consider the following DATR sentence:

```
C:   <> == <A B>.
```

This specifies evaluation via two nested inheritance specifications (A and B) operating completely independently of each other. The results of these evaluations are spliced together to produce the body of a path inheritance specification, which is itself evaluated. If any of A, B or the final path inheritance fails, the entire inheritance fails.[2]

---

[2] We are adopting here Gibbon's (1989) approach to evaluable paths in DATR: in earlier, unpublished work, we only permitted evaluable paths to contain descriptors that evaluated to atoms. To convert value sequences to paths, it was necessary to invoke an explicit sequence-to-path coercion operator. It now seems to us that Gibbon's approach (which dispenses with the operator and allows descriptors to evaluate to value sequences in paths) is syntactically more elegant. The two approaches are equivalent semantically, so no expressive power is lost (or gained) by adopting one rather than another.

We can produce a more elegant and robust implementation of PMI by using this technique and by exploiting the fact that DATR effectively ignores arbitrary extensions to paths not referenced in the definitions. We can ensure that neither A nor B will fail by providing a 'failure-value', and in this case we make it the empty value sequence:

```
A:   <> == ()
     <x> == yes.

B:   <> == ()
     <x> == no
     <y> == yes.
```

Now, consider what happens when we use the evaluable path specification introduced above: the path constructed contains the result from A followed by the result from B. If A defines a value, then that value is a leading subsequence of the elements of the path (followed by the value of B, if any). If A does not define a value, it returns the empty sequence, which disappears when absorbed into the path, so B's value alone is in the path. Either way, the answer we require is a leading subsequence of the path elements. To return the actual result required, we add statements to C, mapping paths with such leading subsequences into their associated values, but ignoring any trailing path elements, produced by inheritance lower down the prioritisation ordering.

```
C:   <> == <A B>
     <yes> == yes
     <no> == no.
```

The derivation of C:<x> now looks like this:

```
C:<x>
C:<A:<x> B:<x> x>     (using C:<> == <A B>)
C:<yes no x>          (using evaluable path instantiation)
yes                   (using C:<yes> == yes)
```

Notice how the result of B:<x> (no) is ignored when mapping to the final result. C:<y> comes out as:

```
C:<y>
C:<A:<y> B:<y> y>     (using C:<> == <A B>)
C:<() yes y>          (using evaluable path instantiation)
C:<yes y>
yes                   (using C:<yes> == yes)
```

This PMI technique will work even when A and B return more complex results. However, it depends on a mapping from these results onto the results actually returned by C. In our example, this is an identity mapping, but nothing forces this: the results of A and B can be viewed more generally as indexes into a table of arbitrary inheritance specifications.

Although elegant, the evaluable path technique has one major drawback: a (finite) table has to be provided, mapping from every possible value returned by A or B onto an appropriate result. This is acceptable for applications that are restricted to a small set of possible results, but may well be impractical for larger finite applications, and is expressively inadequate for applications where the set of possible results is unbounded (as can easily arise when value sequences are returned).

3.4   Prioritising Using Negative Path Extension

Our third technique solves the finite table problem by encoding the successful inheritance source (rather than the result) and then using it to direct the inheritance. Once again we need an explicit value to indicate failure of A or B; however, this time it is not the empty value sequence, but instead an arbitrary but unique result value, undef.

```
A:   <> == undef
     <x> == yes.

B:   <> == undef
     <x> == no
     <y> == yes.
```

Node C is more complicated:[3]

```
C:   <> == <<one_of A B>>
     <one_of> == from_A
     <one_of undef> == from_B
     <one_of undef undef> == nowhere
     <nowhere> == undef
     <from_A> == A:<>
     <from_B> == B:<>.
```

Much as before, the prioritised inheritance operates by evaluating A and B inside an evaluable path and collecting up the results returned, now including undefs for failed queries. The resulting path, prefixed with one_of, is evaluated against a set of definitions which use the presence or absence of undef's to select among tokens from_A, from_B or nowhere. These in turn are evaluated as

---

[3] In a real application, the bulk of this complexity could be stated once at a higher node rather than associated with every lower node that needs to make use of it. But we have located all the machinery at node C here, in order to keep the examples for our three techniques as comparable as possible.

path elements (note the *double* path brackets on the empty path definition in C),
directing inheritance through either A or B, or returning undef as a result. Our
two derivations are now as follows:

```
C:<x>
C:<C:<one_of A:<x> B:<x> x> x>
                        (using C:<> == <<one_of A B>>)
C:<C:<one_of yes no x> x>
                        (using evaluable path instantiation)
C:<from_A x>            (using C:<one_of> == from_A)
A:<x>                   (using C:<from_A> == A:<>)
yes                     (using A:<x> == yes)


C:<y>
C:<C:<one_of A:<y> B:<y> y> y>
                        (using C:<> == <<one_of A B>>)
C:<C:<one_of undef yes y> y>
                        (using evaluable path instantiation)
C:<from_B y>            (using C:<one_of undef> == from_B)
B:<y>                   (using C:<from_B> == B:<>)
yes                     (using B:<y> == yes)
```

Thus the path resulting from evaluation at the parents A and B
is matched against the 'selector' paths, <one_of>, <one_of undef>
and <one_of undef undef>.   When node A returns a value other
than undef, the instantiated path extends neither <one_of undef> nor
<one_of undef undef>, and so inheritance through <one_of> occurs. If
on the other hand A 'fails' and returns undef, <one_of> is ignored and
the same situation applies for the value returned by B matching against
<one_of undef>.

This technique might appropriately be called *negative path extension*. DATR's
default mechanism operates by selecting the statement containing the longest
leading subpath of the query path.   Typically, this is used by specifying a
path containing the particular domain attributes which correspond to the given
definition. Here, however, we have introduced a distinguished value (undef),
not properly part of the descriptive domain of the other path attributes, and used
it in a negative fashion: the 'interesting' paths (at this point in the derivation)
are those which do *not* extend undef, and which are therefore forced to inherit
through the more general (shorter) path.

Although this technique is not the simplest, it has the advantage of working in
completely arbitrary (acyclic) network configurations. There can be an arbitrary
number of parent nodes, arbitrarily related to each other. Furthermore, regardless
of the inheritance specifications in the parents, no context is ever altered by the

prioritisation step: the final inheritance from a parent occurs in the same local and global state as a direct inheritance would.

3.5   Conclusion

The three examples that we have presented above demonstrate how PMI can be implemented in DATR in a variety of ways, using mechanisms already provided in the language for quite different purposes. The three techniques given are illustrative and there may well be other ways of implementing PMI within DATR, quite possibly better ways. Furthermore, we are not seeking to recommend any one of the techniques over the other two, but simply to clarify the differences between them. As we have seen, they differ in flexibility and clarity, and indeed in efficiency, especially when used in implementations of DATR that make use of non-cacheing query algorithms.

We mentioned in the introduction that the approaches we describe differ in kind from techniques such as Touretzky's inferential distance. In effect, the DATR approach is to control conflict by not allowing it to arise: instead of resolving conflicting inherited values, we control the inheritance specifications themselves, directing inheritance deterministically to the appropriate parent. DATR's descriptive mechanisms thus allow an orthogonal, declarative treatment of prioritised multiple inheritance.

But it is also interesting to note that the first example suggests that at least a non-trivial subclass of PMI is almost within the reach of the simplest imaginable OMI systems: the only significant feature of DATR used there is the renaming of the property inherited (the prefixation of <not from_A> to the path) to indicate evaluation failure in A. The latter two analyses, however, exploit the more esoteric facilities of DATR, namely nested evaluation and value to property coercion.

DATR was designed to facilitate OMI analyses of natural language lexicons. The designers of DATR were not persuaded then (or now) that PMI treatments of the lexicon offer significant analytical or descriptive advantages. However, despite their theoretical intentions and analytical prejudices, it seems that DATR is surprisingly well suited to PMI-style lexicons.

Acknowledgements

We are grateful to Dan Flickinger and Susan Warwick-Armstrong for relevant conversations on the topic of this chapter.

4   Some Reflections on the Conversion of the TIC Lexicon into DATR

LYNNE J. CAHILL

Abstract

The Traffic Information Collator (TIC)[1] (Allport, 1988a,b) is a prototype system which takes verbatim police reports of traffic incidents, interprets them, builds a picture of what is happening on the roads and broadcasts appropriate messages automatically to motorists where necessary. Cahill and Evans (1990) described the process of converting the main TIC lexicon (a lexicon of around 1000 words specific to the domain of traffic reports) into DATR (Evans and Gazdar, 1989a,b; 1990). This chapter reviews the strategy adopted in the conversion discussed in that paper, and discusses the results of converting the whole lexicon, together with statistics comparing efficiency and performance between the original lexicon and the DATR version.

4.1   Introduction

The Traffic Information Collator (TIC) is a prototype system which takes verbatim police reports of traffic incidents, interprets them, builds a picture of what is happening on the roads and broadcasts appropriate messages automatically to motorists where necessary. In Cahill and Evans (1990), the basic strategy of defining the structure of lexical entries was described. That paper concentrated on the main TIC lexicon, which was just one part of a collection of different kinds of lexical information and only dealt with a small fragment even of that. The whole conversion involved collating all of that information into a single DATR description. In this chapter we review the structure of the original TIC lexicon; with sections describing the reasons behind the conversion, the conversion itself, some statistics relating to the relative sizes of the lexica and processing times for the two. Finally we provide some conclusions.

---

[1] The TIC was originally developed as part of the Alvey MISC Demonstrator Project.

4.1.1   Structure of the Original TIC Lexicon

The original TIC lexicon was written in POP11,[2] using macros to define different sets of lexical entries. The main lexicon matched words with expressions denoting their syntax and semantics, in the format,

```
WORD CAT=(FEAT1=VAL1, ... FEATn=VALn) # SEMANTICS #
```

where WORD is the word being defined, CAT is the syntactic category to which it belongs and FEAT1 to FEATn are features having the values VAL1 to VALn respectively. The feature/value pairs are optional, although most categories require that at least the feature 'type' is given a value in the lexicon. The semantics is in the form of a list, which consists of propositions expressed in the form of lambda calculus, e.g. [L X [road X]] (the 'L' stands for λ).

In addition to the main lexicon, the original TIC lexicon had sections dealing with phrases, abbreviations, irregular lexical forms and special entries (e.g. car registration numbers, police classification numbers). The lookup procedure involved checking in the special sections first, and then, if no corresponding entry was found there, splitting the word into possible root and ending pairs, by pattern matching. The lookup in the special sections effectively bypassed the root/ending splitting stage, so had to provide root and ending information explicitly. The root was then looked up in the main lexicon, and a set of procedures applied to the root and ending, for example to assign arguments of verbs to subject or object roles.

The phrases were defined as follows:

```
en route .   enroute null
```

where the phrase being defined is everything before the '.', and the two words after the '.' are the root and ending respectively. Abbreviations were defined as triples, with the first 'word' being the abbreviation, the second the root and the third the ending, and irregular forms were defined in the same way as abbreviations, e.g.

```
amb ambulance null
broken break ed
```

The special entries were simple rules which associated with each class of entry a procedure for deriving the syntax and semantics. For example, the procedure for roads (such as a23) generated a syntax of the form,

```
db_road=(type=@road)
```

and a semantics,

```
[L x [and [road x] [called x a23]]].
```

---

[2] The TIC is implemented in a combination of POP11 and Prolog in the POPLOG multi-language programming environment (Hardy, 1982).

4.2   Reasons for the Conversion

The two principal reasons for converting the TIC lexicon into DATR were:

- Ease of adaptation to new domain (and ease of maintenance, since the language used by the police forces, like any language, varies slowly over time);
- More integrated and linguistically accurate definition of all the lexical information.

The original TIC project developed a prototype system with the principal aim to ascertain whether the problem was indeed a tractable one, and was based solely on the Sussex police force. The current project (POETIC – POrtable Extendable Traffic Information Collator,[3] Evans *et al.*, 1990) aims to take the TIC and develop it in such a way as to make it more easily adaptable to new domains, and thus more widely applicable. At present, work is centered on adaptation to the Metropolitan police force. With this in mind, it was felt that a more structured organisation of the lexicon, which is one of the main areas which will need adaptation for a new domain, was desirable. The nature of the DATR representation language means that much information is shared between entries, either by means of abstract nodes or by simple inheritance between terminal nodes. Thus, for example, verbs inherit the structure of their syntactic arguments from the abstract 'VERB' node, while features such as 'type', 'subjtype' are defined at individual nodes. However, a verb like 'request' inherits all of its information from 'ask' because in terms of the syntax and semantics required for the TIC parser they are identical. The first benefit of this type of organisation is thus that when changes need to be made to the lexicon, they do not necessarily need to be made for every affected word, but may be made only at an abstract node from which those words all inherit. This is not always the case, of course, but it is still expected to be of significant benefit in this regard.

Besides this practical reason for the conversion, there is the theoretical desirability of a more integrated and linguistically sound representation of the lexical information needed by the system. The original TIC lexicon system was devised primarily to be functional, with little regard for linguistic niceties (understandably, since the aim of the original TIC project was simply to build a prototype to see whether the basic problem was soluble). Thus the means of handling different types of information, e.g. abbreviations, irregular forms and information carried by endings, are rather *ad hoc*. By using DATR we are able to integrate all of this information into a single DATR description, not only providing a more elegant unified representation of the lexicon, but also meaning that a single, one-pass lexical lookup procedure can be used. As discussed in

---

[3] The POETIC project is a collaborative project between Sussex University, Racal Research Ltd, the Automobile Association and National Transcommunications Ltd., funded by SERC and the DTI, following on from the TIC project.

section 4.4 below, this does not necessarily mean a faster lexical lookup, but speed is not of primary concern to us at this stage.

4.3   The Conversion

4.3.1   Querying the Lexicon

Each query of the lexicon is of a root and ending, as in the original lexicon, and is done by constructing a new node which inherits from the node representing the word in question, but has the path `<init_ending>` (meaning initial ending) defined. For example, to query the lexicon for the syntax with the root/ending pair 'ask/ing', the node,

```
Node1:   <> == Ask
         <init_ending> == ing
         <syntax> = ?? .
```

would be compiled, with the '??' indicating that the value at the path in question is to be evaluated. (See Evans, 1990.)

There are three endings distinguished, 'init_ending', which is the ending in the query, 'ending', which may be defined at some other point in the hierarchy and 'true_ending', which is the resultant ending arising when the other two are considered together. Their relationship, with 'true_ending' having the value of 'init_ending' unless the latter is null and an 'ending' is defined, is defined at the CATEGORY node, the top node of the hierarchy. The reason for the distinction can be seen by considering as an example the word 'children'. The pattern matching procedures would define this as the root/ending pair 'children/null'. The entry for the word 'children' in the lexicon is,

```
Children:<> == Child
         <ending> == s.
```

which says that 'children' inherits from 'child' but has the 'ending' 's'. The true-ending in this case is therefore the same as `<ending>`, i.e. 's', since the initial ending was null. If the initial ending was not null, then this would be the true_ending, since the assignment of endings in the lexicon is only to complete word forms, so we do not allow the overriding of non-null initial endings.

4.3.2   Structure of Entries

Each entry in the main lexicon has a syntax and a semantics, which are of a particular structure. The syntax consists of a major category and a (possibly empty) set of feature/value pairs. The features which are defined for each major category are different. The basic structure of the DATR lexicon is as described in Cahill and Evans (1990). The DATR lexicon top level consists of a CATEGORY node, which is the very top of the hierarchy. This defines the basic structure of any set of syntactic information thus,

```
<syntax> == ({ "<cat>" [ "<synargs>" ] })
<synargs> == ({ type "<type>" })
```

which says that the syntax of a word is a list (in round brackets) which contains a {, the value of the path <cat>, a [, the value of the path <synargs>, a] and a }. With the exception of the outer round brackets which indicate a DATR list, the various brackets are individual elements of the list, which will be interpreted as delimiters of POP11 lists and vectors when the resultant structure is passed to the POP11 procedures in the parser. The quotes around the paths indicate that the path is to be evaluated at the original query node (which may refer by default or explicitly back to other nodes higher up the hierarchy, including the CATEGORY node). What the two lines given above state is that the syntax of a word consists of its category and the 'synargs' or syntactic arguments, which by default consist simply of the word 'type' and the type of that word. The default semantics of a word is defined by the line,

```
<semantics> == ([ L X true ])
```

The full CATEGORY node is,

```
CATEGORY:<> == false
          <cat> == cat
          <synargs> == ({ type "<type>" })
          <syntax> == ({ "<cat>" [ "<synargs>" ] })
          <semantics> == ([ L X true ])
          <true_ending> == <end "<init_ending>">
          <end null> == "<ending>"
          <end> == "<init_ending>"
          <ending> == "<init_ending>".
```

with the word 'false' being the default value for any path not defined elsewhere.

The major categories all inherit from the top node, adding their own 'synargs' to those of CATEGORY, assigning default values to some of these and defining default structures for the semantics. The 'ADJECTIVE' node, for example, is as follows,

```
ADJECTIVE: <> == CATEGORY
       <cat> == adjective
       <type> == @property
       <synargs> == ({ subjtype "<subjtype>" } CATEGORY)
       <semantics> == ([ L X "<rootsem>" ])
       <rootsem> == true.
```

In addition to these, some nodes (notably NOUN and VERB) supply additional information derived from the ending. This is one of the respects in which the DATR lexicon differs from the original lexicon. Since the original (main) lexicon could not refer to the ending, all information derived from the ending had to be provided by procedures run at lookup time. The DATR lexicon can express all of this information in a declarative manner, simply because of the assumption that the query will be in the form of a DATR node which may inherit and disseminate information in exactly the same way as other nodes permanently in the lexicon. The NOUN node defines the feature 'num' as singular or plural depending on the 'true_ending', even though this is only defined for query nodes, not for any of the permanent nodes in the lexicon,

```
NOUN:    <> == CATEGORY
         <cat> == n
         <num> == sing
         <num s> == plur
         <synargs> == ({ num <num "<true_ending>"> } CATEGORY)
         <semantics> == ([ L X [ "<semfunc>" X ] ]).
```

and VERB defines the features 'pass' (which defines whether it is possible that a verb is passive) and 'tense' by the same means,

```
VERB:    <> == CATEGORY
         <cat> == v
         <type> == @event
         <synargs> == ({ subcat "<subcat>" }
                        { subjtype "<subjtype>" }
                        { objtype "<objtype>" }
                        { obj2type "<obj2type>" }
                        { subjprep "<subjprep>" }
                        { objprep "<objprep>" }
                        { obj2prep "<obj2prep>" }
                        { passive "<passive>" }
                        { ending "<true_ending>" }
                        CATEGORY )
         <semantics> == ([ L E L S L 01
                         [ and [ eventtype E "<rootsem>" ]
                           [ time E <tense> ] ] ])
         <passive> == <pass "<true_ending>">
         <pass> == no
         <pass ed> == yes
         <tense> == <ten "<true_ending>">
         <ten> == pres
         <ten ing> == pres_fut
         <ten ed> == past.
```

In addition to the major categories, there are other abstract nodes which inherit from these, which group together sets of words which have other shared information. For example, the 'WEATHER' node inherits from NOUN, but defines the type and the semantics, with a single word, defined by the path <weather> derived from the terminal node. Thus words like 'rain', 'snow' etc.

can inherit everything from the WEATHER node needing only to define the weather condition in question,

```
WEATHER:<> == NOUN
        <type> == @ilpevent
        <semantics> == ([ L E [ eventtype E "<weather>" ] ]).
Rain:   <> == WEATHER
        <weather> == rain.
```

The treatment of abbreviations and irregular forms, as should be obvious, is trivial and needs no extra machinery. An abbreviation simply inherits everything from the word which it is an abbreviation for, e.g.

```
        Amb:    <> == Ambulance.
```

and an irregular form inherits from the root of that form, together with a separately defined ending, as in the example of 'children' above.

Phrases are still handled separately, in the same way as in the old lexicon. This is the only piece of 'lexical' information which is not contained in the DATR theorem.

4.3.3   Coverage of the Conversion

In the conversion, the initial aim was to purely convert the existing lexicon into DATR without making any improvements to it. However, in the course of the conversion, it became apparent that certain changes implemented now would save effort later. For example, it was deemed impractical to produce a DATR lexicon and interface which handled ending information in the same way as the original lexicon, when this would subsequently be changed. Similarly, some entries were omitted from the lexicon since they are now handled by tokenisation (e.g. numbers and punctuation characters) and others were omitted rather than set up distinct abstract nodes to handle them which seemed inappropriate. For example, the original lexicon had an entry for 'smith' as a name, but this was the only name given. To incorporate this would have meant creating an abstract node for the category of 'name', simply for this one word, so it was omitted.

4.4   The Lexica – Some Statistics

In the tables below, the number of 'entries' in each section of the original TIC lexicon is given. These do not correspond entirely with the number of words for which lexical information exists. This is because there is duplication in the representation. A word such as 'report' had two entries in the irregular lexicon,

```
        report report age
        report report null
```

the first of which states that it could have the information associated with the verb 'report' in the main lexicon, with the manipulations entailed by the 'age' ending (the ending used to express nominalisation). The second stated that it could also have the information associated with the verb in the main lexicon with a null ending. This was necessary since the lookup procedures did not allow normal checking of the lexicon if such an entry had been found, so the irregular entries frequently had to have their regular forms specified explicitly in the irregular section in this way.

Original lexicon

Number of entries in main lexicon	786
Number of abbreviation entries	179
Number of irregular entries	129
TOTAL	1094
Total size of files (bytes)	70046

With the figures for the DATR lexicon, the number of nodes is given, and these are divided into total number of nodes, number of abstract nodes and number of terminal nodes. In contrast to the original TIC lexicon, there is a direct correlation here between the number of terminal DATR nodes and the number of words for which lexical information exists. This assumes that 'ambulance' and 'amb' are distinct words, although the latter is an abbreviation of the former. As one would expect with DATR, there is no essential difference in the format, nor the type or amount of information in the different sections of the lexicon. The node for an abbreviation inherits from the node for its full form in exactly the same way as a word inherits from the node for another equivalent (in TIC terms) word.

DATR **lexicon**

Number of nodes in main lexicon	722
Number of nodes in special lexicon	186
(includes abbreviations and irregularities)	
TOTAL	908
Abstract nodes in main lexicon	154
Abstract nodes in special lexicon	7
TOTAL	161
Terminal nodes in main lexicon	568
Terminal nodes in special lexicon	179
TOTAL	747
Total size of files (bytes)	68032

The number of terminal DATR nodes differs from the number of lexical entries in the original lexicon for a number of reasons:

1. Certain entries are unnecessary with the improved morphological (i.e. ending) analysis in the new lexicon. Principally this affects the irregular entries. As discussed below, in the original lexicon, any word which had an irregular entry and a regular entry had to have both entries specified in the irregular section, in addition to having an entry in the main lexicon.

2. A few entries were omitted because they were inappropriate and/or not consistent (e.g. the example of 'smith' given above).

3. Some punctuation characters were included in the original lexicon and have been omitted.

4. The organisation into main, abbreviations and irregulars changed, so that some entries which were in the main lexicon originally are now treated as abbreviations. In addition, many of the irregularities were omitted because they were linguistically unsound, e.g. a set of nouns which inherited their information from the corresponding verbs like collision/collide. This information was constructed by means of some highly convoluted procedures. Any shared information can easily be accounted for in the DATR lexicon by means of inheritance between nodes. In fact, the division between sections of the lexicon, although maintained for ease of adaptation, is redundant in the processing of the DATR lexicon because it is all compiled into a single DATR theorem.

5. The way the lexicon is structured and the way lexical lookup takes place means that entries in the original lexicon do not correspond directly to terminal nodes in the DATR lexicon. Multiple entries are handled using two distinct methods: polysemous entries have a single node which refers to a set of nodes, one for each entry, which are distinguished by lettering, e.g. the verb 'ask' has a node 'Ask' which has a single sentence,

```
Ask:     <> == ([ poly "AskA" "AskB" ]).
```

and the separate senses of the word are dealt with under the nodes 'AskA' and 'AskB'; homographs have distinct nodes which are differentiated by means of numbering, so that the entries for 'close' (meaning a kind of street) and 'close' (meaning 'shut') are represented by two nodes 'Close1' and 'Close2'. The lookup procedures then check for a node which corresponds to the input root (capitalised) and if not found then look for a node which corresponds to the capitalised word with a 1; if this succeeds then it looks for the word, capitalised, with a 2 and so on until it fails. This method of representation has led to an overall decrease in the number of terminal nodes required. The reason for this is that, although for each polysemous entry an extra node has to be used, in many cases there are words which are essentially identical (in terms of the syntax and semantics required for the TIC), and so a word which had seven polysemous entries in the original TIC lexicon, but whose entries were all identical to those of another word, requires only one DATR node, referring to the other word's top node. Thus, although in several cases a single additional node is required, in other cases, six or seven entries in the original lexicon are reduced to a single DATR node. In addition, some polysemous entries can refer directly to abstract nodes. For example,

```
Ford: <> == ([ poly "SMALL_VEH" "VEH_ADJ" ]).
```

where the two entries in the original lexicon were for the use of 'ford' as a noun meaning a make of car or as an adjective applied to a vehicle (as in 'ford transit'). Another similar case which requires fewer DATR nodes than original lexical entries is the situation where the quoted nodes are not abstract nodes, but other terminal nodes, for the definition of other words, e.g.

```
Send:    <> == ([ poly "SendA" "Pass" ]).
```

4.5   Processing Times

The original TIC lexicon was written in POP11 and was pre-compiled into a simple lookup table which was consulted at run-time. The process of compiling involves loading up a set of POP11 files and then building the lexicon onto disc. The total time for this is approximately 6 minutes of which less than a minute is the initial loading of files.

The DATR lexicon uses the DATR implementation written by Roger Evans in Prolog (Evans, 1990) and involves a two-stage compilation. The DATR files containing the lexicon are first compiled into Prolog files, then the Prolog files are compiled into the parser saved image. This could be done in just one stage, with the DATR files compiled directly into the saved image, but this way takes much longer. The compilation directly into the saved image takes about 37 minutes, while the compilation into Prolog files takes approximately 12 minutes, with another 1.5 minutes to compile the Prolog files into the saved image. These times are based on the system running on a SPARC-station1 but are extremely approximate. It should be stressed that the compilation time is not of great concern to us and that the DATR compiler used is non-optimal.

Similarly, efficiency of lexical lookup is not of primary concern at this stage of the project. None of the system code has been written with this kind of optimisation in mind; the whole aim of the project up to now has been simply to show that the problem for the system as a whole is tractable.

Timed tests have shown that lexical lookup in the old lexicon is, as expected, faster than in the DATR lexicon. The times for lookup for the original lexicon ranged from about 0.09 seconds for a word with a simple, small, single entry (e.g. 'rta', 'you') to about 0.5 seconds for a word with polysemous entries (e.g.

'close', 'northbound'). The DATR lookup times ranged from 0.2 seconds to 1.05 seconds for the same words. It was interesting that the times for 'you', which has a relatively complex entry in the DATR lexicon, with reference to two abstract nodes and quoted path inheritance, were not significantly different from those for 'rta' which has a relatively simple inheritance structure. Similarly, the times for 'close' which requires lookup of more than one node name ('Close1', 'Close2'), were not significantly different from those for 'northbound', which has three polysemous entries. It would appear from these times that the complexity of the DATR is of less importance in lookup times than the simple number of different senses of a word, however they are represented. This implies that a large part of the lookup time is actually taken up by the macro expansion procedures, which take the abbreviated forms of syntactic types in the lexical entries and expand them out, for both the DATR and old versions of the lexicon. This also explains why the differences between times of words with multiple entries and those with single entries differed by similar proportions in both the DATR and old lexica.

4.6   Conclusion

Although the times for lexical lookup have not been improved, the conversion of the TIC lexicon into DATR has undoubtedly been worthwhile.

One of the main aims of converting the lexicon into DATR, in addition to the general aim of finding out how feasible it was to code a real application lexicon in DATR, was to improve portability. This has been achieved, since the very structure of the DATR lexicon means that changes to a set of entries or to all entries can very often be done only at a small number of abstract nodes, rather than throughout the lexicon as was previously the case. This is particularly important at the current stage of the project, when we are involved in changing the grammar rules and the semantic representations used on a fairly large scale, as well as developing a lexicon for a new police domain.

5   Norms or Inference Tickets? A Frontal Collision between Intuitions

MICHAEL MORREAU

Abstract

Theories of nonmonotonic reasoning are, on the face of it, of at least two sorts. In *Circumscription*, generic facts like *Birds fly* are taken to be essentially normative, and nonmonotonicity arises when individuals are assumed to be as normal as is consistent with available information about them. In theories like *Default Logic* such facts are taken to be rules of inference, and nonmonotonicity arises when available information is augmented by adding as many as possible of the inferences sanctioned by such rules. Depending on which of the two informal views is taken, different patterns of nonmonotonic reasoning are appropriate. Here it is shown that these different patterns of reasoning cannot be combined in a single theory of nonmonotonic reasoning.

5.1   Introduction

Nonmonotonic reasoning is that which lacks a monotonicity property which has been taken to be a characteristic of logical reasoning. In a theory of nonmonotonic reasoning, the consequences of a set of premises do not always accumulate as the set of premises is expanded. Nonmonotonicity has been researched in artificial intelligence because people reason nonmonotonically, and this in ways which seem directly related to intelligence. One important example of this is in commonsense reasoning about kinds, where jumping to conclusions enables intelligent agents to save time spent on gathering information.

In just what way is such jumping to logically invalid conclusions reasonable? In the artificial intelligence literature essentially two sources of nonmonotonicity have been investigated: reasoning by *inference tickets* about individuals of various kinds, and reasoning by assuming individuals to be as normal representatives of kinds as information available about them allows.

In some theories, hard information is augmented by means of inference tickets like *If something is a bird, and you have no reason to assume that it cannot fly, then assume that it can fly.* Nonmonotonicity comes about because one sometimes must retract such premature conclusions as the gaps in one's information are filled in. On the basis of the above rule one might, lacking information to the contrary, jump to the conclusion that a particular bird can fly. On obtaining information to the contrary, however, there is reason to assume that the bird

58

cannot fly, and the above rule no longer allows this premature assumption to be made.

A second and on the face of it different source of nonmonotonicity is what might be called *norms*. Philosophers of science have reduced dispositional propositions such as *Table salt is soluble in water* to nondispositional terms by invoking the notion of normal circumstances. This particular sentence then comes out as something like *Pieces of table salt dissolve when placed in water under normal circumstances*. Similarly, generic sentences like *Birds fly* have been thought to be true or false depending on the properties of prototypical or normal birds. It is this sort of statement about what normal or ideal individuals are like, or what happens under normal or ideal circumstances, that I mean by norms.

To see how norms give rise to nonmonotonic reasoning, assume the above analysis of the fact that table salt is soluble in water, and suppose that a particular piece of salt has been added to water. Assuming circumstances to be normal then allows the conclusion to be drawn that the salt will dissolve. The reasoning is defeasible because this conclusion must be retracted if the additional information is made available that the circumstances are somehow abnormal, say because the water is frozen. For circumstances can no longer be assumed to be normal once they are known to be abnormal (one can of course under circumstances which are known to be abnormal reason counterfactually about how things would have been if circumstances *had been* normal — but that is different from assuming that they *are* normal).

There are of course some obvious differences between norms and inference tickets. For one thing, whereas norms are obviously the sort of thing which can be true or otherwise, inference tickets are not. Like other rules governing behaviour, an inference ticket is more naturally thought of as something which can be followed, or otherwise. It somehow seems wrong to attribute truth to a rule like *If something is a bird, and you have no reason to assume that it cannot fly, then assume that it can fly*, as it does to attribute truth to the rules of a board game (like say the following 'en passant' rule of chess: *If a white pawn moves two places forward, and a black pawn is positioned so that it could have taken the white one had it moved just one place, then the black pawn may pretend that the white pawn has moved just one place*. It is true of chess that it has this rule. But what could it mean to say that this rule itself is true in chess?) It does of course make sense to assign truth values to statements about the actions of chess players, as it does to assign truth values to statements about the epistemic states of agents who reason according to default rules. But that is different from assigning truth values to the rules themselves.

But when it comes to the nonmonotonic inferences which they sanction, there are also some striking similarities between norms and inference tickets. Both the norm *Pieces of table salt are such that if added to water under normal circumstances, they will dissolve* and a default rule like *If a piece of table salt is added to water and there is no reason to believe that it will not dissolve, then you may assume that it will dissolve* allow the same assumption to be made about a given bit of salt which has been added to a quantity of water: it will dissolve. A glance through the artificial intelligence literature provides more circumstantial evidence that reasoning with normative facts and default reasoning are, if not one and the same, then at least very similar things. The same generic examples involving birds and whether or not they can fly are used to motivate both, and the same general patterns of nonmonotonic reasoning, such as the so-called *Nixon Diamond* and the *Tweety Triangle*, are judged appropriate to both.

It is the purpose of this paper to argue that these appearances to the contrary, nonmonotonic reasoning deriving from assuming maximal normality and that deriving from inference tickets are very different things. I argue that each of these kinds of nonmonotonic reasoning has characteristic properties which make it incompatible with the other.

5.2   A General Format for Nonmonotonic Formalisms

Most theories of nonmonotonic reasoning are of the following format, or can be pressed into it to facilitate comparison. Sets of premises representing the indefeasible or *hard* facts about some domain are stated in a logical language, which is governed by a monotonic inference notion $\models$. This *core* inference notion extracts from a set of premises information, it doesn't add anything. Furthermore, an inference notion $\approx$ is defined which allows additional defeasible or *soft* conclusions to be drawn. To the conclusions drawn by means of $\models$ from a set Γ of premises, $\approx$ adds a periphery of conclusions which do not logically follow from Γ. That is, $\approx$ is nonmonotonic, and *extends* $\models$: for all sets Γ of sentences and for all sentences ϕ, if $\Gamma \models \phi$ then $\Gamma \approx \phi$. In this section, constraints are reviewed which are commonly placed on such notions $\models$ and $\approx$.

In the thirties, Tarski stated quite generally some minimal requirements which a relation $\models$ must fulfill if it is truly to be a logical notion. Tarski's three requirements of reflexivity, idempotence and monotonicity are, in combination, equivalent to the combination of the following three requirements which we place on $\models$. Here Γ and Γ' range over sets of formulas, and ϕ ranges over isolated formulas:

REFLEXIVITY: If $\phi \in \Gamma$, then $\Gamma \models \phi$.

CUT: If $\Gamma \models \Gamma'$ and $\Gamma \cup \Gamma' \models \phi$, then $\Gamma \models \phi$.

MONOTONICITY: If $\Gamma \models \phi$, then $\Gamma \cup \Gamma' \models \phi$.

A relation $\models$ which satisfies these three requirements will be said to be *Tarskian*.

Concerning the nonmonotonic periphery, Gabbay (1985) and Makinson (1989) have stated and investigated some minimal requirements which a relation $\mathrel{|\!\approx}$ should satisfy if it is to be a notion of nonmonotonic logical consequence. Clearly the third of the above requirements must be given up. But, as Gabbay and Makinson suggest, a nonmonotonic logic may reasonably be required to retain at least the little monotonicity which the following notion of *cautious monotonicity* would salvage:

CAUTIOUS MONOTONICITY: If $\Gamma \mathrel{|\!\approx} \phi$ and $\Gamma \mathrel{|\!\approx} \Gamma'$, then $\Gamma \cup \Gamma' \mathrel{|\!\approx} \phi$.

There is no obvious reason why a notion of nonmonotonic logical consequence should not be required to satisfy the first two of the above requirements, reflexivity and cut. And here is a good technical reason for wanting them satisfied: cautious monotonicity and cut (a combination which Makinson refers to as *cumulativity*) together make consequence notions behave themselves. For provided $\mathrel{|\!\approx}$ satisfies these two requirements, it can easily be shown that if $\Gamma \mathrel{|\!\approx} \Gamma'$ and $\Gamma' \mathrel{|\!\approx} \Gamma$, then $\Gamma' \mathrel{|\!\approx} \phi$ iff $\Gamma \mathrel{|\!\approx} \phi$.

For one half of the trivial proof, let (i) $\Gamma' \mathrel{|\!\approx} \Gamma$ and (ii) $\Gamma \mathrel{|\!\approx} \Gamma'$, and suppose (iii) $\Gamma' \mathrel{|\!\approx} \phi$. To be shown is that $\Gamma \mathrel{|\!\approx} \phi$. By cautious monotonicity we have from (i) and (iii) $\Gamma \cup \Gamma' \mathrel{|\!\approx} \phi$. But then with cut and (ii): $\Gamma \mathrel{|\!\approx} \phi$. $\square$

Given that $\mathrel{|\!\approx}$ extends $\models$, cumulativity has in view of the above the consequence that $\models$ and $\mathrel{|\!\approx}$ together satisfy the following constraint of

LOGICALITY: If $\Gamma \models \Gamma'$ and $\Gamma' \models \Gamma$, then $\Gamma' \mathrel{|\!\approx} \phi$ iff $\Gamma \mathrel{|\!\approx} \phi$.

According to this principle, logically equivalent sets of premises have the same nonmonotonic consequences; it is in other words not the syntactic form of a set of premises which counts, but its logical content. Below I need not assume cumulativity. But I do assume logicality, a principle which is obviously desirable quite apart from the fact that it follows from cumulativity.

The above discussion is summarized in the following definition:

Definition 1 *Consequence notions* $\models$ *and* $\mathrel{|\!\approx}$ *together constitute a* nonmonotonic theory *just in case:*

1. $\models$ *(the* monotonic core*) is Tarskian;*
2. $\mathrel{|\!\approx}$ *(the* nonmonotonic periphery*) extends* $\models$*; and*
3. $\models$ *and* $\mathrel{|\!\approx}$ *satisfy logicality.*

One trivial consequence of this definition which we will use later is that the nonmonotonic periphery of a nonmonotonic theory is reflexive.

To bring out the difference between reasoning with inference tickets and norms we must assume that $\mathcal{L}$, the formal language on which the above consequence notions are defined, has a certain minimal expressive power: here, for the sake of simplicity, we assume a conjunction $\wedge$ and a negation $\neg$ to be definable in $\mathcal{L}$ which behave classically. Disjunction, and a material conditional and biconditional are defined in terms of $\wedge$ and $\neg$ in the usual way. I assume also that $\approx\!\!\!\mid$ is closed under modus ponens across the material conditional: if $\Gamma \approx\!\!\!\mid \phi$ and $\Gamma \approx\!\!\!\mid \phi \rightarrow \psi$, then $\Gamma \approx\!\!\!\mid \psi$.

5.3   Inference Tickets

On what I am calling the 'inference ticket' view of nonmonotonic reasoning about kinds, nonmonotonicity arises from strengthening sets of premises by adding conclusions sanctioned by rules of inference. On this view, a natural language generic sentence like *Birds fly* expresses something like the following inference ticket: *If you think something is a bird, and you have no reason to assume that it cannot fly, then you may assume that it flies.* Or, in other words, *A bird may be assumed to be able to fly, unless there is reason to assume otherwise.*

What are some of the characteristic principles of reasoning by inference tickets? Suppose you are following the rule *A ϕ may be be assumed to be a ψ_1 unless there is reason to assume otherwise*, and also the rule *A ϕ may be assumed to be a ψ_2 unless there is reason to assume otherwise*. Suppose in addition that, according to your information, *c is a ϕ, but not a ψ_1* . Then the first of these rules does not enable the assumption to be made that *c is a ψ_1*, since you do have reason to assume that *c is not a ψ_1*. You have reason to assume this since it is a part of the information available to you. But provided the information that *c is a ϕ, but not a ψ_1*, is not a ground for assuming that *c is not a ψ_2*, the second rule does enable the assumption to be made that *c is a ψ_2*.

To facilitate the comparison of different formalisms, let us now introduce a piece of meta-notion, so as to be able to refer to various representations of facts like *Birds fly*. While discussing inference tickets, $\phi > \psi$ will refer to the inference ticket: *A ϕ may be assumed to be a ψ unless there is reason to assume otherwise*. Later, when we come to consider normative systems, $\phi > \psi$ will come to stand for something like *Normal ϕ's are ψ's*.

Then it has just been argued that the following principle of *Independence* is inescapable on an inference ticket view of nonmonotonic reasoning:

$$\phi c, \neg\psi_1 c, \phi > \psi_1, \phi > \psi_2 \approx\!\!\!\mid \psi_2 c$$

The above argumentation for this principle covers only the case where c, ϕ, ψ_1 and ψ_2 are such that the information that c is a ϕ but not a ψ_1 does not provide a ground for assuming that c is not a ψ_2. So clearly this principle must be restricted to formulas ϕ, ψ_1 and ψ_2 which are, in some appropriate sense of the word, independent of each other. Here I won't attempt to characterise completely a suitable notion of independence. The notion of *logical independence* defined below says what it is for predicates to behave logically with respect to each other like different predicate letters. On the basis of the story told above, and in a simple setting where causal and other nonlogical evidential relations are excluded, it is reasonable to take logical independence as a sufficient criterion for independence.

Definition 2 *A* conjunctive context *(in variables ϕ, ψ, and γ) maps any formulas ϕ, ψ, and γ onto the formula $\pm\phi \wedge \pm\psi \wedge \pm\gamma$ (here '$\pm$' indicates that either $\neg$ or nothing may stand at this place in the formula).*

Definition 3 *Monadic predicates ϕ, ψ, and γ are $\models$-independent provided that for all conjunctive contexts $C_1, C_2 \ldots$ in the variables ϕ, ψ, and γ, and all sets $\{c_1, c_2, \ldots\}$ of constants:*

$$\cup_i \{C_i(c_i)\} \text{ is } \models\text{-consistent}$$

Where $\models$ is classical logic, $\models$-independent predicates are said to be *classically independent*. By way of example, any three different monadic predicate letters can easily be seen to be classically independent.

It is a routine matter to verify the following consequence of the fact that negation and conjunction behave classically in the monotonic core $\models$ of our nonmonotonic theories (although we could make do with, say, an intuitionistic core logic):

Fact 1 *If ϕ, ψ and γ are $\models$-independent predicates, then so are ϕ, ψ and $\psi \leftrightarrow \gamma$.*

On the basis of the story told above, and in a simple setting where causal and other nonlogical evidential relations are excluded, it is reasonable to take logical independence as a sufficient criterion for independence:

Definition 4 *The consequence relation $\approx$ satisfies* Independence *relative to $\models$ just in case for all $\models$-independent monadic predicates ϕ, ψ_1, and ψ_2, and for all constants c:*

$$\phi c, \neg\psi_1 c, \phi > \psi_1, \phi > \psi_2 \approx \psi_2 c$$

The above discussion is summarized in the following definition:

Definition 5 *Consequence notions $\models$ and $\approx$ together constitute an* inference ticket theory *just in case:*

1. *$\models$ and $\approx$ form a nonmonotonic theory;*
2. *$\approx$ satisfies Independence, relative to $\models$.*

5.4 An Example: Default Logic

I take Reiter's (1980) *Default Logic* to be an inference ticket theory, in the sense of definition 5. In this section, after briefly presenting a simple version of Default Logic, I will show how to present it as a nonmonotonic theory in the technical sense defined above, using an embedding into modal logic due to Truszczyński (1991). I then verify that Default Logic satisfies the principle of Independence.

Default Logic[1] works with the notion of *default theories*, these being pairs $\langle W, \Delta \rangle$ of which W is a set of first order sentences, and Δ is a set of *closed default rules*. A closed default rule is a rule of the form

$$\frac{\phi : \psi}{\psi}$$

where ϕ and ψ are first order sentences. Note that default rules are not them-selves a part of the object language of Default Logic, which is just that of classical first order logic. For convenience, ϕ may be called the *condition* of the above rule, and ψ its *consequent*. This notation may be extended to monadic predicates ϕx and ψx which share the same free variable, the understanding be-ing that the *open default rule*

$$\frac{\phi x : \psi x}{\psi x}$$

is just shorthand for the collection of all of its instantiations with terms. So, for example, the set

$$\left\{ \frac{\phi x : \psi x}{\psi x} \, , \, \frac{\phi x : \chi x}{\chi x} \right\}$$

of open defaults is just shorthand for the following set of closed defaults:

$$\left\{ \frac{\phi t : \psi t}{\psi t} : t \in TERMS \right\} \bigcup \left\{ \frac{\phi x : \chi x}{\chi x} : t \in TERMS \right\}$$

Here *TERMS* is the set of closed terms of the language in question.

The set W of a default theory $\langle W, \Delta \rangle$ represents hard facts, whose logic is just first order logic, and to which a nonmonotonic periphery is to be added by doing default reasoning. Roughly speaking, the idea is to strengthen W by adding as many conclusions sanctioned by rules in Δ as is possible, without sacrificing consistency. In order to capture this idea, Reiter introduces the notion of an *extension* of a default theory. The extensions of $\langle W, \Delta \rangle$ may be defined to be those sets E of sentences such that

$$E = \bigcup_{i=0}^{i=\infty} E_i$$

---

[1] The simple part of Default Logic presented here is sufficient for illustrative purposes.

where (letting Cn be the classical notion of logical consequence) E_0, E_1, $E_2,\ldots$ are defined as follows:[2]

$$E_0 := W$$

$$E_{i+1} := Cn(E_i) \cup \left\{ \psi : \dfrac{\phi\colon\psi}{\psi} \in \Delta, \text{ and } \phi \in E_i \text{ and } \neg\psi \notin E \right\}$$

Set up in this manner by Reiter, Default Logic is not a nonmonotonic theory in the technical sense of definition 1, and this for two reasons. Firstly, we do not have a background core logic $\models$ defined on default theories, let alone one which can be shown to be Tarskian. We do of course have a logic for the first component of default theories, the sets W of first order formulas. It is just classical logic. But we have nothing which is defined on the sets Δ of defaults. Indeed, it is not obvious that a sensible notion of logical inference could even in principle be defined for default rules. Logical inference almost always invariably involves preserving truth values. But, as we have seen in the introduction, it is not clear what it means to assign truth values to inference tickets. In Default Logic, defaults are not even a part of the object language, but are rules of inference expressed in the metalanguage. The second reason why Default Logic does not yet fit the format of definition 1 is that we do not have a notion of nonmonotonic consequence $\approx$ which allows conclusions to be drawn from default theories. We just have the notion of an extension.

It is, however, possible to set Default Logic up as a nonmonotonic theory and, it turns out, to verify that it satisfies *Independence*. In the rest of this section I show how.

In the introduction it was briefly mentioned that even if rules of behaviour do not have truth values, sentences describing the behaviour of those who follow them do. In the special case of rules of inference, these descriptions have the form of closure conditions on the reasoner's epistemic state, and can be expressed in a language containing suitable epistemic operators. This is what underlies the embeddings of Default Logic into various modal epistemic logics, as first presented by Konolige (1988) and later much improved by Truszczyński (1991). It is these results which allow Default Logic to be cast as a nonmonotonic theory.

Truszczyński works in a language $\mathcal{L}$ for modal sentential logic, with the two modal operators L (necessity) and M (possibility). For the sake of uniformity we choose a first-order language, but since we will not venture outside of its sentential fragment, we can still make use of his results. Let $\mathcal{L}_0$ be the nonmodal part of $\mathcal{L}$, and let δ be a normal default rule in $\mathcal{L}_0$. That is, let δ, for some $\mathcal{L}_0$

---

[2] Note that this is not an inductive definition of E, because of the presence of E in the definition of E_{i+1}.

sentences ϕ and ψ, be of the form

$$\frac{\phi : \psi}{\psi}$$

Truszczyński defines the translation δ^* of δ into $\mathcal{L}$ to be the following sentence:

$$L\phi \wedge LM\psi \to L\psi$$

For an $\mathcal{L}_0$ sentence ϕ, let ϕ^* be defined as $L\phi$. Finally, let the translation function $*$ be extended to sets W of sentences and sets Δ of defaults in the obvious way: W^* is defined as $\{\phi^* : \phi \in W\}$, and Δ^* is defined analogously.

For any set E of $\mathcal{L}_0$ sentences with $E = Cn(E)$, let $st(E)$ be the unique stable expansion of E in $\mathcal{L}$ whose restriction to $\mathcal{L}_0$ is just E. (See Moore, 1985 for Stalnaker's notion of a stable expansion, and the demonstration of uniqueness. Here all that matters is that for any stable set S, if $\phi \in S$ then $L\phi \in S$.) And let $\models$ be any one of a range of well understood modal logics specified by Truszczyński. For details the reader is referred to Truszczyński (1991). Here, all that matters is that:

1. Each such $\models$ is Tarskian. As a result of this, each has the property that $\models$-equivalent sets of premises have the same $\models$-consequences.
2. Each such $\models$ is a conservative extension of classical logic, in the sense that its restriction to $\mathcal{L}_0$ is just classical logical consequence.

As a result, any $\models$-independent $\mathcal{L}_0$ predicates are also classically independent.

As a notational convenience set $Cn_\models(\Gamma) = \{\psi : \Gamma \models \psi\}$. Then one main theorem of the paper mentioned above is:

Theorem 1   *(Truszczyński): For any set $E \subseteq \mathcal{L}_0$ which is closed under classical consequences, the following two statements are equivalent:*

1. *E is an extension of $\langle W, \Delta \rangle$.*
2. *$st(E) = Cn_\models(W^* \cup \Delta^* \cup \{\neg L\phi : \phi \notin st(E)\})$.*

As a further convenience, identify any default theory $\langle W, \Delta \rangle$ with $W \cup \Delta$ (nothing is lost in so doing, since it is always possible to recover $\langle W, \Delta \rangle$ from $W \cup \Delta$). Now a monotonic core and nonmonotonic periphery may be defined as follows:

Definition 6   *Where ϕ is either an $\mathcal{L}_0$ sentence or a default rule in $\mathcal{L}_0$, we define:*

1. *$W \cup \Delta \models \phi$ iff $W^* \cup \Delta^* \models \phi^*$.*
2. *$W \cup \Delta \approx\!\!\!| \phi$ iff for all $E \subseteq \mathcal{L}_0$ such that $st(E) = Cn_\models(W^* \cup \Delta^* \cup \neg L\phi : \phi \notin st(E)) : \phi^* \in st(E)$.*

This definition makes $\models$ ambiguous, but harmlessly so. Note also that *(2)* amounts to a 'cautious' definition of default reasoning, where the consequences of a default theory are those sentences which show up in all of its extensions. In fact, however, everything which is said here about Default Logic holds just as well if a 'credulous' notion of default consequence is adopted instead.

Now the following facts, which follow immediately from the above definition, confirm that the above presents Default Logic in the general format of a nonmonotonic theory in the sense of definition 1:

Fact 2

1. $\models$ *is Tarskian;*
2. *If $W \cup \Delta \models \phi$, then $W \cup \Delta \mathrel{\vert\!\approx} \phi$ (that is, $\mathrel{\vert\!\approx}$ extends $\models$);*
3. *If $W \cup \Delta \models W' \cup \Delta'$ and $W' \cup \Delta' \models W \cup \Delta$, then:*
   $W \cup \Delta \mathrel{\vert\!\approx} \phi$ *iff* $W' \cup \Delta' \mathrel{\vert\!\approx} \phi$ ($\mathrel{\vert\!\approx}$ *and* $\models$ *satisfy logicality).*

Independence I take to be a characteristic pattern of reasoning in inference ticket formalisms. Default Logic I take to be an inference ticket formalism, so it remains to be verified that (modal) Default Logic does in fact satisfy independence. The following fact gets us most of the way:

Fact 3 *Let ϕ, ψ_1 and ψ_2 be classically independent monadic predicates, and let c be any constant. Define:*

$$W := \{\phi c, \neg \psi_1 c\}, \qquad \Delta := \left\{ \frac{\phi: \psi_1}{\psi_1} \;,\; \frac{\phi: \psi_2}{\psi_2} \right\}$$

Then $\psi_2 c \in E$, where E is any extension of $\langle W, \Delta \rangle$.

Proof sketch: Prove first (using the definition of a default extension together with the independence of ϕ, ψ_1 and ψ_2) that for each extension E of $\langle W, \Delta \rangle$: $\neg \psi_2 c \notin E$. Prove second (using the same definition) that because of this $\psi_2 c \in E$. (In fact, for any extension E we have $\psi_2 c \in E_2$.) $\quad\square$

Together with the above theorem of Truszczyński, this fact has the immediate corollary that modal default logic satisfies Independence:

Corollary 1 *Let ϕ, ψ_1 and ψ_2 be $\models$-independent monadic predicates of $\mathcal{L}_I$. Then:*

$$\phi c, \neg \psi_1 c, \frac{\phi: \psi_1}{\psi_1} \;,\; \frac{\phi: \psi_2}{\psi_2} \mathrel{\vert\!\approx} \psi_2 c$$

Proof: Let W and Δ be as in fact 3 above, and suppose for the contradiction that there is some set $E \subseteq \mathcal{L}_I$ such that:

1. $st(E) = Cn_{\models}(W * \cup \Delta^* \cup \{\neg L\phi : \phi \notin st(E)\})$, but such that
2. $(\psi_2 c)^* = L\psi_2 c \notin st(E)$.

By the stability of $st(E)$, (2) implies that $\psi_2 c \notin st(E)$, and so (since $E \subseteq st(E)$) $\psi_2 c \notin E$.

By theorem 1, on the other hand, (1) implies that E is an extension of $\langle W, \Delta \rangle$. Since $\models$ is a conservative extension of classical consequence, ϕ, ψ_1 and ψ_2 are classically independent. So by fact 3, $\psi_2 c \in E$.

We have a contradiction, and have proved the corollary. $\Box$

To summarize: in view of fact 2 and corollary 1, (modal) Default Logic is an inference ticket theory in the sense of definition 5.

5.5   Norms

In this section, the meta-notion $\phi > \psi$ will be used to refer to norms, or sentences which express that normal, or typical, or prototypical ϕ's have the property ψ. Here are some characteristics which I think a theory based on norms must have, if it takes this intended interpretation of normative sentences at all seriously. They are characteristics of the monotonic core, since they follow quite directly from the idea that norms quantify over normal individuals, and have nothing to do with whatever mechanism is used for assuming maximal normality.

CONJUNCTION IN THE CONSEQUENT:
$$\phi > \psi_1, \phi > \psi_2 \models \phi > (\psi_1 \wedge \psi_2)$$

That is, if all normal ϕ's have the property ψ_1, and also the property ψ_2, then all normal ϕ's have the property $\psi_1 \wedge \psi_2$. The following principle likewise follows from the idea that normative sentences quantify over normal individuals:

WEAKENING IN THE CONSEQUENT:
If $\psi x \models \chi x$ then $\phi > \psi \models \phi > \chi$.

Thus if individuals cannot have the property ψ without having the property χ, then this also applies to all normal ϕ's.

Together, these two principles make that which appears on the right of $>$ a *theory*, in the sense that it is closed under logical consequence:

LOGICAL CLOSURE IN THE CONSEQUENT:
If $\psi_1 x, \dots, \psi_n x \models \chi x$ then $\phi > \psi_1, \dots, \phi > \psi_n \models \phi > \chi$.

To recapitulate the justification for this principle on the view that generic sentences express the properties of prototypical or normal individuals is: if individuals which have the properties $\psi_1, \dots, \psi_n$ necessarily have the property χ, and if furthermore normal ϕ's have these properties $\psi_1, \dots, \psi_n$, then normal ϕ's must have the property χ.[3]

---

[3] Veltman offers the following (to my mind, very puzzling) argument *against* logical closure in the consequent in reasoning with norms (Veltman, 1991, pp. 48 and 49): Here are two sets of

I take this principle of logical closure in the consequent to be a characteristic feature of normative theories of nonmonotonic reasoning, so to summarize the discussion of this section:

premises:

Γ: Tigers normally have four legs. Shere Khan is a tiger. Shere Khan does not have four legs.

Γ': Tigers normally have four or five legs. Shere Khan is a tiger. Shere Khan does not have four legs.

According to Veltman, from Γ' it intuitively does, and from Γ it does not, defeasibly follow that Shere Khan has five legs. So letting this sentence be denoted A, according to Veltman (1) does not hold but (2) does:

(1) $\Gamma \not\approx A$

(2) $\Gamma' \approx A$

I think he is right about this; let us suppose that he is. Veltman continues on p. 49, 'It is difficult to see how this could be so if from "tigers normally have four legs" it would follow that tigers normally have four or five legs'. About this I think he is wrong. That a defeasibly drawn conclusion like *Shere Khan has five legs* could be withrawn on substituting a logically stronger sentence like *tigers normally have four legs* for a weaker one like *tigers normally have four or five legs* is precisely the sort of thing that nonmonotonicity makes possible. Furthermore, and more significantly, that this particular conclusion should be withdrawn on moving from this Γ' to Γ follows almost automatically from the dynamic approach which Veltman himself takes.

To see how, consider the following two suggestive cases:

1. Suppose one obtains the information that p holds. Then one's set of epistemic possibilities, or the way one takes the world to be, will include only worlds where p holds. Suppose one then hears that one's previous information was wrong, that in fact (*not p*). And let q be some other proposition about which one had no prior beliefs, and which is independent of (*not p*) (in the sense that each of q and (*not q*) is compatible with (*not p*)).

   There is, on the basis of the above, no obvious way to respond to this new information that (*not p*). But whichever way one responds, one has no reason to start believing the arbitrary independent proposition q.

   Letting p be the proposition that Shere Khan has four legs, letting q be the proposition that Shere Khan has five legs, and substituting for one's epistemic possibilities the smaller set of ways one *presumes* the world to be, one has the outline of a dynamic explanation of the invalidity of the argument (1) above.

2. Suppose that instead of obtaining the information that p holds, one obtains the — logically weaker — information that either p or q holds, these being two incompatible propositions about which one had no prior beliefs. Then one will have, among one's epistemic possibilities, possible worlds where q holds but not p, and worlds where p holds but not q. Suppose that one then learns that in fact p does not hold. Since this new information is consistent with that which was previously available, one will update incrementally, simply excluding from one's epistemic possibilities those possible worlds where p holds. The result will be a set of possible worlds where q holds but not p. Substituting as above, one has the outline of a dynamic explanation of the validity of argument (2) above.

One theory of defeasible reasoning about norms which satisfies logical closure in the consequent and yet distinguishes in the way Veltman wants between argument forms (1) and (2) above, is presented in Asher and Morreau (1991). The above suggests strongly the way in which this theory distinguishes between (1) and (2).

Definition 7 *Consequence notions $\models$ and $\approx$ together constitute a* normative theory *just in case:*

1. $\models$ *and $\approx$ form a nonmonotonic theory ;*
2. $\models$ *satisfies Closure in the Consequent.*

5.6   An Example: Circumscription

McCarthy's (1980, 1986) theory of Circumscription is the most familiar theory from the Artificial Intelligence literature which, with a few reservations which I will come to shortly, may be seen to be a theory of reasoning with norms. In the case of Circumscription, the normative sentences which give rise to the nonmonotonic reasoning are representations in first order logic of generic sentences; the standard example is *Birds normally fly*, which can be represented as follows:

$$\forall x (bird(x) \wedge \neg Ab(x) \to fly(x))$$

Here the monadic first order predicate *Ab* expresses abnormality: an individual falls within its extension just in case it is, intuitively speaking, an abnormal bird.

Another and more sophisticated representation of generic sentences in Circumscription distinguishes different 'respects' in which things can be abnormal. These different respects are treated as abstract objects, allowing the notion of 'abnormality in some respect' to be formalized as a relation between these abstract objects and the individuals of whatever kind one is interested in. So *Ab* becomes a binary relation instead of the above monadic predicate, and *Birds normally fly* is represented

$$\forall x (bird(x) \wedge \neg Ab(\texttt{respect} - \texttt{of} - \texttt{flying}, x) \to fly(x))$$

Here the individual constant `respect-of-flying` is supposed to denote one particular respect in which something can be abnormal. Judging from the literature, which is not explicit on the matter, it seems that there are a great number of these different respects, essentially a different one for each property which one might attribute to birds or other kinds. Models contain lots of different abstract objects, denoted by mnemonically chosen constants `respect-of-flying`, `respect-of-feathers`, `respect-of-laying-eggs`, `respect-of-chirruping`, and so on.

In the case of Circumscription, then, *bird > fly* is shorthand for either of the above first order representations; it will be clear from the context which one, and the monotonic logic $\models$ is just classical logical consequence. So much for the representation of norms using Circumscription, then, and their monotonic core logic. It remains to be said how in Circumscription hard information is strengthened by assuming maximal normality.

In Circumscription, $\models$ is defeasibly strengthened by restricting attention to a subclass of the models of sets of premises. The preferred subclass contains those models of the premises in which the special predicate Ab has a set theoretically minimal extension. The resulting nonmonotonic extension $\approx$ of the classical underlying logic is called minimal entailment. It is a trivial matter to verify that $\models$ is a notion of logical consequence in the sense of Tarski, that $\approx$ is an extension of $\models$, and that together $\approx$ and $\models$ satisfy logicality. So Circumscription is a nonmonotonic theory in the sense of definition 1.

We have taken Circumscription as our example of a normative theory, and it is instructive to check to what extent Closure in the Consequent is satisfied. In fact it is very easy to verify that Circumscription validates this principle on the simpler representation of generic sentences given above, in which Ab is a monadic predicate.

However, it is also easy to see that without making adjustments, Closure in the Consequent is not satisfied on the more sophisticated representation. In fact, *neither* the principle of Conjunction in the Consequent nor the principle of Weakening in the Consequent is satisfied, so these representations of generic sentences have only a very trivial logic. For example, in first order logic the following

$$\forall x(bird(x) \wedge \neg Ab(\texttt{respect-of-flying}, x) \rightarrow fly(x))$$

$$\forall x(bird(x) \wedge \neg Ab(\texttt{respect-of-feathers}, x) \rightarrow feathered(x))$$

do not jointly entail

$$\forall x(bird(x) \wedge \quad \neg Ab(\texttt{respect-of-flying-and-feathers}, x)$$
$$\rightarrow fly(x) \wedge feathered(x))$$

That is, given the more sophisticated representation, from *Birds normally fly* and *Birds normally have feathers*, it does not follow that *Birds normally fly and have feathers*.

Because they destroy Closure in the Consequent, these more sophisticated representations in Circumscription are not faithful to the idea that generic sentences like *Birds normally fly* are about normal (or prototypical, or typical) birds. McCarthy (1986) notes that the 'counterintuitiveness' of these respects in which something can be abnormal is a blight upon the theory. I would add that all of these different respects, whatever they may be, also deprive reasoning about normality in Circumscription of the semantic intuitions which originally made it so attractive among theories of nonmonotonic reasoning.

In fact, the abstract objects were introduced so as to make Circumscription satisfy Independence, which I have taken to be the characteristic of inference ticket formalisms. That this has to be at the cost of the original, normative intuitions is one point of the incompatibility result of the next section.

5.7   Norms Are Not Inference Tickets

I now show that no interesting inference ticket theory of nonmonotonic reasoning is a normative theory. More precisely, I show that Independence is satisfied in a normative theory at best *trivially*:

Definition 8 $\approx$ trivially *satisfies Independence relative to* $\models$ *just in case for any* $\models$-*independent monadic predicates* ϕ, ψ_1, ψ_2 *there is some formula* χ *such that both*

$$\phi c, \neg \psi_1 c, \phi > \psi_1, \phi > \psi_2 \approx \chi, \text{ and } \phi c, \neg \psi_1 c, \phi > \psi_1, \phi > \psi_2 \approx \neg \chi$$

Clearly, Independence is not of interest as a pattern of reasoning if only trivially satisfied. For the sets of premises which are of interest in connection with this principle, like *Birds fly*, *Birds lay eggs*, *Tweety is a bird*, *Tweety does not fly*, are then $\approx$-inconsistent.

Theorem 2   *Let* $\models$ *and* $\approx$ *constitute a nonmonotonic theory, in the sense of definition 1. Let furthermore* $\models$ *satisfy Closure in the Consequent. Then* $\approx$ *satisfy Independence relative to* $\models$ *only if it does so trivially.*

Proof: Assume $\models$ and $\approx$ constitute a nonmonotonic theory. Let $\models$ satisfy Closure in the Consequent. And let $\approx$ satisfy Independence relative to $\models$.

To see that Independence is satisfied trivially, let ϕ, ψ_1, ψ_2 be any $\models$-independent monadic predicates, and let Γ be the set of the following premises: $\phi > \psi_1, \phi > \psi_2, \phi c, \neg \psi_1 c$. It is sufficient to come up with some formula χ such that both $\Gamma \approx \chi$ and $\Gamma \approx \neg \chi$.

To this end, let Γ' be the premises $\phi > \psi_1, \phi > (\psi_1 \leftrightarrow \psi_2), \phi c, \neg \psi_1 c$.

Firstly, since $\models$ satisfies the principle of Closure in the Consequent and is monotonic: $\Gamma \models \Gamma'$ and $\Gamma' \models \Gamma$. From this it follows with Logicality that

(i) $\Gamma \approx \delta$ iff $\Gamma' \approx \delta$.

The predicates ϕ, ψ_1 and ψ_2 are $\models$-independent, so (fact 1) ϕ, ψ_1 and $\psi_1 \leftrightarrow \psi_2$ are too. So since $\approx$ satisfies Independence relative to $\models$:

(ii)

(a) $\Gamma \approx \neg \psi_2 c$, and

(b) $\Gamma' \approx \psi_1 c \leftrightarrow \psi_2 c$.

By (i) above and (ii) (a), $\Gamma' \approx \psi_2 c$. Then with (ii)(b) and "modus ponens" across the biconditional we have $\Gamma' \approx \psi_1 c$. By reflexivity of $\approx$ we, however, also have $\Gamma' \approx \neg \psi_1 c$. Finally, two more applications of (i) give $\Gamma \approx \psi_1 c$ and $\Gamma \approx \neg \psi_1 c$.   □

5.8   Conclusion

Nonmonotonic reasoning which arises from normative statements like *Birds normally fly* is to be distinguished from that which arises from default rules or 'inference tickets', like *If something is a bird, then assume that it can fly unless there is reason to assume the contrary.* These two kinds of nonmonotonic reasoning, exemplified respectively by circumscription and default logic, give rise to distinctive patterns of reasoning which would conflict were they to be combined in one theory.

All inference ticket theories of nonmonotonic reasoning that I know of, including default logic, the theory of nonmonotonic inheritance, and the theory of defaults in update semantics, are largely motivated with reference to norms like the example above. The result proved here suggests that such theories cannot (and indeed should not) do justice to this motivation. They cannot do justice to patterns of reasoning which are appropriate to such normative statements because they are in a different business.

Similarly, in developing a theory of nonmonotonic reasoning based on norms, one should be wary of principles of reasoning such as the principle of *independence* discussed above, for which I can think of no justification other than that which appeals to inference tickets.

Lastly, theorists on both sides of the norms-inference ticket divide have taken themselves to be explicating the meaning of natural language generic statements like *Lions eat meat* and *Boys don't cry.* Apparently it can't be that both sides are right.

6   Issues in the Design of a Language for Representing Linguistic Information Based on Inheritance and Feature Structures

RÉMI ZAJAC

Abstract

In this chapter, we address some issues in the design of declarative languages based on the notion of inheritance. First, we outline the connections and similarities between the notions of object, frame, conceptual graph and feature structures and we present a synthetic view of these notions. We then present the Typed Feature Structure (TFS) language developed at the University of Stuttgart, which reconciles the object-oriented approach with logic programming. We finally discuss some language design issues.

6.1   Convergences

Developing large NLP software is a very complex and time consuming task. The complexity of NLP can be characterized by the following two main factors:

1. NLP is data-intensive. Any NLP application needs large amounts of complex linguistic information. For example, a realistic application has typically dictionaries with tens of thousands of lexical entries.
2. Sophisticated NLP applications such as database interfaces or machine translation build very complex and intricate data structures for representing linguistic objects associated to strings of words. Part of the complexity also lies in the processing of such objects.

6.1.1   Object-oriented Approaches

An object-oriented approach to linguistic description addresses these two sources of complexity by providing:

1. facilities to manage the design process: data abstraction and inheritance.
2. facilities for capturing directly the interconnections and constraints in the data: properties, relations and complex objects.

These features are common to object-oriented languages (OOL), object-oriented database management systems (OODBMS) or knowledge representation languages (KRL). There are more than superficial similarities between the notions of classes, types and concepts: they are all organized in inheritance

74

hierarchies with some broad consensus on the abstract interpretation of such hierarchies (usually logical implication or set-inclusion), but with as many finer distinctions as there are specific languages. Likewise, there are strong relationships between the different data models for objects: frames, complex (recursive) records, nested tuples or conceptual graphs.

Typically, these languages offer:

- Complex objects can be represented as graphs where edges are labeled by roles and nodes by concept names;
- Multiple inheritance;
- Role-value restrictions;
- Role-value equality;
- Classification.

6.1.2 Logic Programming

Computation is usually done either by providing a fully integrated procedural programming language (e.g. Smalltalk) or by providing an adequate interface to some programming language (e.g. LISP or C for O_2, (Lécluse *et al.*, 1988). A very few systems provide a declarative component for computation: e.g. FOOPlog (Goguen and Meseguer, 1987) or CLASSIC (Borgida *et al.*, 1989). In these systems, procedural method/message passing is replaced with a logical rule-based component (in CLASSIC) or generic modules (in FOOPlog), which offer a much cleaner integration of the data component and the computational component. The evolution towards declarativity is motivated by Goguen and Meseguer (1987, p. 7) as follows:

> We believe that the many advantages claimed, including simplicity, clarity, understandability, reusability and maintainability, are all compromised to the degree that a programming language fails to correspond to a pure logic.

All these advantages are crucial in the development of NLP systems. Ideally, a linguistic formalism should be an object-oriented logic formalism. Feature structures, as used in unification-based grammar formalisms, provide the link between the object-oriented world and the logic programming world. Objects bear strong similarities with feature structures. For example, the O_2 data model has a notion of identity between parts of objects Lécluse *et al.*, 1988), which is equivalent to the notion of 'sharing' or 'reentrancy' in feature structures. In his PhD dissertation, Aït-Kaci (1984, 1986) bridged the gap between these models. He synthesized the notions of inheritance, types and feature structure in a unique data structure, typed feature structures (called 'ψ-terms'), and gave them a formal declarative semantics.

6.1.3   *Typed Feature Structures*

Assume the existence of an (abstract) informational domain, for example the set of linguistic objects. *Feature terms* describe objects of this universe by specifying values for attributes of objects. More precisely, as feature terms can provide only partial information about the objects they describe, a feature term denotes a *set* of objects in this universe. Feature terms are ordered by a subsumption relation: a feature term f_1 subsumes another feature term f_2 iff f_1 provides *less information* than f_2: $f_1 \geq f_2$. In our universe, this means that the set described by f_1 is *larger* than the set described by f_2. Note that there can be feature terms that describe objects which are not comparable (with respect to the subsumption relation), for example, a feature term describing verb phrases and a feature term describing noun phrases: the intersection of the sets they denote is empty.

As different sets of attribute-value pairs make sense for different kinds of objects, we also divide our feature terms into different types, which we call *feature types*. These types are ordered by a subtype relation: a type t_1 is a *subtype* of another type t_2 if t_1 provides *more information* than t_2. For example, if one assumes that a verb phrase is a phrase, then the set of verb phrases is included in the set of phrases. Using types to model this taxonomic hierarchy, the type symbol VP denotes the set of verb phrases, the symbol PH denotes the set of phrases, and we define VP as a subtype of PH.

This description implies of course that, if we know that a linguistic object is a verb phrase, we can deduce that it is a phrase. This deduction mechanism is expressed in our type system as *type inheritance*. Furthermore, with each type we associate *constraints* expressed as feature terms, thereby defining an inheritance hierarchy of typed feature terms: if a feature term is of type t_1 and there exist supertypes of t_1, then t_1 inherits all the attribute-value pairs of the feature terms associated with the supertypes. A feature term of type VP describing a verb phrase can have an embedded verb phrase: the definition of the type VP is recursive, and this recursivity will give us the necessary expressive power to describe any complex linguistic object.

Given a typed feature term inheritance hierarchy, we can query the system and ask if some feature term belongs to the hierarchy. To produce the answer, the system will check the necessary and sufficient conditions such that all subterms of the query belong to the hierarchy. An answer will be the set of substitutions used to check these conditions: the answer will be printed as a set of feature terms subsumed by the query where all necessary and sufficient conditions hold. In that sense, the answer will give the best approximation of the set of objects denoted by the query, giving a formal basis of the traditional interpretation of feature structures as representing partial information.

A language based on typed feature structures extends object-oriented programming with relational logic programming features:

- logical variables,
- non-determinism with backtracking,
- existential queries;

and conversely, it extends logic programming with the following features:

- typed complex objects with role-value restrictions,
- multiple inheritance,
- classification.

Such a language is an attempt to combine the best of two worlds: declarativity and referential transparency from logic programming, modularity through inheritance and complex objects from object-oriented programming. Furthermore, based on feature structures, it is a good candidate as a computational linguistics formalism.

The basic approach described in this chapter is based on original work by Aït-Kaci (1984, 1986) on the KBL language and has been influenced by the work on HPSG by Pollard and Sag (1987) and Pollard and Moshier (1990). The presentation in this chapter is rather informal, and a more technical account can be found in Emele and Zajac (1990a) and Zajac (1990). Among the growing literature on the semantics of feature structures, many relevant results and techniques have been published by Smolka (1988, 1989), Smolka and Aït-Kaci (1988) and Aït-Kaci and Podelski (1991). Based on Pollard and Sag (1987), Pollard (1990) and Pollard and Moshier (1990), a computational formalism, very close to the TFS formalism, is currently under design at CMU for implementing HPSG (Carpenter, 1990, and Franz, 1990). The TFS formalism presented in the following section has been designed and implemented at IMS by Martin Emele and the author.

6.2 The TFS Language

6.2.1 Types

The universe of feature terms is structured in an inheritance hierarchy which defines a partial ordering on kinds of available information. The backbone of the hierarchy is defined by a finite set of type symbols $\mathcal{T}$ together with a partial ordering $\leq$ on $\mathcal{T}$: the partially ordered set (poset) $\langle \mathcal{T}, \leq \rangle$. The ordering $\leq$ defines the subtype relation: for A, B in $\mathcal{T}$ we read $A \leq B$ as 'A is a subtype of B'.

In order to have a well-behaved type hierarchy, we require that $\langle \mathcal{T}, \leq \rangle$ be such that:

- $\mathcal{T}$ contains the symbols $\top$ and $\bot$, where $\top$ is the greatest element and $\bot$ is the least element of $\mathcal{T}$.
- Any two type symbols A and B of $\mathcal{T}$ have a greatest common lower bound called the infimum of A, B and written $inf\{A, B\}$. A poset where

this property holds is a meet semi-lattice: we introduce a new operation $A \wedge B = inf\{A, B\}$, where $A \wedge B$ is called the *meet* of A and B.

The tuple $\langle \mathcal{T}, \leq, \wedge \rangle$ is formally a meet semi-lattice. A technicality arises when two types A and B have more than one infimum: in that case, the set of infimums is interpreted disjunctively. We call the smallest types of $\mathcal{T}$, the minimal types.

A type hierarchy is interpreted set-theoretically, subtyping corresponding to set inclusion.

- $\top$ is interpreted as the whole universe.
- $\bot$ is interpreted as the empty set.
- Any type of the hierarchy is interpreted as a subset of the universe.
- $\leq$ is interpreted as set inclusion: a subtype inherits all information of all its supertypes.
- $\wedge$ is interpreted as set intersection.

6.2.2   Feature Terms

As different combinations of attribute-value pairs make sense for different kinds of objects, we divide our feature terms into different types. Types are closed in the sense that each type defines a specific collection of features (and restrictions on their possible values) which are appropriate for it, expressed as a feature structure (the definition of the type). Since types are organized in an inheritance hierarchy, a type inherits all the features and value restrictions from all its supertypes. This type-discipline for feature structures enforces the following two constraints:[1] a type cannot have a feature which is not appropriate for it and conversely, a feature-value pair should always be defined for some type. Thus a feature term is always typed.

As a notational convention, we use the attribute-value matrix (AVM) notation for feature terms and we write the type symbol for each feature term in front of the opening square bracket of the AVM. A type symbol which does not have any feature defined for it is called atomic. All other types are complex. In the remainder of this section, we shall implicitly refer to some given signature $\langle \mathcal{T}, \leq, \wedge, \mathcal{F} \rangle$ where $\langle \mathcal{T}, \leq, \wedge \rangle$ is a type hierarchy, and $\mathcal{F}$ is a set of feature symbols, and we shall also assume a set of variables V.

A feature term t is an expression of the form

$$\#x = A[f_1 : t_1, \ldots, f_n : t_n]$$

where $\#x$ is a variable in a set of variables V, A is a type symbol in $\mathcal{T}, f_1, \ldots, f_n$ (with $n \geq 0$) are features in $\mathcal{F}$ and $t_1, \ldots, t_n$ are feature terms.

We have to add some restrictions that capture properties commonly associated with feature structures:

---

[1] Which can be checked at compile time.

1. A feature is a selector that gives access to a subterm: it has to be unique for a given term.
2. ⊥ represents inconsistent information: is it not allowed in a term.
3. A variable is used to capture equational constraints ('reentrancy') in the term: there is at most one occurrence of a variable #x in a term which is the root of a term different from #y = ⊤.

Given a signature $\langle \mathcal{T}, \leq, \wedge, \mathcal{F} \rangle$, feature terms are partially ordered by a subsumption relation. This captures the intuitive notion that a term containing a lot of information is more specific, and describes a smaller set than a term which contains less information. A feature term t subsumes a term t', $t \geq t'$ iff:

1. All the paths in t are in t'.
2. All equational constraints in t hold in t'.
3. For a given path in t, its type is greater or equal than the corresponding type in t'.

Since we have a partial order on feature terms, the meet operation between two feature terms t and t' is defined in the usual way as the greatest common lower bound of t and t'. It is computed using a typed unification algorithm. A feature term is represented as a graph where each node has a type, an equivalence class used to represent equational constraints ('co-references') and a set of outgoing arcs. The unification algorithm uses the union/find procedure on an inverted set representation of the equivalence classes adapted by Aït-Kaci (1984) after Huet (1976). The actual algorithm used in the system is optimized using several different techniques in order to minimize copying and to behave as efficiently as a pattern-matcher in cases when no information needs to be added (Emele, 1991).

6.2.3   *Inheritance Network of Feature Terms*

Type Equations

An inheritance network of feature terms is specified by a set of type definitions (type equations). A type definition has the following form: the type symbol to be defined appears on the left-hand side of the equation. The right-hand side is an expression of conjunctions and disjunctions of typed feature terms. Conjunctions are interpreted as meets on typed feature terms. The definition may have conditional constraints expressed as a logical conjunction of feature terms. These conditions are introduced by ':-'. The right-hand side feature term may contain the left-hand side type symbol in a subterm (or in the condition), thus defining a recursive type equation which gives the system the expressive power needed to describe complex linguistic structures. A simple example of a type definition is shown in Figure 6.1, and the corresponding partial order is displayed in Figure 6.2 using Hasse diagrams.

```
LIST = NIL | CONS.
CONS = [first: T, rest: LIST].

APPEND0 = APPEND[1: NIL, 2: #1= LIST, 3: #1].
APPEND1 = APPEND[1: CONS[first: #x, rest: #l1],
                 2: #l2=LIST,
                 3: CONS[first: #x, rest: #l3]]
          :- APPEND[1: #l1, 2: #l2, 3: #l3].
```

Figure 6.1: Type definitions for LIST and APPEND using the TFS syntax

A subtype inherits all constraints of its supertypes monotonically: the constraints expressed as feature terms are conjoined using typed unification; the conditions are conjoined using the logical conjunction. The compiler makes sure that we have specified an inheritance hierarchy, building an internal representation where for any two types such that $A \leq B$ we have $def(A) \leq def(B)$. If this cannot be done, the hierarchy is inconsistent and an error is reported.

In a feature type definition $s = F$, the equality symbol that separates the left-hand side type symbol s from the right-hand side feature term F is interpreted as an equivalence. Assume that $\underline{F}$ is the meet of F and all feature type definitions of the supertypes of s. The two directions of the biconditional are:

$\Rightarrow$ all feature terms of type s are subsumed by the feature term $\underline{F}$;
$\Leftarrow$ all feature terms which are subsumed by $\underline{F}$ are of type s.

The $\Leftarrow$ part of the condition is checked statically at compile-time, and the $\Rightarrow$ part is checked dynamically at run time. A feature term where all subterms obey these two typing constraints is a well-typed feature term.

Closed Terms and Static Type Inference

Typed feature terms are always interpreted as *closed terms*: this is a consequence of the fact that a type definition defines an equivalence relation. All features of a feature term associated with a type are declared to be valid for that type and for all its subtypes only. This is a closure constraint: it is not possible to add through unification (which is the only operation used on these data structures) an arbitrary feature to a term during computation, but only those declared for the type of the term. Given the information that all features are declared for a type and possibly have specific value restrictions, the compiler is able to infer the most specific type for any given feature term. Before presenting the inference rule for checking the $\Leftarrow$ condition, let us introduce a logical notion for feature terms.

A logical feature expression is an expression of either of the form:

$X:A$
$X \doteq Y$
$X.l \doteq Y$
$\phi_1 \wedge \phi_2$

where X and Y are variables, A is a type symbol, l is a feature and ϕ_i are logical expressions. The first three expressions are read 'X is of type A', 'X is equal to Y' and 'the value of the feature l of X is Y'. The operator $\wedge$ is the logical conjunction. A term $\#x = A[f_1: B_1, f_2: B_2]$ will be written as the expression $X:A \wedge X.f_1 \doteq Y_1 \wedge X.f_1 \doteq Y_2 \wedge Y_1: B_1 \wedge Y_2: B_2$.

The inference rule for checking the $\Leftarrow$ condition is defined as follows. With each feature f which appears in the definition of type A and which has the type restriction B, we associate the expression $X:A \wedge X.f \doteq Y \wedge Y:B$. With every feature which does not appear in the definition of any type, we associate the expression $X: \perp \wedge X.f \doteq Y \wedge Y: \perp$. The collection of those expressions for a set of type definitions for feature f is

$$\bigvee_i X_i: A_i \wedge X_i.f \doteq Y_i \wedge Y_i: B_i$$

Then, a term is correctly typed if adding this type information using the following rule preserves consistency (the result should be different from $\perp$):

$$\frac{X.f \doteq Y \qquad\qquad \bigvee_i X_i: A_i \wedge X_i.f \doteq Y_i \wedge Y_i: B_i}{X.f \doteq Y \ \wedge \ \bigvee_i X \doteq X_i \wedge Y \doteq Y_i \wedge X_i: A_i \wedge X_i.f \doteq Y_i \wedge Y_i: B_i}$$

6.2.4   The Meaning of Typed Feature Structures

A ground feature term is a term where all type symbols in this term are minimal types (the lowest types in the hierarchy immediately above $\perp$). A well-typed feature term is a term which obeys the type equivalence relation defined by the set of type definitions. The meaning (denotation) of a feature term is represented by the set of all well-typed ground feature terms which are subsumed by it. If this set is empty, the feature term is inconsistent with regard to the set of type definitions. The denotation can be finite, e.g. in the case of a dictionary, but it can also be infinite in the case of recursive types: for example, the set of ground terms subsumed by LIST is the set of all possible ground lists. However, the symbol LIST is itself the best *finite approximation* of the *infinite set* of all possible lists. Thus, instead of enumerating all ground feature terms of the denotation of a non-ground feature term, we will describe its denotation by a set of *approximations*, themselves represented as feature structures.

Evaluation in the TFS system amounts to finding the necessary and sufficient conditions for describing exactly the denotation of an input feature term (the

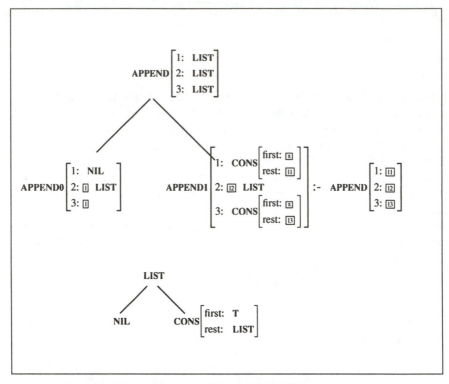

Figure 6.2: Type hierarchy for LIST and APPEND (⊤ and ⊥ omitted)

'query') modulo a set of type equations. Given an inheritance network, the necessary conditions are always checked in a finite amount of time: these are basically type constraints, and the procedure is the same as the one used at compile time to check the consistency of the network. But this is not enough, since the input term will usually describe a subset (maybe empty) of the denotation of its type. Thus, we also want to find sufficient conditions that describe this subset. These conditions will be produced as specializations of the query: a set of well-typed feature terms which are subsumed by the input term.

6.2.5   The TFS Abstract Rewrite Machine

In this section, we describe an abstract rewrite machine for evaluating feature terms. The rewrite mechanism is based on a variant of narrowing adapted to feature terms.

A set of type definitions defines an inheritance hierarchy of feature terms which specifies the available approximations. Such a hierarchy is compiled into a rewriting system as follows: each direct link between a type *A* and a subtype

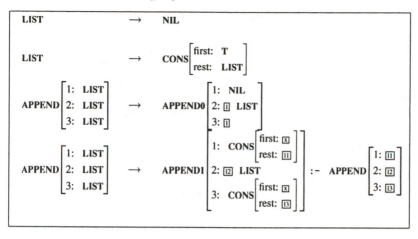

Figure 6.3: Rewrite rules for LIST and APPEND

B generates a rewrite rule of the form $A[a] \rightarrow B[b]$ where $[a]$ and $[b]$ are the definitions of A and B, respectively (see Figure 6.3).

The interpreter is given a 'query' (a feature term) to evaluate: this input term is first type-checked. If it is consistent, it is already an approximation of the final solution, although a very rough one. The idea is then to incrementally add more information to that term using the rewrite rules in order to get step by step closer to the solution: we stop when we have the best possible approximation.

A rewrite step for a term t is defined as follows: if u is a subterm of t and u is of type A, and there exists a rewrite rule $A[a] \rightarrow B[b]$ such that $A[a] \wedge u \neq \bot$, then the right-hand side $B[b]$ is unified with the subterm u, giving a new term t' which is more specific than t. Rewrite steps are applied non-deterministically everywhere in the term until all types are minimal and no further rule is applicable.[2]

Actually, the rewriting process stops either when no rule is applicable or when all subterms in a term correspond exactly to some approximation defined by a type in the hierarchy and the fixed-point is reached. A term is 'solved' when any of its subterms is either

- more specific than the definition of a minimal type, or
- does not give more information than the definition of its type.

This defines an *if and only if* condition for a term to be a solved-form, where any addition of information will not bring anything new. This condition is implemented using a *lazy rewriting* strategy: the application of a rule at a

---

[2] Conditions do not change this general scheme (they are evaluated using the same rewriting mechanism) and are omitted from the presentation here for the sake of simplicity. See, for example, Dershowitz and Plaisted (1988) on conditional rewrite systems, and Klop (1991) for a survey.

subterm is triggered only when the subterm gets more specific than the left-hand side of the rule. More precisely, given a subterm u of type A and a rewrite rule $A[a] \to B[b]$, the application of the rule is triggered if $A[a] \wedge u \leq A[a]$.

This lazy rewriting strategy implements a fully data-driven computation scheme and avoids useless branches of computation. Thus, there is no need to have a special treatment to avoid what corresponds to the evaluation of uninstantiated goals in PROLOG, since a general treatment based on the semantics of the formalism itself is built into the evaluation strategy of the interpreter.

The lazy evaluation mechanism has an almost optimal behavior on the class of problems that have an exponential complexity when using the 'generate and test' method. It is driven by the availability of information: as soon as some piece of information is available, the evaluation of constraints in which this information appears is triggered. Thus, the search space is explored 'intelligently', never following branches of computation that would correspond to uninstantiated PROLOG goals.[3]

The choice of which subterm to rewrite is only partly driven by the availability of information (using the lazy rewriting scheme). When there are several subterms that could be rewritten, the computation rule is to choose the outer-most ones (inner-most strategies are usually non-terminating). If there are several outer-most candidates, they are all rewritten in parallel. This is in contrast with PROLOG which evaluates the goals in a clause one after the other, from left to right.[4] Such a parallel outer-most rewriting strategy has interesting termination properties, since there are problems on which any fixed order of rewriting would not terminate where a parallel strategy does.[5]

For a given subterm, the choice of which rule (actually which set of rules) to apply is done non-deterministically, and the search space is explored depth-first using a backtracking scheme. This strategy is not complete, though in association with the parallel outer-most rule and with the lazy evaluation scheme, it terminates on 'well-defined' problems (a complete breadth-first search strategy can be used for debugging purposes).

6.3   Language Design Issues

In this section, we discuss some issues in the design of a language based on feature structures and inheritance. We distinguish between two broad levels

---

[3] The lazy evaluation mechanism is not yet fully implemented in the current version (March 1991) of TFS, but with the partial implementation we have, a gain of 50% in speed for parsing has already been achieved in comparison with the previous implementation that used only the outer-most parallel rewriting strategy.

[4] This parallel rewriting strategy is similar to hyper-resolution in logic programming. The lazy evaluation mechanism is related to the 'freeze' predicate of, e.g. PROLOG-II and Sicstus PROLOG, though in PROLOG, it has to be called explicitly.

[5] E.g. the problem of left-recursive rules in naive implementations of DCGs.

in such a language: the object level, related to feature structures, their syntax and semantics, and the network level, related to the organization of feature structures into an inheritance hierarchy of types of feature structures. Since this basis provides a very general framework with all necessary computational expressive power, any enhancement or extensions (other than simple syntactic sugar) can be done by providing new type constructors with the associated unification algorithms.

6.3.1 The Network Level

Using the TFS syntax, there are two means of specifying an inheritance network. The first is to use disjunctive specifications:

     BOOL = TRUE | FALSE.

This expression specifies that the type BOOL covers the two types TRUE and FALSE. Moreover, this expression specifies exhaustively the set of types covered by BOOL. Using disjunctive specifications, the network is described in a top-down fashion.

It is also possible to use conjunctive specifications to describe a network in a bottom-up fashion.

     GREEN = BLUE & YELLOW.

In the current TFS syntax, the two means can be combined with an interpretation which is unfortunately not very intuitive. The following set of definitions

     A = A1 | A2.
     B = B1 | B2.
     X = A & B & C & D.

is equivalent to

     A = A1 | A2.
     B = B1 | B2.
     X = (A1 | A2) & (B1 | B2) & C & D.

and a partial order is derived using the factorization of the disjunctive normal form. This allows us to specify in a concise way cross-classifications that would need to be expanded explicitly otherwise.

Specialized syntax can be used for specifying networks. Two linguistic examples are HPSG inheritance hierarchies (Pollard and Sag, 1987) and Systemic Networks (see e.g. Mellish, 1988). Carpenter (1992) shows how partial orders can be extracted from such kinds of specifications.

The simplest and most general means of specifying an inheritance network is to use a covering relation: x covers y, notated $x \triangleright y$, when there is no z different from x and y such that $x \leq z \leq y$. A unique partial order is constructed as the transitive closure of the covering relation. If the set of elements in the network is finite, it is always possible to embed such a partial order into a lattice that preserves the meets using a powerset construction, as used in the TFS system.

$$\langle\rangle == PERSON$$
$$\langle name \rangle == ID$$
$$\langle name\ first \rangle == Jo$$
$$\langle name\ last \rangle == Brown$$
$$\langle spouse \rangle == PERSON$$
$$\langle spouse\ name \rangle == ID$$
$$\langle spouse\ name\ first \rangle == Judith$$
$$\langle spouse\ name\ last \rangle == \langle name\ last \rangle$$
$$\langle spouse\ spouse \rangle == \langle\rangle$$

Figure 6.4: Path equations.

$$X_0: PERSON \wedge$$
$$X_0.name \doteq X_1 \wedge X_1: ID \wedge$$
$$X_1.first \doteq X_2 \wedge X_2: Jo \wedge$$
$$X_1.last \doteq X_3 \wedge X_3: Brown \wedge$$
$$X_0.spouse \doteq X_4 \wedge X_4: PERSON \wedge$$
$$X_4.name \doteq X_5 \wedge X_5: ID \wedge$$
$$X_5.first \doteq X_6 \wedge X_6: Judith \wedge$$
$$X_5.last \doteq X_3 \wedge$$
$$X_4.spouse \doteq X_0$$

Figure 6.5: Expression of a feature logic.

6.3.2   The Object Level

There are three different kinds of syntax for describing feature structures: path equations as in PATR-II (Figure 6.4), logical expressions of the feature logic (Figure 6.5), and feature terms using the AVM notation as used in the TFS syntax (Figure 6.6).

The TFS syntax allows any expression in place of a term. A TFS expression

```
#x=PERSON[name:   ID[first: Jo,
                     last: #y=Brown],
              spouse: PERSON[name: ID[first: Judith,
                                       last: #y],
                             spouse: #x]]
```

Figure 6.6: Feature term.

is of one of the forms

$e1 \,\&\, e2$
$e1 \mid e2$
$e1 \setminus e2$
$e1 : - e2$

where $\&$ is the meet operator, $\mid$ the join operator, $\setminus$ the relative pseudo-complement operator and $: -$ the conditional operator.

6.3.3 Linking the Two Levels: Network of Objects

The inheritance network of typed feature structures is built from a partial order on type symbols and an equivalence relation between type symbols and feature structures specified as a type equation. For example, the TFS definition
APPEND0 = APPEND[1: NIL, 2: #1=LIST, 3: #1].
specifies in a single expression these two kinds of information:[6]

$APPEND0 \lhd APPEND$

$X : APPEND0 \Leftrightarrow X.1 \doteq U \,\wedge\, U : NIL \wedge X.2 \doteq V \,\wedge\, V : LIST \wedge X.3 \doteq V$

Furthermore, the axioms on the domain and image restrictions for features are also extracted from the same definition:

- $X.1 \doteq Y \wedge X : APPEND0 \wedge Y : NIL$
- $X.2 \doteq Y \wedge X : APPEND0 \wedge Y : LIST$
- $X.3 \doteq Y \wedge X : APPEND0 \wedge Y : LIST$

This choice leads to a very concise syntax. It could nevertheless be interesting to separate the specification of the partial order on type symbols from the specification of the equivalence relation. This separation would allow a more modular scheme of compilation. The partial order on type symbols could be defined using different kinds of syntax such as the covering relation, the Systemic Network notation or HPSG hierarchies, and specialized graphical interfaces could be used without changing the syntax for the type definition (equivalence relation and feature restrictions). Another advantage is that a type definition can be recompiled without necessarily recompiling the entire network.

6.3.4 Extensions

There are three ways of extending the language. The first one is to provide additional notation with the same underlying semantics, e.g. logical expressions. The second is to provide a library of pre-defined types that could be defined in

---

[6] The logical interpretation of the covering relation is the implication: $X : APPEND0 \Rightarrow X : APPEND$.

the language, but could be implemented in a more efficient way. The last is to provide new types that cannot be defined in the language, together with the associated unification algorithms.

Logical Expressions

Since the feature term and the logical notations are equivalent (see e.g. Aït-Kaci and Podelski, 1991), we can use both in our concrete syntax. The compiler will then compile these mixed expressions into a unique normal form used by the interpreter. Changes are located at the compiler level and no modification of the interpreter is required. Logical expressions are specially useful to express complex conditions that are more difficult to specify using only the meet, join and complement operators.

Built-in Types

Some types commonly used can be specified directly in the TFS language, but they can advantageously be defined as built-in types and be more efficiently implemented. Examples of such types are characters, strings of characters, or numbers, together with their associated operations (concatenation, addition, etc.). Thus, the semantic of such extensions can be precisely defined in the TFS language itself, and their implementation realized in the underlying implementation language. The interface to these types can then be defined and documented using the TFS syntax, and a specific syntax could be used for ground objects.

For example, we could define a type STRING as:

```
STRING = EMPTY-STRING | NON-EMPTY-STRING.
NON-EMPTY-STRING = [first: ASCII, rest: STRING].
```

which defines both the interface and the semantics of that type. A LISP implementation could use directly LISP lists, and the general unification algorithm can be modified to work directly on lists instead of the general internal representation for feature terms. Extensions are located at the compiler level and for efficiency purposes, also in the unification algorithm. A syntax for ground strings is:

```
EMPTY-STRING                                     →    ""
NON-EMPTY-STRING[first:  a, rest:  EMPTY-STRING]  →    "a"
```

Semantic Extensions

Extensions that cannot be easily expressed in the language itself are more significant. For example, a type string where the concatenation operator is associative needs associative unification (this problem is also known as the resolution of word equations), which is significantly more complex than the unification on feature terms. Thus, this kind of extension leads to non-trivial changes in the language and its implementation. Such a string type would be useful for expressing, for example, morphological patterns as string patterns.

An associative unification algorithm (see e.g. Abdulrad and Pécuchet, 1990) would solve the equation $cons(a, X) = cons(Y, b)$, where the set of strings beginning with an a is equated with the set of strings ending with b, the solution describing the set of strings beginning with a and ending with b. Using the axiom of associativity

$$cons(cons(X, Y), Z) = cons(X, cons(Y, Z))$$

and introducing a new variable, we have

$$cons(a, cons(Z, b)) = cons(cons(a, Z), b)$$

The set of substitutions describing the answer to the problem is

$$\{X = cons(Z, b), \quad Y = cons(a, Z)\}$$

Extensions which can be treated as the introduction of a new built-in type, even if they modify the semantics of the language, modify it in a coherent and conservative way. They can be accommodated without changing the basic design of the language.

6.4   Conclusion

The TFS language is a formalism based on typed feature structures and it synthezises some of the key concepts of object-oriented languages (abstraction and multiple inheritance, complex objects, classification) and relational languages (logical variables, non-determinism with backtracking, existential queries). The language is fully declarative: the notions of inheritance, type checking, classification, and evaluation are all based on unification of feature structures extended with types.

Based on feature structures, the language is expressive enough to accommodate very different styles of grammars, and as a 'lingua franca' for computational linguistics, it can help to bridge the gap between different approaches to linguistic description.

Acknowledgements

Research reported in this chapter is partly supported by the German Ministry of Research and Technology (BMFT, Bundesminister für Forschung und Technologie), under grant No. 08 B3116 3. The views and conclusions contained herein are those of the author and should not be interpreted as representing official policies.

7 Feature-Based Inheritance Networks for Computational Lexicons

HANS-ULRICH KRIEGER AND JOHN NERBONNE

Abstract

The virtues of viewing the lexicon as an inheritance network are its succinctness and its tendency to highlight significant clusters of linguistic properties. From its succinctness follow two practical advantages, namely its ease of maintenance and modification. In this chapter we present a feature-based foundation for lexical inheritance. We shall argue that the feature-based foundation is both more economical and expressively more powerful than non-feature-based systems. It is more economical because it employs only mechanisms already assumed to be present elsewhere in the grammar (viz., in the feature system), and it is more expressive because feature systems are more expressive than other mechanisms used in expressing lexical inheritance (cf. DATR). The lexicon furthermore allows the use of default inheritance, based on the ideas of default unification, defined by Bouma (1990a).

These claims are buttressed in sections sketching the opportunities for lexical description in feature-based lexicons in two central lexical topics: inflection and derivation. Briefly, we argue that the central notion of paradigm may be defined directly in feature structures, and that it may be more satisfactorily (in fact, immediately) linked to the syntactic information in this fashion. Our discussion of derivation is more programmatic; but here, too, we argue that feature structures of a suitably rich sort provide a foundation for the definition of lexical rules.

We illustrate theoretical claims in application to German lexical structure. This work is currently under implementation in a natural language understanding project (DISCO) at the German Artificial Intelligence Center (Deutsches Forschungszentrum für Künstliche Intelligenz).

7.1 Introduction

The best inheritance mechanisms for representing lexical information have been Flickinger, Pollard and Wasow's (1985) work on 'structured lexicons', and Evans and Gazdar's (1990) work on DATR. Both Flickinger's work and DATR aim to supplement feature-based grammars, but both require an explicit translation step to convert lexical information into grammatical features. Furthermore, they are both hampered in expressive power, so that they accommodate some

90

sorts of information poorly, even information which is standardly found in feature systems, e.g. disjunction, negation and complex feature structures used as values.

The present proposal draws both from the work above on default inheritance networks and from the lexical ideas of feature-based theories in general (cf. the section on PATR-II lexicons in Shieber, 1986, pp. 54–61). PATR-II present lexicons via a collection of *templates* or *macros*, which are purely syntactic abbreviations for feature-structure descriptions. Pollard and Sag's (1987) sketch of the lexicon in Head-Driven Phrase Structure Grammar (hence HPSG) and Sag and Pollard (1987) extended these ideas by interpreting lexical definitions as feature-structure descriptions and inheritance specifications as subsumption statements, rather than treating them in a purely syntactic fashion. Pollard and Sag (chap. 8.2) furthermore suggest a use of lexical rules which brings their work closer to standard linguistic views (e.g. LFG, Bresnan, 1982).

This and most other work on feature structures, on the other hand, has failed to allow the use of *defaults* or *overwriting*, which is crucial for a practical lexical tool.[1] The key advantage of default specifications is that they allow the description of *subregularities*, classes of items whose properties are largely, but not perfectly, regular. In a system with default inheritance, these may be regarded not as anomalous, but rather as imperfectly regular, or regular within limits. We shall employ default inheritance regularly, perhaps most crucially in the specification of derivational relations (cf. below and Flickinger *et al.*, 1985; Gazdar, 1987, 1990; and Flickinger and Nerbonne, 1992, for arguments supporting the use of defaults in lexical specifications). This has seemed suspicious within the context of feature systems because these were developed (in part) to allow monotonic processing of linguistic information, and the use of defaults leads to nonmonotonicity.[2] But, as Bouma (1990a, p. 169) points out, the use of lexical defaults is a fairly harmless form of nonmonotonicity, since the lexicon is nonmonotonic only with respect to lexical development—the syntactic use of information specified via lexical default leads to none of the problems associated with nonmonotonic reasoning; e.g. inferences about phrases never need to be retracted, and the NL system may be configured to be perfectly monotonic at run-time. If we employ default inheritance for the specification of lexical information, then the inheritance hierarchy does *not* correspond to a subsumption or

---

[1] But cf. Pollard and Sag (1987, p. 194, note 4); Sag and Pollard (1987, p. 24) and Shieber (1986, pp. 59–61).

[2] It is probably worth noting that there have nonetheless been several attempts at using nonmonotonic inference rules in unification-based systems. Kay's FUG (Kay, 1985) included an ANY value, which defaulted to $\perp$ unless unified with, in which case it was $\top$; Shieber (1986, p. 59) presents a scheme for the default interpretation of feature structure templates; Kaplan and Bresnan (1982) present nonmonotonic 'constraining equations' for LFG; and Gazdar *et al.* (1985), p. 29 *et passim* propose nonmonotonic *feature specification defaults*.

subtyping hierarchy—information may be overwritten which renders subsumption invalid. Care needs to be taken that the two notions of hierarchy—the classes involved in the default inheritance relationship and the feature structure types defined there—not be confused (cf. Cook, Hill and Canning, 1990). The mechanism we shall employ for the default combination of lexical information is the *default unification* developed by Bouma (1990a); we may employ this within the lexicon, even while eschewing its use for parsing and generation.

The present work is closest to Pollard and Sag's in that it proceeds from a view of the lexicon in which feature structures bear the burden of linguistic description. It differs from their work in advocating the use of default inheritance, and perhaps more significantly, in using *only* feature structure descriptions to represent lexical information, including especially lexical rules. Where Pollard and Sag viewed lexical rules as operators on feature structures, we propose defining lexical rules purely in terms of feature structures. On our view, one need not assume a distinct sort of linguistic entity, lexical rule, which maps feature structures into feature structures. Instead, one begins with feature structures and a description language for them, and this suffices to characterize lexical rules. Lexical rules are thus an emergent phenomenon in language, ultimately reducible to feature-structures (cf. section 7.4 for a discussion of alternative views of lexical rules).

Our purpose in this chapter is to present the feature-based lexicon not as a linguistic theory of lexical structure, but rather as a framework within which such theories may be formulated, i.e. a tool for lexical description. This means that we shall at points demonstrate the formulation of competing views of lexical phenomena, e.g. matrix-based and form-based views of the inflectional paradigm, and inflectional and derivational views of the passive. It is also worth noting that, although we are quite interested in the question of efficiently processing feature-based descriptions—especially the question of lexical access for generation and recognition, we will not have anything to say about it in this paper.

It is probably worth sketching here in broad strokes the sorts of advantages we shall claim for our proposals. These lie primarily in the expressive power of the feature formalisms. The added expressive capacity is exploited in order to characterize both inflectional paradigms and derivational word formation rules as first-class linguistic objects—feature structures—of the same sort as words or phrases. We believe this proposal is made here for the first time, certainly the first time in a formalized theory. We illustrate the advantages of the added expressive power in analyses of inflectional paradigms as disjunctive further specifications of abstract lexemes, and in analyses of derivationally complex forms as instantiations of rules, where the latter are given a feature-based interpretation.

Our proposals are couched in HPSG terms, both because this is often readily understandable but also because HPSG—and to a lesser extent, FUG (Kay, 1984,

1985)—have most vigorously explored the hypothesis that feature structures are a sufficient representation scheme for all linguistic knowledge. The idea is that feature structures (also called 'functional structures' in FUG, 'attribute-value matrices' in HPSG) can encode not only syntactic information, but also semantic, pragmatic, morphological and lexical information. In HPSG, even recursively structured aspects of syntax such as syntactic rules and phrase structure trees are ultimately characterized as constraints on feature structures, so that the attempt to construe lexical information strictly within the limits provided by feature structures would not seem inappropriate.

We commence from the treatment of the lexicon in HPSG I (Pollard and Sag, 1987, chap. 8) as an inheritance structure, which we accept (with minor modifications noted below). Now, HPSG I invoked 'lexical rules' as operations or functions *on* feature structures, but this proposal in many ways violates the spirit which infuses HPSG, that of demonstrating that all linguistic knowledge can be modeled directly in feature structures. Our proposed construal of lexical rules as feature structures obviates any use of lexical rules as operations— also familiar from LFG (Bresnan, 1982) and PATR-II (Shieber *et al.*, 1983), especially D-PATR (Karttunen, 1986).[3] We believe therefore that the present chapter is a contribution to feature-based theories, as well, in that it shows how lexical rules can be construed in terms of feature-structure. This reduces the theoretical inventory, which is by itself desirable, and, as we argue below, it has significant descriptive advantages as well.

The structure of the chapter is as follows: we first continue the introduction with a discussion of the distinction between morpheme- and lexeme-based analyses. In section 7.2, we summarize the use we shall make of feature structures, which is essentially that provided by HPSG. We then explore the advantages of feature-based lexicons in two central lexical topics: the treatment of inflection and derivation. (There is, of course, an influential school of linguistic thought which denies the significance of this distinction, and our tools do not presuppose the distinction—we too can generalize all lexical rules to 'word formation' à la Sadock's 'autolexical syntax' (Sadock, 1985). But feature structures offer interesting alternatives for inflection.)

7.1.1 Lexemes and Morphemes

Before we examine the feature-based analysis of inflection and derivation in more detail, it is worth reminding ourselves that the developing research paradigm of computational lexicology—within which this paper might be located—differs from computational morphology (e.g. two-level or finite-state

---

[3] And nearly everywhere else: GPSG metarules (Gazdar *et al.*, 1985) and Categorial Morphology treatments (Hoeksema, 1985) are quite similar in treating lexical rules as fundamentally distinct from lexical entries.

morphology) in that the former takes a *lexeme*-based view of lexical variation (such as inflection and derivation), while the latter generally takes a *morpheme*-based view. While we do not aim here to settle any debate over which is preferable, it may be useful to sketch the differences.[4]

A lexeme is an abstract unit which characterizes what is common among the inflectional variants of a word. It contains, for example, what is common among the variants of the verb *institute (institutes, instituting, instituted)*, etc, but *not institution, institutional, reinstitute, . . .*, all of which are related, but distinct lexemes. Note that the lexeme is an abstract unit, which need not even be associated with any particular form. The lexeme-based view of lexical processes such as inflection and derivation maintains that these processes are based on properties of lexemes. We clarify this below after sketching the morpheme-based alternative. A morpheme is also an abstract unit which is the minimal unit to which meaning is attached. Note that a lexeme may contain meaningful parts, e.g. *ab-* + *leit-* + *bar*—this is a lexeme with its own set of inflectional variants (the case, gender, number, grade paradigm of German adjectives). The question of whether lexical processes are morpheme-based or lexeme-based thus centers on the analysis of such complex words. Are these optimally analyzed solely in terms of component morphemes (morpheme-based), or must one take into account intermediate lexemes (lexeme-based)? In the example *ableitbar*, can one derive all properties from *ab-*, *leit-* and *-bar*, or must one take into account the intermediate lexeme *ableiten*?

Returning to our English example to clarify further the distinction between the morpheme-based and lexeme-based views, we note that it is very unlikely that *institute* could be divided into further meaningful parts, so that we may examine the morpheme *institute* (which constitutes all of the material of the lexeme above), and which also appears in *institution, institutional, reinstitute, institutionalize . . . .* As we see, a single morpheme may be shared by many lexemes (but never *vice versa*). The morpheme-based view analyzes lexical processes as depending on the properties of morphemes.

There is a fairly clear division among the practitioners of each type of analysis. Linguists are fairly unanimous in seeing lexical processes as lexeme-based, while computational linguists have generally conducted morpheme-based analyses. The computational advantage of morpheme-based analysis is fairly easy to see: one can develop procedures for isolating the morphemes in a given form, and assign properties to the form based on these. Lexemes, involving (as they potentially do) nontransparent combinations of morphemes, are more difficult to recognize, are therefore more frequently stored *in toto* and are thus ultimately more demanding of memory resources—there are simply many more lexemes than morphemes (perhaps an order of magnitude more).

---

[4] Cf. Matthews (1974, pp. 20ff) for a much more thorough defense of this material; cf. Anderson (1988a, 1988b) and Zwicky (1985, 1990) for more recent defenses of the lexeme-based view.

Linguists have been assiduous in turning up cases where the larger number of lexemes seems useful in analyzing lexical processes. The suffixation of *-bar* in German, which we examine below in detail, provides examples of the most important sorts of cases.[5] The crucial observation is always of the form that important properties of complex words depend *not* on the morphemes of the complex, but rather on the lexemes. Wellformedness is one such important property. And it turns out that the wellformedness of forms with the suffix *-bar* cannot be predicted only on the basis of the component morphemes. We find patterns such as the following:

morpheme	lexeme 1	lexeme 2
meid-	**meidbar*	*vermeidbar* 'avoidable'
lad-	**ladbar*	*aufladbar* 'loadable'
hab-	**habbar*	*handhabbar* 'manageable'
stell-	**stellbar*	*einstellbar,* 'adjustable' *vorstellbar* 'imaginable'
meß-	*meßbar* 'measurable'	**bemeßbar*
arbeit-	**arbeitbar*	*bearbeitbar* 'workable'

This table demonstrates that the wellformedness of *-bar* derivatives cannot be predicted on the basis of the stem morphemes with which they combine, and the last pair suggests that prefix morphemes are likewise poor predictors. (This is true, but we won't adduce further evidence here. It is trivial, but very tedious, for a German speaker with a dictionary to collect this evidence.) It is worth anticipating one reaction to the evidence above: one might object that there are perfectly respectable accounts of the illformedness of some of the examples here—some are not derived from transitive verbs, for example. But this sort of objection is merely a more detailed diagnosis of the same problem: the illformedness arises when the lexeme source of a derived word is not transitive. There is no claim made here that these patterns are ultimately inexplicable, merely that they are inexplicable on the basis of morphemic analysis. The hypothesis of a lexeme base enables more exact hypotheses in this area (e.g. about transitivity).

A second important property of derived words is their meaning, and here again, the best predictor of derived meaning is the meaning of component lexemes rather than that of component morphemes. We can illustrate the evidence for this using the same suffix, *-bar*. The general meaning accruing to a *-bar* adjective is that it describes the property of something which could stand (in

---

[5] A great deal of what we analyze below may be found in a very thorough study of this process, Jindrich Toman's *Wortbildung* (Toman, 1983).

object position) in the relation denoted by the verb. Thus something is *faxbar* if one can fax it. The cases which demonstrate the lexeme basis of derivation all involve some irregularity in meaning. For example, German *eßbar* 'edible' involves a slight narrowing in meaning from the verb *essen* 'eat', since something must be capable of being safely eaten to be *eßbar*. More complicated derivatives involving these two morphemes could either preserve this narrowing, in which case they would appear to support the hypothesis of a lexeme basis, or they might fail to preserve it. The example of *Eßbarkeit* 'edibility' indicates that the narrowing is exactly preserved. And in general, meaning changes are persistent in further derivation. For a further example, note *Kostbarkeit* 'valuableness' derived from the semantically irregular *kostbar* 'valuable'.

A third important property of derived words is their form, and form is likewise lexeme-dependent. The form of the argument here is the same as that above: irregularity is persistent throughout further derivation. Thus irregular *sichtbar* 'visible' (instead of **sehbar*) is found further in *Sichtbarkeit*.[6]

It is worth noting that *-bar* suffixation is a derivational process, and that most of the evidence for a lexeme basis has been accumulated from studies of derivation. We shall likewise present a lexeme-based treatment of inflection below, however. The same sorts of evidence for a lexeme basis may be adduced in the case of inflection, but rather less of it than in the case of derivation. There are, e.g. verbs whose paradigms differ from those of their component morphemes, e.g. the weak verbs *handhaben* and *veranlassen*, which are derived from the strong *haben* and *lassen*. If inflection depends on morphemes, these examples must be analyzed as involving distinct pairs of morphemes.[7] Matthews (1974, chap. VIII) presents arguments of a different sort that inflection should not be reduced to manipulations of morphemes.

We have continued at some length to justify our choice of lexeme-based analysis here, in order to emphasize that this is a deliberate, and not merely a customary, assumption. Morpheme-based work has its purpose under this scheme, however. In particular, since our treatment of derivation allows regular derivations not to be listed in the lexicon, we need a method of recognizing the parts of a regular derivation in order to assign the correct properties to it. As we see it, a fully regular derivation such as *faxbar* 'faxable' need not appear in the lexicon at all. Its properties are fully specified under the specifications for the lexeme *fax-* 'to telefax', the suffix *-bar*, and the morpholological head-complement rule scheme. But in order to recognize *fax-* and *-bar* in *faxbar*,

---

[6] One would expect irregular syntactic properties to show the same persistence through derivation, but we do not know of relevant studies.

[7] A further sort of example may be forthcoming if one examines perfect participle formation in German. The generalization to be captured is that a prefix *ge-* is employed when stress is on the first stem syllable (stem or inseparable prefix) of the lexeme. The argument is complicated by the fact that this is often—perhaps always—predictable on the basis of the morphemes involved.

some analysis must be performed, and morpheme-based processing seems well-suited for this purpose.

7.1.2 Morphotactics and Allomorphy

There is a traditional distinction in morphology between *morphotactics*, the arrangement of morphological elements into larger structures, and *allomorphy* or *morphophonemics*, variations in the shape of morphological units (cf. Anderson, 1988b, p. 147). It is our goal here to show how morphotactics may be subsumed into the lexicon, and we shall discuss this at length in sections 7.3 and 7.4 below. But we shall deliberately have very little to say about morphophonemics, which we do not intend to treat here. We take up this distinction more concretely in section 7.3.1 below, but only to reinforce the point here: we do not propose subsuming morphophonemics into the lexicon.

7.2   Background

In this section we review the background material in the theory of feature-based description. This section may be skipped over by those familiar with feature structure theory and HPSG.

7.2.1   Feature Structures

The fundamental analytic tool of *feature-based* or *unification-based* theories is the feature structure, represented by the attribute-value matrix (AVM)—a set of pairs of *attributes* (such as PER) and *values* (such as FIRST, SECOND or THIRD). Shieber (1986) is the standard introductory reference to feature-based grammars, and we assume basic familiarity with this sort of analysis; here we review only the bare essentials needed for the lexical analysis below. Feature structures are mathematical objects which model linguistic entities such as the utterance tokens of words and phrases. It is important to note that values may themselves be feature structures, so that we allow that an AGR attribute may specify its value using the complex AVM below, resulting in a hierarchical AVM:

$$\left[\quad \text{AGR} \quad \left[\begin{array}{l} \text{PER THIRD} \\ \text{NUM SG} \end{array} \right] \quad \right]$$

A useful conceptualization of feature structures is that of rooted, directed labeled graphs, where values correspond to nodes, attributes to labeled edges, and where the AVM as a whole describes the root. This conceptualization is particularly useful when it comes to specifying values within complex structures, which we do by concatenating attributes to form paths from the root into the interior of the structure. Because AVM descriptions can quickly become quite large, we will employ path descriptors, abbreviating, e.g. the person information in the AVM above to simply:

$$[\quad \text{AGR|PER THIRD} \quad]$$

We shall even take the liberty occasionally of suppressing prefixes where no confusion arises, and specifying (as equivalent to the above):

$$[\quad \text{PER THIRD} \quad]$$

But we shall take care to do this only where the type of the AVM is clear (so that it is the type of AVM in which AGR occurs, as opposed to one in which HEAD|AGR occurs, etc.). Such abbreviations are generally disambiguated when interpreted in the light of type information. They reduce the complexity of AVM's a great deal, making them easier to read and write.

We shall have frequent occasion to employ AVM's with *disjunctive* value specifications. These are descriptions of objects whose value is included in one of the disjuncts, i.e. it is FIRST or THIRD:

$$[\quad \text{AGR|PER } \{ \text{ FIRST, THIRD} \} \quad]$$

In order to link particular choices with formal elements, we make extensive use of *distributed disjunctions*, investigated by Backofen *et al.* (1990) and Dörre and Eisele (1989). This technique was developed because it (normally) allows more efficient processing of disjunctions, since it obviates the need to expand them to disjunctive normal form. It adds no expressive power to a feature formalism (assuming it has disjunction), but it abbreviates some otherwise prolix disjunctions:

$$
\begin{bmatrix} \text{PATH1} \; \{_{\$1} \; a, b\} \\ \text{PATH2} \; \{_{\$1} \; \alpha, \beta\} \\ \text{PATH3} \; [\; \ldots \;] \end{bmatrix}
=
\left\{
\begin{bmatrix} \text{PATH1} \; a \\ \text{PATH2} \; \alpha \\ \text{PATH3} \; [\; \ldots \;] \end{bmatrix}
,
\begin{bmatrix} \text{PATH1} \; b \\ \text{PATH2} \; \beta \\ \text{PATH3} \; [\; \ldots \;] \end{bmatrix}
\right\}
$$

The two disjunctions in the feature structure on the left bear the same name '$1', indicating that they are a single alternation. The sets of disjuncts named covary, taken in order. This may be seen in the right-hand side of the equivalence. Two of the advantages of distributed disjunctions may be seen in the artificial example above. First, covarying but non-identical elements can be identified as such, even if they occur remotely from one another in structure, and second, feature structures are abbreviated. The amount of abbreviation depends on the number of distributed disjunctions, the lengths of the paths PATH1 and PATH2, and—in at least some competing formalisms—on the size of the remaining structure (cf. [PATH3:   ] above).[8]

---

[8] Cf. Backofen *et al.* (1990) for a discussion of a third advantage of distributed disjunctions, namely a normal increase in processing efficiency.

A final point to be appreciated about the use of feature structures is that two different attributes may be specified as having the same value, even when that value is unknown. For example, we might specify subject verb agreement in the following fashion, where the boxed numbers are just 'tags' that identify the values as being the same:

$$\left[\begin{array}{l} \text{AGR} \boxed{1} \\ \text{SUBJECT} \left[\begin{array}{l} \text{AGR} \boxed{1} \end{array} \right] \end{array} \right]$$

Returning to the graph conceptualization above, the need for this sort of specification demonstrates that the class of graphs we're interested in are not simply trees, but objects of the more general class of directed graphs.

What we have written above are AVM's or *feature descriptions*—they describe the abstract objects (feature structures) we use to model linguistic phenomena. Attribute-value descriptions such as the ones above are standardly interpreted in one of two ways: either directly, as descriptions of linguistic objects (cf. Johnson, 1988; Smolka, 1988), or algebraically, as specifications of *feature structures* (cf. Pollard and Sag, 1987, chap. 2; Carpenter, 1992, chap. 17), which then may be regarded as models of the linguistic objects. The distinction is mathematically interesting, but it will not be pursued here, since it is irrelevant to grammars and lexicons written in this notation. Indeed, we shall often speak informally of the AVM's as if they were the linguistic objects, as is common.

Unification is the normal means of combining the compatible information in two or more feature structures into a single one. Unification fails when there is incompatible information. We shall not provide a formal definition of the notion here, even though it is used frequently below, since it is defined in the works cited above. Here is an example of two AVM descriptions which are compatible, and a further example of two which are not:

$$\left[\begin{array}{l} \text{AGR} \left[\begin{array}{l} \text{PER THIRD} \end{array} \right] \end{array} \right] \sqcap \left[\begin{array}{l} \text{AGR} \left[\begin{array}{l} \text{NUM SG} \end{array} \right] \end{array} \right] =$$

$$\left[\begin{array}{l} \text{AGR} \left[\begin{array}{l} \text{PER THIRD} \\ \text{NUM SG} \end{array} \right] \end{array} \right]$$

$$\left[\begin{array}{l} \text{AGR} \left[\begin{array}{l} \text{PER THIRD} \\ \text{NUM PL} \end{array} \right] \end{array} \right] \sqcap \left[\begin{array}{l} \text{AGR} \left[\begin{array}{l} \text{NUM SG} \end{array} \right] \end{array} \right] = \bot$$

(Note the incompatible specification of the value at the AGR|NUM path.)

One point about the use of coreference and disjunction is worth special mention: there is 'normally' no way to specify that structure is shared between one disjunct of a (possibly distributed) disjunction and anything outside the disjunction. Thus the feature structure below is misleading:

(1) $$\left[\begin{array}{l} \text{ATTR1} \boxed{1} \\ \text{ATTR2} \left\{ \left[\begin{array}{l} \text{ATTR3} \boxed{1} \end{array} \right], \left[\begin{array}{l} \text{ATTR4} \boxed{1} \end{array} \right] \right\} \end{array} \right]$$

We said that there is 'normally' no such allowable specification, but this should be clarified: the semantics of the formula here is clear enough (it can be readily reduced to disjunctive normal form), but two things must be noted. First, the formulation is somewhat deceptive, in that the value in [ATTR1 $\boxed{1}$] in the formula above is implicitly disjunctive. This may be seen if one considers the result of unifying the above with a (nondisjunctive) description:

$$\left[\begin{array}{cc} \text{ATTR2} & \left[\begin{array}{c} \text{ATTR3 } a \\ \text{ATTR4 } b \end{array} \right] \end{array} \right]$$

which yields:

$$\left[\begin{array}{cc} \text{ATTR1 } \{a, b\} \\ \text{ATTR2} & \left[\begin{array}{c} \text{ATTR3 } a \\ \text{ATTR4 } b \end{array} \right] \end{array} \right]$$

This is perhaps not immediately appreciated when such structures are encountered. The second point is related, namely, that the administration of coreference which spans disjunction can become fairly involved. It is worth noting that neither of these points calls the legitimacy of the coreference spanning disjunction into question; they merely point out that it is a sensitive area. For this reason, we shall not avoid it completely here. It will allow us more succinct representations.

The reason why a restriction against coreference spanning disjunction is not felt to hinder expressivity is clear: there is a reasonably succinct alternative to the form (1) above:

$$\left[\begin{array}{c} \text{ATTR1 } \{\$1 \ \boxed{1}, \boxed{2} \} \\ \text{ATTR2 } \{\$1 \ [\ \text{ATTR3 } \boxed{1} \ ] \ , \ [\ \text{ATTR4 } \boxed{2} \ ] \ \} \end{array} \right]$$

Notice that coreferences do not span disjunctions here, since we employ coreferences only within single alternatives of a distributed disjunction.

The significance of feature structures for the present work is twofold: first, contemporary grammatical work in computational linguistics is nearly universally conducted in feature-based grammars, so that it is important that lexical specifications for feature-based theories be clearly interpretable. The present work also aims to provide a lexicon for feature-based grammar, where the lexicon may be viewed as a (disjunctive) collection of feature descriptions. Feature structures will be the only content of the lexical specifications in the lexicon; in other words, specifications associate word class types with feature structure descriptions.

This brings us to the second point of connection between feature-based theories and lexicon theory. The work on 'structured lexicons' cited in the introduction by Flickinger *et al.* (1985), Flickinger (1987) and Evans and Gazdar (1990) emphasized the value of lexicons in which specifications were as free as possible of redundancy, and these works eliminated redundancy by exploiting a relation of *inheritance* between lexical classes, realized as a relation between nodes in a directed graph (inheritance hierarchy). In structured lexicons, the word class *transitive verb* inherits properties from the word class *verb* as well as the word class *transitive*. The usual formulation in feature-based theories takes the inverse relation 'bequeath' as primitive. This relation is very naturally characterized in feature-based theories as the relation 'less-informative-than', or *subsumption*, which we symbolize '$\sqsupseteq$'. For example, the feature structures below stand in this relation:

$$\left[\ \text{AGR}\ \left[\ \text{NUM SG}\ \right]\ \right]\ \sqsupseteq\ \left[\ \text{AGR}\ \left[\begin{array}{l}\text{PER THIRD}\\\text{NUM SG}\end{array}\right]\ \right]$$

We shall therefore formulate statements about inheritance (the inverse of bequeath) using '$\sqsubseteq$'. We implement this notion of inheritance using a procedure, 'unify' (or 'default-unify'), which unifies the information of every superclass with *local* idiosyncratic information to determine a fully expanded prototype of the class in question. Feature description languages thus provide a natural formalization for work in structured lexicons.

A final aspect of modern feature theories that we shall have cause to exploit is their use of *typing* (cf. Carpenter, 1992, for a presentation). A type system imposed on a system of feature structures has several tasks: first, it provides a means of referring to *classes* of feature structures of a given restricted sort. We shall put this to good use, e.g. in representing derivational relationships as complex inheritance. Second, attributes are restricted by their types to being appropriate on a limited class of feature structures; thus the attribute VFORM will be limited in appropriateness to objects of type *verb* or *verbal-head*. Third and finally, the values of attributes will be restricted by type.

7.2.2   HPSG

Although most of what we propose might be realized in formalisms weaker than HPSG, it is worth noting that we shall employ *recursive type specifications* of a kind found in HPSG, but generally not elsewhere. In HPSG the type *sign* has an attribute SYNTAX|LOCAL|SUBCAT which is restricted in value to lists of signs. This attribute encodes *subcategorization* information, which is lexically based in HPSG, much as it is in Categorial Grammar (Bach, 1988). Grammatical heads specify the syntactic and semantic restrictions they impose on their complements and adjuncts. For example, verbs and verb phrases bear a feature SUBCAT whose content is a (perhaps ordered) set of feature structures representing their unsatisfied subcategorization requirements. Thus the feature structures associated with transitive verbs include the information:

$$\left[\begin{array}{l}\textit{trans-verb}\\[4pt]\text{SYN|LOC|SUBCAT}\ \left\langle\left[\begin{array}{l}\textit{NP}\\\text{CASE ACC}\end{array}\right],\left[\begin{array}{l}\textit{NP}\\\text{CASE NOM}\end{array}\right]\right\rangle\end{array}\right]$$

(where *NP* is the type of noun phrase signs, and *trans-verb* the type of transitive verb sign).

The significance of subcategorization information is that the subcategorizer may combine with elements listed in its SUBCAT feature (perhaps only in a particular order) in order to form larger phrases. When a subcategorizer combines with a subcategorized-for element, the resultant phrase no longer bears the subcategorization specification—it has been discharged (cf. Pollard and Sag, 1987, p. 71, for a formulation of the HPSG *subcategorization principle*). We shall have cause to return to subcategorization in our presentation of derivation.

In order to appreciate the point about recursive specification, let us regard the subcategorization list as represented in [FIRST, REST] form (so that every SUBCAT either is null or occurs in [FIRST, REST] form). Then, the important point is to note that we have a type *list*, one of whose attributes, REST, is restricted to values of type *list*, including the empty list. This is a recursive type specification. In general, SUBCAT is restricted to taking values which are of the type *list(sign)*—and this attribute occurs within signs. A similar recursion obtains when we define the type *tree* as a *lexical-sign* or a *sign* whose attribute DAUGHTERS is a list of signs of the type *tree*. We shall employ recursive type specifications in a proposal for the representation of derivational relationships.

7.3   Inflection

We turn our intention here to the treatment of inflectional paradigms as exemplified by verbal, adjectival and nominal paradigms in German. We illustrate with a fairly traditional representation of the inflectional endings used in the present active paradigm of weak verbs below (and we explore alternatives to this below):

	sg	pl
1st	+ e, *kriege*	+ en, *kriegen*
2nd	+ st, *kriegst*	+ t, *kriegt*
3rd	+ t, *kriegt*	+ en, *kriegen*

7.3.1   Interface to Morphophonemics

It is worth noting here that the forms found in paradigms may be more complex than simple concatentations of stems and the inflectional endings specified in paradigms. Full forms cannot always be derived from simple concatenation since internal sandhi rules, i.e. rules of morphological juncture of various sorts, may need to be applied. In fact, this is the case in the simple example here. For weak verb stems ending in alveolar stops, a rule of schwa-epenthesis must be invoked in the third-singular position (and this is *not* a general phonological process in German).

	sg	pl
1st	arbeit + e	arbeit + en
2nd	arbeit + st	arbeit + t
3rd	arbeit + t,	arbeit + en
	arbeitet	

The status of *umlaut* in strong conjugations (*ich schlage, du schlägst*) is similarly sensitive to morphological juncture—thus it is triggered by the second singular present /st/, but not by the second singular preterite /st/.

We draw attention to these phenomena only to emphasize that, while we are aware of such complications, we do not intend to treat them here because a proper treatment involves morphophonemic detail, which is not our primary focus here.[9] Our focus here will be on the morphological interface to syntax, rather than on the interface to morphophonology.

The interface to allomorphy is then quite simple:

$$\left[\text{MORPH} \left[\begin{array}{l} \text{STEM } \boxed{2} \\ \text{ENDING } \boxed{3} \\ \text{FORM } \boxed{2} \& \boxed{3} \end{array} \right] \right]$$

where '&' designates the concatentation operation between morphs. It is the task of the allomorphy to 'spell out' the combination under FORM. We also emphasize that we indulge below in the convenient fiction that the inputs to allomorphy can be adequately specified using strings—even though we are convinced that a more abstract characterization (e.g. in feature structures) is necessary.

We shall not provide a detailed proposal—either here or in the following section on derivation—about the interface of the lexeme-based lexicon to morphophonemics. The main issue we see as significant here is the relationship between the lexeme-based lexicon and morpheme-based generalizations which might arise in morphophonemics. This is a subject of current investigation.

7.3.2 Approaches to Inflection

The dominant approaches to the treatment of inflection in computational linguistics have been either (i) to model inflection using collections of lexical rules, or (ii) to employ two-level morphology. The deployment of lexical rules may be

---

[9] For the theorist who would like to maintain the interesting claim that feature structures can represent *all* linguistic knowledge, the feature-based treatment of morphophonemics is of great potential interest (cf. Bird, 1990). For efficiency reasons, however, a second path might be chosen, viz., the employment of a hybrid feature-based two-level morphology. This has efficiency advantages, and it is our intention to pursue this line (cf. Trost, 1990). A third possibility would be to simply anticipate the effects of morphophonemics in the specification of paradigms (even if this results in the multiplication of paradigms).

found in Flickinger's approach (cf. Flickinger, 1987, pp. 107–110), in the Alvey tools project (cf. Ritchie *et al.*, 1987, p. 298) and in HPSG (cf. Pollard and Sag, 1987, pp. 209–213). Paradigmatic morphology improves upon these ideas by defining the paradigm as a sequence of lexical rules on which subsumption relations can be defined (cf. Calder, 1989), but the fundamental analytical tool is still the lexical rule.

In this view, the inflectional paradigm above is described by postulating rules which relate one paradigm element to another (or relating it to another form), including perhaps a rule to derive first singular forms from infinitives. While nothing would prohibit a lexical rule from operating on abstract stems to create forms, this was seldom done (cf. Karttunen's LFG-style treatment of passive in D-PATR, Karttunen, 1986, pp. 12–14, for an exception). In the following section on derivation (section 7.4), we sketch a feature-based theory of lexical rules within which these notions of the paradigm could be recast, but we prefer to demonstrate the flexibility of the feature-based approach here by developing a more purely paradigmatic view. While it would clearly be possible to formulate a rule-based view of the paradigm in feature structures, the analytically more challenging task is to describe directly the abstract variations which constitute paradigms—i.e. to try to characterize paradigms directly without recourse to lexical rules.

The two-level approach to inflection may be found in Koskenniemi (1983) (for an interesting extension in the direction of feature-based processing, cf. Trost, 1990). This differs from the current proposal in being morpheme-based. It is, however, compatible with various lexical structures, as is demonstrated by its use in the Alvey project, noted above (Ritchie *et al.*, 1987).

The direct characterization of the paradigm has been the alternative approach both in linguistics (cf. Matthews, 1972, chap. IV) and in computational linguistics (cf. Evans and Gazdar's DATR, 1990, and Russell *et al.*'s ELU lexicon, 1991). The fundamental idea in our characterization is due to the work in DATR, in which paradigms are treated as alternative further specifications of abstract lexemes. We express the same fundamental idea in feature structures by defining paradigms as large disjunctions which subsume appropriate lexical nodes. Each disjunct represents conceptually one element of the paradigm, and specifies what is peculiar to that element. The fundamental person-number verb paradigm in German is just an association of forms with the six disjuncts in the disjunctive normal form of the following disjunction:

$$\left[\text{AGR} \left[\begin{array}{l} \text{PER} \{1 \text{ ST}, 2 \text{ ND}, 3 \text{ RD}\} \\ \text{NUM} \{ \text{ SG, PL}\} \end{array} \right] \right]$$

7.3.3   A 'Word and Paradigm' Approach

We may now employ distributed disjunctions (cf. section 7.2) to link the fundamental alternation in (1) to the expression of forms. We obtain the following description of the present weak paradigm:

$$
\left[
\begin{array}{l}
\text{MORPH} \quad
\left[
\begin{array}{l}
\text{STEM } \boxed{2} \\
\text{ENDING } \boxed{3} \left\{ \$_1 \quad \text{``e''}, \ \text{``st''}, \ \text{``t''}, \ \text{``n''}, \ \text{``t''}, \ \text{``n''} \right\} \\
\text{FORM } \boxed{2} \ \& \ \boxed{3}
\end{array}
\right] \\[3em]
\text{SYN|LOCAL|HEAD|AGR} \ \left\{ \$_1 \
\left[
\begin{array}{ll}
\text{PER} & 1 \ \text{ST} \\
\text{NUM} & \text{SG}
\end{array}
\right],
\left[
\begin{array}{ll}
\text{PER} & 2 \ \text{ND} \\
\text{NUM} & \text{SG}
\end{array}
\right], \cdots ,
\left[
\begin{array}{ll}
\text{PER} & 3 \ \text{RD} \\
\text{NUM} & \text{PL}
\end{array}
\right] \right\}
\end{array}
\right]
$$

Each of the disjunctions tagged by '$1' constitutes effectively the same set of alternatives, taken in sequence. Thus we understand the feature structure above as denoting a disjunction of six disjuncts, the first of which has "e" as a value for MORPH|ENDING AND [PER 1 ST, NUM SG] (1st-sing) as a value of SYN|LOCAL|HEAD|AGR; etc. This node may be inherited by all German weak verbs.

In general, in representing a paradigm, the *exponents* of the paradigm are listed as alternatives under [MORPH|ENDING {$_n$...}], while their associated *properties* appear elsewhere within the feature structure under the same distributed disjunction '{$_n$...}' (for this terminology, cf. Matthews, 1974).

One advantage of representing paradigms in this fashion—as opposed to representations via lexical rules, as in Flickinger (1987) or in the other rule-based approaches cited above—is that the paradigm is represented in the same formalism in which word classes and lexemes are represented. A paradigm may thus participate in the same inheritance relationships that relate word classes and individual lexemes. We may, e.g. represent modal paradigms as inheriting by default from standard paradigms, modifying only the 'morph' value:

$$
\left[\ \text{MORPH|ENDING} \ \left\{ \$_1 \ \text{``''}, \ \text{``st''}, \ \text{``''}, \ \text{``n''}, \ \text{``t''}, \ \text{``n''} \right\} \ \right]
$$

(Note that we assume that the co-naming of disjunctions is inherited, so that the endings specified above are still to be understood as covarying with syntactic agreement features. The specification may be this compact because it exploits the nonlocal information in naming disjunctions.) The modal verb *sollen* is an example of this subparadigm:

	sg	pl
1st	soll +	soll + n
2nd	soll + st	soll + t
3rd	soll +	soll + n

The example is misleading in that we have shown the only modal paradigm with just this distinction from standard paradigms. We are aware that modal paradigms are in general also characterized by stem vowel alternations *kann*, *können*, etc., and we should have to represent this information as well. We could, e.g. allow lexemes to have a present singular stem and a present plural stem which are normally identical, but which are distinguished for these modals (and a very few other verbs such as *wissen*), or we might even try to describe the vowel alternations directly, if this were not going further into the morphophonemics than we care to (at least in this paper).

Genuine *suppletion* we likewise propose to treat via default overwriting:

$$
\left[
\begin{array}{l}
\text{MORPH} \quad \left[
\begin{array}{l}
\text{STEM} \\
\text{ENDING} \\
\text{FORM} \left\{ _{\$1} \ \text{"bin", "bist", "ist", "sind", "seid", "sind"} \right\}
\end{array}
\right] \\[2em]
\text{SYN|LOCAL|HEAD|AGR} \ \left\{ _{\$1} \left[\begin{array}{l} \text{PER 1ST} \\ \text{NUM SG} \end{array} \right], \left[\begin{array}{l} \text{PER 2ND} \\ \text{NUM SG} \end{array} \right], \ldots, \left[\begin{array}{l} \text{PER 3RD} \\ \text{NUM PL} \end{array} \right] \right\}
\end{array}
\right]
$$

Here we exploit default overwriting to describe the suppletive forms of *sein*. Note that we avoid the sticky question here of what the STEM and ENDING of such suppletive word forms ought to be. Perhaps a more graceful means of avoiding this question would be to deny that the forms are concatenations of STEM and ENDING (which we have not done above—we merely fail to identify them).

A *defective paradigm*, e.g. that of the verbs *dünken* 'to think', or *jemandem an etwas liegen* '(for something) to be important to someone', which occur only in the 3rd person singular, may be analyzed as a more extreme instance of overwriting inheritance—the entire disjunction is eliminated. (It is worth noting that non-overwriting analyses may also be formulated here, just as in most other places.)

$$
\left[
\text{SYN|LOCAL|HEAD|AGR} \ \left\{ _{\$1} \ \bot, \bot, \left[\begin{array}{l} \text{PER 3RD} \\ \text{NUM SG} \end{array} \right], \bot, \bot, \bot, \right\}
\right]
$$

Of course, one can formulate alternative linguistic descriptions of the requirement that this verb appear only in the third-person singular. For example, rather than say that the other forms do not exist, which is roughly the content of the specification above, one could postulate that impersonal verbs subcategorize for an (abstract) subject which is 3rd-sg. Our goal here is not to defend these particular 'paradigmatic gap' analyses, but rather to show that the phenomenon may be satisfactorily formulated in feature structures.[10] A further alternative would be to overwrite the AGREEMENT value nondisjunctively. There are probably alternative descriptions available.

These examples of paradigm inheritance point out limitations to the technique worth noting, even if they eventually prove to be convivial. First, although we

---

[10] Better candidates for genuine paradigmatic gaps in German are e.g. *Eltern* 'parents', which lacks a singular (except in the speech of biologists), or the verb *verscholl, verschollen* 'to get lost', which lacks all finite present forms. The English auxiliaries *come* and *go* are also frequently cited to demonstrate the existence of gaps in paradigms. Thus *I come/go see her daily; *He comes/goes see her daily*, even though *He wants to come/go see her daily.*

can allow the inheritance of distributed disjunctions to model the inheritance of paradigms, there is no way to make sense of an inherited paradigm being larger or smaller than the ancestor from which it inherits—so that we cannot sensibly construe a four-element paradigm as inheriting from a six-element one, or *vice versa*. This limitation arises because a distributed disjunction is always an alternation of elements in order. Second, there is no way to note that a single form in a paradigm is exceptional without respecifying the entire paradigm—the disjunction must be respecified as a whole. This stems from the fact that there is no way to identify a particular alternation within the distributed disjunction. Thus the defective paradigm above had to respecify the entire paradigmatic disjunction (this suggests perhaps using features to identify forms, which is the technique employed in DATR).

This in general is the case, and it brings us to a slight modification of the style of representation we shall employ. We examine this in the following section.

7.3.4   Matrix- vs. Form-based Approaches

The specifications above are written in what might be called the 'matrix' style of the word-and-paradigm model—every cell in the matrix of cross-cutting paradigmatic distinctions is specifically assigned a form value. The incorporation of a further dimension with n distinctions would increase paradigm size by a factor of n—even if *no* new forms were introduced. This is the presentation preferred in didactic grammars. Thus we might view a determiner or nominal paradigm in the fashion shown in Figure 7.1.

Opposed to this 'matrix-based' view of the paradigm is a 'form-based' view— only distinct forms are assigned feature specifications. The same (weak present) paradigm can be represented as an alternation of only four forms, two of which are (disjunctively) underspecified for agreement values (note that we employ nested distributed disjunctions in order to reduce the top-level 6-set to a 4-set). In general, this is the presentation used by linguists:

$$
\begin{bmatrix}
\text{MORPH} & \begin{bmatrix} \text{STEM} \\ \text{ENDING} \ \{_{\$1} \ \text{``e''}, \ \text{``st''}, \ \text{``t''}, \ \text{``n''}\} \end{bmatrix} \\[2em]
\text{SYN}|\text{LOCAL}|\text{HEAD}|\text{AGR} & \begin{bmatrix} \text{PER} \ \{_{\$1} \ \text{1ST}, \ \text{2ND}, \{_{\$2} \ \text{3RD}, \ \text{2ND}\}, \ \{ \ \text{1ST}, \ \text{3RD}\}\} \\ \text{NUM} \ \{_{\$1} \ \text{SG}, \ \text{SG}, \{_{\$2} \ \text{SG}, \ \text{PL}\}, \ \text{PL}\} \end{bmatrix}
\end{bmatrix}
$$

Which representation is preferable? A feature-based lexicon need not distinguish between these two representations; indeed, they are provably equivalent within the formalism, even if they illustrate two distinct styles in representing paradigms.

This assertion of equivalence concerns the properties of the feature structures only. The two representations are distinct in their default inheritance properties (which are thus in a sense intensional), so that overwriting defaults from the

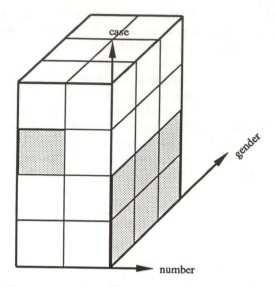

Figure 7.1: A three-dimensional view of the German determiner (or nondeclinable noun) paradigm, with dimensions corresponding to person, number and case

one or the other structure would be different. But the representations describe the same structures.[11]

7.3.5   *Complex Paradigmatic Elements*

In traditional treatments of the paradigm, the passive is normally listed as one of the elements in the paradigm. But passive and active forms differ not merely in the assignment of agreement features (of fairly simple structure) but also in the subcategorization classes to which they belong, and these are quite complex when expressed as feature structures, involving lists of feature structures. The representation of passive as an inflectional variant is something of a challenge for lexical representation schemes.

It is therefore worth noting that even paradigmatic elements as complex as passive may be described as inflectional variants using distributed disjunctions in the way just sketched. That is, we may describe not only the covariation between inflectional affix and a syntactic feature [PASSIVE ±], but even the effect of passive, e.g. on an HPSG subcategorization feature. We hasten to add that feature-based lexicons are not forced to this point of view—one could likewise formulate a derivational rule of passive (cf. section 7.4), nor do we

---

[11] While it is pleasant to obtain the intuitively correct result, it also means that there is no way to distinguish the structures described. Any putative distinction related to the two types of representation would have to be explained in another fashion.

wish to advocate the inflectional analysis at this time.[12] But there are clearer examples of languages with passives which are paradigm elements, e.g. Latin (cf. Allen and Greenough, 1903), and our primary goal is to establish that this (traditional) analysis is formulatable in a feature-based lexicon. It seems impossible to formulate in other structured lexicons.

$$
\begin{bmatrix}
\text{MORPH} & \begin{bmatrix} \text{STEM} \\ \text{PREFIX } \{_{\$1} \text{ ``''}, \text{ ``ge''}\} \\ \text{ENDING } \{_{\$1} \{_{\$2} \text{ ``e''}, \ldots, \text{ ``n''}\}, \text{ ``n''}\} \end{bmatrix} \\
\text{SYN}|\text{LOCAL} & \begin{bmatrix} \text{SUBCAT } \{_{\$1} \langle \text{ NP[ACC]}_{\boxed{4}}, \text{ NP[NOM]}_{\boxed{3}}\rangle, \\ \langle(\text{ PP[VON]}_{\boxed{3}},) \text{ NP[NOM]}_{\boxed{4}}\rangle \} \\ \text{HEAD}|\text{AGR } \{_{\$2} \begin{bmatrix} \text{PER } 1\text{ST} \\ \text{NUM } \text{SG} \end{bmatrix}, \ldots, \begin{bmatrix} \text{PER } 3\text{RD} \\ \text{NUM } \text{PL} \end{bmatrix}\} \end{bmatrix} \\
\text{SEM} & \begin{bmatrix} \text{PRED} \\ \text{SOURCE } \boxed{3} \\ \text{THEME } \boxed{4} \end{bmatrix}
\end{bmatrix}
$$

where NP[ACC] abbreviates [*np*, CASE ACC], etc. The structure above provides for two alternate (sets of) forms, active and passive.[13] This alternation is indicated by the disjunction name '$1'. The second, passive alternative correlates with a subcategorization in which, e.g. an optional PP[von] phrase fills the same semantic argument slot as the active subject. The first, active alternative in $1 is simply the active paradigm sketched above.[14]

The version of passive shown here is the version typically used to demonstrate grammatical analysis, i.e. passive is taken to be a variant of transitive verbs only, and no connection between passive and perfect participle is noted, even though these are never distinguished in form. Both of these flaws may be remedied, by what amount to essentially disjunctive specifications. For example, we may allow that the second alternative in $1 above correspond either to the passive syntactic structure (given) or to a perfect participle. It is worth clarifying that we do not claim that anything particularly insightful is gained by a disjunctive

[12] Cf. Kathol (1991) for a third, perhaps most interesting analysis, under which a single participial form serves in both active and passive voices, so that passive is neither an inflection nor a derivational alternation.

[13] But it is clear that a description such as the one above cannot hold of the Latin *deponent* forms—those with passive inflection, 'active' meaning and no active counterpart (*loquor*).

[14] It would be useful to find a way to allow the active paradigm not merely to be reused, but actually to be inherited in cases such as this (Latin). We have not seen a way of specifying this, since it amounts to specifying that a value be inherited as one of several disjuncts 'to be further specified'.

analysis of this sort; for insight we need some more detailed work in linguistic analysis. It is nonetheless worth noting the possibility of the further (disjunctive) detail, given the program of specifying all inflectional variants of a given lexeme as alternative further specifications of the lexeme. These further disjunctive and perhaps uninsightful specifications do not stand in the way of realizing this program.

7.3.6   Alternative Frameworks

We discussed above why we prefer *not* to analyze inflectional variation as an employment of lexical rules (but cf. section 7.4 for a proposal for representing in feature structures relations which linguists normally designate as 'lexical rules'). There are two similar proposals in inheritance-based, computational lexicons for analysing inflectional variation as the further specification of an abstract lexeme. We discuss these in the present section.

DATR (cf. Evans and Gazdar, 1990) is a graph description language (and inference engine) which can encode information about lexical items. DATR provides a formally clean version of the sort of default inheritance first advocated in de Smedt (1984) and Flickinger *et al.* (1985), and as such represents a significant advance in the understanding of default lexical inheritance. Although DATR superficially resembles feature notation, its semantics are in some ways different, so that an interface between DATR and a feature system is required, if DATR is to be used as a lexicon in combination with a feature-based parser (or morphological processor)—in keeping with the intention of DATR's developers. The fundamental advantage of our approach over that of DATR is that no such interface is required: lexical structures are exactly the structures required in syntax (and morphology).[15]

A further advantage accrues to feature-based approaches, because they come with a logic which has proven useful in linguistic description. Cf., for example, the extensive employment of disjunction above. Disjunction could probably be added to a system such as DATR, but it does not seem that anyone is trying to do this. A more subtle point is the status of coreference, a notion which feature logics are designed to treat in a very particular way, but which seems inexpressible in DATR.[16]

---

[15] For a rather bleak view of prospects for interfaces between DATR and feature formalisms, cf. the proposal in Kilbury *et al.* (1991).

[16] What makes this point subtle is that DATR does allow the expression of 'path equivalences', e.g. a statement such as $\langle agr \rangle == \langle subject\ agr \rangle$. Thus, if $\langle subject\ agr\ person \rangle =$ first AND $\langle subject\ agr\ number \rangle =$ sg then the same values will accrue to agr. But the relation is not symmetric; assignment of values to agr either overrides or is overridden by the above. (DATR's '==' is like the assignment operator in imperative programming languages, not like the identity relation.) A further refinement is that, even in the direction in which this does work (like identity) no distinction is made between two paths which have the same values and those

A final point of divergence is the degree of complexity which an inflectional specification may be allowed to have. The DATR scheme is to use specifications of the form:

< path >==< value >

to encode dependencies between properties and exponents, e.g.

< present first plural >== "en"

and this works fine as long as the properties involved fit neatly along a simple path. If properties become complex, on the other hand, as they seem to in the case of the (at least the Latin) passive, then this scheme breaks down. The feature-based model using distributed disjunctions is freer: dependent properties may be distributed in various positions in a feature structure.

The ELU lexicon (Russell *et al.*, 1991) uses equations describing feature structures for the most part, but the equations are divided into a 'main set' and a 'variant set', the latter of which (monotonically) describe inflectional variants. The paradigm is then described using a set of implicational equations, expressing information such as 'if x = [pers: 3, num: sg], then y ='s' '.[17] The use of distributed disjunctions seems to be a more concise method of specifying inflectional alternatives, but the underlying logic of the ELU approach is very similar to ours.[18]

7.4   Derivation

Looking at work done in the area of word formation, various formalisms and theories can be ordered according to different dimensions. One possible dimension of classification is, for instance, the distinction between procedural vs. declarative formulation of rules relating phonological, morphological and orthographic phenomena (cf. Calder, 1989).[19] Classifying specific treatments is subjective. Most linguists will interpret lexical rules procedurally. But lexical

which have distinct, but equivalent, values. But such 'structure-sharing' is very widely exploited in feature-based linguistic analyses.

[17] Information in variant sets is not subject to default overwriting, for reasons which are not explained. Although we find the proposal that some information not be subject to default overwriting congenial, it would seem desirable to view the specification of alternations as an orthogonal point.

[18] We have also benefited from the opportunity to examine unpublished work of Andreas Kathol at Ohio State University, who has independently developed a similar treatment of inflectional variation—this one based on constrained relations.

[19] Our briefly sketched treatment of derivation (and inflection) in the introductory section is in its essence declarative, because linguistic knowledge is encoded in terms of feature structures only and unification is the sole information-building operation.

rules can also be regarded purely declaratively, even if the procedural view is the most prominent one.[20]

7.4.1   *External vs. Internal Lexical Rules*

Instead of treating the issue of declarative vs. procedural formulations, we want to turn our attention to another dimension of classification: *Where does word formation take place—within or without the lexicon? without* means that the form of lexical rules is different from the structure of lexical entries (lexemes, also possibly morphemes). Lexical rules in PATR-II (Shieber, 1983) or D-PATR (Karttunen, 1986), for example, look like feature structures and are represented via a collection of path equations, but their interpretation is completely different from that of (normal) feature structures. The same is true, if we move to other theories: *f-structures* differ in form (syntax) and interpretation (semantics) from lexical rules stated in LFG (cf. the articles in Bresnan, 1982). This same observation holds for HPSG (Pollard and Sag, 1987, chap. 8.2),[21] for the Alvey tools project (Ritchie *et al.*, 1987), for the early days of HPSG (Flickinger *et al.*, 1985), for the work of Flickinger (1987), and also for Hoeksema's (1985) Categorial Morphology.

By its nature, an *external* lexical rule sets up a relation between two lexemes (or classes of lexemes)—or, in the case of feature-based theories, between two feature structure descriptions. But specifying the exact meaning of this mapping is an open question—nearly all theories have different viewpoints when interpreting (external) lexical rules:

- Are external lexical rules functions or perhaps even relations?
- If functions, do they take one argument or arbitrarily many? (*Mutatis mutandis* for relations)
- Are they unidirectional or bidirectional?
- If unidirectional, will they be interpreted declaratively (AVM_1 implies a corresponding AVM_2) or procedurally (lexical rule as an instruction, to build AVM_2 out of AVM_1)?

---

[20] Interesting to note, Pollard and Sag, 1987, p. 209, suggest a third interpretation of lexical rules coming directly from the field of many-sorted abstract data types—an *algebraic* perspective on lexical rules.

[21] Feature structures descriptions and lexical rules (form: $AVM_1 \longmapsto AVM_2$) in HPSG have nothing in common, because they differ in form as well as in interpretation. This remark is supported by the following observation: feature structures in HPSG are always typed, and these types can be ordered (partially) via subsumption. But this isn't true for lexical rules. A lexical rule as a whole does not have a type and there's no way to relate it to other feature structures. Under the assumption that a lexical rule can in principle be typed and resides in the lexicon, this type ought to be a subtype of *lexical-sign* according to Pollard and Sag (1987) and ought to have exactly the three top-level attributes PHON, SYN and SEM—but this isn't the case.

Instead of treating external lexical rules further, we'd like to propose a novel interpretation of lexical rules, which we call *internal*. An internal lexical rule is an information-bearing object, indistinguishable in its form and meaning from other entries of the lexicon—strictly speaking, it just *is* a lexical entry.

Derivational rules will be modeled as feature structure descriptions, just as lexical entries are. This is aesthetically pleasing, and has the further advantage of formal clarity. Perhaps most importantly, however, the fact that lexical rules and lexical entries are of the same formal type allows one to liberate yet another level of linguistic structure from *procedural* considerations and therefore allows one to interleave, e.g. morphological and phrasal processing in a way that is otherwise prohibited.[22]

It is worth noting that there is no one-to-one correspondence between traditional lexical rules (what linguists have called lexical rules) and single objects (feature structures) in our approach. Rather, the information in a lexical rule is distributed among lexical entries, principles, and morphological dominance schemata—our closest analogue to 'rule'.

In general, internal (or external) lexical rules cannot be realized as independent lexemes (or morphemes); instead rules serve as *filters* (in the sense of well-formedness conditions), used to rule out ill-formed structures (to fail to parse or generate them). A treatment of this kind will be presented here for the field of *derivation*. Another approach, which is also distinguished by its use of internal lexical rules, can be found in the ELU system (Russell *et al.*, 1991).[23]

7.4.2 Our Treatment of Derivation

In HPSG-I linguistic knowledge about word formation is encoded through a family of lexical rules, which are not feature structures, but rather essentially external operators working on feature structures. This (for us) unsatisfactory view appears even more questionable given the view of most linguists that form and meaning are much harder to describe for sentences and phrases than for words. If this is the case, one may ask, why does HPSG treat word formation

---

[22] One can quibble about our choice of terminology here. Given the possibility of interleaving processing in the way we describe, it might seem as if what we are calling *internal* lexical rules are rather more external than other construals would have it. Or one can insist on the standard construal of derivation as a mapping from lexical entries to lexical entries, which implies that the term *internal* lexical rule is misleading, since this insistence effectively equates the notion 'lexical rule' with that of an external mapping, always taking a set of feature structures and yielding a feature structure. Our own preference for the term 'internal lexical rule' arises because we see the lexicon in general as constituted by a set of feature structure descriptions—with no fundamental distinction between lexical rules and lexical entries. Lexical rules are simply a particular kind of feature structure description.

[23] ELU treats inflection as well as derivation by means of pure inheritance. We are convinced, however, that this approach is not strong enough for derivation (cf. below).

via external lexical rules rather than in a purely feature-based way? Why not formulate *rules* and *principles* for word grammar similar to those stated by Pollard and Sag (1987) for phrasal and sentential grammar? We think, there are at least three replies this question might provoke:

1. HPSG is a theory capable only of capturing the form and meaning of sentences in feature structure descriptions, but incapable of describing morphotactical aspects of language.

2. Trying to handle lexical structures (morphotactics) in terms of feature structure descriptions (i.e. via rules and principles) only leads to inefficient implementations.

3. HPSG is a conglomerate of different formalisms and theories (cf. Sag and Pollard, 1987, p. 1, and Pollard and Sag, 1987, p. 1), saying little or nothing about morphotactics. In the theories from which HPSG borrows, morphotactics were stated in form of external lexical rules. HPSG assumed this view somewhat nonreflectively, because HPSG's primary purpose is the description of phrasal and sentential syntax and semantics.

We're convinced that the first thesis is simply *wrong*, and that the second one is (at the moment) probably true (because procedural implementations of lexical rules can be very efficient), while the third statement is definitely correct. Summing up, we think it's a promising task to approach *derivation* purely in terms of feature structure descriptions—just in the spirit of HPSG. Recall the two equations in Pollard and Sag (1987, p. 147),

(2) $UG = P_1 \sqcap ... \sqcap P_n$

(3) $English = P_1 \sqcap ... \sqcap P_{n+m} \sqcap (L_1 \sqcup ... \sqcup L_p \sqcup R_1 \sqcup ... \sqcup R_q)$

These may be understood in the following way: universal grammar (UG) consists of a set of principles $P_1, ..., P_n$, whose conjunction (or unification) must hold true of every structure in every language. In addition, a given language may impose the language-specific constraints $P_{n+1}, ..., P_{n+m}$. Finally, the grammar requires that every structure instantiate some lexical entry $L_1, ..., L_p$, or phrasal pattern (rule) $R_1, ..., R_q$—since a structure need satisfy only one of the lexical or rule descriptions in order to be a well-formed phrase, these constraints obtain disjunctively. A language is then just the set of structures which simultaneously conform not only to all the principles, both universal and language-specific, but also to at least one of the lexical or phrasal descriptions. These fundamental equations define an HPSG grammatical theory for phrases and sentences, and we propose to apply a similar methodology to derivation, relying extensively on *rules*, *principles* and unification-based *inheritance* (for an explanation of (2) and (3), cf. Pollard and Sag, 1987, p. 147).

In contrast to inflection, derivation cannot rely on *naive* inheritance alone. Here, 'naive' means that a word like the German *weglaufen* is defined by inheriting (unifying) all the properties from the prefix *weg-*, the verb *laufen* plus additional idiosyncratic properties of the new complex lexeme, i.e.

(4)   weglaufen = [*weg*] ⊓ [*laufen*] ⊓ [......].

ELU's treatment of derivation (cf. Russell *et al.*, 1991, p. 218) is done in such a way, and it may be a reasonable tack to take for the treatment at hand, that of the German separable prefixes. Applied generally, an approach like this leads to several insurmountable problems:

- If we relied on naive inheritance as the (sole) descriptive means, it would seem impossible to explain how the iteration of derivational processes could ever lead to different results. If *anti-* (or take the German *vor-*) is a derivational prefix, and its effect on a stem is described via inheritance, then the effect of inheriting it should be the same, whether there are one, two or more instances of the *same* prefix in a word because unification is *idempotent* and inheritance defines itself through unification. Thus a complex word like *anti-missile* (or *Vor+version*) would be predicted to be the same as *anti-anti-missile* (or *Vor+vor+version*).[24] Likewise, such an approach is not capable of explaining the *indirect* recursion occurring in complex compounds such as *institu+tion+al+isa+tion*.

- Sole reliance on naive inheritance leaves little opportunity to explain the hierarchical structure often found in morphology, e.g. the difference in bracketing one finds in complex words containing at least two affixes, e.g. [*un-* [*do -able*]] as opposed to [[*un- do*]-*able*]. Because inheritance is associative and monotonic (in the absence of overwriting), other mechanisms must be at play. Naive inheritance seems incapable of accounting for any structure, let alone ambiguous hierarchical structure.

- Simple examination of derivational results suggests that treating all of them via naive inheritance from a single lexeme will lead to unwieldy lexicons: a form such as German *Ableit+bar+keit* (derivability) would seem to require that verbal, adjectival and nominal paradigms be found as heirs of the single lexeme (recall that we dealt with this above by modeling it via mapping from lexeme to lexeme).

- It turns out also that there are technical problems connected with the treatment of derivation as inheritance. These may be summarized, albeit cryptically, in the following way: we should prefer that the result of a category-changing derivational process, e.g. the process which

---

[24] Permitting iteration of derivational prefixes only to a certain depth (which seems *prima facie* plausible since, e.g. words such as German *Vor+vor+vor+version* are questionable) will solve this problem, if every element of the finite set of complex prefixes is coded as a lexical entry. But this attempt at repair is (i) extremely unsatisfying theoretically and (ii) incomplete, because the depth of composition is a subjective measure.

derives *derive+able* from *derive* and *-able*, be a full-fledged member of the target category (of the derivational process)—in this case, the class of adjectives. Now, if the derivational process is modeled by naive inheritance only, then *derive+able* ought to inherit from the class of verbs (through *derive*), as well. It is easy to continue this line of reasoning further (consider *derive+abil+ity*) to see how this sort of explanation leads one to the postulation of lexemes of dubious lineage, inheriting from too many ancestors (this point is essentially just the converse of the last).

Treating *derivation* in our approach will lead to complex morphs (e.g. words) consisting of a head daughter HEAD-MORPH and a complement daughter COMP-MORPH (e.g. (5)). The task of the 'morphological-daughters' feature is to encode morphological structure, similarly to how HEAD-DTR and COMP-DTRS do this on the phrasal level (cf. Pollard and Sag, 1987). This is in analogy to the HPSG formulation of phrase structure in features, yielding tree structures.[25]

(5)

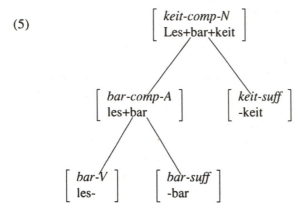

We include this as an example of the hierarchical structure whose analysis is beyond the descriptive reaches of *naive* inheritance. The objections to the description of derivation in terms of naive inheritance do not apply here, since, e.g. tree adjunction is not idempotent—so that, e.g. *Vorversion* may be distinguished from *Vorvorversion*; tree adjunction generates hierarchical structures (evident here), and, as we shall see, it distinguishes inheritance (sharing properties) from the requirements that sublexemes come from particular word classes or types (so that the tree structure above cannot be interpreted to mean that the noun *Lesbarkeit* is in any sense a verb of the same type as *lesen* or an adjective

---

[25] Binary trees (together possibly with unary ones for ∅ derivation) seem to suffice, at least for derivation. Of course, this is an assumption that will be put to the test in applications of this lexical work.

of the same type as *lesbar*). The hierarchy here is a *part-of* hierarchy in contrast to the inheritance hierarchy, which constitutes an IS-A hierarchy. The distinction is crucial: the parts of a complex word do not bequeath their properties to the words derived from them.

In general, the head daughter is a bound morpheme of type *affix*, while the complement daughter is of type *word* and is free (cf. Figure 7.2). HEAD-MORPH and COMP-MORPH are put together under the label MORPHS (cf. DTRS). With these assertions in mind, we postulate, in analogy to the phrasal 'rules' in HPSG (cf. Pollard and Sag, 1987, p. 149), the following morphological rule schema:

(6) $[\text{LEX} +] \longrightarrow \text{H, C}[\text{LEX} +]$

or more formally as a typed feature structure ('$\equiv$' is used for definitional expressions):

$$(7) \quad \text{MHCR} \equiv \begin{bmatrix} complex \\ \text{SYN|LOC|LEX} + \\ \text{MORPHS} \begin{bmatrix} morph\text{-}head\text{-}struct \\ \text{HEAD-MORPH} \ [affix\ ] \\ \text{COMP-MORPH} \ [part\text{-}of\text{-}speech\ ] \end{bmatrix} \end{bmatrix}$$

Just as Pollard and Sag proclaim universal as well as language-specific principles, we will define four 'principles', which are consistent with our linguistic data and specified as typed implications. We don't suppose that these principles will not be overturned by wider ranges of analyses, but we do suppose that they illustrate how the HPSG style of analysis can be extended to word-internal structure. The formulation of the principles presupposes that the underlying feature logic (along the lines of Kasper and Rounds, 1986, Rounds and Kasper, 1986; cf. the section on feature structures and HPSG) is extended by adding *functional dependencies* (functionally dependent values; for a motivation, cf. Pollard and Sag, 1987, pp. 48–49; for a formal definition, cf. Reape, 1991, pp. 73ff).

All morphological HEAD features, as well as (morphological) *subcategorization* will be defined, for simplicity, under the path SYN|LOC.[26] PHON will be replaced by MORPH|FORM and *headed-structure* is replaced by *morph-head-struct* (morphologically headed structure) which has at least the attributes HEAD-MORPH and COMP-MORPH. The symbol *complex* (complex word) corresponds to the *type* of the same name in the subsumption lattice (cf. Fig. 7.2). The *constituent order principle* (Pollard and Sag, 1987, pp. 169)

---

[26] There are good reasons to introduce, at least for affixes, an (additional) morphological subcategorization feature under the path MORPH, but we shall not pursue this here. This approach is investigated in Krieger (1991).

was taken over directly from HPSG (MCOP).[27]

$$(8) \qquad \text{MCOP} \equiv \left\{ \begin{array}{l} \left[\begin{array}{l} complex \\ \text{MORPHS} \ [morph\text{-}head\text{-}struct \ ] \end{array} \right] \Longrightarrow \\ \left[\begin{array}{l} complex \\ \text{MORPH|FORM} \ \ \text{order-constituents(} \ \boxed{1}) \\ \text{MORPHS} \ \ \boxed{1} \end{array} \right] \end{array} \right.$$

Likewise for derivation, the formulation of the *head feature principle* in HPSG (Pollard and Sag, 1987, p. 58) is used directly (MHFP), and only certain attributes and type names were altered. Among other things, MHFP is responsible for deducing the category of the new word from the category of the head daughter.

$$(9) \qquad \text{MHFP} \equiv \left\{ \begin{array}{l} \left[\begin{array}{l} complex \\ \text{MORPHS} \ [morph\text{-}head\text{-}struct \ ] \end{array} \right] \Longrightarrow \\ \left[\begin{array}{l} complex \\ \text{SYN|LOC|HEAD} \ \ \boxed{1} \\ \text{MORPHS|HEAD-MORPH|SYN|LOC|HEAD} \ \ \boxed{1} \end{array} \right] \end{array} \right.$$

The *semantics principle* may be taken in its simplest form and slightly modified (Pollard and Sag, 1987, p. 99): the semantics of the mother is equal to the semantics of the head daughter.

$$(10) \qquad \text{MSP} \equiv \left\{ \begin{array}{l} \left[\begin{array}{l} complex \\ \text{MORPHS} \ [morph\text{-}head\text{-}struct \ ] \end{array} \right] \Longrightarrow \\ \left[\begin{array}{l} complex \\ \text{SEM} \ \ \boxed{1} \\ \text{MORPHS|HEAD-MORPH|SEM} \ \ \boxed{1} \end{array} \right] \end{array} \right.$$

The use of binary trees and the head-complement structure for derivation leads to a *subcategorization principle* which looks (and is) completely different from the one proposed in HPSG-I for phrases (Pollard and Sag, 1987, p. 71). Identifying the values of MORPHS|COMP-MORPH and MORPHS|HEAD-MORPH|SYN|LOC|SUBCAT in MSCP (cf. (11)) guarantees that the head takes the right complement and binds it. In addition, the function construct-subcat assembles the subcategorization information of the new morphological phrase. The elements of the subcategorization list under path SYN|LOC|SUBCAT are essentially those of the complement—however, construct-subcat regroups them, perhaps omitting some of them (cf. examples). The result of this modification

---

[27] The function order-constituents in MCOP has to be sensitive to the type of its argument. If the argument is of type *morph-head-struct* (see below), the function is being applied in derivation instead of working on the sentence level. Thus, in contrast to the version of order-constituents in Pollard and Sag (1987), our version of order-constituent is overloaded with respect to its argument—we employ an *ad hoc polymorphism*. Cf. Cardelli and Wegner (1985). Alternatively, we could specify a second function, order-morph-constituents.

depends not only on the type of the attribute MORPHS|HEAD-MORPH, but also on the sort of the complement morpheme:

$$(11) \quad MSCP \equiv \left\{ \begin{array}{l} \begin{bmatrix} complex \\ \text{MORPHS } [morph\text{-}head\text{-}struct] \end{bmatrix} \implies \\ \begin{bmatrix} complex \\ \text{SYN|LOC|SUBCAT construct-subcat(} \boxed{1}) \\ \text{MORPHS } \boxed{} \begin{bmatrix} \text{HEAD-MORPH|SYN|LOC|SUBCAT } \boxed{2} \\ \text{COMP-MORPH } \boxed{2} \end{bmatrix} \end{bmatrix} \end{array} \right.$$

Although Pollard and Sag (1987) strictly type the attributes of feature structures in general, they do not explicitly state that *principles* as well as *rules* may also be regarded as types. But we may interpret them as types which have to satisfy the *subsumption* relation only.[28] In taking this step, one has to integrate them consistently into the subsumption lattice (cf. Figure 7.2).

With respect to equation (3), we extend the set of principles and the set of rules by adding MCOP, MHFP, MSP, MSCP and MHCR. Finally, in typing the antecedents (of the implications), we must take care, since not every principle can be combined with every rule or lexical entry.

Because only morphological head-complement structures are examined in this chapter, equation (3) allows us to unify the types associated with (the right-hand sides of) MCOP, MHFP, MSP, MSCP and MHCR (call the result *HCR&Ps*), and to regard this feature structure as a restriction for all feature structures belonging to this new (conjunctive) type. All complex morphs (morphs having the attribute MORPHS) must satisfy this type restriction, i.e. must be of the type *HCR&Ps*.

$$(12) \quad HCR\&Ps = MHFP \sqcap MSCP \sqcap MSP \sqcap MCOP \sqcap MHCR$$

$$(13) \quad HCR\&Ps \equiv$$

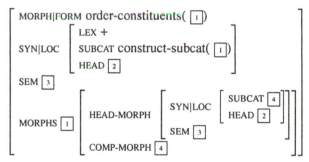

Trying to encode rules and principles explicitly as elements of a type subsumption lattice (inheritance network) along the lines of HPSG (Pollard and Sag,

---

[28] Principles constrain existing types and so must be interpreted as supertypes. In translating a principle—usually expressed as a conditional—into a type, we use only the right side of the conditional, the consequent. For a motivation, see below.

1987, chap. 8) requires a *rewriting* step: Because of their implicative nature, we cannot state principles *directly* as types—we must rewrite them. 'Rewriting' means, first, that only the right side (the consequent) of an implication will be regarded as a type. Second, in order to obtain the force of the antecedent, the type associated with the conjunctive feature structure representing the consequent has to be integrated into the 'right' position in the lattice (cf. *HCR&Ps* in Figure 7.2), where 'right' is determined by *taking care that the subsumption relation holds*.[29] Even an equation like (3), containing lots of implications, can then be compiled to form an inheritance hierarchy, consisting only of conjunctive feature types.[30]

The idea of reducing implications to conjunctive types will lead us directly to the structure of the (type/class) subsumption lattice (cf. Figure 7.2). Notice that, regarding the laws of feature algebras, we're allowed to 'multiply out' information stored in certain normal forms. This additional step of transformation is necessary to construct hierarchies like that shown in Figure 7.2.

In the following, we will further motivate and exemplify our approach to derivation by applying it to examples of (morphological) *suffixation* and *prefixation*.

7.4.3   *-bar* **and** *-keit* **Suffixation**

The treatment of German *-bar* (and also of *-keit*) suffixation is interesting from different points of view and presents severe problems, which can, however, be adequately solved in our approach:

sporadic applicability   *-bar* suffixes many verbs, but not all.

partial regularity   Many *-bar* derivatives have regular forms and irregular semantics.

category change   *-bar* suffixation changes (syntactic) category: Verb $\rightsquigarrow$ Adjective.

subcategorization change   The subcategorization list of Verb+*bar* changes: the arity is that of the verb minus 1; the semantic ar-

---

[29] In general, there's only *one* right position—*the most general position at which the subsumption relation holds*. But this is true only if we assume a (subsumption) lattice where subsumption is *strict*, i.e. where it is not possible to have two different types standing in a subsumption relation, even though their denotation is the same.

[30] The rewriting step is subtle in that it moves information from object-language implicational statements into restrictions in the type hierarchy which forms the skeleton of the interpretation. On the one hand, because of general laws of interpretation for feature logics, we have the following inference for *Ante, Conseq* feature structure terms: from the principle *Ante* $\Rightarrow$ *Conseq*, we know that $[\![Conseq]\!] \supseteq [\![Ante]\!]$. On the other hand, the principles always *add* information to a feature structure description to which they are applied, so that *Ante* always subsumes *Conseq*, i.e. $[\![Ante]\!] \supseteq [\![Conseq]\!]$. This leads to an effective identification of *Ante* and *Conseq* which is realized in the type hierarchy.

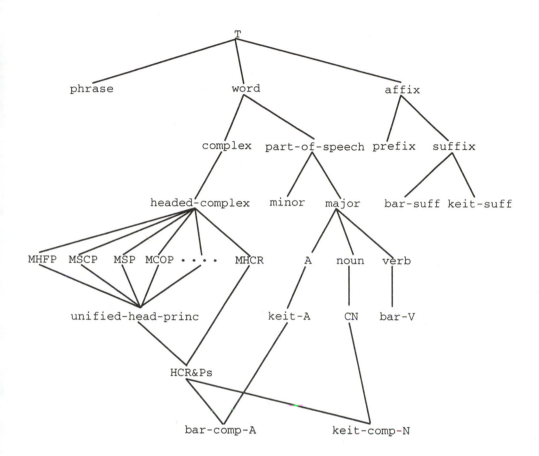

Figure 7.2: Structure of the inheritance network in case of *-bar* and *-keit* suffixation, including morphological principles and rules. Note that we additionally impose *local* constraints on certain classes, especially on *bar-comp-A* and *keit-comp-N*; for motivation, see text. Note further that, although the class of adjectives formed using *-bar* inherits from A (adjective) and from *HCR&Ps*, it does *not* inherit from either of its component morphs—*bar-V* or *bar-suffix*.

gument positions in the scope of the *-bar* semantics, on the other hand, do *not* change.

Starting with a verb like the German *lesen* (to read), where *-bar* suffixation is regular, we may construct a possible lexicon entry with respect to the inheritance network of Figure 7.2.

$$
(14) \quad lesen \equiv \begin{bmatrix} bar\text{-}V \\[4pt] \text{MORPH} \begin{bmatrix} \text{STEM} & \text{``les''} \\ \text{PARADIGM} & [\,\dots\,] \end{bmatrix} \\[10pt] \text{SYN|LOC} \begin{bmatrix} \text{SUBCAT} & < \dots, (\,NP_{\boxed{2}}\,), \; NP_{\boxed{1}} > \\ \text{LEX} & + \\ \text{HEAD|MAJ} & V \end{bmatrix} \\[14pt] \text{SEM} \begin{bmatrix} \text{RELN} & read' \\ \text{SOURCE} & \boxed{1} \\ \text{THEME} & \boxed{2} \end{bmatrix} \end{bmatrix}
$$

Notice that although *lesen* is syntactically classified as a verb (this is the import of the feature specification [SYN|LOC|HEAD|MAJ   V]), more specifically, it is an instance of the class *bar-V* (verbs that may combine with *-bar*). Note also that we employ here the *lexeme lesen* rather than, e.g. the infinitive in *lesen*'s paradigm—this is compatible with the fact that only the stem *les-* is found in the derived word.

Moving now to *-bar*, we regard *-bar* (cf. (15)) as the HEAD of the morphological complex with category *adjective* (A); it may function as a head even though it fails to appear as a *free* word. Instead, it occurs only as a *bound* morpheme (instance of the class *bar-suff*; cf. Figure 7.2). As a result of the *head feature principle* the mother obtains automatically the category of the head daughter—and this is exactly what we want, since *les+bar* (*readable*) is an adjective. The head-complement rule, the subcategorization principle and the specification of SYN|LOC|SUBCAT to be an (underspecified) instance of *bar-V* additionally guarantee that *-bar* only combines with *-bar* verbs. Note too, that the value of the attribute LEX in (15) is *unspecified*.[31]

Semantically, *-bar* functions as a modal operator, working on the propositional semantics of *lesen* 'read' to create a proposition asserting the possibility of reading. We note here the co-specification between the semantics of the subcategorized element and the value of the SCOPE attribute in the modal proposition.

---

[31] Under the assumption of Carpenter's 'total well-typing' (Carpenter, 1991), it may be useful to drop the attribute LEX in (15).

These assumptions lead us to postulate the following structure for *-bar*:

(15)   bar ≡

$$
\begin{bmatrix}
\textit{bar-suff} \\
\text{MORPH|FORM} \quad \text{"bar"} \\
\text{SYN|LOC} \quad \begin{bmatrix} \text{LEX} \\ \text{HEAD|MAJ} \quad \text{A} \\ \text{SUBCAT} \quad \text{bar-V}_{\boxed{1}} \end{bmatrix} \\
\text{SEM} \quad \begin{bmatrix} \text{OPERATOR} \quad \diamond \\ \text{SCOPE} \quad \boxed{1} \end{bmatrix}
\end{bmatrix}
$$

The entries for *lesen* and *-bar* together with the head-complement rule and the morphological principles permit us therefore to construct a well-formed feature structure for *lesbar*, and also to reject ill-formed feature structures, so that we can show that (16) is the predicted structure. This meshing of mechanisms ensures that *lesbar* has the right internal structure. The function order-constituents, for instance, determines on the basis of the values of HEAD|MORPH and COMP|MORPH (more exactly, on the basis of the types restricting the attributes) that it has to perform a concatenation (&) (cf. 16). Additionally, the semantics principle is responsible for the semantics of *lesbar* coming directly from the head daughter *-bar*, while *-bar* takes the complete semantics of *lesen* to fill its attribute SCOPE.

(16)   lesbar ≡

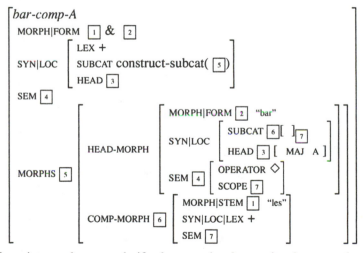

At this point, we have to clarify the complex interaction between the *subcategorization principle* and the *semantics principle*. The scope on which *-bar* semantically operates is the semantics of *lesen*. The SOURCE role of *lesen* (cf. (14)), whose value is identical to the semantics of the *subject* of *lesen*, won't be filled by a phrase licensed by *lesbar* directly, so that it is possible that the SOURCE role in *lesbar* is unfilled. This occurs when no agentive *von* phrase occurs in construction with the adjective, but the attribute is present even where the value is not. In this case, the SOURCE role contains the semantics of an underspecified NP, and the proposition within which it occurs holds whenever there is some value for the NP semantics for which the proposition holds (cf. Flickinger and Nerbonne, 1992 for a similar treatment of the semantics of the *for* phrase licensed by *easy* adjectives and Karttunen, 1986, for an analysis of the semantics of the passive *by* phrase along these lines). The intention behind this approach can be appreciated in a concrete example: the sentence *Das Buch ist lesbar* 'The book is readable' doesn't *explicitly* state for whom it is possible to read the book. Instead, the reader is mentioned only *implicitly*, so that the filler of SOURCE role of *lesbar* might be suspected from extralinguistic context, or from the preceding or following discourse, but is not specified directly by the sentence itself.[32] The subcat list of *lesbar* therefore does not include the subject of *lesen*, at least not as an obligatory complement. The object of *lesen* fills the same role filled by the subject of *lesbar*, of course. This is exactly what the function construct-subcat has to accomplish, taking over all other entries from the subcat list of *lesen* to build the right subcategorization list for *lesbar* (cf. (16)).

We provide a single sketch to suggest the possibility of a more involved hierarchical structure. In order to construct the word *Les+bar+keit* (*readability*) out of *lesbar*, we have to specify the entry for the suffix *-keit* and the *keit-suff* class (cf. Figure 7.2), i.e. it is necessary to state the idiosyncratic properties of *-keit*.

$$
(17) \quad keit \equiv
\begin{bmatrix}
keit\text{-}suff \\
\text{MORPH|FORM} \quad \text{"keit"} \\
\text{SYN|LOC}
\begin{bmatrix}
\text{HEAD|MAJ} \quad N \\
\text{SUBCAT} \quad keit\text{-}A_{\boxed{1}}
\end{bmatrix} \\
\text{SEM}
\begin{bmatrix}
\text{VAR} \quad \boxed{2} \\
\text{RESTRICTION} \quad \boxed{1}
\begin{bmatrix}
\text{PRED} \quad \ldots \\
\text{EVENT} \quad \boxed{2}
\end{bmatrix}
\end{bmatrix}
\end{bmatrix}
$$

By means of the morphological principles and the head-complement rule we may now build an entry for *Lesbarkeit* in the same way shown above (for *lesbar*) with the morphological constituent structure shown in (5).

Among *-bar* verbs such as *lesen*, having perfectly regular *-bar* adjectives (i.e. complex adjectives, containing *-bar* as their head, e.g. *lesbar*), there are others whose derived adjectives are partially irregular, for example with respect to their semantics. As an additional complication, some *-bar* adjectives of these verbs are provided with an additional regular, but non-standard reading. Take

---

[32] By contrast, there may be a syntactic binding in examples such as *Ich finde das Buch lesbar* 'I find the book readable'.

for instance the German verb *essen* (to eat):

$$(18) \quad \textit{essen} \equiv \begin{bmatrix} \textit{bar-V} \\ \text{MORPH|FORM} \quad \text{"essen"} \\ \text{SYN|LOC|SUBCAT} \quad < \; ..., \; (\; \text{NP}_{\boxed{2}}), \; \text{NP}_{\boxed{1}} \; > \\ \text{SEM} \quad \begin{bmatrix} \text{RELN} \quad \text{eat}' \\ \text{SOURCE} \quad \boxed{1} \\ \text{THEME} \quad \boxed{2} \end{bmatrix} \end{bmatrix}$$

The non-standard (semantically regular) reading of *eßbar* can be built in a regular way by means of the mechanisms described above, taking *essen* and *-bar* to form a complex word.

$$(19) \quad \textit{eßbar}^{non-stand} \equiv \begin{bmatrix} \textit{bar-comp-A} \\ \text{SEM} \; \boxed{1} \begin{bmatrix} \text{OPERATOR} \quad \diamondsuit \\ \text{SCOPE} \begin{bmatrix} \text{RELN} \quad \text{eat}' \\ \text{SOURCE} \quad ... \end{bmatrix} \end{bmatrix} \\ \text{MORPHS|HEAD-MORPH|SEM} \; \boxed{1} \end{bmatrix}$$

The standard reading of *eßbar*, on the other hand, is 'edible' (the property of an object which can *safely* be eaten). Constructing the standard reading (with irregular semantics) for *eßbar* can be done in our approach in two different ways:

1. We do *not* regard *eßbar* as an instance of the class *bar-comp-A*; instead, *eßbar* is entered separately into the lexicon. We then have to specify at least that the semantics of (20) is different from that of (19), although the MORPH and SYN properties seem to remain the same. A treatment of this kind leads us to the question of whether the feature structure (20) actually will have MORPH daughters—since no use need be made of the structure.

2. The semantics of (19) (the entry which was built regularly) is modified by using *overwriting*, *default unification* or other non-monotonic mechanisms to enforce the standard reading. In this case, *eßbar* (21) belongs to the class *bar-comp-A*, because all other properties remain the same. We would follow Bouma (1990a) in the use of default unification (as a basis for default inheritance).

$$(20) \quad \textit{eßbar}^{stand} \equiv \begin{bmatrix} \textit{?-A} \; \wedge \; \neg \textit{bar-comp-A} \\ \text{SEM} \begin{bmatrix} \text{RELN} \quad \text{safely-eat}' \\ \text{SOURCE} \quad ... \end{bmatrix} \\ \text{MORPHS} \quad \text{???} \end{bmatrix}$$

$$\text{eßbar}^{stand'} \equiv \text{eßbar}^{non-stand} \oplus \left[\text{SEM} \left[\begin{array}{ll} \text{RELN} & \text{safely-eat}' \\ \text{SOURCE} & \ldots \end{array} \right] \right]$$

(21)

$$= \left[\begin{array}{l} \textit{bar-comp-A} \\ \text{SEM} \; \boxed{1} \left[\begin{array}{ll} \text{RELN} & \text{safely-eat}' \\ \text{SOURCE} & \ldots \end{array} \right] \\ \text{MORPHS|HEAD-MORPH|SEM} \quad \neg \boxed{1} \end{array} \right]$$

The advantage of the second approach is that regular properties of partially regular derivations need not be specified redundantly, as would be the case in the first approach. The use of default specifications thus obtains the same advantages in *derivation* that Flickinger *et al.* (1985) and Evans and Gazdar (1990) have shown in word-class definitions. Defaults, together with the possibility of overwriting defaults in more specific definitions, may turn out to be even more important in connection with the analysis of derivational relationships, since these are notoriously irregular in morphological form, syntactic feature assignment and semantics (cf. Toman's, 1983, book-length study on *-bar* adjectives for ample illustration).

The typed approach to *-bar* suffixation allows us to prevent ill-formed *-bar* adjectives; e.g. we have to rule out the combination of *haben* (to have) together with *-bar*. This is very easy to achieve under the assumption that *haben* doesn't belong to the *-bar* verb class *bar-V* , but instead to another class (say *?-V*), thus preventing *haben* from combining with *-bar*—therefore *hab+bar* is disallowed.

(22) $\text{haben} \equiv \left[\begin{array}{l} \textit{?-V} \; \wedge \; \neg\textit{bar-V} \\ \ldots\ldots \\ \ldots\ldots \end{array} \right]$

It is nevertheless possible to construct *handhab+bar* 'manageable' out of *handhaben* 'to handle, manage', since *haben* and *handhaben* are distinct lexemes. By explicitly encoding *handhaben* as an entry of type *bar-V*, we can move to a legal description of *handhabbar*.

(23) $\text{handhaben} \equiv \left[\begin{array}{l} \textit{bar-V} \\ \ldots\ldots \\ \ldots\ldots \end{array} \right]$

(24) $\text{handhabbar} \equiv \left[\begin{array}{l} \textit{bar-comp-A} \\ \ldots\ldots \\ \ldots\ldots \end{array} \right]$

The structure of the class hierarchy (cf. Figure 7.2) ultimately leads us to a treatment of suffixation, esp. *-bar* and *-keit* suffixation (and also of prefixation in general), where the whole process can be described within the framework of *unification-based inheritance reasoning*. On what grounds are we allowed to state such a thesis? At first sight, this statement seems to stand in contrast with the claim made above, that *naive* inheritance is not enough. But we do not rely on naive inheritance as the only mechanism. So we turn now to an examination of why this is so.

We noted earlier that *les+bar* and *Les+bar+keit* are legal lexemes because they satisfy all principles whose left sides they match (implying that they have to meet the right sides too), and because they are composed out of lexicon entries by means of rules. In doing realistic parsing or generation, we might assume additional *control machinery* outside of the grammar/lexicon, which uses principles and rules to accept or reject, or alternatively, to generate well-formed (complex) phrases.

Because we regard principles as well as rules as types, equation (3) allows us to employ the laws of feature algebras to construct new types (call them *precategories*), which are subsumed by all principles having a more general left side and by at least one rule (cf. equations (12) and (13)). Complex words/morphemes like *lesbar*, on the other hand, will then be subsumed by such precategories.

It is now easy to see that the processes described up to now can be represented entirely via inheritance of a sophisticated kind (effectively constraint resolution). This very interesting observation is motivated as follows: it is possible to define new legal complex word classes by inheriting from precategories as well as from simple lexical categories (cf. subtypes of *part-of-speech* in Figure 7.2) and by stating additional local constraints for the class in question. Looking at Figure 7.2, *bar-comp-A* (complex adjectives with head daughter *-bar*) and *keit-comp-N* (complex nouns with head daughter *-keit*) are classes of such a kind.

Let's have a closer look at *bar-comp-A* and *keit-comp-N*: *bar-comp-A* inherits from *HCR&Ps* and *A*, but also enforces idiosyncratic constraints, which have to be satisfied by words that are members of this class:

$$
\text{(25)} \quad \text{bar-comp-A} = \text{HCR\&Ps} \wedge A \wedge \left[\text{MORPHS} \left[\begin{array}{l} \text{HEAD-MORPH} \ [\ \textit{bar-suff}\ ] \\ \text{COMP-MORPH} \ [\ \textit{bar-V}\ ] \end{array} \right] \right]
$$

It's very important to constrain HEAD-MORPH and COMP-MORPH to be of type *bar-suff* resp. *bar-V* respectively,[33] in order to get the right feature structure for *bar-comp-A*. We also require that the adjective class *A* is associated with the

---

[33] Strictly speaking: The value of HEAD-MORPH is a fully expanded instance of type *bar-suff*, whereas COMP-MORPH is bound to an underspecified instance of type *bar-V*, because for instance the value of MORPH|FORM is unspecified.

following feature structure.

$$(26) \quad A \equiv \begin{bmatrix} \text{MORPH} & \cdots \cdots \\ \text{SYN|LOC} & \begin{bmatrix} \text{LEX} & + \\ \text{MOD} & < \ldots, & \text{NP} > \\ \text{HEAD|MAJ} & A \end{bmatrix} \\ \text{SEM} & \cdots \cdots \end{bmatrix}$$

Since furthermore *HCR&Ps* (cf. (13)) is also associated with a feature structure, it's not difficult to construct the prototypical feature structure for *bar-comp-A* by unifying all the information. But once this is achieved, we may construct an entry for *lesbar* by creating an *instance* of the class *bar-comp-A* and stating that the complement daughter of this instance is *lesen*, i.e. COMP-MORPH must have as value a feature structure equal to that of the lexeme *lesen* (cf. (14)).

$$(27) \quad \text{lesbar} = \text{bar-comp-A} \land [\text{ MORPHS|COMP-MORPH } \textit{lesen}]$$

Notice that the feature structure for (27) corresponds to the one for *les+bar* (cf. (16)) provided earlier. In entirely the same fashion, we might *instantiate* feature structures for new words like *Les+bar+keit*, which belong to the class *keit-comp-N*. For that purpose, we have to define the class *CN*, which *keit-comp-N* inherits from (cf. Figure 7.2).

$$(28) \quad CN \equiv \begin{bmatrix} \text{MORPH} & \cdots \cdots \\ \text{SYN|LOC} & \begin{bmatrix} \text{LEX} & + \\ \text{SUBCAT} & < \ldots, & \{ \text{ Det, PosP} \} > \\ \text{HEAD|MAJ} & N \end{bmatrix} \\ \text{SEM} & \cdots \cdots \end{bmatrix}$$

With these definitions in mind, we're able to state the dependence of the complex word class *keit-comp-N* on *HCR&Ps* and *A*, in perfect analogy to equation (25):

$$(29) \quad \text{keit-comp-N} = \text{HCR\&Ps} \land \text{CN} \land \\ \begin{bmatrix} \text{MORPHS} & \begin{bmatrix} \text{HEAD-MORPH} & [\, \textit{keit-suff}\,] \\ \text{COMP-MORPH} & [\, \textit{keit-A}\,] \end{bmatrix} \end{bmatrix}$$

We may then represent a feature structure like *Lesbarkeit* by instantiating *keit-comp-N* and imposing a local constraint on this instance:

$$(30) \quad \text{Lesbarkeit} = \text{keit-comp-N} \land [\text{ MORPHS|COMP-MORPH } \textit{lesbar}]$$

The restriction that COMP-MORPH must be of type *keit-A* (cf. (29)) also allows that COMP-MORPH may be an instance of type *bar-comp-A* defined earlier (cf. (25)) because *keit-A* is a supertype of *bar-comp-A* (cf. Figure 7.2).[34]

---

[34] What we said up to now isn't the whole truth. There's an additional restriction we're faced with: given what we have said up till now, nothing prevents us from creating instances which

This last point should only be seen as a remark to practitioners working on computational lexicons. To enforce, for instance, that elements of the lexicon *must* have their PHON attributes filled, one can use the mechanisms discussed in footnote 34.

At the beginning of this section we listed four analytical problems for the description of *-bar* adjectives. During the course of this section we have proposed solutions to these which we summarize here:

Problem	Solution via internal lexical rules
sporadic applicability	use type restrictions
partial regularity	apply non-monotonic mechanisms or introduce additional classes
category change	treat affix as head of morphological complex
subcategorization change	employ functional dependencies

Before closing this section, we would like to note that the derivational view of passive, which we promised to sketch in the introduction, may be developed straightforwardly on the basis of the analysis of *-bar* sketched here. In particular,

---

are *underspecified* with respect to certain attributes. Such instances do not represent real words and therefore must be forbidden.

Take for instance *CN*, the class of common nouns. We might create an instance without specifying the value for MORPH|FORM. Although this instance would be of class *CN*, it couldn't be used by any speaker. Trying to build an instance of type *word* (*lexical-sign*; the most general type of the lexical subsumption hierarchy), which is only constrained to possess the attributes PHON, SYN and SEM according to Pollard and Sag, would be an extreme case of this shortcoming. This observation holds for *phrasal signs* too, because it is possible to generate sentences without any phonological content, when assuming lexical entries (instances) which are empty with respect to their PHON attribute. As these examples suggest, the possibility of creating underspecified instances depends on there being incorrect grammatical specifications. There are at least two *non-monotonic* approaches in order to repair this defect:

1. We introduce a special type, say *undefined*, whose extension is a unique constant (call it NONE). Those attributes we require to be filled at run time (instantiation time) are assigned the type restriction ¬ *undefined* and the contradictory value NONE at definition time. Now, if we carry out a type check at run time, we're able to recognize whether the critical attributes have been assigned real values (by overwriting NONE with a different value), i.e. not to be of type *undefined*.

2. We classify the relevant attributes with a special atom called ANY, which functions in the same way as the ANY works in Kay's FUG: ANY may successfully unify with every object, except ⊥ (Bottom); i.e. the semantics of ANY is that of ⊤ (Top). But when the instantiation of a word is done, all ANYs have to be removed (must be unified 'out'), because ANY henceforth behaves like ⊥. (Dörre and Eisele, 1991, p. 18, give a formalization of ANY in terms of so-called *meta-constraints*.)

There will be a third possibility of repair, if the underlying (feature) logic allows us to state that certain (underspecified) types (classes) *cannot* be instantiated. Instead, these classes only serve as choice points in our linguistic ontology—reflecting the distinction between *regularities*, *subregularities*, and *exceptions* and enabling a finer granularity of lexical knowledge.

the class of verbs involved here is very nearly the same, and the effects on subcategorization (via construct-subcat) identical.

7.4.4   *Vor-* **Prefixation**

In this section we investigate the phenomenon of *prefixation*, focusing for further depth on a specific prefix, namely *vor-*.[35] What prefixes and suffixes have in common is that they serve as heads in our simple head-complement approach. *Vor-* prefixation is in many respects different from *-bar* suffixation and has special properties that make it interesting for expository purposes:

> **sporadic applicability**   *Vor-* prefixes many nouns (e.g. *Vorversion, Vorgaben, Vorzelt, Vorzimmer* and *Vorabend*), but not all.
>
> **partial regularity**   Many *Vor-* derivatives have regular morphological forms and irregular semantics.
>
> **category constant**   The (syntactic) category of the *Vor-* derivative does not change.
>
> **subcategorization constant**   The subcategorization list of the derived complex word (*Vor*+Noun) is taken over from the complement, the noun and does not undergo any changes.
>
> **iterability**   The prefix *Vor-* can be applied iteratively.

Let's examine a noun that may combine with *Vor-* to form a complex noun, viz., the German *Version* 'version':

$$
(31) \qquad Version \equiv \begin{bmatrix} vor\text{-}N \\ \text{MORPH|FORM} \quad \text{``Version''} \\[4pt] \text{SYN|LOC} \quad \begin{bmatrix} \text{SUBCAT} \quad < \ldots, \{\ \text{Det}\ ,\ \text{PosP}\} > \\ \text{LEX} \ + \\ \text{HEAD|MAJ} \quad N \end{bmatrix} \\[4pt] \text{SEM} \quad \begin{bmatrix} \text{PRED} \quad version' \end{bmatrix} \end{bmatrix}
$$

Trying to encode *Vor-* is a bit harder, because *Vor-* works not only on nouns, but also on certain verbs (e.g. *vorgehen, vorarbeiten* or *vorlaufen*). In order to represent this fact, we again make use of distributed disjunctions, which were

---

[35] As we mentioned above, we have taken the prefix *Vor-* as an example to show how certain phenomena can be handled in our approach. The assumption that *Vor-* functions semantically as an operator, working on the semantics of the noun (cf. (32)), is of course not an in-depth analysis and may not be useful in real applications. There are other prefixes like *Anti-* or *Ur-* having similar properties, but their semantics is even more complicated.

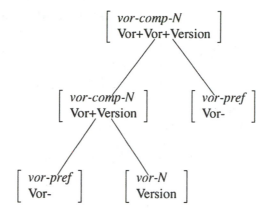

Figure 7.3: Derivational morphotactics defined through lexical type specifications

employed in section 7.3 above to encode inflectional paradigms.

$$
(32) \quad \text{Vor} \equiv
\begin{bmatrix}
\text{vor-pref} \\
\text{MORPH}|\text{FORM} \quad \text{"Vor"} \\
\text{SYN}|\text{LOC} \quad
\begin{bmatrix}
\text{HEAD}|\text{MAJ} \ \{\, \text{s1} \quad \text{N}, \quad \text{V} \,\} \\
\text{SUBCAT} \ \{\, \text{s1} \quad \text{vor-N}_{\boxed{1}}, \quad \text{vor-V}_{\boxed{2}} \,\}
\end{bmatrix} \\
\text{SEM} \quad
\begin{bmatrix}
\text{OPERATOR} \quad \text{vor}' \\
\text{SCOPE} \ \{\, \text{s1} \quad \boxed{1}, \boxed{2} \,\}
\end{bmatrix}
\end{bmatrix}
$$

It is important to understand the intention behind the use of the distributed disjunction in *Vor-*: if *Vor-* combines with a *Vor-* noun, it will be classified as a noun, but if it binds a *Vor-* verb, it creates a verb. Moreover, the head feature principle takes care that the mother of the morphological phrase will be assigned the same category that the prefix *Vor-* bears. That's the main reason why recursion is possible—the new word, e.g. *Vor+Version*, will again be classified as a noun and could then combine with a new *Vor-* (cf. Figure 7.3) in the same way as described before (actually it is now a *complex* noun with internal structure; cf. Figure 7.4).

The value of SCOPE under path MORPHS|HEAD-MORPH|SEM now will be assigned by means of structure sharing, coming directly from the semantics of the value of SYN|LOC|SUBCAT, no matter which value of the distributed disjunction is taken (cf. (32)). Finally, by virtue of the semantics principle, *Vorversion* will get its semantics from its head daughter *Vor-*; construct-subcat is again responsible for constructing the right subcategorization list for *Vorversion*: because *Vor-* is the head morph, construct-subcat can detect that the value of SYN|LOC|SUBCAT has to be equal to the entire subcat list of the complement. With these things in mind, we may now construct, with the assistance of the above mentioned principles and the head-complement rule, an admissible feature structure for *Vorversion*, which has the following form:

(33)   Vorversion ≡

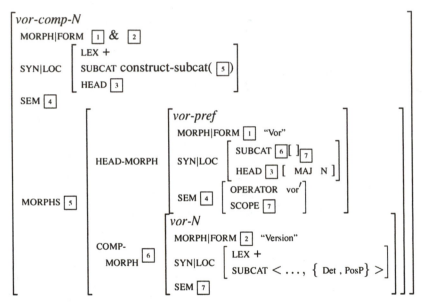

It may be useful to split up the entry for *Vor-* (cf. (32)), distributing its semantics among two feature structures—one (Vor[1]), which combines only with nouns, another one (Vor[2]), which binds instead verbs. But this kind of representation is rather a matter of style.

(34)   Vor[1] ≡

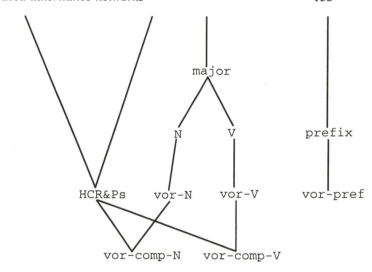

Figure 7.4: Structure of the inheritance network in case of *Vor-* prefixation, regarding the principles and the rule. Note that we additionally impose *local* constraints on certain classes, especially on *vor-comp-N* and *vor-comp-V*

$$(35) \quad \text{Vor}^2 \equiv \begin{bmatrix} \textit{vor-pref} \\ \text{MORPH|FORM} \quad \text{"Vor"} \\ \text{SYN|LOC} \begin{bmatrix} \text{HEAD|MAJ} \quad \text{V} \\ \text{SUBCAT} \quad \text{vor-V}_{\boxed{1}} \end{bmatrix} \\ \text{SEM} \begin{bmatrix} \text{OPERATOR} \quad \text{vor}'' \\ \text{SCOPE} \quad \boxed{1} \end{bmatrix} \end{bmatrix}$$

We described *-bar/-keit* suffixation above by means of unification-based inheritance; once we assume an inheritance network such as Figure 7.4, we may analyze *Vor-* prefixation (including recursion) similarly.

Analogous to (25) and (29), we may state the right definitions for *vor-comp-N* and *vor-comp-V* with respect to Figure 7.4.

$$(36) \quad \begin{aligned} \text{vor-comp-N} &= \text{HCR\&Ps} \wedge \text{vor-N} \wedge \\ & \begin{bmatrix} \text{MORPHS} \begin{bmatrix} \text{HEAD-MORPH} \; [\; \textit{vor-pref} \;] \\ \text{COMP-MORPH} \; [\; \textit{vor-N} \;] \end{bmatrix} \end{bmatrix} \end{aligned}$$

$$(37) \quad \begin{aligned} \text{vor-comp-V} &= \text{HCR\&Ps} \wedge \text{vor-V} \wedge \\ & \begin{bmatrix} \text{MORPHS} \begin{bmatrix} \text{HEAD-MORPH} \; [\; \textit{vor-pref} \;] \\ \text{COMP-MORPH} \; [\; \textit{vor-V} \;] \end{bmatrix} \end{bmatrix} \end{aligned}$$

The iterated application of *Vor-* will be guaranteed by using the *recursive* type definition of *vor-comp-N*: the value of the attribute MORPHS|COMP-

MORPH in *vor-comp-N* is required to be of type *vor-N*. Because *vor-N* subsumes *vor-comp-N*, we're allowed in particular to require that the value of MORPHS|COMP-MORPH should be an instance of type *vor-comp-N*, and this corresponds to a potentially infinite iteration of *Vor-*. But how do we block infinite recursion in cases of concrete words? Only instances of minimal type *vor-N* will stop parsing or generation, because those instances don't have any internal constituent structure (no MORPHS attribute), i.e. there's no way to expand them further.[36] It is the indirect self-reference that is responsible for the recursive nature of *vor-comp-N*. If we now still require that the value of MORPHS.COMP-MORPH not be underspecified, the aim of describing *Vor-*prefixation by inheritance only is fully realized.

Constructing an entry for *Vorversion* is done in a trivial way by instantiating *vor-comp-N* and by imposing an additional restriction on that instance, namely that the complement daughter must hold a feature structure representing *Version*.

(38)   Vorversion = vor-comp-N $\wedge$ [MORPHS|COMP-MORPH *Version*]

7.5   Summary and Conclusion

In this section we summarize the results of the present study, pointing out areas which we have yet to investigate, but which seem pertinent or promising; the further investigation of these areas offers the best practical means to advances in this approach to computational lexicology.

The results of the present study may be viewed as follows: feature-based formalisms (such as PATR-II or the HPSG formalism) have been successful in the description of *syntagmatic* grammatical relations—the relations between the various syntactic parts of an utterance token. The present study attempts to demonstrate that the feature description languages developed for this purpose may also be applied fruitfully to *paradigmatic* relations—the relations between words and their common alternatives in utterances.[37] We have examined proposals here for the representation of inflectional and derivational relations. These relations are purely lexical, since they may never result in syntactic relations, so that a distinctly lexical status accrues to them even in a highly 'lexicalized theory' such as HPSG. This is the sense in which the present contribution claims to develop further the theory of the *lexicon* for feature-based theories of language. It is of course clear to us that several aspects of this theory—most clearly its syntactic content—have been under development for some time, but the larger theoretical picture had not been clarified.

---

[36] When we say *an instance of minimal type vor-N*, we exclude instances of types more specific than *vor-N*. This corresponds roughly to *classification* in KL-ONE-like knowledge representation systems. By making a distinction between class and instance, and assuming totally well-typed feature structures, this goal is easily reached.

[37] We appreciate Carl Pollard's suggesting this contrast to us.

We have attempted to provide that clarification, so that our proposals here have thus been programmatic, but we provide concrete elaborations in two central areas of paradigmatic relations, inflection and derivation. Our proposal for inflection may be seen as a variant of one first proposed in DATR: we characterize the inflectional variants of a lexeme as alternative (disjunctive) realizations. The basic insight of DATR is easily accommodated within the language of feature structure descriptions. Alternative realizations of lexemes—paradigms—are represented using the technical tool of distributed disjunctions (although there are several equivalent means of representation). Our proposal for derivation may be seen as an application of the HPSG treatment of syntactic structure in feature structure formalism. Just as HPSG characterizes phrase structure rules via descriptions of the output phrases created by the rule, so we propose characterizing (derivational) word formation rules via recursive constraints on complex lexemes—those which linguists would regard as created by the 'rule'. This contrasts with the usual treatment in feature-based theories, which construes derivational rules (in fact, normally *all* lexical rules) as mappings within the algebra of feature structures. The latter proposal relies on subsidiary functions or relations to characterize lexical rules, while our own characterization remains within the language of feature-structure description. Our proposal is probably preferable in direct proportion to the degree to which derivational structure employs mechanisms which feature formalisms describe well—inheritance, typing, and shared structure. We suggest that the inheritance exploited in structured lexicons finds very apt application in derivation as well.

We do not imagine that this paper represents a mature presentation of what a feature-based lexicon ought to be capable of. In particular, we continue to puzzle over several areas: the correct representation of compounding; the treatment of idioms; the most attractive analysis of so-called 'zero-derivation' (e.g. the relation between verbal participles and the adjectives derived from them); the proper interface to allomorphy—both theoretically and practically; the role of morpheme-based generalizations; and the question of flexible access (for both parsing and generation) to lexical structure. We regard these as challenging issues for future work in feature-based lexical analysis.

The further investigation of these areas, together with continuing work on elaborations and alternatives to the analyses suggested here, offers the best practical means to advances in this approach to computational lexicology.

Acknowledgements

We thank Rolf Backofen, Stephan Busemann, Bob Carpenter, Bob Kasper, Andreas Kathol, Klaus Netter, Carl Pollard and Harald Trost for conversations about this work. We have also benefited from the reactions of audiences where we presented different parts of it (in the Spring of 1991), in particular at the ACQUILEX Workshop, Cambridge; The ASL Workshop on DATR, Bielefeld; and the Linguistics Colloquium at The Ohio State University. This work was supported by a research grant, ITW 9002 0, from the German Bundesministerium für Forschung und Technologie to the DFKI DISCO project.

8   A Practical Approach to Multiple Default Inheritance for Unification-Based Lexicons

GRAHAM RUSSELL, AFZAL BALLIM, JOHN CARROLL AND
SUSAN WARWICK-ARMSTRONG

8.1   Introduction

Natural language lexicons form an obvious application for techniques involving default inheritance developed for knowledge representation in artificial intelligence (AI). Many of the schemes that have been proposed are highly complex – simple tree-form taxonomies are thought to be inadequate, and a variety of additional mechanisms are employed. As Touretzky *et al.* (1987) show, the intuitions underlying the behaviour of such systems may be unstable, and in the general case they are intractable (Selman and Levesque, 1989).

It is an open question whether the lexicon requires this level of sophistication – by sacrificing some of the power of a general inheritance system one may arrive at a simpler, more restricted, version, which is nevertheless sufficiently expressive for the domain. The particular context within which the lexicon described here has been devised seems to permit further reductions in complexity. It has been implemented as part of the ELU[1] unification grammar development environment for research in machine translation, comprising parser, generator, lexicon, and transfer mechanism.

8.2   Overview of Formalism

An ELU lexicon consists of a number of 'classes', each of which is a structured collection of constraint equations and/or macro calls encoding information common to a set of words, together with links to other more general 'superclasses'. Lexical entries are themselves classes,[2] and any information they contain is standardly specific to an individual word; lexical and non-lexical classes differ in that analysis and generation take only the former as entry points to the lexicon.

---

[1] 'Environnement Linguistique d'Unification' (Estival, 1990). See also Johnson and Rosner (1989) for a description of the earlier UD system on which ELU is based.

[2] Thus no distinction is made between classes and 'instances', as in e.g. KL-ONE (Schmolze and Lipkis, 1983)

Class Definition

A class definition consists of the compiler directive '#Class' (for a non-lexical class) or '#Word' (for a lexical class), followed by:

1. the name of the class
2. a (possibly empty) list of its direct superclasses
3. a (possibly empty) 'main' equation set
4. zero or more 'variant' equation sets

Superclass Declaration

The superclass declaration is a list of the names of any direct superclass of the current class. This is used in computing the relative precedence of classes in the lexicon for the purpose of default inheritance (see section 8.2.2); it may be empty if the class has no superclasses, i.e. if it is one of the most general in the lexicon, and thus inherits no information. More specific classes appear to the left of more general ones.

Main Equation Set

Following the superclass declaration are zero or more equations or macro calls representing *default* information, which we refer to as the 'main' equation set. These may be overridden by conflicting information in a more specific class. Each equation in a main set functions as an independent constraint, in a manner which will be clarified below.

Variant Equation Sets

Following the (possibly empty) main equation set are zero or more sets of e-quations or macro calls representing variants within the class which, loosely speaking, correspond to alternatives at the same 'conceptual level' in the hierarchy. Equations within a variant set are absolute constraints, in contrast to those in the main set; if they conflict with information in a more specific class, failure of unification occurs in the normal way. Also, unlike the main set, each variant set functions as a single, possibly complex, constraint (see section 8.3). A feature structure is created for each variant set that successfully unifies with the single structure resulting from the main set. Each variant set is preceded by the vertical bar '|'.

String Concatenation

Construction and decomposition of complex words are carried out by the string concatenation operator '&&'. An equation of the form

    X = Y && Z

unifies X nondeterministically with the result of concatenating Y and Z.

8.2.1 Multiple Inheritance and Ambiguity

A class may inherit from more than one direct superclass. In general, multiple inheritance of this kind necessitates more complex methods of searching a hierarchy; much of the complexity of inheritance reasoners lies in finding and determining what to do in these cases of *ambiguity*.[3] Multiple inheritance is not an *a priori* necessity for lexical specification, so it is worth considering whether any phenomena occur in this domain that might make multiple inheritance desirable, rather than the simpler tree-structured hierarchy.

However, natural language lexicons do appear to require description in terms of 'tangled hierarchies', at least if certain types of generalization are not to go unexpressed. It has often been observed, for example, that syntactic and morphological properties are in many respects disjoint; the subcategorization class of a verb cannot be predicted from its conjugation class, and vice versa. Multiple inheritance permits the two types of information to be kept separate by isolating them in distinct sub-hierarchies. This compartmentalization is implicitly related to the independence of the sub-hierarchies; if superclasses B and C of some class A are independent in this way, no conflict will arise when A inherits from B and C.

The present system disallows ambiguity of inheritance by enforcing a total ordering on the superclasses of any given class or word, and by making clear to users how this ordering is derived, so that they may more accurately control and exploit it in the organization of the hierarchy. As a substitute, the variant set mechanism is introduced; this allows variants to be represented directly within a class, rather than by creating alternate, unordered, superclasses, and corresponds to a strong element in traditional grammatical description, that such mutually exclusive variant classes should nevertheless be grouped together in a single compound statement or paradigm. A concrete version of this may be seen in the inflection tables to be found in reference and pedagogical grammars of foreign languages.

Users are able to simulate ambiguity when required, but are responsible for determining when this should occur. In effect, the ELU lexicon abandons some of the generality of an inheritance reasoner (that it reasons correctly over arbitrary inheritance networks according to certain 'intuitions') by making creators of lexicons perform the 'intuitive' work themselves. The creator of the lexicon is then forced to consider the desired relations, rather than relying on the semantics of the inheritance system to produce them.

---

[3] Cf. examples of cascaded ambiguity and On-Path versus Off-Path preemption in Touretzky *et al.* (1987).

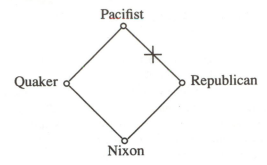

Figure 8.1: The Nixon Diamond

8.2.2   Class Precedence

A system such as the ELU lexicon, which permits the defeasible inheritance of information from more than one superclass, must provide a way of resolving the conflicts that arise when information present in two or more superclasses is mutually incompatible, e.g. when the result obtained when A inherits from one superclass B before inheriting from another, C, differs from that obtained by inheriting first from C and then from B. It is in such cases that the notion of 'precedence' comes into play; if the system is constrained so that information is inherited first from B, we say that B 'has precedence over', or 'is more specific than' C.

A familiar example of this type of situation from the AI literature is the so-called 'Nixon Diamond' (Touretzky, 1986). Nixon is both a Quaker and a Republican; Quakers are (typically) pacifists, while Republicans are (typically) not; the question to be answered is whether Nixon is a pacifist. This problem may be represented by the configuration shown in Figure 8.1. If the links to the 'Pacifist' class are both defeasible, which should take precedence, the positive link from 'Quaker', or the negative link from 'Republican'?

Within the ELU lexicon, a natural way of representing the same information is to dispense with a 'Pacifist' class, and instead to make (non-) pacifisthood a defeasible property of Quakers and Republicans, as shown in the example below:

```
#Word  Nixon (Quaker Republican)
     |
     <name> = 'Nixon'

#Class Quaker ()
     <pacifist> = yes
     |
     <denomination> = 'Quaker'

#Class Republican ()
     <pacifist> = no
     |
     <party> = 'Republican'
```

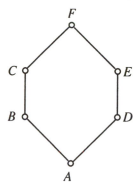

Figure 8.2: A partially ordered set of classes

Here, the 'lexical class' Nixon has two immediate superclasses, Quaker and Republican – as we shall see below, the order in which these are declared is significant. It also contains the constraint that the value of the <name> path must be Nixon. Quaker imposes two constraints; the value of <denomination> must be Quaker, and the value of <pacifist> must be yes, unless that would conflict with a value assigned in some more specific class. The constraints embodied in Republican are that the value of <party> must be Republican, while, again unless differently assigned in a more specific class, <pacifist> has the value no.

What will be the result of looking up 'Nixon' in this lexicon? The paths <name>, <party> and <denomination> are unproblematic; the only conflict arises with <pacifist>. As indicated above, its value will depend on which of the two superclasses of Nixon is the more specific; the declaration (Quaker Republican) states not only what the immediate superclasses of Nixon are, but also that Quaker is to be regarded as more specific than Republican. Thus it is Quaker that will provide the value for <pacifist>. If the opposite answer were required, the appropriate declaration would be (Republican Quaker).

The ELU lexicon employs the class precedence algorithm of the Common Lisp Object System (CLOS) to derive a total order on the superclasses of each lexical class.[4] The resulting 'class precedence list' (CPL) contains the lexical class itself and all of its superclasses, from most specific to most general, consistent with the local order given by class declarations. The effect of the CPL can be seen most clearly in connection with a graphical representation like that in Figure 8.2, which represents the partial order generated by the local immediate superclass ordering constraints in a lexicon.

Note that the left-to-right order of the two 'branches' in Figure 8.2 reflects

---

[4] See Steele (1990, pp. 728ff.) for a precise statement of the algorithm, and Keene (1989; pp. 118ff.) for discussion.

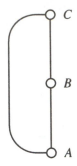

Figure 8.3: An impossible hierarchy

the order in which B and D appear in the superclass declaration of A. The CPL is constructed by traversing the graph in a depth-first, left-to-right manner, at any joins (such as F in this case) splicing in the next leftmost path before continuing with depth-first computation. The CPL of A in Figure 8.2 is therefore $\langle A, B, C, D, E, F \rangle$. This procedure deterministically selects one total ordering from the set of orderings compatible with the superclass declarations; if none can be derived, the system gives an error during compilation.

Patterns of inheritance between superclasses of a lexical class are determined solely by the linear CPL. Note that this scheme excludes a number of configurations that have featured in the AI literature. Dual paths from one class to another, of the sort shown in Figure 8.3, cannot arise in the compiled lexicon; given a CPL $\langle c_1, \ldots c_n \rangle$, the only path from c_i to c_k is through every c_j, $0 \leq i < j < k \leq n$.

Another consequence is that cyclic hierarchies are precluded – no total order can be constructed in which $A < B$ and $B < A$. Intuitively, there is no reason for defining a network with cyclic paths when traversing the same portion of the network repeatedly can add no more information.

Nor is there any means of expressing negative links of the kind shown in Figure 8.1. The significance of this point is that the presence of exception links is another factor in the complexity of a hierarchy; moreover, this type of negation is of dubious utility in the present context, for two reasons. First, the precedence of default information from subclasses enables exceptionality to be expressed without explicit negation of inheritance. The second reason is connected with the nature of unification. The absence of a path-value pair $P = <p, v>$ in an FS F cannot be interpreted as a positive constraint that (some extension of) F does not have the property represented by P; a later unification may lead to P being added to F. The desired effect can only be achieved by the presence in F of a distinct path-value pair $<p, v'>$, where v and v' do not unify. Conflicting information of this type can be introduced by means of the standard positive inheritance link.

In comparison with inheritance systems in general, then, the ELU lexicon is rather restrictive. Hierarchies are constrained to be acyclic, unipolar and unambiguous, these limitations reflecting the desire not only to reduce the complexity of the system, but also to eliminate from it inessential or redundant aspects.

8.2.3 *An Informal Account of Lexical Access*

Lookup of a lexical item with CPL $\langle c_1, \ldots c_n \rangle$ proceeds as follows: starting with an empty FS, the system first applies any default equations in c_1, then applies any variant sets in c_1 to the result. The system then repeats this process on each resulting FS, for the classes c_{i+1} to c_n in turn. The result of lookup is the set of FSs produced by the most general class c_n; this set we term the *global extension* of the lexical class c_1.

A set of default equations $D = \{d_1, \ldots d_n\}$ applies to an FS F as follows: each d_i that does not conflict with some existing information in F is unified with F, subject to the condition that any reentrant substructure of F should be compatible with D, and that any reentrant subset of D should be compatible with F.[5] A set of equations that satisfies this condition may be applied without regard to order. Any variant sets that exist in the current class are then applied to the resulting FS F'.

The result of applying variant sets $v_1, \ldots v_n$ to an FS F is the set of FSs $\{f_1, \ldots f_m\}$, where each f_i is the result of successfully unifying F with some different v_j. Unification failure in variant sets produces a null result, so $m \leq n$. Variant sets have two effects: they enforce strict constraints which cannot be overridden, and multiple variant sets 'multiply' FSs, e.g. to produce different members of an inflectional paradigm.

8.3   The System in More Detail

Following the relatively informal presentation in the previous section, we continue by refining some of the notions introduced there.

We define the *global extension* of a lexical class in terms of two auxiliary notions, *default extension* and *superclass extension*.[6]

Default Extension

The *default extension* of an FS ϕ with respect to a set of FSs Ψ is

$$\phi \sqcup \bigsqcup \{\psi \in \Psi \mid \phi \sqcup \psi \neq \bot\}$$

---

[5] Bouma (1990a, p. 166) discusses the motivation for this condition.

[6] '$A \sqcup B$' here denotes the unification of A and B, '$\top$' denotes the most general, 'empty' FS, which unifies with all others, and '$\bot$' denotes the inconsistent FS, equated with failure of unification.

if both $R(\phi) \sqcup \bigsqcup \Psi \neq \bot$ and $\phi \sqcup R(\bigsqcup \Psi) \neq \bot$, and $\bot$ otherwise, where $R(\phi)$ denotes the restriction of ϕ to reentrant paths, i.e. the most general FS such that $\forall p,q \, [\phi(p) \equiv \phi(q) \rightarrow R(\phi)(p) \equiv R(\phi)(q)]$.[7]

Each of the FSs in Ψ that can unify with ϕ does so – those that cannot, because they conflict with information already present, are ignored. This is the basis of the defaulting behaviour of the lexicon. The condition referring to reentrant paths takes account of the potential order-sensitivity of the defaulting operation – only those main sets having this property can be applied without regard to the relative order of the individual constraints within them. If the condition is met then the application of defaults always succeeds, producing a feature structure which, if no member of the set of equations is applicable, is identical to ϕ; otherwise the lookup fails.

Superclass Extension

The *superclass extension* of an FS ϕ with respect to a class C having a main equation set M and variant sets $v_1, \ldots v_n$ is

$$\Sigma(\phi, C) = \{\psi \mid 1 \leq i \leq n \wedge v_i' \sqcup \phi' = \psi \wedge \psi \neq \bot\},$$

where M' is the smallest set of FSs such that each $m \in M$ describes some $m' \in M'$, ϕ' is the default extension of ϕ with respect to M', and v_i' is the feature structure described by v_i.

$\Sigma(\phi, C)$ is formed by applying to ϕ any default equations in the main set of C, and then applying to the result each variant set in C; for variant sets $v_1, \ldots v_n$, the result of this second stage is the set of FSs $\{\psi_1, \ldots \psi_m\}$, where each ψ_i is the result of successfully unifying ϕ with some different v_j.

Global Extension

The *global extension* of a lexical class L having the CPL $C = \langle c_1, \ldots c_n \rangle$ is Γ_n, where $\Gamma_0 = \{\top\}$, and

$$\Gamma_{i>0} = \bigcup \{\Psi \mid \forall \phi \in \Gamma_{i-1}, \Psi = \Sigma(\phi, c_i)\}.$$

To speak in procedural terms, $\top$ is the empty FS which is input to C; each c_i in C yields as its superclass extension a set of FSs, each member of which is input to the remainder of C, $\langle c_{i+1}, \ldots c_n \rangle$. The global extension of L is then the yield of the most general class in its CPL – expressed in a slightly different way, the global extension of L is the result of *applying* to $\top$ the CPL of L. The set of lexical items admitted by a lexicon consists of the union of the global extensions of all lexical classes in the lexicon.

---

[7] Here, '$\phi(p)$' denotes the value of the path p in the FS ϕ, and '$\equiv$' denotes token-identity of its operands.

The implementation of defaults in ELU ensures the monotonicity of structure-building – given a CPL $\langle c_1, \ldots c_n \rangle$, any FS F admitted by a class c_i subsumes every FS that can be created by applying to F the classes $\langle c_{i+1}, \ldots c_n \rangle$. Shieber (1986, pp. 59ff) and Karttunen (1986, p. 76) describe default inheritance systems based on a nonmonotonic 'overwriting' operation; in both cases, the statements exhibiting default behaviour are ones that have the ability to override others over which they have precedence, whereas in the approach presented here the default statements are ones that can be overridden by others which have precedence over them.

8.4   An Example Analysis

This section briefly illustrates some aspects of the ELU lexicon introduced above with an analysis of English verbal morphology.

In most cases, lexical items that realize certain morphosyntactic properties in irregular forms do not also have regular realizations of those properties; thus *sinked*, on the analogy of e.g. *walked*, is not a well-formed alternative to *sank* or *sunk*. This phenomenon has frequently been discussed in both theoretical and computational morphology, under the title of 'blocking', and it appears to provide clear motivation for a default-based hierarchical approach to lexical organization. There are exceptions to this general rule, however, and inheritance mechanisms must be sufficiently flexible to permit deviation from the strict pattern.

Consider the small class of English verbs including *dream*, *lean*, *learn* and *burn*; for many speakers, these have alternate past finite and past participle forms: e.g. *dreamed* and *dreamt*. The following simplified fragment produces the correct analyses, in which the value of <morph> expresses inflectional information, and that of <form> is the corresponding word-form:

```
#NLexicon Eng-Irreg-Verbs

#Word walk (Verb)
        <stem> = walk

#Word sink (Verb)
        <stem> = sink
        P_Fin_Form = sank              PSP_Form = sunk

#Word dream (DualPast Verb)
        <stem> = dream

#Class DualPast ()
        |
        PSP_Form = <stem> && t
        P_Fin_Form = <stem> && t
        <morph> = pastfinite/pastnonfinite
        |

#Class Verb (VFin VNonFin)
        <cat> = v
```

```
#Class VFin ()
      P_Fin_Form = <stem> && ed
      |
      <morph> = present_nonsg3        <form> = <stem>
      |
      <morph> = present_sg3           <form> = <stem> && s
      |
      <morph> = pastfinite            <form> = P_Fin_Form
      |
      <morph> = pastnonfinite

#Class VNonFin ()
      PSP_Form = <stem> && ed
      |
      <morph> = pastnonfinite         <form> = PSP_Form
      |
      <morph> = present_nonsg3/present_sg3/pastfinite
```

Being the lexical class of a regular verb, walk contains a minimum of idiosyncratic information, *viz.* that the value of the feature <stem> is the string *walk*. Its direct superclass, Verb, contributes the information that the value of <cat> is v, and in turn specifies inheritance from its direct superclasses, VFin and VNonFin. Each of these contains a single main set equation, assigning a default value to a variable; both P_Fin_Form and PSP_Form, having no conflicting value, are set to the concatenation of *walk* and *ed*. The first three variant sets of VFin establish correspondences between values of <morph> and <form>, while the third unifies with variants treated by VNonFin. The latter class contains just two variant sets, the first of which produces the correct form for past nonfinite verbs, while the second permits analysis of the finite forms treated by VFin – it contains a disjunctive constraint, to the effect that the value of <morph> must unify with at least one of present_nonsg3, present_sg3 and pastfinite.

The main set equations in sink assigning values to P_Fin_Form and PSP_Form override those in its superclasses VFin and VNonFin, so that the variants in the latter class which give rise to past participle and past tensed forms associate the appropriate information with the strings *sunk* and *sank*, respectively.

The lexical class dream is exceptional in having as one of its direct superclasses DualPast, which contains two variant sets, the second of which is empty (recall that variant sets are preceded by the vertical bar '|'). Moreover, this class is more specific than the other superclass Verb, and so the equations in the first variant set assigning to PSP_Form and P_Fin_Form the string formed by concatenating the value of <stem> and *t* (e.g. *dreamt*) have precedence over the contradictory statements in the main sets of VFin and VNonFin. The absence of contradictory specifications in the second variant set permits the equations in the main sets of VFin and VNonFin to apply. In addition to specifying exceptional properties, therefore, the definition of DualPast also permits the inheritance of properties from more general classes, i.e. those of regular verbs like *walk*; among these is that of forming the two past forms by suffixing *ed* to the stem, which produces the regular (*dreamed*, etc.) past forms.

8.5 Summary

The popularity of unification as a tool for computational linguistics stems from its declarative, monotonic semantics; however, the price to be paid for the benefits of a pure unification framework is the lack of a satisfactory treatment of exceptions (negation, defaults, etc.). The popularity of default inheritance as a tool for knowledge representation stems from its ability to encode, in a straightforward manner, the type of nested generalization with exceptions that natural language lexicons exhibit; however, in achieving this expressive power one introduces a degree of order-dependence into the system. The approach presented here attempts to combine the advantages of unification and default inheritance, while minimizing the disadvantages arising from their interaction.

Properties of general default systems that lead to intractability are absent; the total ordering imposed on superclasses by the CPL eliminates cycles, ambiguity and the redundancy of multiple paths, while the suppression of negative inheritance links removes a further source of complexity. Facilities have been dispensed with not only because they are computationally problematic, but also as a result of the application in question – as we observe in sections 8.2.1 and 8.2.2, ambiguity and negation are redundant in the present context.

9   The ACQUILEX LKB: An Introduction

ANN COPESTAKE, ANTONIO SANFILIPPO, TED BRISCOE AND
VALERIA DE PAIVA

9.1   Introduction

This chapter and those following describe the LKB, a lexical knowledge base
system which has been designed as part of the ACQUILEX project to allow the
representation of syntactic and semantic information semi-automatically extracted from machine readable dictionaries (MRDs) on a large scale. An overview
of the ACQUILEX project is given by Briscoe (1991).

Although there has been previous work on building lexicons for Natural Language Processing (NLP) systems from MRDs (e.g. Carroll and Grover, 1989),
most attempts at extracting semantic information have not made use of a formally defined representation language; typically a semantic network or a frame
representation has been suggested, but the interpretation and functionality of the
links has been left vague. Several networks based on taxonomies extracted from
MRDs have been built (following Amsler, 1980) and these are useful for tasks
such as sense-disambiguation, but are not directly utilisable as NLP lexicons.
For a lexicon to be genuinely (re)usable, a declarative, formally specified, representation language is essential. A large lexicon has to be highly structured;
it is necessary to be able to group lexical entries and to represent relationships
between them, both in order to capture linguistic generalisations and to achieve
consistency and conciseness. But, unless these notions of structure are properly
specified, a lexicon based on them is in danger of being incomprehensible except
(perhaps) to its creators. We therefore take semantic structuring seriously, and
use taxonomic information as one of the ways of providing such structure, but
we do this within the context of a formally specified representation language.

The LKB's knowledge representation language (LRL) can be viewed as an
augmentation of a typed graph-based unification formalism with minimal default
inheritance; default inheritance is formalised in terms of default unification of
feature structures (see e.g. Carpenter, this volume). We chose to use a graph
unification based representation language (e.g. Shieber, 1986) for the LKB, because this offered the flexibility to represent syntactic and semantic information,
and the interaction between them, in a way which could be easily integrated
with much current work on unification grammar, parsing and generation. In
contrast to DATR (Evans and Gazdar, 1990) for example, the LRL has not been
designed specifically for lexical representation. This made it much easier to

incorporate a parser in the LKB (which is almost essential for developing a type system and for testing lexical entries) and to experiment with notions such as lexical rules and inter-lingual links between lexical entries. Although this means that the LRL is perhaps too general for its main application, the type system provides a way of flexibly constraining the representation according to the particular linguistic treatment adopted.

The main structure of the lexicon is given by the type system. Our typed feature structure language is based on Carpenter's (1990, 1992) work on the HPSG formalism, although there are some significant differences. The type system can be regarded as a way of providing (non-default) inheritance, combined with error-checking. The notion of types, and features appropriate for a given type, gives some of the functionality of frame representation languages, such as KL-ONE; in particular, classification of a feature structure is possible.

We augment the typed feature structure language with a default inheritance mechanism. This can be used to organise the lexicon in a completely user-defined way, to allow morphological or syntactic information to be concisely specified, for example, as has been done with DATR and other systems (for example, Russell *et al.* and Krieger and Nerbonne's chapters in this volume). However much of the motivation behind our formalisation of default inheritance comes from consideration of the sense-disambiguated taxonomies semi-automatically derived from MRDs, which we are using to structure the LKB. The top level of the inheritance structure, which cannot be automatically derived from MRDs, is, in effect, given by the type system.

Thus the operations that the LRL supports are (default) inheritance, (default) unification and lexical rule and translation link application. It does not support any more general forms of inference and is thus designed specifically to support processes which concern lexical rather than general reasoning. The type system provides the non-default inheritance mechanism and constrains default inheritance. We use lexical rules as a further means of structuring the lexicon, in a flexible, user definable manner, but lexical rules are also constrained by the type system.

In the remainder of this introduction we provide an informal account of the type system and other aspects of the LKB including the lexical rule and translation link mechanisms. Other chapters in this volume discuss various aspects of the LRL in more depth and describe two applications in detail. De Paiva discusses the theoretical background to typed feature structures and the way that they are formalised in the LRL. Sanfilippo describes the type system which has been used in the ACQUILEX project to represent lexical entries for verbs, using information extracted from MRDs. Copestake completes the description of the LRL by considering the default unification and default inheritance mechanisms and the way they interact with the type system, and discusses the use of the default system in the representation of taxonomic information extracted from MRDs. Vossen and Copestake continue the discussion of the representation

$$\left[\begin{array}{l} \textbf{lex-count-noun} \\ \text{ORTH} = \textbf{lamb} \\ \text{CAT} = \boxed{\textbf{noun-cat}} \\ \text{SEM} = \left[\begin{array}{l} \textbf{unary-formula-entity-arg1} \\ \text{IND} = \boxed{0}\ \textbf{entity} \\ \text{PRED} = \textbf{lamb\_L\_1\_1} \\ \text{ARG1} = \boxed{0} \end{array}\right] \\ \text{QUALIA} = \left[\begin{array}{l} \textbf{animal} \\ \text{SEX} = \textbf{gender} \\ \text{PHYSICAL-STATE} = \textbf{solid} \\ \text{FORM} = \left[\begin{array}{l} \textbf{physform} \\ \text{SHAPE} = \textbf{individuated} \end{array}\right] \end{array}\right] \end{array}\right]$$

Figure 9.1: Simplified LKB lexical entry for *lamb*

of taxonomic information, and show how more problematic examples may be tackled. Appendix 13.8 is a bibliography of relevant papers produced under ACQUILEX. Appendix 13.8 gives a full description of the syntax of the LKB's feature structure description language.

9.2   An Informal Introduction to Typed Feature Structures

The feature structure shown in Figure 9.1 is a (highly simplified) example of a lexical entry in the LRL which illustrates the notational conventions which we will use in this group of chapters. Bold font is used for types, features are capitalised. A box round a type indicates that that portion of the feature structure is not shown. The lexical entry as shown has four components; ORTH is the orthography, CAT the syntactic information (not shown), SEM the formal semantic structure. This essentially corresponds to the expression, $\lambda x[\text{lamb\_L\_1\_1}(x)]$, where the predicate indicates that the sense corresponds to a particular dictionary sense, in this case *lamb*[1] *1* in LDOCE (*Longman Dictionary of Contemporary English*, Procter, 1978). The feature QUALIA introduces the lexical semantic information, the representation of which is loosely based on Pustejovsky's (1989, 1991) notion of qualia structure. The basic structure of the lexical entry is determined by the type system.

The type system can be described as having two components; the type hierarchy and the constraint system. The type hierarchy defines a partial ordering (notated $\sqsubseteq$) on the types and specifies which types are *consistent*. Only feature structures with mutually consistent types can be unified — two types which are unordered in the hierarchy are assumed to be inconsistent unless the user explicitly specifies a common subtype. Every *consistent* set of types $S \subseteq$ TYPE has a unique greatest lower bound or meet (notation $\sqcap S$). This condition allows feature structures to be typed deterministically — if two feature structures of types **a** and **b** are unified the type of the result will be $\textbf{a} \sqcap \textbf{b}$, which must be unique if it exists. If $\textbf{a} \sqcap \textbf{b}$ does not exist unification fails. Thus in the fragment of a type hierarchy shown in Figure 9.2 **artifact** and **physical** are consistent; **artifact** $\sqcap$ **physical** = **artifact_physical**. We will use a very simplified type sys-

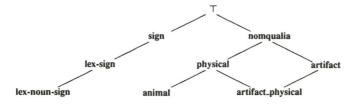

Figure 9.2: A fragment of a type hierarchy

tem in this introduction for ease of exposition; for more realistic type systems see the chapters by Sanfilippo and by Vossen and Copestake in this volume.

Our system differs somewhat from that described by Carpenter (1990, 1992) in that we adopt a different notion of well-formedness of typed feature structures. In our system every type must have exactly one associated feature structure which acts as a constraint on all feature structures of that type, by subsuming all well-formed feature structures of that type. The constraint also defines which features are *appropriate* for a particular type; a well-formed feature structure may only contain appropriate features. Constraints are inherited by all subtypes of a type, but a subtype may introduce new features (which will be inherited as appropriate features by all its subtypes). A constraint on a type is a well-formed feature structure of that type; all constraints must therefore be mutually consistent. Constraints can be seen as extending the PATR-II notion of templates (e.g. Shieber, 1986) in that the inheritance of constraints allows concise definitions of all feature structures, not just lexical entries; but in an untyped system, such as PATR-II, there is no restriction on the features that can occur in a feature structure.

For example the unexpanded constraint associated with the type **artifact** might be:

$$\begin{bmatrix} \text{artifact} \\ \text{TELIC} = \text{formula} \end{bmatrix}$$

This constraint states that any feature structure of type **artifact** must have a feature structure of type **formula** as the value for its TELIC (purpose) feature. The type **formula** is intended to represent a formula in predicate logic; it therefore would have a complex constraint itself:

$$\begin{bmatrix} \text{formula} \\ \text{IND} = \text{entity} \\ \text{PRED} = \text{logical-pred} \\ \text{ARG1} = \text{sem} \end{bmatrix}$$

The full constraint associated with a type is found by expanding the constraints associated with all the types inside the constraint feature structure, thus the expanded constraint for artifact would be:

$$\begin{bmatrix} \textbf{artifact} \\ \text{TELIC} = \begin{bmatrix} \textbf{formula} \\ \text{IND} = \textbf{entity} \\ \text{PRED} = \textbf{logical-pred} \\ \text{ARG1} = \textbf{sem} \end{bmatrix} \end{bmatrix}$$

The type **physical** might have constraint:

$$\begin{bmatrix} \textbf{physical} \\ \text{PHYSICAL-STATE} = \textbf{state} \\ \text{SHAPE} = \textbf{shape} \end{bmatrix}$$

Here **shape** and **state** are both atomic types, and have no appropriate features. For example the constraint on **state** is simply the atomic feature structure [**state**]. The constraint on **artifact_physical** will contain information inherited from both parents, thus:

$$\begin{bmatrix} \textbf{artifact\_physical} \\ \text{PHYSICAL-STATE} = \textbf{state} \\ \text{SHAPE} = \textbf{shape} \\ \text{TELIC} = \begin{bmatrix} \textbf{formula} \\ \text{IND} = \textbf{entity} \\ \text{PRED} = \textbf{logical-pred} \\ \text{ARG1} = \textbf{sem} \end{bmatrix} \end{bmatrix}$$

Given that **solid** is an atomic subtype of **state**, and that **entity** is an atomic subtype of **sem**, the feature structure below is well-formed. It contains all the appropriate features and no inappropriate ones, it is subsumed by the constraints on its type and all its substructures are well-formed.

$$\begin{bmatrix} \textbf{artifact\_physical} \\ \text{PHYSICAL-STATE} = \textbf{solid} \\ \text{SHAPE} = \textbf{shape} \\ \text{TELIC} = \begin{bmatrix} \textbf{formula} \\ \text{IND} = \boxed{0} \ \textbf{entity} \\ \text{PRED} = \textbf{logical-pred} \\ \text{ARG1} = \boxed{0} \end{bmatrix} \end{bmatrix}$$

Since the type system gives us a concept of a well-formed feature structure it follows that non well-formed feature structures can be detected, allowing error checking. This is particularly important for our particular application where mistakes may occur, either because of errors in the original dictionary entries, or because of problems in the automatic extraction processes.

Typing also allows for a form of classification; a feature may only be introduced as appropriate at one point in the type hierarchy (and will be inherited as an appropriate feature by all subtypes of that type); it follows from this that there is a unique maximal type for any set of features, and therefore an untyped feature structure can always be typed deterministically. For example, assuming the type system introduced above, the attribute value specification:

```
< PHYSICAL-STATE > = solid
< TELIC : IND > = < TELIC : ARG1 >
```

would be expanded out into the feature structure just shown. (Full details of the feature structure description language are given in Appendix B.) The type of the feature structure is determined automatically; since the features PHYSICAL-STATE and TELIC are specified, its type has to be **artifact_physical** (or some subtype of that type).

9.2.1 Limitations of Error Checking and Classification

Error checking and classification with respect to a type system in the LKB are computationally efficient but have limitations. One disadvantage of the system as described is that it is not possible in general to enforce co-occurrence restrictions, even of a quite limited sort. For example, Sanfilippo's representation of verb semantics in the LKB (Sanfilippo, this volume) involves using thematic roles and encoding restrictions on arguments of a predicate by sorting the variables. In order to do this a type **theta-formula** is defined to have the following constraint:

$$
\begin{bmatrix}
\text{theta-formula} \\
\text{IND} = \boxed{1} \quad \text{eve} \\
\text{PRED} = \text{theta-relation} \\
\text{ARG1} = \boxed{1} \\
\text{ARG2} = \text{obj}
\end{bmatrix}
$$

To classify psychological predicates thematic predicates such as **theta-sentient** are used; in this case the second argument to any formula whose predicate is **theta-sentient** should denote a sentient entity; i.e. if the value of PRED is **theta-sentient** then the value of ARG2 is **e-sentient**. But the nearest we could get to achieving this would be to define a subtype of **theta-formula**, e.g. **theta-sentient-formula**, with constraint:

$$
\begin{bmatrix}
\text{theta-sentient-formula} \\
\text{IND} = \boxed{1} \quad \text{eve} \\
\text{PRED} = \text{theta-sentient} \\
\text{ARG1} = \boxed{1} \\
\text{ARG2} = \text{e-sentient}
\end{bmatrix}
$$

and to define other subtypes for the other possible theta relations. This does not really achieve the desired result, however — for example:

$$
\begin{bmatrix}
\text{theta-formula} \\
\text{IND} = \boxed{1} \quad \text{eve} \\
\text{PRED} = \text{theta-sentient} \\
\text{ARG1} = \boxed{1} \\
\text{ARG2} = \text{e-plant}
\end{bmatrix}
$$

is still a well-formed feature structure, despite the fact that it cannot be extended to be a well-formed structure with a type corresponding to that of any leaf node in the type hierarchy (assuming that **e-plant** $\sqcap$ **e-sentient** $= \perp$). This seems undesirable; the type system is supposed to be complete, so intuitively we might expect such a feature structure to be ill-formed in some sense. It seems clear that we cannot check for such cases efficiently in general, because to do so would, in the worst case, involve attempting to unify the feature structure with the constraints of all leaf types which were subtypes of its type.

We refer to a feature structure which can be extended to a well-formed structure where every type is a leaf type as 'ultimately well-formed', and we can enforce such co-occurrence restrictions when automatically acquiring lexical entries from the MRDs by checking for ultimate well-formedness. This does not impose an unreasonable overhead in practice, since a lexical entry need only be acquired and checked once.

A related issue is that classification of a feature structure with respect to a type system is also limited, in that the procedure only takes account of the top level features in a structure and not their values. Even if the only subtype of **binary-formula** which had a value for PRED which was compatible with **theta-relation** was **theta-formula**, the following feature structure would be classified as a **binary-formula** rather than a **theta-formula**:

$$
\begin{bmatrix}
\textbf{top} \\
\text{IND} = \boxed{1} \quad \textbf{entity} \\
\text{PRED} = \textbf{theta-relation} \\
\text{ARG1} = \boxed{1} \\
\text{ARG2} = \textbf{obj}
\end{bmatrix}
$$

Again, although full classification would be expensive computationally, allowing such a procedure to be invoked when lexical entries are being created is a practical option which has considerable advantages in allowing augmentation of automatically acquired information.

9.2.2   *Extensions to the Language*

A type system in the LKB has, essentially, to be fully defined before lexical entries can be built. This causes obvious problems with respect to atomic types representing orthography and predicate names, for example, where it is unrealistic to assume that the complete set can be known in advance. To get round this we allow any string as a valid LKB type; all strings are assumed to be subtypes of the predefined atomic type **string**, but to be unordered with respect to one another. Particular features such as ORTH, which are specified as having value **string**, thus in effect take arbitrary string values.

Although many feature structure based languages allow disjunctive feature structures, we have avoided this in the LKB. Arbitrary disjunction can result in a computationally intractable system and it is not clear whether it is in fact necessary, given that the type system can be set up in a way which, in effect, allows a constrained form of disjunction. For example, given the types shown in Figure 9.2, rather than stating that a feature had value **animal** or **artifact_physical**, we would state its value to be **physical**. In general new types might have to be created in order to do this; thus given, for example, that the type **person** was defined to have the subtypes **first, second, third**, a new type would have to be inserted in the hierarchy in order to express the equivalent of the disjunction **second** or **third**.

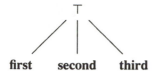

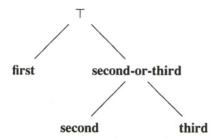

In the particular case of atomic types we do allow disjunction in the language, with an effect which is formally similar to creating an additional type in this way. We express this as a list of values, for example, (**second third**).

The flexibility of the LKB is enhanced by allowing feature structures to be described in terms of other feature structures. Particular feature structures may have identifiers associated with them; feature structures representing complete lexical entries are identified by a combination of orthography plus sense information. Lexical and grammar rules also have associated names, and in general any feature structure may be defined with an associated identifier. We refer to all such named feature structures as *psorts*; the significance of this is the use of such structures in the description of other feature structures. Feature structure descriptions are not just local; relationships between feature structures may be set up in a variety of ways. The simplest of these relationships conceptually is non-default inheritance, (notated <=); a feature structure may be described as inheriting information from a psort. For example, we could define the feature structure corresponding to the lexical entry for *ewe* as inheriting its qualia structure from a particular sense of *sheep*, but further specifying the SEX to be **female**:

```
<> = lex-count-noun
< QUALIA > <= sheep_L_0_1 < QUALIA >
< QUALIA : SEX > = female
```

Non-default inheritance is simply implemented by unification of the feature structure with a copy of the relevant part of the psort.[1]

---

[1] Formally the ordinary attribute value language may be regarded as describing feature structures, and the feature structure which is built is the minimal satisfier of this set of descriptions (see de Paiva, this volume, for example). Non-default inheritance from another feature structure is equivalent to adding the set of descriptions of which it is the minimal satisfier to the locally defined set.

We also allow a feature structure to be specified as being identical (modulo alphabetic variance) to a psort (notated as ==).[2] (The non-default inheritance relationship can be seen as a constraint that the daughter feature structure is subsumed by the psort feature structure; the equality relationship corresponds to a mutual subsumption constraint.) The default inheritance relationship (notated as <) allows for values to be overridden, thus we could (albeit somewhat perversely) specify *ram* as inheriting information by default from *ewe*, but override the value for SEX:

```
<> = lex-count-noun
< QUALIA > < ewe_L_0_0 < QUALIA >
< QUALIA : SEX > = male
```

Psort feature structures may also be combined by unification and generalisation,[3] or transformed by lexical rule application. For details, and some examples of use of these operations in the lexical representation language, see Copestake (this volume) and Vossen and Copestake (this volume).

9.3   Lexical Rules

The lexical rule mechanism, and the translation link mechanism which will be discussed in the next section, involve no further extensions to the LRL, but indicate how typing and inheritance may be applied to feature structures other than lexical entries. We encode grammar and lexical rules as typed feature structures, which represent relationships between two or more signs. Here we will just consider lexical rules; further details can be found in Copestake and Briscoe (1991) and Briscoe and Copestake (1991). A lexical rule is a feature structure of type **lexical-rule** which is a subtype of **rule**. The expanded constraints for the types are:

$$
\begin{bmatrix} \textbf{rule} \\ 0 = \textbf{sign} \\ 1 = \textbf{sign} \end{bmatrix}
\begin{bmatrix} \textbf{lexical\_rule} \\ 0 = \textbf{lex\_sign} \\ 1 = \textbf{lex\_sign} \end{bmatrix}
$$

Thus all lexical rules have to have the features 0 and 1 which must both have values which are of type **lex_sign**. Lexical rules can be regarded as a means of generating new lexical signs; if a lexical entry can be unified with the feature structure at the end of the path <1> in the lexical rule then the feature structure at the end of the path <0> is a new lexical sign. Alternatively they can be regarded statically, as expressing the relationship between two existing lexical signs. We use lexical rules both to represent morphological derivation and sense extension.

---

[2] Earlier versions of the LKB used == for non-default inheritance.

[3] The generalisation operation is the opposite of unification; it produces a feature structure which contains only the information which is common to both of its arguments (see, for example, de Paiva, this volume, for a formal definition). In contrast to disjunction it always yields a single feature structure; this may be equivalent to the disjunction, but in general will be less specific.

An example of a productive sense extension process which we represent as a lexical rule is that which transforms animal denoting (count) nouns to (mass) nouns denoting their meat (e.g. *lamb*). Because lexical rules are typed feature structures, we can make use of the LKB's inheritance mechanism in their representation. In this case we regard the animal/meat sense extension as a special case of 'grinding'. It is well known that any count noun denoting a physical object can be used in a mass sense to denote a substance derived from that object, when it occurs in a sufficiently marked context. We refer to this as 'grinding' because the context normally suggested is the 'Universal Grinder' (see Pelletier and Schubert, 1986). So if *a table* is ground up the result can be referred to as *table* (*there was table all over the floor*). Several regular sense extensions can be regarded as special cases of 'grinding', where the extension may have become conventionalised; besides the animal/meat examples, trees used for wood (*beech*) have a sense denoting the wood, and so forth.

A general type for grinding lexical rules can be specified in the LKB as follows:

grinding ⊑ lexical_rule

$$
\begin{bmatrix}
\textbf{grinding} \\
1 = \begin{bmatrix} \textbf{lex-count-noun} \\ \text{ORTH} = \boxed{1} \\ \text{QUALIA} = \begin{bmatrix} \textbf{physical} \\ \text{FORM} = \begin{bmatrix} \textbf{physform} \\ \text{SHAPE} = \textbf{individuated} \end{bmatrix} \end{bmatrix} \end{bmatrix} \\
0 = \begin{bmatrix} \textbf{lex-uncount-noun} \\ \text{ORTH} = \boxed{1} \\ \text{QUALIA} = \begin{bmatrix} \textbf{physical} \\ \text{FORM} = \begin{bmatrix} \textbf{physform} \\ \text{SHAPE} = \textbf{unindividuated} \end{bmatrix} \end{bmatrix} \end{bmatrix}
\end{bmatrix}
$$

The effect of this rule is to transform a count noun with the qualia structure properties appropriate to an individuated physical object into a mass noun with properties appropriate for a substance. Thus the core component of grinding is a linguistic operation which affects syntactic realisation, such as the ability to appear without a determiner, correlated with an abstract and underspecified semantic operation.

We specialise the grinding rule to allow for cases such as the animal/meat regular sense extension explicitly. The typed framework provides us with a natural method of characterising the subparts of the lexicon to which such rules should apply. The lexical rules can, in effect, be parametrised by inheritance in the type system. Thus animal_grinding can be described as follows:

$$
\text{animal\_grinding} \quad
\begin{bmatrix}
\textbf{grinding} \\
1 = \begin{bmatrix} \text{QUALIA} = \textbf{animal} \end{bmatrix} \\
0 = \begin{bmatrix} \text{QUALIA} = \textbf{food\_substance} \end{bmatrix}
\end{bmatrix}
$$

We treat the lexical rule as fully productive across the appropriate subset of the lexicon and account for cases of 'blocking', where an existing lexeme (e.g. *pork*) appears to render the sense extension highly marked (c.f. *pig*), by a separate mechanism which detects the presence of an existing lexical entry comparable to the extended sense (see Briscoe *et al.*, in press). (This relies on the lexical semantic specification of lexical entries being considerably more fine-grained than that shown here.) Thus, the use of *pig* to mean the meat is possible, but tends to suggest that the substance is in some way inferior, or that the speaker is adverse to (this type of) meat.

9.4   Representation of Translation Equivalence

In this section we complete the overview of the LKB by introducing the techniques which we use for encoding translation equivalence between lexical entries. A more detailed description, and a discussion of how translation links might be used in machine translation is given in Copestake *et al.* (1992) and Sanfilippo *et al.* (1992).

We define lexical translation equivalence in terms of cross-linguistic links, *tlinks*, between the lexical entries in the monolingual lexicons. In general there may be a many-to-many equivalence between word senses, but each possibility is represented by a single tlink. In the simplest and commonest cases unmodified pairs of lexical entries can be treated as translation equivalents, and it is unnecessary to augment the monolingual information, other than simply to assert that a link is present (see **simple-tlink**, below). However in general we have to allow for 'mismatches' such as differences in argument ordering, plurality, and specificity of reference, and for 'lexical gaps', where a word sense in one language has to be translated by a phrase in the other. The tlink mechanism allows the monolingual information to be augmented with translation specific information, in a variety of ways, in order to cope with such problems. We use inheritance from both lexical entries and rules in tlinks; this makes them compact while ensuring that the multilingual and monolingual components are compatible.

A tlink is simply a feature structure of type **tlink**, which is to be read as stating that two feature structures (the 'output structures') are to be regarded as translation equivalents. The tlink encodes the relationship between the input word senses and these output structures; it can be viewed as describing how lexical entries may be transformed into translation equivalent pairs. A complete tlink is essentially a relationship between two **rule**s (as defined above) where the rule inputs have been instantiated by the representations of the word senses in the source and target languages which are to be linked and where the rule outputs are translation equivalent. A level of indirection is thus involved in stating the equivalence between lexical entries, and this allows 'mismatches' to be treated.

The type **tlink** is defined as follows:

```
tlink (top)
< TLINK-ID > = tlink-id
< SFS > = rule
< TFS > = rule
< SFS : 0 : SEM : IND > = < TFS : 0 : SEM : IND >.
```

The third line indicates equivalence of the variables in the two output structures in the particular monolingual encoding of semantic information that we are currently adopting. For all tlinks the feature structures at the end of the paths < SFS : 0 > and < TFS : 0 > will be translation equivalent. For all tlinks at least the paths < SFS : 1 > and < TFS : 1 > have to be instantiated by lexical entries to produce the complete tlink.[4]

By defining types of tlinks the concept of translation equivalence can be constrained and generalisations can be encoded. The commonest and simplest cases of translation equivalence can be represented as **simple-tlink**s.

```
simple-tlink (tlink)
< SFS : 0 > = < SFS : 1 >
< TFS : 0 > = < TFS : 1 >.
```

A **simple-tlink** is applicable in the case where two lexical entries which denote single place predicates (nouns etc.) are straightforwardly translation equivalent, without any transformation being necessary. (For verbs more argument equivalence specifications are necessary; see Sanfilippo *et al.*, 1992.) Like lexical rules tlinks can be regarded statically or dynamically; given a feature structure in one language, and an appropriate tlink, unification with the feature structure at the end of the appropriate path (e.g. < SFS : 0 >) in the tlink will result in the feature structure at the end of the other output path being returned (e.g. < TFS : 0 >).

Assuming that the LDOCE sense *chocolate* 1 4, is translation equivalent to the Van Dale *chocolade* 0 2, we would have the tlink:

```
simple-tlink
< SFS : 1 > <= chocolate_L_1_4 <>
< TFS : 1 > <= chocolade_V_0_2 <> .
```

where <= indicates non-default inheritance from the lexical entries.

Some restrictions on translation can be expressed by making the target or source feature structures more specific. For example, both *maestro* and *maestra* in Spanish can be translated as *teacher* in English; the restriction that *maestro* denotes a male teacher and *maestra* a female one can be encoded as follows:

```
simple-tlink
< SFS : 1 > <= teacher_1 <>
< TFS : 1 > <= maestro_1 <>
```

---

[4] Tlinks and lexical rules are both symmetrical and reversible; we use the terminology source (sfs), target (tfs), input (1) and output (0) solely for ease of exposition.

```
< SFS : 0 : QUALIA : SEX > = male.

simple-tlink
< SFS : 1 > <= teacher_1 <>
< TFS : 1 > <= maestra_1 <>
< SFS : 0 : QUALIA : SEX > = female.
```

Alternatively we can define a type **human-tlink** and state as a constraint that the values for the SEX feature must be equivalent in the translation equivalent feature structures.

```
human-tlink (simple-tlink)
< SFS : 0 : QUALIA : SEX > = < TFS : 0 : QUALIA : SEX >.
```

The restrictions would then follow, assuming that the Spanish lexical entries were appropriately instantiated, and would apply to the whole class.

Somewhat rarer and more complex cases of linking arise when the changes to the feature structures are those such as pluralisation, which is a process that has to be represented separately, and which has to be viewed as a transformation of a feature structure rather then a simple restriction. For example, a lexical/morphological rule for plural formation, which would be required anyway for the monolingual grammar, can be used in a tlink: we encode the idea that the equivalence is to be defined between a basic lexical entry and a lexical entry after rule application by instantiating one half of the tlink with the appropriate lexical rule.

For example, *furniture* can be encoded as translation equivalent to the plural *muebles* by specifying that the named rule 'plural' has to be applied to the base sense in Spanish.

```
tlink
< SFS : 1 > <= furniture_1 <>
< TFS : 1 > <= mueble_1 <>
< SFS : 0 > = < SFS : 1 >
< TFS > <= plural <> .
```

This tlink can be represented diagrammatically as shown in Figure 9.3; unlabelled arrows indicate token identity between FSs. Since the singular form of *mueble* would not unify with the feature structure at the end of the output path < TFS : 0 >, a translation of *mueble* as *furniture* would not be generated by this tlink.

In some cases the existence of a tlink between two lexical items implies a further translation relationship. For example, a similar sense extension rule to that of animal_grinding described in the previous section applies to Italian (Östling, 1991) but in Dutch a compound is generally used (*lam*, *lamsvlees*), although the semantic process is apparently equivalent. To represent the relationship between these lexical rules we define the type **tlink-rule**:

Figure 9.3: Diagrammatic representation of translation link

```
tlink-rule (top)
< ID > = tlink-rule-id
< TO > = tlink
< T1 > = tlink
< SRULE > = lexical-rule
< SRULE : 1 > = < TO : SFS : 1 >
< SRULE : 0 > = < T1 : SFS : 1 >
< TRULE > = lexical-rule
< TRULE : 1 > = < TO : TFS : 1 >
< TRULE : 0 > = < T1 : TFS : 1 >
```

By stating that the lexical rule for animal-grinding is linked with that for compounding with *vlees*, we can, for example, automatically generate the relationship between *lamb_2* and *lamsvlees* from a simple tlink between *lamb_1* and *lam*; see Figure 9.4.[5] There are many examples of such correspondences; for example, the English sense extension between trees and their fruits (*pear*, etc.) is mirrored in Italian with a gender distinction; the trees are masculine but the fruits feminine (*pero*, *pera*).[6]

9.5 Conclusion

In this introduction we have outlined the functionality of the ACQUILEX LKB. A description of the software system and its use in the ACQUILEX project is given in Copestake (1992b). In the remaining chapters we give a more detailed description of the LRL and some of the uses to which it has been put.

The aim of the ACQUILEX project is to demonstrate that substantial amounts of lexical information can be acquired semi-automatically from MRDs and represented in a way that makes it usable by a range of NLP systems. The first essential for this is a well-defined representation language, which is efficiently

---

[5] Since we are just making use of the monolingual sense extension mechanism here we can rely on that to handle cases where the sense extension is blocked.

[6] It does not necessarily matter for translation purposes whether the rule can fully predict the effects of the sense extension; even if the rule is used statically to encode the regular aspects of the relationship between two lexicalised items, an appropriate translation link will be generated if the monolingual processes are sufficiently similar.

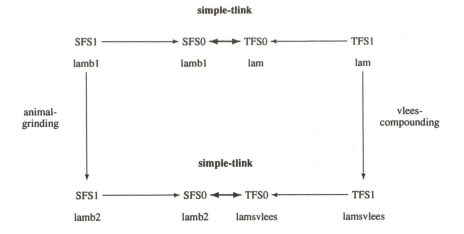

Figure 9.4: Tlink rule for animal grinding and compounding with *vlees*

implementable. We have chosen to use an LRL which is relatively 'theory-neutral' in the same sense as PATR-II (Shieber, 1986); it could be used to implement different linguistic theories. The second essential requirement is to have some theory of the data to be represented which can be encoded in the LRL. Sanfilippo's chapter describes one such theory for verbs; it also illustrates one advantage that our LRL has over PATR-II, in that the type system makes the encoding of the theory more explicit. It would be, however, possible to make use of the information encoded even if a different treatment were adopted; for example, deriving a verb lexicon for a system which did not rely on theta roles to express semantic argument structure would be straightforward, because this information could simply be ignored.

Clearly linguistic theories, their encoding in the LRL and even the LRL itself may have to be modified in response to the data. It is not currently possible to construct a large lexicon which incorporates lexical semantic information without developing the linguistic theory, since formal lexical semantics is a relatively undeveloped field. In our discussion of defaults in the LRL we will show that there are problematic areas, where modifications are required. However, even if further changes are made to the LRL, most, if not all, of the existing data will be reusable, because the current language has been explicitly specified.

Acknowledgements

This work and that reported in the subsequent chapters was supported by Esprit grant BRA 3030. We are grateful to our colleagues on ACQUILEX in the

Universities of Pisa and Amsterdam, University College Dublin and the Universitat Politecnica de Catalunya, Barcelona, for discussions on the LKB, to John Carroll for his advice and help on the design and construction of the software and to Bob Carpenter for his detailed comments on our use of typed feature structures.

10 Types and Constraints in the LKB

VALERIA DE PAIVA

Introduction

This chapter describes — from a mathematical perspective — the system of typed feature structures used in the ACQUILEX Lexical Knowledge Base (LK-B). We concentrate on describing the type system the LKB takes as input, making explicit the necessary conditions on the type hierarchy and explaining how — mathematically — our system of constraints works. It is assumed that the reader is familiar with basic unification-based formalisms like PATR-II, as explained in Shieber (1986). It must also be said from the start that our approach draws heavily on the work on *typed feature structures* by Carpenter (1990, 1992).

The LKB works basically through unification on (typed) feature structures. Since most of the time we deal with *typed* feature structures (defined in section 10.2) we will normally drop the qualifier and talk about feature structures. When necessary, to make a distinction, we refer to structures in PATR-II and similar systems as *untyped* feature structures. Feature structures are defined over a (fixed) *finite* set of features FEAT and over a (fixed) type hierarchy $\langle \text{TYPE}, \sqsubseteq \rangle$. Given FEAT and $\langle \text{TYPE}, \sqsubseteq \rangle$ we can define $\mathcal{F}$ the collection of all feature structures over FEAT and $\langle \text{TYPE}, \sqsubseteq \rangle$. But we are interested in feature structures which are *well-formed* with respect to a set of constraints. To describe constraints and well-formedness of feature structures we specify a function $C: \text{TYPE} \rightarrow \mathcal{F}$, which corresponds to an association of a constraint feature structure $C(t_i)$ to each type t_i in the type hierarchy TYPE. The constraint feature structure $C(t_i)$ imposes conditions on all well-formed feature structures of type t_i. We call the combination of FEAT, $\langle \text{TYPE}, \sqsubseteq \rangle$ and the constraint function C the *type system*.

Initially we define the type hierarchies $\langle \text{TYPE}, \sqsubseteq \rangle$ we deal with and then formalise our notion of feature structures and some operations over them. Next we describe our kind of constraints and what it means for a feature structure to be well-formed in our system. Then we discuss briefly internal and external logics of feature structures. A short section concludes comparing this with related work, especially Carpenter's.

10.1 The Type Hierarchy

The type hierarchy is a partially ordered set (or poset) $\langle \text{TYPE}, \sqsubseteq \rangle$ with two extra properties. Before describing these properties we recall that if $\langle \text{TYPE}, \sqsubseteq \rangle$ is a poset, it satisfies:

- (reflexivity) For any t in TYPE, $t \sqsubseteq t$.
- (anti-symmetry) If $t \sqsubseteq s$ and $s \sqsubseteq t$ in $\langle \text{TYPE}, \sqsubseteq \rangle$, then $s = t$.
- (transitivity) If $t_1 \sqsubseteq t_2$ and $t_2 \sqsubseteq t_3$ then $t_1 \sqsubseteq t_3$.

We adopt the convention that the most general type appears at the top of any diagram. The type hierarchy is ordered by $\sqsubseteq$ (which can be read 'is more specific than'). For example:

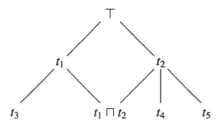

It is a straightforward consequence of the definition of a poset that the order '$\sqsubseteq$' has *no cycles*, i.e if $t_1 \sqsubset t_2$ then $t_2 \not\sqsubseteq t_1$ — where we write $t_1 \sqsubset t_2$ for $t_1 \sqsubseteq t_2$ and $t_1 \neq t_2$. (Suppose it had a cycle, i.e. $t_2 \sqsubseteq t_1$; then using $t_1 \sqsubseteq t_2$ and anti-symmetry we have $t_1 = t_2$, a contradiction!)

Following Carpenter we call a subset $S \subseteq \text{TYPE}$ *consistent*[1] iff there is some t_0 in TYPE such that $t_0 \sqsubseteq t$ for any t in S. In the example above, for instance, the sets $\{t_1, t_2\}$ and $\{t_2, t_4\}$ are consistent sets, but $\{t_4, t_5\}$ is not, so the first two sets have meets, respectively $t_1 \sqcap t_2$ and t_4, while the third set has not. Then we can define:

Definition 1 *A type hierarchy* $\langle \text{TYPE}, \sqsubseteq \rangle$ *is a (non-empty) poset with two extra properties:*

1. *Every* consistent *set of types* $S \subseteq \text{TYPE}$ *has a* unique *greatest lower bound or meet (notation* $\sqcap S$ *).*
2. *The partial order* $\langle \text{TYPE}, \sqsubseteq \rangle$ *has no unary branches, i.e. no type may have exactly one immediate subtype. If* $t_2 \sqsubset t_1$ *and there is no intermediate type* s *such that* $t_2 \sqsubset s$ *and* $s \sqsubset t_1$ *then there must be some other subtype* t_3 *such that* $t_3 \sqsubset t_1$ *and* $t_3 \not\sqsubseteq t_2$.

Note that the empty set is (vacuously) consistent, as for any t_0 in TYPE it satisfies the condition that $t_0 \sqsubseteq t$ for all t's in the empty set. Hence the partial

---

[1] The usual term in Lattice Theory is bounded, but consistent seems more expressive.

order $\langle \text{TYPE}, \sqsubseteq \rangle$ must have a maximal element $\top$ which is the meet of the (consistent) empty set, $\top = \sqcap \emptyset$. This element $\top$ is such that $t \sqsubseteq \top$ for any t in TYPE. The first property says that the type hierarchy $\langle \text{TYPE}, \sqsubseteq \rangle$ is (the dual of) a bounded complete poset, cf. definition in Gunther and Scott (1991). This property could be re-stated as saying that $\langle \text{TYPE}, \sqsubseteq \rangle$ is a 'consistently complete meet-semilattice'.[2]

If $\langle \text{TYPE}, \sqsubseteq \rangle$ is finite then all (non-empty) joins are defined. Thus we have a poset $\langle \text{TYPE}, \sqsubseteq \rangle$ with two operations, a *partial* operation of taking binary meets $\sqcap$ - or greatest lower bounds - and a total operation of taking joins $\sqcup$ - or lowest upper bounds.

The prohibition of unary branches means that posets like

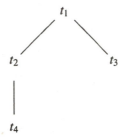

are not allowed. The no-unary-branching condition is desirable because the type system must be 'intuitively complete', where by complete we mean that whatever is said in the partial-order is all that can be said about the types being described. Hence if we say

the interpretation we have in mind is that t_2 things are t_1 and t_3 things are t_1 and things which are t_1 are either t_2 or t_3 but nothing else. Thus if we did have the situation above where t_4 is the only subtype of t_2 we would be stating that everything which was of type t_2 was also of type t_4 (as well as the inverse). To specify both in the hierarchy could lead to inconsistency (with respect to the specification of constraints, for example) so unary branches are disallowed.

We can make the meet $\sqcap$ operation total if we add the join of the empty-set $\bot = \sqcup \emptyset$ to $\langle \text{TYPE}, \sqsubseteq \rangle$. But even if we do add $\bot$ to make $\langle \text{TYPE}, \sqsubseteq \rangle$ a lattice, this lattice need not be distributive, not even modular, as the example below from Carpenter (1990) shows

---

[2] Note that a consistently complete meet-semilattice is *not* a meet-semilattice, since it does not have all binary meets, only the *consistent* ones.

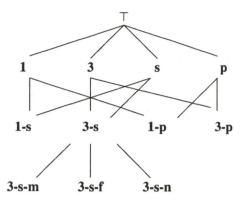

Adding $\perp$ to the poset above, we have:

$$(\textbf{3-s-m} \sqcup \textbf{3-s-f}) \sqcap \textbf{3-s-n} = \textbf{3-s-n}$$

$$\neq (\textbf{3-s-m} \sqcap \textbf{3-s-n}) \sqcup (\textbf{3-s-f} \sqcap \textbf{3-s-n}) = \perp$$

Some implementations of systems similar to ours assume a lattice of types and a lattice of feature structures. This can always be achieved by a process of completion of the partial order and several different completion processes are possible; see, for instance, Davey and Priestley (1990). If we do add *only* $\perp$ to $\langle \mathsf{TYPE}, \sqsubseteq \rangle$, we call the resulting type hierarchy $\langle \mathsf{TYPE}, \sqsubseteq \rangle_\perp$. In this case we have an inclusion,

$$\langle \mathsf{TYPE}, \sqsubseteq \rangle \xrightarrow{\ incl\ } \langle \mathsf{TYPE}, \sqsubseteq \rangle_\perp$$

Condition 1 on the definition of the type hierarchy $\langle \mathsf{TYPE}, \sqsubseteq \rangle$ seems necessary for the constructions we want to make, at least if one insists on a unique value for the unification of feature structures. Condition 2, on the other hand, is interesting, but not necessary. In his most recent work Carpenter drops this condition and, in effect, so do we, since the introduction of unary branches cannot practically be avoided while developing a type system.

10.2   Feature Structures

In this section we define formally the feature structures we shall be dealing with and compare our definition with the traditional (untyped) PATR-II style one, as in Moshier and Rounds (1987). We define the collection $\mathcal{F}$ of feature structures over the (fixed) set of features FEAT and the (fixed) type hierarchy $\langle \mathsf{TYPE}, \sqsubseteq \rangle$. Our feature structures are an acyclic variant of Carpenter's (typed) *quasi-feature structures*.

Definition 2   *A feature structure is a tuple* $F = \langle Q, q_0, \delta, \alpha \rangle$ *where*

- Q *is a (non-empty) finite set of (connected, acyclic) nodes;*

- $q_0 \in Q$ *is the initial (or root) node;*
- $\alpha \colon Q \to$ TYPE *is a* total *node typing function and* $\langle$TYPE$, \sqsubseteq\rangle$ *is a type hierarchy as in the previous section;*
- $\delta \colon Q \times$ FEAT $\to Q$ *is a partial transition function, where* FEAT *is a (non-empty) finite set.*

The collection of all possible feature structures for a given set FEAT *and poset* $\langle$TYPE$, \sqsubseteq\rangle$ *is denoted* $\mathcal{F}$.

An example of a feature structure F_1 in attribute-value matrix notation is:

$$
\begin{bmatrix}
\textbf{phrase} \\
\text{AGR} = \begin{bmatrix}
\textbf{agr} \\
\text{PERS} = \textbf{1} \\
\text{NUM} = \textbf{sing}
\end{bmatrix}
\end{bmatrix}
$$

In this case the set of nodes consists of $\{q_0, q_1, q_2, q_3\}$, where $\alpha(q_0) = \textbf{phrase}$, $\alpha(q_1) = \textbf{agr}$, $\alpha(q_2) = \textbf{1}$, $\alpha(q_3) = \textbf{sing}$, $\delta(q_0, \text{AGR}) = q_1$, etc. A notational convention is that types are written in **boldface** and features are written in SMALL CAPITALS within attribute-value matrices (with the exception of the type $\top$). In mathematical definitions t's are used as variables for types, f's as variables for features and F's as variables for feature structures.

The intuition behind this definition goes back to Kasper and Rounds' formalisation of the logic of feature structures; the main idea being that an attribute-value matrix like:

$$
\begin{bmatrix}
\text{AGR} = \begin{bmatrix}
\text{PERS} = \textbf{3} \\
\text{NUM} = \textbf{sing}
\end{bmatrix}
\end{bmatrix}
$$

could be thought of as a deterministic automaton (Kasper and Rounds, 1986). By a 'connected set of nodes' we mean that every node $q \in Q$ is reachable from the initial node q_0 by using the transition function δ. More precisely, there exists a sequence of features $\langle f_1 \ldots f_{n-1}\rangle$ in FEAT* and a sequence of nodes $\langle q_0, q_1, \ldots q_n\rangle$ such that $\delta(q_i, f_{i+1}) = q_{i+1}$ and $q_n = q$.

Recall that in the traditional definition of a feature structure as in, for instance, Carpenter's paper in this volume (after Moshier and Rounds, 1987), one has a *partial (injective) atomic value* function α from nodes to atoms. But only nodes for which no features are defined by the transition function can have atomic values, so that if $\alpha(q)$ is defined then $\delta(q, f)$ is undefined for all f in FEAT. Some types in the definition above will correspond to the 'nodes that do not have features' in the traditional definition and we shall call them *atomic* types. For instance **sing** and **1** in the example above are atomic types.

The main differences between the traditional definition and the one above are that:

- In our definition *all* nodes, not only *some* of the terminal ones, have types.
- The set of types TYPE is now endowed with a partial order.

People of a very abstract turn of mind could write the Moshier-Rounds definition as a triple of functions,

$$1 \xrightarrow{\;q_0\;} Q \times \text{FEAT} \xrightarrow{\;\delta\;} Q \xrightarrow{\;\alpha\;} \text{ATOMS}$$

where a map $1 \xrightarrow{q_0} Q$ picks up one object, q_0, in the set Q; the arrows $\rightharpoonup$ for δ and α are partial maps; α is injective and the domain of definition of α is given by

$$dom(\alpha) = \{q \in Q \mid \delta(q,f) \text{ is undefined } \forall f \in \text{FEAT}\}$$

They could also write our definition as

$$1 \xrightarrow{\;q_0\;} Q \times \text{FEAT} \xrightarrow{\;\delta\;} Q \xrightarrow{\;\alpha\;} \langle \text{TYPE}, \sqsubseteq \rangle$$

where, in contrast, the function α is total and TYPE is endowed with a partial order. Pollard and Moshier's (1990) *ordinary feature structures* are slightly different in that the function α is partial, non-terminal nodes can have *SORTS* (and *SORTS* may have a partial ordering on them) and the acyclicity condition is dropped. In all cases one should remember that the set Q is 'rooted' (or connected) by the transition function.

One of the immediate consequences of our definition is that, as every feature structure has a unique initial node q_0, every feature structure has a type. We say that

Definition 3 *The type of the feature structure $F = \langle Q, q_0, \delta, \alpha \rangle$ is the type of its initial node, that is, $\alpha(q_0)$.*

Note that this definition induces a function *type-of*: $\mathcal{F} \rightarrow$ TYPE. For example the type of feature structure F_1 in the example above is **phrase**.

Corresponding to the distinction between atomic and non-atomic types we have atomic and non-atomic feature structures. The feature structure F_1 in the example above is a non-atomic feature structure, whereas the feature structure consisting of the single type [**sing**] is an atomic one.

One similarity between the definitions above is that they can be extended to 'paths' π in FEAT*. That is, every feature structure F over FEAT gives rise to a map

$$Q \times \text{FEAT}^* \xrightarrow{\;\delta^*\;} Q$$

where

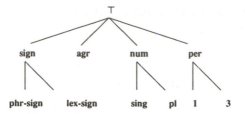

Figure 10.1: An example of a type hierarchy

- $\delta^*(q, \lambda) = q$ if λ is the empty path,
- $\delta^*(q, \pi.f) = \delta^*(\delta^*(q, \pi), f)$.

10.3   Subsumption of Feature Structures

In this section we describe the order on the collection $\mathcal{F}$ of feature structures and describe the operation of restricting a feature structure F to a node q or a path π over FEAT.

It is clear that, as in the traditional setting, we have a natural order in the collection of feature structures $\mathcal{F}$. We call this order $\sqsubseteq$, overloading the symbol. Intuitively $\sqsubseteq$ means is subsumed by ('is-more-specific-than'). Subsumption is like usual subsumption of feature structures, with the added condition that the order on types is 'preserved' (see precise definition below).

For example, given the type hierarchy in Figure 10.1, we have:

$$\begin{bmatrix} \textbf{phr-sign} \\ \text{AGR} = \begin{bmatrix} \textbf{agr} \\ \text{PERS} = 1 \\ \text{NUM} = \textbf{sing} \end{bmatrix} \end{bmatrix} \sqsubseteq \begin{bmatrix} \textbf{sign} \\ \text{AGR} = \begin{bmatrix} \textbf{agr} \\ \text{PERS} = 1 \\ \text{NUM} = \top \end{bmatrix} \end{bmatrix}$$

If F_1 and F_2 are feature structures of types t_1 and t_2 respectively, then $F_1 \sqsubseteq F_2$ only if $t_1 \sqsubseteq t_2$. Another example:

$$\begin{bmatrix} \textbf{agr} \\ \text{PERS} = 1 \\ \text{NUM} = \textbf{sing} \end{bmatrix} \sqsubseteq \begin{bmatrix} \textbf{agr} \\ \text{PERS} = 1 \end{bmatrix}$$

But note that the subsumption order is not simply a containment order. For example, in the feature structures below, F_1 contains F_2, but $F_1 \not\sqsubseteq F_2$.

$$F_1 = \begin{bmatrix} \textbf{sign} \\ \text{AGR} = \begin{bmatrix} \textbf{agr} \\ \text{PERS} = 1 \\ \text{NUM} = \textbf{sing} \end{bmatrix} \end{bmatrix} \qquad F_2 = \begin{bmatrix} \textbf{agr} \\ \text{PERS} = 1 \end{bmatrix}$$

This order in the collection of feature structures $\mathcal{F}$ is mathematically expressed using feature structure morphisms, following Moshier and Rounds.

Definition 4   *Given feature structures F_1 and F_2, $\langle Q_1, q_0, \delta_1, \alpha_1 \rangle$ and $\langle Q_2, q_0', \delta_2, \alpha_2 \rangle$, respectively, in $\mathcal{F}$ we say a total map $h: Q_1 \to Q_2$ is a feature structure morphism iff*

- *h sends the initial node q_0 of F_1 to the initial node q_0' of F_2, that is, $h(q_0) = q_0'$.*
- *h preserves the partial map structure of F_1, that is, the following diagram 'commutes',*

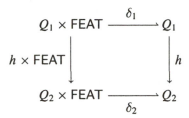

this means that if $\delta_1(q,f)$ is defined (written as '$\delta_1(q,f) \downarrow$') then $\delta_2(h(q),f) \downarrow$ and $h(\delta_1(q,f)) = \delta_2(h(q),f)$.
- *h 'preserves' the order in $\langle \mathsf{TYPE}, \sqsubseteq \rangle$, that is, $\alpha_2(h(q)) \sqsubseteq \alpha_1(q)$.*

For feature structures F_1 and F_2 in $\mathcal{F}$, we say $F_1 \sqsubseteq F_2$ iff there is a feature structure morphism $h: F_2 \rightarrow F_1$.

Note the 'opposite' of the Carpenter (or Pollard and Moshier, 1990) order in the definition above. With our definition of feature structures, the least informative feature structure is $[\top]$, that is, $F \sqsubseteq [\top]$ for any F in $\mathcal{F}$.

This notion of morphism is a natural extension of the definition of homomorphism of untyped feature structures in Moshier and Rounds. The main difference is that for untyped feature structures, if $\alpha_1(q)$ is defined, then $\alpha_2(h(q))$ is defined and *equal* (rather than less than or equal) to $\alpha_1(q)$.

Looking at the definition of morphism of feature structures abstractly we have:

$$
\begin{array}{ccccccc}
1 & \longrightarrow & Q_1 \times \mathsf{FEAT} & \xrightarrow{\delta_1} & Q_1 & \xrightarrow{\alpha_1} & \mathsf{TYPE} \\
\| & & \big\downarrow {\scriptstyle h \times \mathsf{FEAT}} & & \big\downarrow {\scriptstyle h} & \sqsubseteq & \| \\
1 & \longrightarrow & Q_2 \times \mathsf{FEAT} & \xrightarrow[\delta_2]{} & Q_2 & \xrightarrow[\alpha_2]{} & \mathsf{TYPE}
\end{array}
$$

First note that the order in $\mathcal{F}$ is *not* a partial order, but only a *pre-order*. We can have $F_1 \sqsubseteq F_2$ and $F_2 \sqsubseteq F_1$ without F_1 and F_2 being the same; in this case they are called alphabetic variants, which we write as $F_1 \sim F_2$, following Carpenter. We can make this pre-order a poset by taking equivalence relations the usual way. The equivalence classes of feature structures are called by Moshier (1988) *abstract feature structures*.

We need some extra easy definitions. Given a feature structure $F = \langle Q, q_0, \delta, \alpha \rangle$ and a node q in Q we can define $F|_q$, the restriction of F to q, as the feature structure that starts in q and is the restriction of F - as a partial map. More formally:

Definition 5   *Given a feature structure F of the form $\langle Q, q_0, \delta, \alpha \rangle$ and a node q in Q we define $F|_q$ the restriction of F to q, as the feature structure $F' = \langle Q', q_0', \delta', \alpha' \rangle$, such that:*

1. *The new initial node q_0' is q,*
2. *The set of nodes Q' is the subset of the set Q of nodes of F, reachable from q, i.e.*

$$Q' = \{q \in Q \mid \delta(q, \pi) \text{ is defined, for all } \pi \in \mathsf{FEAT}^*\}$$

3. *The transition function $\delta'(q, f)$ is the restriction of δ to Q'.*
4. *The typing function α' is the restriction of α to Q'.*

We can also define the restriction $F@\pi$ of a feature structure F to a path $\pi \in \mathsf{FEAT}^*$. The definition above would only change in the two first clauses; the new initial node is $q_0' = \delta(q_0, \pi)$ and the new set of nodes is the subset of Q reachable from q_0'. Viewed this way each feature f or path π determines a partial function from feature structures to feature structures, the basis of other formalisations of feature structure logics (cf. Smolka, 1988).

Another definition extracts features from a node.

Definition 6   *Given a feature structure F and a node q in F, we define features of the node q in F or $Feat(\langle F, q \rangle)$, as the set of features labelling the edges coming out of the node q. Thus if F is given by $\langle Q, q_0, \delta, \alpha \rangle$ and $\delta(q, f)$ is defined then the feature f is in $Feat(\langle F, q \rangle)$ or*

$$Feat(\langle F, q \rangle) = \{f \in \mathsf{FEAT} \mid \delta(q, f) \text{ is defined}\}$$

We call $Feat_0(F)$ the set of features that appear on the top level of the feature structure F, that is, $Feat_0(F) = Feat(\langle F, q_0 \rangle)$.

It is reasonable to ask *why* do we want the morphisms in $\mathcal{F}$ in the direction of definition 4, which is not the direction chosen by Carpenter or Pollard and Moshier. The same question could be asked about the direction of the order on TYPE. The answer is given by the use of feature structures. The main operation one wants to perform with feature structures is *unification*, which we describe in the next section. Unification of F_1 and F_2 is the *conjunction* of the information contained in F_1 and F_2. Taking the order on TYPE and the morphisms as defined here, unification corresponds to 'meet' $\sqcap$ in the pre-order $\mathcal{F}$, the natural choice for logical conjunction.

10.4 Operations on Feature Structures

We want to define two main operations on feature structures, *generalisation* and *unification*. We give algebraic definitions of both unification and generalisation, following Carpenter, but since algebraically *generalisation* is easier, we start with this operation.

The operation of generalisation $\sqcup: \mathcal{F} \times \mathcal{F} \to \mathcal{F}$ is much more natural from the algebraic viewpoint than the more useful unification. Given feature structures F_1 and F_2, respectively, $\langle Q_1, q_0, \delta_1, \alpha_1 \rangle$ and $\langle Q_2, q_0', \delta_2, \alpha_2 \rangle$ in $\mathcal{F}$, we can take the product $\delta_1 \times \delta_2$ of the partial maps δ_1 and δ_2 and transform it in a 'product of automata' as follows:

$$
\begin{array}{ccc}
1 & & \text{TYPE} \\
\Big\downarrow {\scriptstyle\langle q_0, q_0' \rangle} & & \Big\uparrow {\scriptstyle\sqcup} \\
(Q_1 \otimes Q_2) \times \text{FEAT} \xrightarrow{\ \delta_1 \otimes \delta_2\ } Q_1 \otimes Q_2 \xrightarrow{\ \alpha_1 \times \alpha_2\ } \text{TYPE} \times \text{TYPE}
\end{array}
$$

To be precise:

Definition 7 *Given feature structures F_1 and F_2 their generalisation is the feature structure $F_1 \sqcup F_2$ given by:*

$$F_1 \sqcup F_2 = \langle Q_1 \otimes Q_2, \langle q_0, q_0' \rangle, \delta_1 \otimes \delta_2, \alpha_1 \otimes \alpha_2 \rangle$$

- *The initial node of $F_1 \sqcup F_2$ is the pair $\langle q_0, q_0' \rangle$.*
- *The transition function $\delta_1 \otimes \delta_2$ of $F_1 \sqcup F_2$ is the restriction of the product function $\delta_1 \times \delta_2$ given by the composition:*

$$Q_1 \times Q_2 \times \text{FEAT} \xrightarrow{\Delta} Q_1 \times Q_2 \times \text{FEAT} \times \text{FEAT} \xrightarrow{\delta_1 \times \delta_2} Q_1 \times Q_2$$

Thus $\delta_1 \otimes \delta_2$ is given by restricting $\delta_1 \times \delta_2$ to the pairs

$$\langle \delta_1(q_1, f), \delta_2(q_2, f') \rangle$$

where the feature 'read' is the same, i.e $f = f'$.
- *The set of nodes $Q_1 \otimes Q_2$, is the subset of $Q_1 \times Q_2$ rooted by the transition function $\delta_1 \otimes \delta_2$ above. Thus (q_1, q_2) is in $Q_1 \otimes Q_2$, if there exists a path $\pi \in \text{FEAT}^*$ such that*

$$\delta_1 \otimes \delta_2(\langle q_0, q_0' \rangle, \pi) = (q_1, q_2)$$

- *The typing function $\alpha_1 \otimes \alpha_2$ is given by the composition of the product $\alpha_1 \times \alpha_2$ with the function generalisation on types $\sqcup: \text{TYPE} \times \text{TYPE} \to \text{TYPE}$ restricted to the nodes in $Q_1 \otimes Q_2$.*

An easy example should help to make things clear. Suppose we have F_1 and F_2 below and we know **phr-sign** $\sqsubseteq$ **sign**,

$$
F_1 = \begin{bmatrix} \textbf{phr-sign} \\ \text{AGR} = \begin{bmatrix} \textbf{agr} \\ \text{PERS} = \textbf{1} \\ \text{NUM} = \textbf{sing} \end{bmatrix} \\ \text{RGA} = \top \end{bmatrix}
\qquad
F_2 = \begin{bmatrix} \textbf{sign} \\ \text{AGR} = \begin{bmatrix} \textbf{agr} \\ \text{PERS} = \textbf{1} \\ \text{NUM} = \textbf{pl} \end{bmatrix} \end{bmatrix}
$$

Generalising, we end up with $F_1 \sqcup F_2$ given by:

$$
F_1 \sqcup F_2 = \begin{bmatrix} \textbf{sign} \\ \text{AGR} = \begin{bmatrix} \textbf{agr} \\ \text{PERS} = \textbf{1} \\ \text{NUM} = \textbf{num} \end{bmatrix} \end{bmatrix}
$$

Thus generalisation corresponds to taking the product of the partial maps restricting to the diagonal in FEAT and making the resulting structure 'rooted', i.e. getting rid of the unreachable nodes. In the example above we have 20 nodes in $Q_1 \times Q_2$, but 16 are isolated, thus only 4 appear in $Q_1 \otimes Q_2$.

Note that $F_1 \sqcup F_2$ is the *lowest upper bound* of F_1 and F_2 in the subsumption order. That is, $F_1 \sqsubseteq F_1 \sqcup F_2$ and $F_2 \sqsubseteq F_1 \sqcup F_2$ and if $F_1 \sqsubseteq G$ and $F_2 \sqsubseteq G$ then $F_1 \sqcup F_2 \sqsubseteq G$. Generalisation is a *total* function; the feature structure $[\top]$ will always be an upper bound.

Another operation we could define looks very much like generalisation, but uses the 'meet' $\sqcap$ operation on types, which makes it a partial map, if we use the type hierarchy $\langle \text{TYPE}, \sqsubseteq \rangle$,

$$\oplus: \mathcal{F} \times \mathcal{F} \rightharpoonup \mathcal{F}$$

$$
\begin{array}{ccc}
1 & & \text{TYPE} \\[0.5em]
\Big\downarrow \langle q_0, q'_0 \rangle & & \Big\uparrow \sqcap \\[0.5em]
(Q_1 \otimes Q_2) \times \text{FEAT} \xrightarrow{\ \delta_1 \otimes \delta_2\ } Q_1 \otimes Q_2 \xrightarrow{\ \alpha_1 \times \alpha_2\ } \text{TYPE} \times \text{TYPE}
\end{array}
$$

But if we use $\langle \text{TYPE}, \sqsubseteq \rangle_\perp$ it is another total operation. In the example above, we end up with $F_1 \oplus F_2$ as

$$
\begin{bmatrix} \textbf{phr-sign} \\ \text{AGR} = \begin{bmatrix} \textbf{agr} \\ \text{PERS} = \textbf{1} \\ \text{NUM} = \perp \end{bmatrix} \\ \text{RGA} = \top \end{bmatrix}
$$

The operation $\oplus$ has not been discussed in the literature, probably because it is not clear that it has any linguistic utility.

10.4.1 Unification

Unification of feature structures is defined as a *partial* function denoted by $\sqcap: \mathcal{F} \times \mathcal{F} \rightharpoonup \mathcal{F}$. The definition for (typed) feature structures follows broadly the definition for untyped feature structures. Carpenter presents a very simple algorithm — attributed to Moshier — to compute it. Intuitively, the difference from untyped feature structures unification is that:

> If F_1 and F_2 are feature structures of types t_1 and t_2 respectively, then $F_1 \sqcap F_2$ has to have type $t_1 \sqcap t_2$. Thus if $t_1 \sqcap t_2$ does not exist then unification fails.

If in F_1 and F_2 below **phr-sign** $\sqsubseteq$ **sign**:

$$
F_1 = \begin{bmatrix} \textbf{phr-sign} \\ \text{AGR} = \begin{bmatrix} \textbf{agr} \\ \text{PERS} = 1 \end{bmatrix} \end{bmatrix} \quad
F_2 = \begin{bmatrix} \textbf{sign} \\ \text{AGR} = \begin{bmatrix} \textbf{agr} \\ \text{NUM} = \textbf{pl} \end{bmatrix} \end{bmatrix}
$$

Then

$$
F_1 \sqcap F_2 = \begin{bmatrix} \textbf{phr-sign} \\ \text{AGR} = \begin{bmatrix} \textbf{agr} \\ \text{PERS} = 1 \\ \text{NUM} = \textbf{pl} \end{bmatrix} \end{bmatrix}
$$

But if F_1 and F_2 are as below and **sing** $\sqcap$ **pl** $= \perp$:

$$
F_1 = \begin{bmatrix} \textbf{phr-sign} \\ \text{AGR} = \begin{bmatrix} \textbf{agr} \\ \text{PERS} = 1 \\ \text{NUM} = \textbf{sing} \end{bmatrix} \end{bmatrix} \quad
F_2 = \begin{bmatrix} \textbf{sign} \\ \text{AGR} = \begin{bmatrix} \textbf{agr} \\ \text{PERS} = 1 \\ \text{NUM} = \textbf{pl} \end{bmatrix} \end{bmatrix}
$$

The unification $F_1 \sqcap F_2$ fails, as the information F_1 and F_2 convey about the feature NUM is not consistent. Finally unifying

$$
F_1 = \begin{bmatrix} \textbf{phr-sign} \\ \text{AGR} = \begin{bmatrix} \textbf{agr} \\ \text{PERS} = 1 \\ \text{NUM} = \textbf{sing} \end{bmatrix} \end{bmatrix} \quad
F_2 = \begin{bmatrix} \textbf{sign} \\ \text{AGR} = \begin{bmatrix} \textbf{agr} \\ \text{PERS} = \top \\ \text{NUM} = \textbf{sing} \end{bmatrix} \end{bmatrix}
$$

we end up with:

$$
F_1 \sqcap F_2 = \begin{bmatrix} \textbf{phr-sign} \\ \text{AGR} = \begin{bmatrix} \textbf{agr} \\ \text{PERS} = 1 \\ \text{NUM} = \textbf{sing} \end{bmatrix} \end{bmatrix}
$$

Now we define unification algebraically in two steps. Recall that to unify feature structures F_1 and F_2 we want to 'union' the partial maps δ_1 and δ_2, making sure that

- the two initial nodes are made the 'same';
- if a feature f appears in both feature structures in a consistent way, this feature appears only once in the unification.

Trying to make the initial nodes the same, we have to check that the relation δ_3 that arises from this 'identification' and subsequent ones is really a partial map, not a relation. Note that, given two feature structures F_1 and F_2, we can (without loss of generality) consider the sets of nodes Q_1 and Q_2 disjoint. We then write $Q_1 + Q_2$ for the disjoint union of Q_1 and Q_2.

Define the union $\delta_1 + \delta_2$ of the transition functions δ_1 and δ_2 by

$$(Q_1 + Q_2) \times \mathsf{FEAT} \xrightarrow{\;\;\delta_1 + \delta_2\;\;} (Q_1 + Q_2)$$

As a graph the partial map $\delta_1 + \delta_2$ is disconnected; it has two initial nodes, and a feature f may appear in both components. Thus to make the initial nodes the same we define an equivalence relation on the set of nodes $Q_1 + Q_2$. Given feature structures $F_1 = \langle Q_1, q_0, \delta_1, \alpha_1 \rangle$ and $F_2 = \langle Q_2, q_0', \delta_2, \alpha_2 \rangle$ in $\mathcal{F}$, we define the equivalence relation '$\bowtie$' on the set $Q_1 + Q_2$ as the least equivalence relation such that:

- $q_0 \bowtie q_0'$;
- $\delta_1(q, f) \bowtie \delta_2(q', f)$ iff both are defined and $q \bowtie q'$.

Because we need to identify nodes in a coherent fashion, the unification operation is more complicated from the algebraic point-of-view than the operation of generalisation. One observation is that having a (partial or not) map $f : A \to B$ and an equivalence relation on A, we could define an induced map $[f]$ on the equivalence classes of A by saying that $[f]([a]) = [f(a)]$ if whenever $a \sim a'$ then $f(a) = f(a')$. This is to take the identity equivalence relation on B and it is exactly what is done with unification of untyped feature structures, where B is the set of *ATOMS* and the map α names the atomic nodes. When we merge the graphs of F_1 and F_2 (as untyped feature structures), we say $F_1 \sqcap F_2$ is defined if $\alpha([q']) = a$ for any $q' \in [q]$. But since we have a partial order on the set of types TYPE there are more possibilities.

We define the unification of typed feature structures F_1 and F_2 as follows:

Definition 8 *Given feature structures* $F_1 = \langle Q_1, q_0, \delta_1, \alpha_1 \rangle$ *and* $F_2 = \langle Q_2, q_0', \delta_2, \alpha_2 \rangle$ *in* $\mathcal{F}$, *their unification* $F_1 \sqcap F_2$ *is the feature structure*

$$F_1 \sqcap F_2 = \langle Q_\bowtie, [q_0], \delta_\bowtie, \alpha_\bowtie \rangle$$

- *The set of nodes* $Q_\bowtie$ *is given by the set of equivalence classes* $(Q_1 + Q_2)/\bowtie$.
- *The new initial node is the equivalence class* $[q_0]$.
- *The transition function* $\delta_\bowtie$ *is given by the equivalence class of the union of the transition functions* $\delta_1 + \delta_2$, *when it is defined, that is:*

$$\delta_\bowtie([q], f) = [\delta_1 + \delta_2(q, f)] \text{ if } \delta_1 + \delta_2(q, f) \text{ is defined}$$

- *The new typing function $\alpha_\bowtie$ is the 'meet' of the types in the equivalence class of q, that is $\alpha_\bowtie([q]) = \sqcap\{\alpha_i(q')|q' \bowtie q\}$*

provided that $F_1 \sqcap F_2$ is not cyclic. If $F_1 \sqcap F_2$ is cyclic we say that unification fails.

In the same way we could do generalisation with $\sqcup$ or $\sqcap$ on types, we can do unification with either. Looking at it from the graph-theoretical viewpoint we are glueing or merging the graphs, if they are consistent, and then choosing either $\sqcup$ or $\sqcap$ for the result type. The operation described above — true unification — chooses the meet $\sqcap$ of types. We could as well define an operation $\oslash: \mathcal{F} \times \mathcal{F} \longrightarrow \mathcal{F}$, doing unification of graphs but choosing the join $\sqcup$ of types.

Unification could also be defined through the subsumption order of feature structures, which is a theorem in Carpenter (1992). The unification may FAIL, but if it does succeed, the result of the unification is the meet (or *greatest lower bound*) of the feature structures being unified. Thus $F_1 \sqcap F_2 \sqsubseteq F_1$ and $F_1 \sqcap F_2 \sqsubseteq F_2$ and if $G \sqsubseteq F_1$ and $G \sqsubseteq F_2$, then $G \sqsubseteq F_1 \sqcap F_2$. That is intuitively reasonable, as the unification gives us the *conjunction* of the information in F_1 and F_2, if they are consistent.

It is worth noting that a product is used for 'join' of information and a coproduct, albeit a complicated one, is used for a 'meet' of information. This is reminiscent of the situation in Domain Theory; the similarity between feature structures and domains has been pointed out and used by several people in different ways; see Pereira and Shieber (1984), Carpenter (1990, 1992) and Pollard and Moshier (1990) .

10.4.2 Comparing Feature Structures

The structure on the type hierarchy TYPE repeats itself on the collection of feature structures $\mathcal{F}$, which is why we have used the same symbols. Thus $\langle \text{TYPE}, \sqsubseteq \rangle$ is a partial order, where $\sqcap$ is called unification of types and $\sqcup$ is called generalisation of types. Also $\langle \mathcal{F}, \sqsubseteq \rangle$ is a pre-order, where $\sqcap$ is given by unification and $\sqcup$ is given by generalisation. The same way two types are consistent if $t_1 \sqcap t_2$ exists, we say that F_1 and F_2 are consistent if their unification $F_1 \sqcap F_2$ exists. Moreover $\langle \mathcal{F}, \sqsubseteq \rangle$ is a bounded complete pre-order. If $F \sqsubseteq F_1$ and $F \sqsubseteq F_2$ then $F_1 \sqcap F_2$ exists and $F \sqsubseteq F_1 \sqcap F_2$. If we deal with $\langle \text{TYPE}, \sqsubseteq \rangle_\perp$ we can say that types are consistent if $t_1 \sqcap t_2$ exists and is different from $\perp$.

Apart from being typed, the feature structures above are very similar to the traditional ones in Shieber's book (1986). In particular, we do not support *cyclic* feature structures, so, as mentioned before, the set of nodes Q is an *acyclic* connected or rooted graph. There are two main reasons to allow cyclic feature structures. One is implementational, since the check for cycles (no occurs-in check) during unification is computationally expensive. The other one is more conceptual, as mathematically one of the problems with the assumption that feature structures are acyclic is that you can start with two acyclic feature structures, and their unification is cyclic. This problem can be 'solved' by checking for cyclicity a posteriori, which is not very elegant.

On the other hand, if one accepts cyclic feature structures, apart from problems with checking for well-formedness (next section), one does not have a meet semi-lattice if the set of nodes is finite (cf. Pollard and Moshier, 1990, p. 297). Also, as Pollard and Sag (1987) put it

> In general, cyclic graphs present certain mathematical and computational complexities which are best avoided, although linguistic applications for them have been suggested from time to time.

One of the differences between the feature structures here and the ones in PATR-II is that, because of the type hierarchy, we can support in the formalism disjunction of atomic values. That happens because we can 'complete' the hierarchy $\langle \mathsf{TYPE}, \sqsubseteq \rangle$ with more 'generic' types. For example we can add a type **num** above the types **sing** and **pl**, which stands for either of the types singular or plural. In the traditional definition of a feature structure, since $\delta: Q \times \mathsf{FEAT} \to Q$ is a partial map, to say that the feature NUMBER could have values **sing** or **pl** on a node q would not be possible — a partial map cannot have two values at some node. Another way to deal with this problem is to introduce a notion of *set-valued* feature structure. This is done, using distinct, but similar, approaches in Pollard and Moshier (1990).

If we write $\langle \mathcal{UF}, \sqsubseteq \rangle$ for PATR-II untyped feature structures (using the Moshier–Rounds definition) and their subsumption order, then we have a map that 'forgets' the (non-atomic) types and the ordering among them

$$\langle \mathcal{F}, \sqsubseteq \rangle \overset{Erase}{\longrightarrow} \langle \mathcal{UF}, \sqsubseteq \rangle$$

but preserves subsumption. We also have a function

$$\langle \mathcal{UF}, \sqsubseteq \rangle \overset{trivtyp}{\longrightarrow} \langle \mathcal{F}, \sqsubseteq \rangle$$

which assigns the trivial type 'T' to every non-terminal node.

10.5   Constraints

So far the typing of feature structures is only providing an ordering on values. Any arbitrary assignment of types is possible and this is intuitively too unconstrained. Types should tell you which features to expect, in principle. Thus the idea here is to 'carve out' from the pre-order of all feature structures $\langle \mathcal{F}, \sqsubseteq \rangle$ a subset, the subset of the *well-formed* feature structures $\langle \mathcal{WF}, \sqsubseteq \rangle$ and these will be well-formed with respect to a given constraining function.

Here we depart substantially from Carpenter's work. Carpenter describes an 'appropriateness specification', that is, a partial map

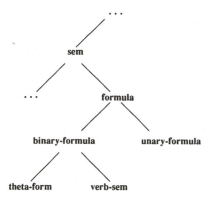

Figure 10.2: Fragment of a type hierarchy

Approp: TYPE × FEAT → TYPE

(satisfying some conditions) which says that for certain types some features are appropriate and yield some other types. This is one possible formalisation of the idea in Pollard and Sag (1987).

The partial map *Approp* is equivalent to a total function

$$\bar{Approp}: \text{TYPE} \to [\text{FEAT} \to \text{TYPE}]$$

which corresponds to associating to each type a list of its appropriate features with types. But a list of features with types can be seen as a very simple (one-level only) feature structure. For example, if we have a fragment of a type hierarchy as in Figure 10.2, then an appropriateness specification for the type **formula**, which has features IND, PRED and ARG1, could be:

$$\begin{bmatrix} \text{formula} \\ \text{IND} = \text{entity} \\ \text{PRED} = \text{logical-pred} \\ \text{ARG1} = \text{sem} \end{bmatrix}$$

and by the way we wrote the list, one can see that it is, in fact, a very simple feature structure. Hence the idea is to generalise appropriateness specifications, by using feature structures instead of one-level only ones.

We generalise the idea of appropriateness specification by associating with each type a whole feature structure in our constraint specification function. Thus every type in ⟨TYPE, ⊑⟩ must have exactly one associated feature structure which acts as a constraint on all feature structures of that type. This associated feature structure is given by the function

$$C: \langle \text{TYPE}, \sqsubseteq \rangle \to \langle \mathcal{F}, \sqsubseteq \rangle$$

but one can think about the constraint specification function C as the set of basic feature structures $C(t_1), C(t_2), \ldots, C(t_k)$ — the constraint feature structures — corresponding to the enumeration of the types $t_1, t_2, \ldots, t_k$ in ⟨TYPE, ⊑⟩.

We think of appropriateness conditions as being (indirectly specified) information which can be extracted from the constraint feature structures $C(t_i)$ by reading only their first level. We actually refer to the 'appropriate features' of a type meaning the top level features of the constraint feature structures $C(t_i)$. Clearly, having feature structures as constraints on types gives us an extra degree of flexibility, as we can impose *re-entrant* constraints.

Any association of types to (their appropriate) features must satisfy some conditions. We proceed to describe the conditions we impose on the constraining function. Similar conditions are imposed by Carpenter and by Pollard and Sag (1987).

The constraints imposed on a type are inherited by all subtypes of this type. In mathematical terms that means that the function C is monotonic, a very reasonable assumption, since its domain is the poset $\langle \mathsf{TYPE}, \sqsubseteq \rangle$ and its codomain the pre-order $\mathcal{F}$ ordered by subsumption $\langle \mathcal{F}, \sqsubseteq \rangle$. Thus:

Monotonicity   Given types t_1 and t_2 if $t_1 \sqsubseteq t_2$ then $C(t_1) \sqsubseteq C(t_2)$

Of course, a subtype may introduce new features — thus if we have the same fragment of a type hierarchy as before and the type **formula** had as its constraint feature structure the previous example, then its subtype **binary-formula** could have as constraint:

$$\begin{bmatrix} \textbf{binary-formula} \\ \text{IND} \;=\; \text{entity} \\ \text{PRED} \;=\; \text{logical-pred} \\ \text{ARG1} \;=\; \text{sem} \\ \text{ARG2} \;=\; \text{sem} \end{bmatrix}$$

But not all monotonic functions $C: \langle \mathsf{TYPE}, \sqsubseteq \rangle \rightarrow \mathcal{F}$ determine a constraint function. Another obvious condition on constraints is:

Type   For a given type t, if $\langle Q, q_0, \delta, \alpha \rangle$ is the feature structure F given by $C(t)$ then $\alpha(q_0) = t$.

Mathematically this means that composing the function C with the function *type-of* gives the identity on the set TYPE; in other words we have a retraction,

$$\mathsf{TYPE} \; \underset{C}{\overset{\textit{type-of}}{\rightleftarrows}} \; \mathcal{F}$$

The condition **Type** is part of the 'modelling convention' in Pollard and Moshier (1990). We also want a condition saying that a feature can only be introduced at one (maximal) point in the type hierarchy — it will be inherited as an appropriate feature by subtypes of that type. (This condition allows us to carry out type inference; see the next section.) Recall from section 10.3 that $Feat_0(F)$ is the set of features that appear on the top level of the feature structure F and that $F|_q$ is the feature structure F starting from the node q.

Given a type $t \in \mathsf{TYPE}$ and a candidate constraint function $C(t)$ let the set of *appropriate features of the type t* be the set of features $AppFeat(t)$ that appear on the top level of the constraint $C(t)$, that is, $Feat_0(C(t))$.

> **Maximal Introduction**   Given *AppFeat* obtained from $C(t)$, say C satisfies a maximal introduction condition if for every feature $f \in \mathsf{FEAT}$ there is a unique type $t = Maxtype(f)$ such that $f \in AppFeat(t)$ and there is no type s such that $t \sqsubset s$ and $f \in Appfeat(s)$.

An appropriateness specification has to satisfy two conditions; the first corresponds to **Monotonicity** and the second to **Maximal Introduction**. Our condition **Type** is not necessary in Carpenter's approach because for each type he gives directly the list of appropriate features and their types.

Another condition on the constraining function C seems very reasonable. This condition says that the constraining feature structures $C(t_i)$ must be compatible with each other.

> **Compatibility**   If $C(t_1) = F_1$ and some t_2 appears in F_1, that is, if F_1 is the feature structure $\langle Q_1, q_0, \delta_1, \alpha_1 \rangle$ and $\alpha_1(q) = t_2$ for some q in Q_1, then $C(t_2) = F_2$ is such that $F_1|_q \sqsubseteq F_2$. Moreover, $Feat_0(F_1|_q) = Feat_0(F_2)$.

The compatibility condition is reminiscent of Sheaf Theory (Tennison, 1975), as it says that *where* the constraining feature structures $C(t_1), C(t_2), \dots, C(t_k)$ overlap they agree with each other.

The compatability condition implies that no constraint feature structure $C(t) = F$ can strictly contain a feature structure of type t or any subtype of t. That is, if F is given by $\langle Q, q_0, \delta, \alpha \rangle$, then for all non-initial nodes $q \in Q$, $q \neq q_0$ the type of the node $\alpha(q) \not\sqsubseteq t$. If such a node existed it would have to be the initial node of a feature structure $F|_q$ which was more specific than F, i.e. $F|_q \sqsubseteq F$, and would therefore itself have to contain such a node, and so on. Thus such a constraint could only be satisfied by a cyclic or infinite structure, and we disallow both of these possibilities.

Note that consistency of the constraining feature structures $C(t_i)$, for *consistent types* t_i is enforced simply by monotonicity of the function C. If types t_1 and t_2 are consistent — as types — $t_1 \sqcap t_2$ exists and $t_1 \sqcap t_2 \sqsubseteq t_1$ and $t_1 \sqcap t_2 \sqsubseteq t_2$. Since the constraining function C is monotonic $C(t_1 \sqcap t_2) \sqsubseteq C(t_1)$ and $C(t_1 \sqcap t_2) \sqsubseteq C(t_2)$. Thus the unification of $C(t_1)$ and $C(t_2)$ as feature structures, $C(t_1) \sqcap C(t_2)$ exists ($\mathcal{F}$ is bounded complete) and is such that $C(t_1 \sqcap t_2) \sqsubseteq C(t_1) \sqcap C(t_2)$. Thus the constraint feature structures $C(t_1)$ and $C(t_2)$ are consistent as feature structures, simply by monotonicity of C.

Definition 9   *A function* $C: \langle \mathsf{TYPE}, \sqsubseteq \rangle \to \langle \mathcal{F}, \sqsubseteq \rangle$ *is a constraint specification function with respect to* FEAT *and* $\langle \mathsf{TYPE}, \sqsubseteq \rangle$ *if it satisfies* **Monotonicity**, **Type**, **Maximal Introduction** *and* **Compatibility**.

Definition 10   *A feature structure* $F = \langle Q, q_0, \delta, \alpha \rangle$ *in the collection of feature structures* $\mathcal{F}$ *is a* well-formed feature structure *with respect to a given constraint specification* C *iff for all* $q \in Q$,

- $F|_q \sqsubseteq C(\alpha(q))$ *and*
- $Feat_0(F|_q) = Feat_0(C(\alpha(q)))$.

We call the collection of all well-formed feature structures $\mathcal{WF}$. $\mathcal{WF}$ *is a pre-order, as the order in* $\langle \mathcal{F}, \sqsubseteq \rangle$ *restricts to* $\mathcal{WF}$.

Recap:

1. We wanted to carve out from the collection of all feature structures $\langle \mathcal{F}, \sqsubseteq \rangle$ a collection of well-formed ones $\langle \mathcal{WF}, \sqsubseteq \rangle$ with good properties.
2. To define well-formed feature structures we use a constraining function $C: \text{TYPE} \rightarrow \langle \mathcal{F}, \sqsubseteq \rangle$. To calculate whether any feature structure F is well-formed we have to calculate some subsumptions and some sets of features.
3. But not any function $C: \text{TYPE} \rightarrow \mathcal{F}$ is a constraining function. To be a constraining function C must satisfy the four conditions **Monotonicity**, **Type**, **Compatibility** and **Maximal Introduction**.

Note that the constraint feature structures $C(t_i)$ are all well-formed by definition, using the compatibility condition, but the definitions are not circular, as the process of checking compatibility of $C(t_i)$'s terminates at the atomic types. Also the function *AppFeat* that we used to define **Maximal Introduction** could be obtained by forgetting some information present in *AppSpec*, namely the target type.

10.5.1   *Type Checking and Type Inferencing*

As mentioned by Copestake *et al.* (this volume) the maximal introduction condition on features makes a form of type inference possible, whereby a feature structure is given the most general type which is consistent with its top level features. As each feature in FEAT has a maximal type $Maxtype(f)$ at which it can be introduced, given a set of features $S \subseteq \text{FEAT}$, either the set $T = \{Maxtype(f) \mid f \in S\}$ is inconsistent or it has a greatest lower bound $\sqcap T$ where that set of features S will become valid. To show that one uses the bounded completeness of TYPE again. This is interesting because we are not assuming any structure on the set of features, FEAT, but the maximal introduction condition induces a notion of 'consistency' of sets of features.

We have a *Well-formed Inference* proposition, analogous to Carpenter's Type Inference theorem, which says:

Proposition 1   *Given a constraint specification function* C *there is a partial map*

$$Fill: \langle \mathcal{F}, \sqsubseteq \rangle \rightarrow \langle \mathcal{WF}, \sqsubseteq \rangle$$

such that for each F in $\langle \mathcal{F}, \sqsubseteq \rangle$, Fill returns a well-formed feature structure $F' = Fill(F)$ or fails.

But note that the procedure to transform any feature structure into a well-formed one may fail.

10.5.2 Unification of Well-Formed Feature Structures

Unification of two well-formed feature structures will involve, in general, unifying with the constraint feature structure associated with the meet of their types in order to produce a well-formed result.

If F_1 and F_2 are well-formed feature structures of types t_1 and t_2 respectively, then $F_1 \sqcap F_2$, if it exists, has type $t_1 \sqcap t_2$. Since F_1 and F_2 are well-formed, in particular we know that $F_1 \sqsubseteq C(t_1)$ and $F_2 \sqsubseteq C(t_2)$. Thus if F_1 and F_2 are consistent, $F_1 \sqcap F_2 \sqsubseteq C(t_1) \sqcap C(t_2)$. But to be well-formed $F_1 \sqcap F_2$ has to satisfy $F_1 \sqcap F_2 \sqsubseteq C(t_1 \sqcap t_2)$ and $C(t_1 \sqcap t_2)$ might be more specific than $C(t_1) \sqcap C(t_2)$.

Consider the following example of a type hierarchy:

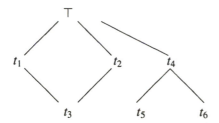

Assume that the types t_4, t_5 and t_6 are atomic (i.e. they have constraints $[t_4]$, $[t_5]$ and $[t_6]$, respectively) and the constraints on types t_1, t_2 and t_3 are:

$$C(t_1) = \begin{bmatrix} t_1 \\ f_1 & = & t_4 \end{bmatrix} \quad C(t_2) = \begin{bmatrix} t_2 \\ f_2 & = & \top \end{bmatrix} \quad C(t_3) = \begin{bmatrix} t_3 \\ f_1 & = & t_5 \\ f_2 & = & \top \\ f_3 & = & \top \end{bmatrix}$$

We then have

$$C(t_1) \sqcap C(t_2) = \begin{bmatrix} t_3 \\ f_1 & = & t_4 \\ f_2 & = & \top \end{bmatrix}$$

Thus $t_3 = t_1 \sqcap t_2$ but $C(t_3) \sqsubset C(t_1) \sqcap C(t_2)$ If we have the following well-formed feature structures

$$F_1 = \begin{bmatrix} t_1 \\ f_1 & = & t_6 \end{bmatrix} \quad F_2 = \begin{bmatrix} t_2 \\ f_2 & = & \top \end{bmatrix}$$

then their unification exists:

$$F_1 \sqcap F_2 = \begin{bmatrix} t_3 \\ f_1 & = & t_6 \\ f_2 & = & \top \end{bmatrix}$$

But $F_1 \sqcap F_2$ is not a well-formed feature structure of type t_3, as $F_1 \sqcap F_2 \not\sqsubseteq C(t_3)$. Moreover it cannot be extended to a well-formed feature structure, because its value for f_1 is inconsistent with the constraint for t_3. Note that the same situation could arise with Carpenter's appropriateness specifications.

The problem of starting with well-formed feature structures and not getting a well-formed unification can be solved by saying that the well-formed unification of F_1 and F_2 is the well-formed feature structure $F_1 \sqcap F_2 \sqcap C(t_1 \sqcap t_2)$, if it exists. Another possibility would be to ask C to preserve meets $C(t_1 \sqcap t_2) \sim C(t_1) \sqcap C(t_2)$, but this is too constraining, since it would also have to apply to the cases where t_1 and t_2 were not immediate parents of $t_1 \sqcap t_2$. Thus the unification operation is not a closed operation in $\mathcal{WF}$. Well-formed unification of well-formed feature structures will result in a structure which is totally well-typed (strongly typed) in Carpenter's sense in that all the features which are possible for that type will be present in the feature structure.

This example illustrates that although the ordering on constraints given by subsumption must be consistent with the type hierarchy, that is, $t_1 \sqsubseteq t_2$ implies $C(t_1) \sqsubseteq C(t_2)$, we do not have that $C(t_1 \sqcap t_2) \sim C(t_1) \sqcap C(t_2)$ nor that $t_1 \sqsubset t_2$ implies $C(t_1) \sqsubset C(t_2)$.

10.6   Internal and External Logics

One can think about logic in the context of feature structures in two rather different ways. One way is to think about the collection $\mathcal{F}$ as a set with some algebraic operations and try and see how these operations compare with the algebraic interpretations of traditional logical connectives. In this sense every set which has the structure of a Boolean algebra is a model of classical propositional logic, any set which has a Heyting algebra structure is a model of intuitionistic propositional logic, any meet-semilattice is a model of a logic of conjunction, etc. That is what we are calling the 'internal logic', as it is logical structure that is already present in the algebraic definitions.

The second way is to produce a logical calculus (or a set of formulas) from the feature structures. Thus we can read the paths in feature structures as atomic formulae and *add* the traditional logical connectives linking these formulae; this was Kasper and Rounds' approach in their seminal paper (1986). Subsequent work has been done to add more logical connectives; for instance, Moshier and Rounds (1987) add intuitionistic implication and negation to the logic of feature structures. To make a clear distinction between the feature structures and the formulae built using the same attributes one talks about the language of attribute-value 'descriptions'. Descriptions are then a neat notation for picking up feature structures and we can talk about disjunctive descriptions — even if they cannot be represented by a single feature structure.

10.6.1 Internal Logic

When the collection of feature structures is regarded as a set with algebraic structure, where we look for the intrinsic logical operators, an unusual propositional logic emerges, where conjunction (or unification) is partial; that is, conjunction only exists for certain pairs of feature structures, the consistent ones. Recall that $[\top]$ behaves as the identity for unification as $F \sqcap [\top] = [\top] \sqcap F = F$ for any F in $\mathcal{F}$.

Note that even with partial conjunction, we could talk about one feature structure implying another $F_1 \Rightarrow F_2$, where we would define $F_1 \Rightarrow F_2$ as the greatest (or least informative) feature structure X such that $F_1 \sqcap X \sqsubseteq F_2$, when $F_1 \sqcap X$ is defined (Pollard and Sag, 1987). Then we have a (closed) logic of 'partial implication and partial conjunction'.

Generalisation gives us a 'kind of' disjunction. But the logical operation given by generalisation in $\mathcal{F}$ is not logical disjunction. For instance, assume that F_1 and F_2 are as below, and **1, 2, 3** are immediate subtypes of **per**,

$$
F_1 = \begin{bmatrix} \text{phr-sign} \\ \text{AGR} = \begin{bmatrix} \text{agr} \\ \text{PERS} = \textbf{1} \\ \text{NUM} = \textbf{sing} \end{bmatrix} \end{bmatrix}
\quad
F_2 = \begin{bmatrix} \text{phr-sign} \\ \text{AGR} = \begin{bmatrix} \text{agr} \\ \text{PERS} = \textbf{2} \\ \text{NUM} = \textbf{sing} \end{bmatrix} \end{bmatrix}
$$

Then intuitively one expects that $F_1 \vee F_2$ should be

$$
\begin{bmatrix} \text{phr-sign} \\ \text{AGR} = \begin{bmatrix} \text{agr} \\ \text{PERS} = \text{`}\textbf{1} \vee \textbf{2}\text{'} \\ \text{NUM} = \textbf{sing} \end{bmatrix} \end{bmatrix}
$$

But $F_1 \sqcup F_2$ is

$$
\begin{bmatrix} \text{phr-sign} \\ \text{AGR} = \begin{bmatrix} \text{agr} \\ \text{PERS} = \textbf{per} \\ \text{NUM} = \textbf{sing} \end{bmatrix} \end{bmatrix}
$$

Hence $(F_1 \vee F_2) \sqsubseteq (F_1 \sqcup F_2)$, which means that $\sqcup$ is not fine-grained enough to model disjunction of information. Thinking about the internal logic of feature structures in $\mathcal{F}$ one is reduced to a logic of partial conjunction, partial implication and total (but very strange) 'form-of-disjunction'.

We can make conjunction total, by adding an inconsistent feature structure. Supposing we have $\langle \text{TYPE}, \sqsubseteq \rangle_\perp$ instead of $\langle \text{TYPE}, \sqsubseteq \rangle$ we have an atomic feature structure $[\perp]$. We could use this feature structure to make unification total, that is, we could define $F_1 \sqcap F_2 = [\perp]$, if $F_1 \sqcap F_2$ fails. This is analogous to the situation with types.

But $[\perp]$ is not an identity for generalisation. If an identity I for generalisation existed it should satisfy $I \sqsubseteq F$, for all F's in $\mathcal{F}$, the characteristic of *false*, the identity for disjunction, hence we should have a morphism of feature structures

$F \rightarrow I$. We also want to complete the definition of I by saying which is the partial map $?: 1 \times \text{FEAT} \rightarrow 1$ making the diagram below commute.

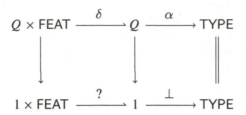

But there is only one map $Q \rightarrow 1$ and if the diagram above were a morphism of feature structures '$?(!(q),f)$' would have to be defined and equal to '$!(\delta(q,f))$' for any feature $f \in \text{FEAT}$. That means that the partial map '$?$' would have $?(*,f) = *$ for all features and that is not a partial map, hence not a feature structure.[3] Even if $[\perp]$ is not ideal as 'the' inconsistent feature structure, say, F_1 and F_2 are consistent if $F_1 \sqcap F_2$ exists and is different from $[\perp]$.

Thus if we use $\langle \text{TYPE}, \sqsubseteq \rangle_{\perp}$ we have total conjunction, but no constant *false*, and disjunction and generalisation are not the same — a very poor logical set up. But of course there are external logics. One of the first external logics was described by Kasper and Rounds and is the subject of the next section.

10.6.2   *Logic of Descriptions*

In this section we introduce a restriction of the logical attribute-value language that several researchers, notably Kasper and Rounds (1986, 1990) and Carpenter (1992) employ to *describe* feature structures. Much more powerful description languages are used by researchers who prefer *feature algebras*, and a comparison between these two approaches is not attempted here.

Definition 11   *The set of* descriptions *over the poset* $\langle \text{TYPE}, \sqsubseteq \rangle$ *of types and the collection* FEAT *of features is the least set* DESC *such that*

- $t \in \text{DESC}$ *if* $t \in \text{TYPE}$
- $\pi : \phi \in \text{DESC}$ *if* $\pi \in \text{FEAT}^*$ *and* $\phi \in \text{DESC}$
- $\pi_1 \doteq \pi_2 \in \text{DESC}$ *if* $\pi_1, \pi_2 \in \text{FEAT}^*$
- $\phi \wedge \psi \in \text{DESC}$ *if* ϕ *and* $\psi \in \text{DESC}$

The idea of providing descriptions as formulae of a logic to be satisfied by some feature structures is introduced by Pereira and Shieber (1984), but they, as well as many other researchers, have a richer set of formulae.

---

[3] Note that we assume that the set FEAT has at least two elements.

Since we restricted the formulae in DESC to the $\wedge$-fragment of propositional logic in the definition above, it does not matter how satisfaction is defined, as the $\wedge$-fragment of classical logic is equivalent to the $\wedge$-fragment of intuitionistic logic. But if we want to add disjunction or implication or negation to DESC, a choice of logical framework becomes necessary. Also different notions of satisfaction will lead to different logical formalisms, which explains why there are so many papers in the literature on this topic.

Definition 12 *The* satisfaction relation *relates the collection of feature structures $\mathcal{F}$ and the set of descriptions* DESC. *It is the least relation '$\models$' such that, if F is the feature structure $\langle Q, q_0, \delta, \alpha \rangle$ and $\phi \in$* DESC

- $F \models t$ *if* $t \in$ TYPE *and* $\alpha(q_0) \sqsubseteq t$
- $F \models \pi : \phi$ *if* $F@\pi \models \phi$
- $F \models \pi_1 \doteq \pi_2$ *if* $\delta(q_0, \pi_1) = \delta(q_0, \pi_2)$
- $F \models \phi \wedge \psi$ *if* $F \models \phi$ *and* $F \models \psi$

Note that the type $\top$, which is already in DESC by definition, behaves as the constant *true* for this logic. It is satisfied by any feature structure $F \models \top$, because for all $F \in \mathcal{F}$, $\alpha(q_0) \sqsubseteq \top$. Recall as well the following usual logical definition,

Definition 13 *Consider the set of all feature structures that satisfy a certain description ϕ, that is $Sat(\phi) = \{F \in \mathcal{F} | F \models \phi\}$.*

If ϕ is a formula in DESC, *say that ϕ is* satisfiable *if there exists a feature structure F that satisfies it, that is the set $Sat(\phi)$ is not empty.*

We have the traditional result:

Proposition 2 *If $F_1 \models \phi$ and $F_2 \sqsubseteq F_1$ then $F_2 \models \phi$ (monotonicity).*

For every satisfiable formula ϕ there is a most general feature structure $MGSat(\phi)$ that satisfies it.

For any feature structure in $\mathcal{F}$ there is a description Desc(F) *such that*

$$F \cong MGSat(\text{Desc}(F))$$

The results and definitions above are all in Kasper and Rounds, the only reason to recall them here is to remind the reader that these results are another way of expressing the existence of the internal logic. In other words, within this small fragment of propositional logic, we have a notion of entailment '$\vdash$' and as entailment is reflexive and transitive, we can think of $\langle$DESC, $\vdash\rangle$ as a pre-order, where meet $\sqcap$ is given by conjunction and $\top$ is the constant *true*. Clearly, given any feature structure F, we can write it as a big conjunction of descriptions, hence the existence of the the function Desc in the proposition above and the diagram below:

$$
\begin{array}{ccc}
\langle \mathrm{DESC}, \vdash \rangle & \xrightarrow{i} & \langle \mathrm{DESC}, \vdash \rangle_{\perp} \\[2mm]
\Big\uparrow \text{\small Desc} & & \Big\downarrow \\[2mm]
\langle \mathcal{WF}, \sqsubseteq \rangle \xrightarrow{i} \langle \mathcal{F}, \sqsubseteq \rangle & \xrightarrow{i} & \langle \mathcal{F}, \sqsubseteq \rangle_{\perp} \\[2mm]
\Big\downarrow \text{\small type-of} & & \Big\downarrow \\[2mm]
\langle \mathrm{TYPE}, \sqsubseteq \rangle & \xrightarrow{i} & \langle \mathrm{TYPE}, \sqsubseteq \rangle_{\perp}
\end{array}
$$

Having established a minimum common denominator one could extend the set of descriptions to accommodate several formalisms. If we choose intuitionistic logic, we can have the Moshier and Rounds (1987) approach. If we choose three-valued logic we can use Dawar and Vijay-Shanker's (1989) formalism. If we choose classical logic, we can have the Kasper and Rounds (1986, 1990) system and Carpenter's (1990, 1992) system (both have classical disjunction). Still using classical logic but at right angles, we have Smolka's (1988, 1989) and Johnson's (1988) systems where DESC has variables and negation. Reape (1991) also adds variables, but he wants to consider the features in paths of the form $\langle f_1 : \phi \rangle$ as modal (possibility)[4] operators, thus getting a poly-modal logic.

10.7   Conclusion

We presented a rigorous *mathematical* definition of a system of well-formed typed feature structures. Our system is very similar to Carpenter's system, but we allow more expressive constraints to be made over types. In our system each type t_i is constrained by a whole, possibly re-entrant, constraint feature structure $C(t_i)$, while using Carpenter's appropriateness specifications each type is constrained by a list of features and types — a one-level only feature structure. On the other hand, Carpenter allows (general) 'disjunctive constraints' which we do not handle at the moment. It should be noted that we could not use Carpenter's appropriateness specifications alone to give the sort of functionality for inheritance in the type system that we needed, thus the generalisation to well-formedness.

We also pointed out where somewhat different choices could be made in the formalisation of typed feature structures and presented two new operations that

---

[4] This also seems to be the case for the Category Structures of Gazdar *et al.* (1988).

one could consider over feature structures looking at them from the mathematical viewpoint only. Finally we briefly discussed one of the reasons why there are many different logics of feature structures in the literature, but for a survey of these logics the reader is referred to the substantial works of Carpenter, Reape and Johnson.

Acknowledgements

Many of the basic ideas and intuitions in this chapter are due to Ann Copestake, Ted Briscoe and Antonio Sanfilippo. The way in which these ideas have been formalised is the responsibility of the author, as are any mistakes in the formalisation.

11   LKB Encoding of Lexical Knowledge

ANTONIO SANFILIPPO

Introduction

In setting up a lexical component for natural language processing systems, one finds that a considerable amount of information is often repeated across sets of word entries. To make the task of grammar writing more efficient, shared information can be expressed in the form of partially specified templates and distributed to relevant entries by inheritance. Shared information across sets of partially specified templates can be factored out and conveyed using the same technique. This makes it possible to avoid redefining the same information structures, thus reducing a great deal of redundancy in the specification of word forms. For example, general properties of intransitive verbs concerning subcategorization and argument structure can be simply stated once, and then inherited by lexical entries which provide word specific information, e.g. orthography, predicate sense, aktionsart, selectional restrictions. Likewise, properties which are common to all verbs (e.g. part of speech, presence of a subject) or subsets of the verb class (presence of a direct object for transitive and ditransitive verbs) can be defined as templates which subsume all members of the verb class or some subset of it. This approach to word specification provides a highly structured organization of the lexicon according to which the properties of related word types as well as the relation between word types and specific word forms are expressed in terms of structure sharing and inheritance (Flickinger, Pollard and Wasow, 1985; Flickinger, 1987; Pollard and Sag, 1987, pp. 191–209).

Following the general insights of this treatment, the goal of this chapter is to describe a system of verb types for English where inheritance and structure sharing are expressed in the representation language of the ACQUILEX LKB (see Copestake, this volume and de Paiva, this volume). In section 11.1, a general characterization of word forms is given along with the specification of a grammar formalism which can be used to demonstrate the appropriateness of lexical representations in a parsing context. In sections 11.2 and 11.3 specific templates are described which encode subcategorization and argument structure for a large subset of English verbs. In section 11.4, the syntactic and semantic templates described in sections 11.2 and 11.3 are integrated to yield sign-based representations of verb types. The chapter concludes with an indication of how to specify inheritance of default features in the lexical domain considered.

190

11.1 A Sign-Based Approach to Lexical Specification

While our description of verb types is meant to be compatible with several theoretical approaches, it is obvious that reference to a specific grammar framework is necessary if we wish to test the fragment built. We have chosen to use a radically lexical theory of grammar since this ensures that lexical entries contain as much information as can be appropriately captured in the lexicon. Consequently, modification for a different framework should be a process of (automatically) removing or transforming information, but not (manually) adding more.

In keeping with a sign-based approach to linguistic analysis (Pollard and Sag, 1987; Zeevat *et al.*, 1987), words and phrases are represented as (typed) feature structures where orthographic, syntactic and semantic information is simultaneously represented as a conjunction of attribute-value pairs forming a **sign**:[1]

$$
\begin{bmatrix}
\text{sign} \sqsubset \top \\
\text{ORTH} = \textbf{orth} \\
\text{CAT} = \textbf{cat} \\
\text{SEM} = \textbf{sem}
\end{bmatrix}
$$

Lexical signs include a further attribute, **sense-id**, which encodes dictionary information about word senses:

$$
\begin{bmatrix}
\text{lex-sign} \sqsubset \text{sign} \\
\text{ORTH} = \textbf{orth} \\
\text{CAT} = \textbf{cat} \\
\text{SEM} = \textbf{sem} \\
\text{SENSE-ID} =
\begin{bmatrix}
\textbf{sense-id} \\
\text{FS-ID} = \textbf{string} \\
\text{LANGUAGE} = \textbf{language} \\
\text{DICTIONARY} = \textbf{string} \\
\text{LDB-ENTRY-NO} = \textbf{string} \\
\text{HOMONYM-NO} = \textbf{string} \\
\text{SENSE-NO} = \textbf{string}
\end{bmatrix}
\end{bmatrix}
$$

Syntactic properties of signs concerning part of speech and subcategorization are expressed using a Categorial Grammar approach to category specification (Zeevat *et al.*, 1987). The category attribute of a sign is either basic or complex. Basic categories are binary feature structures consisting of a category type, and a series of attribute-value pairs encoding morphosyntactic information:[2]

$$
\begin{bmatrix}
\text{basic-cat} \sqsubset \text{cat} \\
\text{CAT-TYPE} = \textbf{cat-type} \\
\text{M-FEATS} = \boxed{\textbf{m-feats}}
\end{bmatrix}
$$

---

[1] The square subset sign and type label(s) following the outermost type label of a feature structure specify the type(s) from which the feature structure inherits; e.g. **lex-sign** $\sqsubset$ **sign** implies that all feature-value pairs in **sign** are found in **lex-sign**.

[2] A box enclosing a non-atomic type label, as in the case of **m-feats** in (1), signals that the attribute-value pairs associated with the type have not been expanded. Occasionally, attribute-value pairs in expanded type descriptions will be selectively omitted for ease of exposition.

Three basic categories are defined according to whether category type is **n** (noun), **np** (noun phrase) or **sent** (sentence); each category is related to a specific group of morphosyntactic features (**nominal-feats** for **n** and **np**, and **sent-feats** for **sent**):

$$
\begin{bmatrix}
\text{noun-cat} \sqsubseteq \text{basic-cat} \\
\text{CAT-TYPE} = \textbf{n} \\
\text{M-FEATS} = \begin{bmatrix}
\textbf{nominal-m-feats} \\
\text{REG-MORPH} = \textbf{boolean} \\
\text{AGR} = \begin{bmatrix}
\textbf{agr} \\
\text{PERS} = \textbf{person} \\
\text{NUM} = \textbf{number} \\
\text{GENDER} = \textbf{gender} \\
\text{DIM} = \textbf{boolean}
\end{bmatrix} \\
\text{NOMINAL-FORM} = \textbf{nominal-form} \\
\text{CASE} = \textbf{case} \\
\text{COUNT} = \textbf{boolean}
\end{bmatrix}
\end{bmatrix}
$$

$$
\begin{bmatrix}
\text{np-cat} \sqsubseteq \text{basic-cat} \\
\text{CAT-TYPE} = \textbf{np} \\
\text{M-FEATS} = \boxed{\textbf{nominal-m-feats}}
\end{bmatrix}
$$

$$
\begin{bmatrix}
\text{sent-cat} \sqsubseteq \text{basic-cat} \\
\text{CAT-TYPE} = \textbf{sent} \\
\text{M-FEATS} = \begin{bmatrix}
\textbf{sent-m-feats} \\
\text{REG-MORPH} = \textbf{boolean} \\
\text{VFORM} = \textbf{vform} \\
\text{COMP-FORM} = \textbf{comp-form} \\
\text{PRT} = \textbf{string} \\
\text{DIATHESES} = \boxed{\textbf{alternations}}
\end{bmatrix}
\end{bmatrix}
$$

Complex categories are recursively defined by letting the type **cat** instantiate a feature structure with attributes RESULT, DIRECTION and ACTIVE. RESULT can take as value either a basic or complex category, ACTIVE is of type **sign**, and the direction attribute encodes order of combination relative to the active part of the sign (e.g. **forward** or **backward**).

$$
\begin{bmatrix}
\text{complex-cat} \sqsubseteq \text{cat} \\
\text{RESULT} = \textbf{cat} \\
\text{DIRECTION} = \textbf{direction} \\
\text{ACTIVE} = \boxed{\textbf{sign}}
\end{bmatrix}
$$

The semantics of a sign is a formula. A formula consists of an index, a predicate and at least one argument:

$$
\begin{bmatrix}
\text{formula} \sqsubseteq \text{sem} \\
\text{IND} = \textbf{entity} \\
\text{PRED} = \textbf{logical-pred} \\
\text{ARG1} = \textbf{sem}
\end{bmatrix}
$$

The index of a formula is an **entity** which provides partial information about the ontological type denoted by the formula. At present, it will suffice to consider two basic semantic entities — eventualities (**eve**) and individual objects (**obj**) — plus a contentless entity, **dummy**, employed in the semantic characterization of pleonastic noun phrases (see footnote 3). Both **formula** and **entity** are subtypes of **sem** (semantics). The predicate of a formula is an atomic type which can instantiate either a logical constant (e.g. **and**) or a lexical predicate (e.g. *sleep*).

Various subtypes of **formula** can be defined according to predicate arity as shown in (1).

(1)
$$\begin{bmatrix} \text{unary-formula} \sqsubset \text{formula} \\ \text{IND} = \text{entity} \\ \text{PRED} = \text{logical-pred} \\ \text{ARG1} = \text{sem} \end{bmatrix} \qquad \begin{bmatrix} \text{binary-formula} \sqsubset \text{formula} \\ \text{IND} = \text{entity} \\ \text{PRED} = \text{logical-pred} \\ \text{ARG1} = \text{sem} \\ \text{ARG2} = \text{sem} \end{bmatrix}$$

Lexical and phrasal signs are combined to form phrasal signs through rules of forward and backward function application. Function application allows a functor sign to combine with an adjacent argument sign just in case the information contained in the active sign of the functor is compatible with the information encoded in the argument sign. The result is a sign whose orthography is a binary feature structure encoding the functor and argument orthographic values, semantics correspond to the semantics of the functor, and category is equal to the category of the functor with its active sign removed. This is shown in (2) with reference to the forward version of the rule where the argument sign occurs to the right of the functor.

(2)
$$\begin{bmatrix} \text{grammar-rule} \\ 0 = \begin{bmatrix} \text{sign} \\ \text{ORTH} = \begin{bmatrix} \text{complex-orth} \\ \text{ORTH1} = \boxed{0} \ \text{orth} \\ \text{ORTH2} = \boxed{1} \ \text{orth} \end{bmatrix} \\ \text{CAT} = \boxed{2} \ \text{cat} \\ \text{SEM} = \boxed{3} \ \text{sem} \end{bmatrix} \\ 1 = \begin{bmatrix} \text{sign} \\ \text{ORTH} = \boxed{0} \\ \text{CAT} = \begin{bmatrix} \text{complex-cat} \\ \text{RESULT} = \boxed{2} \\ \text{DIRECTION} = \text{forward} \\ \text{ACTIVE} = \boxed{4} \begin{bmatrix} \text{sign} \\ \text{ORTH} = \boxed{1} \\ \text{CAT} = \text{cat} \\ \text{SEM} = \text{sem} \end{bmatrix} \end{bmatrix} \\ \text{SEM} = \boxed{3} \end{bmatrix} \\ 2 = \boxed{4} \end{bmatrix}$$

The derivation for the phrasal sign *red book* in Figure 11.1 provides a concrete example of how the rule operates.

A third rule type, **backward-wrapping**, allows the next to last active sign of a functor to be consumed before the outermost active sign is. This rule is needed for transitive verbs which take a clausal complement or oblique object (see sections 11.3 and 11.4); a sample application relative to the derivation of the phrasal sign *gives a book* is given in Figure 11.2.

Note that noun phrases are treated as polymorphic type-raised complements, following Zeevat *et al.* (1987). As indicated in Figures 11.2 and 11.3, these are functor signs which combine with either verbs or verb phrases to form verb phrases or sentences. Consequently, a verb combines with its subject through forward function application and with its objects through backward function application. Insofar as the raised NP inherits directionality relative to its active sign from the verb (phrase) with which it combines — as indicated by the two

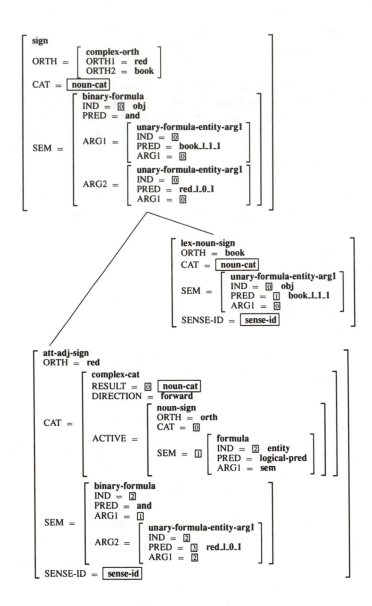

Figure 11.1: Derivation of *red book*

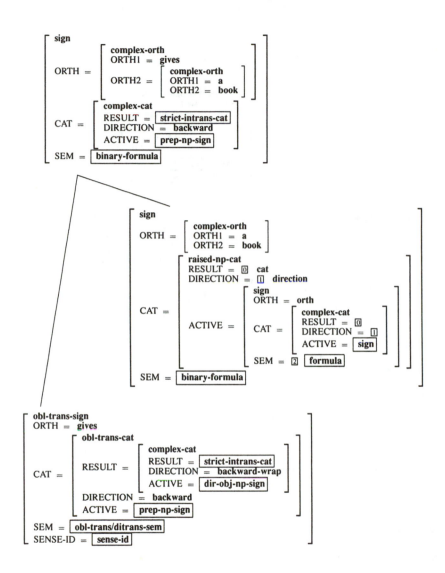

Figure 11.2: Derivation of *gives a book*

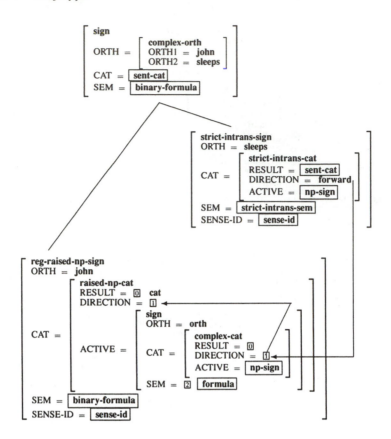

Figure 11.3: Derivation of *John sleeps*

twisted arrows in Figure 11.3 — the direction value relative to a subject in verb categories must be of type **forward** and the direction value relative to an object must be **backward**.

11.2   Verb Semantics

One of the crucial tasks in providing a semantic characterization of verbs regards the specification of arguments in terms of thematic roles. It is now often recognized that the Neo-Davidsonian elaboration of verb semantics proposed by Parsons (1980, 1990) provides an effective way of executing this task as it assigns thematic roles a central function in the association of a verb with its grammatical arguments (Carlson, 1984; Dowty, 1989; Sanfilippo, 1990). According to Parsons, verbs denote properties of eventualities, and thematic roles

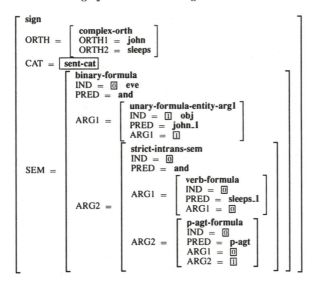

Figure 11.4: Semantics for *john sleeps*

are relations between eventualities and individuals. The logical form of a sentence involves event quantification over these two types of eventuality-denoting expressions, e.g.

(3) $\exists e[sleep(e) \wedge agent(e,john)]$

The appearance of participant role predicates in logical form is thus granted, as these are indispensable in combining verb and noun phrase meanings into sentence meanings (Carlson, 1984). A specification of this approach to verb semantics and predicate-argument association can be easily expressed in the formalism adopted here, as indicated in Figure 11.4 where the reentrancies relative to the event variable encode the event binding which in (3) is represented through existential quantification.[3]

Following Dowty (1991), the semantic content of thematic relations is expressed in terms of prototypical 'cluster-concepts' determined for each choice of predicate through attribution of selected entailments which qualify the relative agentive strength and affectedness of event participants. Dowty assumes that there are only two 'thematic-role-like concepts' whose functionality in grammar is essentially limited to argument selection: the *proto-agent* and *proto-patient* roles defined with reference to the properties in (4) and (5) (Dowty 1991, p. 572).

(4)   Contributing Properties for the Agent Proto-Role:

---

[3] In the grammar fragment assumed, proper names are treated as properties of individuals rather than simplex individuals as in (3).

a   volitional involvement in the event or state
b   sentience (and/or perception)
c   causing an event or change of state in another participant
d   movement (relative to the position of another participant)
e   (exists independently of the event named by the verb)

(5)   Contributing Properties for the Patient Proto-Role:
        a   undergoes change of state
        b.—   incremental theme
        c   causally affected by another participant
        d   stationary relative to movement of another participant
        e   (does not exist independently of the event)

We depart from these assumptions in two major regards. First, we introduce a third proto-role **prep** for prepositional objects — i.e. contentful verbal arguments which cannot be classified as either proto-patient or proto-agent roles (Sanfilippo, 1990) — and the contentless predicate **no-theta** to characterize the relation between a pleonastic NP to its governing verb. Second, we formalize proto-roles as supersets of specific clusters of meaning components which are instrumental in the identification of semantic verb classes. Consider, for example, the characterization of role content with reference to psychological verbs. As is well known (Levin, 1989; Jackendoff, 1990), verbs which belong to this semantic class can be classified according to the following parameters:

- affect is positive (*admire, delight*), neutral (*experience, interest*) or negative (*fear, scare*)
- stimulus argument is realized as object and experiencer as subject, e.g. *admire, experience, fear*
- stimulus argument is realized as subject and experiencer as object, e.g. *delight, interest, scare*

Psychological verbs with experiencer subjects are 'non-causative'; the stimulus of these verbs can be considered to be a 'source' to which the experiencer 'reacts emotively'. By contrast, psychological verbs with stimulus subjects involve 'causation'; the stimulus argument functions as a 'causative source' by which the experiencer participant is 'emotively affected'. Six subtypes of psychological verbs can thus be distinguished according to semantic properties of the stimulus and experiencer arguments as shown in (6).

(6)

STIMULUS	EXPERIENCER	EXAMPLE
non-caus. source	neu., reactive, emotive	*experience*
non-caus. source	pos., reactive, emotive	*admire*
non-caus. source	neg., reactive, emotive	*fear*
neu., caus. source	neu., affected, emotive	*interest*
pos., caus. source	pos., affected, emotive	*delight*
neg., caus. source	neg., affected, emotive	*scare*

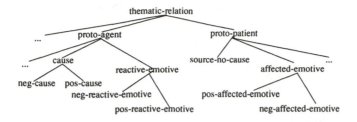

Figure 11.5: Prototype thematic roles

The clusters of meaning components which form the basis for this classification can be thought of as specific instantiations of Dowty's proto-roles, as indicated in Figure 11.5. This adaptation of Dowty's notion of prototype thematic roles provides a richer account of role content which is suitable for the treatment of grammatical phenomena other than argument selection, e.g. control and anaphora.

In keeping with Carlson (1984) and Dowty (1989), the argument structure of verbs is expressed with reference to meaning postulates which specify for each verb the participant roles (and clausal complements) which are necessarily associated with that verb, e.g.

$$\forall e \,\Box[delight(e) \rightarrow \exists x[pos\text{-}cause(e,x)] \land \exists y[pos\text{-}affected\text{-}emotive(e,y)]]$$

The relation between a verbal predicate and its thematic (clausal) entailments is captured lexically by encoding the semantics of all verbs as a conjunctive formula, **verb-sem**. The first argument in **verb-sem** is a unary formula (**verb-formula**) which characterizes the verbal predicate as a property of eventualities. The second argument is a formula which encodes the semantics of subcategorized arguments.

$$
\left[
\begin{array}{l}
\text{verb-sem} \sqsubset \text{binary-formula} \\
\text{IND} = \boxed{0} \ \ \text{eve} \\
\text{PRED} = \ \text{and} \\
\text{ARG1} = \left[\begin{array}{l}
\text{verb-formula} \\
\text{IND} = \boxed{0} \\
\text{PRED} = \ \text{logical-pred} \\
\text{ARG1} = \boxed{0}
\end{array}\right] \\
\text{ARG2} = \left[\begin{array}{l}
\text{formula} \\
\text{IND} = \boxed{0} \\
\text{PRED} = \ \text{logical-pred} \\
\text{ARG1} = \ \text{sem}
\end{array}\right]
\end{array}
\right]
$$

A primary semantic classification of verb types is obtained by specifying how many arguments are encoded in the second subformula of **verb-sem**. Further distinctions are made according to what kind of verbal arguments are encoded:

- proto-agent, e.g. *John* in *John sleeps* and the sentences below
- proto-patient, e.g. *a book* in *John read a book*
- prepositional

- oblique/indirect, e.g. *to Mary* in *John gave a book to Mary*
- objective, e.g. *Mary* in *John gave Mary a book*

- non-thematic, e.g. *Bill* in *Bill seems to be sad*
- pleonastic, e.g. *It* in *It bothers Bill that Mary left*
- predicative (XCOMP), e.g. *to leave* in *John wishes to leave*
- sentential (COMP), e.g. *that Mary left* in *John said that Mary left*

With strict intransitive verbs (*John sleeps*), the second argument in **verb-sem** is an atomic formula encoding a proto-agent role; the index of the proto-agent formula is equated to the index of the verb formula to indicate that the proto-agent functions as a participant of the eventuality described by the verb.

$$
\begin{bmatrix}
\text{strict-intrans-sem} \sqsubset \text{verb-sem} \\
\text{IND} = \boxed{0}\ \text{eve} \\
\text{PRED} = \text{and} \\
\text{ARG1} = \begin{bmatrix}
\text{verb-formula} \\
\text{IND} = \boxed{0} \\
\text{PRED} = \text{logical-pred} \\
\text{ARG1} = \boxed{0}
\end{bmatrix} \\
\text{ARG2} = \begin{bmatrix}
\text{p-agt-formula} \\
\text{IND} = \boxed{0} \\
\text{PRED} = \text{p-agt} \\
\text{ARG1} = \boxed{0} \\
\text{ARG2} = \text{obj}
\end{bmatrix}
\end{bmatrix}
$$

Other verbs have semantics of type **trans/intrans-sem** where the second argument is a conjunctive formula whose ARG1 is either a proto-agent or a non-thematic formula (**p-agt-or-no-theta**) and ARG2 can instantiate one or more argument roles. As for strict intransitives, the index or the proto-agent/non-thematic formula is equal to the eventuality argument of the verbal predicate.

$$
\begin{bmatrix}
\text{trans/intrans-sem} \sqsubset \text{verb-sem} \\
\text{IND} = \boxed{0}\ \text{eve} \\
\text{PRED} = \text{and} \\
\text{ARG1} = \begin{bmatrix}
\text{verb-formula} \\
\text{IND} = \boxed{0} \\
\text{PRED} = \text{logical-pred} \\
\text{ARG1} = \boxed{0}
\end{bmatrix} \\
\text{ARG2} = \begin{bmatrix}
\text{binary-formula} \\
\text{IND} = \boxed{0} \\
\text{PRED} = \text{and} \\
\text{ARG1} = \begin{bmatrix}
\text{p-agt-or-no-theta} \\
\text{IND} = \boxed{0} \\
\text{PRED} = \text{theta-relation} \\
\text{ARG1} = \boxed{0} \\
\text{ARG2} = \text{dummy-or-obj}
\end{bmatrix} \\
\text{ARG1} = \text{sem}
\end{bmatrix}
\end{bmatrix}
$$

The presence of a single argument in addition to the proto-agent, defines three major subtypes of **trans/intrans-sem**. The type **trans/intrans-no-comp/xcomp-sem** describes verbs which take a single non-clausal complement other than the proto-agent; the subject of these verbs is thematic. The index of the added thematic formula and top index are made to share the same variable to enforce event binding across the verb and its thematic conjuncts.

$$\begin{bmatrix} \text{trans/intrans-no-comp/xcomp-sem} \sqsubset \text{trans/intrans-sem} \\ \text{IND} = \boxed{0} \ \text{eve} \\ \text{PRED} = \text{and} \\ \text{ARG1} = \boxed{\text{verb-formula}} \\ \text{ARG2} = \begin{bmatrix} \text{binary-formula} \\ \text{IND} = \boxed{0} \\ \text{PRED} = \text{and} \\ \text{ARG1} = \boxed{\text{p-agt-formula}} \\ \text{ARG2} = \begin{bmatrix} \text{theta-formula} \\ \text{IND} = \boxed{0} \end{bmatrix} \end{bmatrix} \end{bmatrix}$$

Verbs of this semantic type which encode a proto-patient are strict transitives (*read a book*), while those which have a prepositional role correspond to intransitives which subcategorize for an oblique object (*talk to Bill*):

$$\begin{bmatrix} \text{strict-trans-sem} \sqsubset \text{trans/intrans-no-comp/xcomp-sem} \\ \text{IND} = \boxed{0} \ \text{eve} \\ \text{PRED} = \text{and} \\ \text{ARG1} = \boxed{\text{verb-formula}} \\ \text{ARG2} = \begin{bmatrix} \text{binary-formula} \\ \text{IND} = \boxed{0} \\ \text{PRED} = \text{and} \\ \text{ARG1} = \boxed{\text{p-agt-formula}} \\ \text{ARG2} = \begin{bmatrix} \text{p-pat-formula} \\ \text{IND} = \boxed{0} \\ \text{PRED} = \text{p-pat} \\ \text{ARG1} = \boxed{0} \\ \text{ARG2} = \text{obj} \end{bmatrix} \end{bmatrix} \end{bmatrix}$$

$$\begin{bmatrix} \text{intrans-obl-sem} \sqsubset \text{trans/intrans-no-comp/xcomp-sem} \\ \text{IND} = \boxed{0} \ \text{eve} \\ \text{PRED} = \text{and} \\ \text{ARG1} = \boxed{\text{verb-formula}} \\ \text{ARG2} = \begin{bmatrix} \text{binary-formula} \\ \text{IND} = \boxed{0} \\ \text{PRED} = \text{and} \\ \text{ARG1} = \boxed{\text{p-agt-formula}} \\ \text{ARG2} = \begin{bmatrix} \text{prep-formula} \\ \text{PRED} = \text{string} \\ \text{ARG2} = \text{obj} \\ \text{IND} = \boxed{0} \end{bmatrix} \end{bmatrix} \end{bmatrix}$$

The remaining two subtypes of **trans/intrans-sem** are for intransitive verbs which take a clausal complement represented by the last formula of the feature structures in (9). These are distinguished according to whether the subject is thematic or non-thematic:[4]

(7) Thematic Subject: **p-agt-subj-intrans-xcomp-comp-sem**, e.g.
John intended to come
Bill thought that John would come

---

[4] Both raising and pleonastic argument NPs have thematic relation **no-theta**. With raising NPs the second argument of **no-theta** is an object variable, while with pleonastic NPs it is the contentless entity **dummy** (cf. section 11.1). (Either instantiation is possible for **no-theta-subj-intrans-xcomp/comp-sem** in (9) since **dummy-or-obj** is defined as the join of **dummy** and **obj**.) This characterization is meant to capture the fact that raising NPs are non-thematic but make reference to some object entity which is assigned a participant role elsewhere in the sentence, while pleonastic NPs are neither thematic nor referential.

(8)   Non-Thematic Subject: **no-theta-subj-intrans-xcomp/comp-sem**

    a   Subject Raising Verbs, e.g.
            John seems to have solved the problem

    b   Intransitives which take a pleonastic subject, e.g.
            It seems that John might not come
            It won't hurt to remind him

Note that in both cases there is no reentrancy between the top index and the index of the formula representing the semantics of the clausal complement. This is simply because the event described by a clausal complement is generally distinct from that described by the matrix verb, although there may be partial overlap or coincidence.

(9)

$$
\begin{bmatrix}
\text{p-agt-subj-intrans-xcomp/comp-sem} \sqsubseteq \text{trans/intrans-sem} \\
\text{IND} = \boxed{0}\ \text{eve} \\
\text{PRED} = \text{and} \\
\text{ARG1} = \boxed{\text{verb-formula}} \\
\text{ARG2} = \begin{bmatrix}
\text{binary-formula} \\
\text{IND} = \boxed{0} \\
\text{PRED} = \text{and} \\
\text{ARG1} = \boxed{\text{p-agt-formula}} \\
\text{ARG2} = \boxed{\text{formula}}
\end{bmatrix}
\end{bmatrix}
$$

$$
\begin{bmatrix}
\text{no-theta-subj-intrans-xcomp/comp-sem} \sqsubseteq \text{trans/intrans-sem} \\
\text{IND} = \boxed{0}\ \text{eve} \\
\text{PRED} = \text{and} \\
\text{ARG1} = \boxed{\text{verb-formula}} \\
\text{ARG2} = \begin{bmatrix}
\text{binary-formula} \\
\text{IND} = \boxed{0} \\
\text{PRED} = \text{and} \\
\text{ARG1} = \begin{bmatrix}
\text{no-theta-formula} \\
\text{IND} = \boxed{0} \\
\text{PRED} = \text{no-theta} \\
\text{ARG1} = \boxed{0} \\
\text{ARG2} = \text{dummy-or-obj}
\end{bmatrix} \\
\text{ARG2} = \boxed{\text{formula}}
\end{bmatrix}
\end{bmatrix}
$$

Verbs which take more than two arguments[5] have semantic type **intrans/trans/obl-trans/ditrans-sem**:

$$
\begin{bmatrix}
\text{intrans/trans/obl-trans/ditrans-sem} \sqsubseteq \text{trans/intrans-sem} \\
\text{IND} = \boxed{0}\ \text{eve} \\
\text{PRED} = \text{and} \\
\text{ARG1} = \boxed{\text{verb-formula}} \\
\text{ARG2} = \begin{bmatrix}
\text{binary-formula} \\
\text{IND} = \boxed{0} \\
\text{PRED} = \text{and} \\
\text{ARG1} = \boxed{\text{p-agt-or-no-theta}} \\
\text{ARG2} = \boxed{\text{formula}}
\end{bmatrix}
\end{bmatrix}
$$

These are further classified according to whether or not there is a direct object role, i.e. a proto-patient or a non-thematic role other than the subject argument (**p-pat-or-no-theta**). A sizeable group of those which do not encode a direct

---

[5] Here, only verbs which take a maximum of three arguments will be discussed.

object correspond to verbs which take a clausal complement and an oblique object represented by the types **formula** and **prep-formula** in (10).

(10)

$$
\begin{bmatrix}
\text{intrans-xcomp/comp-obl-sem } \sqsubset \text{ intrans/trans/ditrans-sem} \\
\text{IND} = \boxed{0} \ \text{eve} \\
\text{PRED} = \ \text{and} \\
\text{ARG1} = \boxed{\text{verb-formula}} \\
\text{ARG2} =
\begin{bmatrix}
\text{binary-formula} \\
\text{IND} = \boxed{0} \\
\text{PRED} = \ \text{and} \\
\text{ARG1} = \boxed{\text{p-agt-or-no-theta}} \\
\text{ARG2} =
\begin{bmatrix}
\text{binary-formula} \\
\text{IND} = \boxed{0} \\
\text{PRED} = \ \text{and} \\
\text{ARG1} = \ \text{formula} \\
\text{ARG2} = \boxed{\text{prep-formula}}
\end{bmatrix}
\end{bmatrix}
\end{bmatrix}
$$

Two subtypes of **intrans-xcomp/comp-obl-sem** can be distinguished according to whether the subject is thematic or non-thematic:

(11)   Thematic Subject: **p-agt-subj-intrans-xcomp/comp-obl-sem**, e.g.
       John agreed with Mary to go fishing
       John promised (to) me that his car would not break down

(12)   Non-Thematic Subject: **no-theta-subj-intrans-xcomp/comp-obl-sem**
       a   Subject Raising Verbs, e.g.
               John seems to me to have solved the problem
       b   Intransitives which take a pleonastic subject, e.g.
               It will be hard for John to win the race
               It seems to Mary that Bill will not come

$$
\begin{bmatrix}
\text{p-agt-subj-intrans-xcomp/comp-obl-sem } \sqsubset \text{ intrans-xcomp/comp-obl-sem} \\
\text{IND} = \boxed{0} \ \text{eve} \\
\text{PRED} = \ \text{and} \\
\text{ARG1} = \boxed{\text{verb-formula}} \\
\text{ARG2} =
\begin{bmatrix}
\text{binary-formula} \\
\text{IND} = \boxed{0} \\
\text{PRED} = \ \text{and} \\
\text{ARG1} = \boxed{\text{p-agt-formula}} \\
\text{ARG2} =
\begin{bmatrix}
\text{binary-formula} \\
\text{IND} = \boxed{0} \\
\text{PRED} = \ \text{and} \\
\text{ARG1} = \ \text{formula} \\
\text{ARG2} = \boxed{\text{prep-formula}}
\end{bmatrix}
\end{bmatrix}
\end{bmatrix}
$$

$$
\begin{bmatrix}
\text{no-theta-subj-intrans-xcomp/comp-obl-sem } \sqsubset \text{ intrans-xcomp/comp-obl-sem} \\
\text{IND} = \boxed{0} \ \text{eve} \\
\text{PRED} = \ \text{and} \\
\text{ARG1} = \boxed{\text{verb-formula}} \\
\text{ARG2} =
\begin{bmatrix}
\text{binary-formula} \\
\text{IND} = \boxed{0} \\
\text{PRED} = \ \text{and} \\
\text{ARG1} = \boxed{\text{no-theta-formula}} \\
\text{ARG2} =
\begin{bmatrix}
\text{binary-formula} \\
\text{IND} = \boxed{0} \\
\text{PRED} = \ \text{and} \\
\text{ARG1} = \ \text{formula} \\
\text{ARG2} = \boxed{\text{prep-formula}}
\end{bmatrix}
\end{bmatrix}
\end{bmatrix}
$$

Transitives which take a clausal or prepositional complement and ditransitives are jointly characterized by the presence of a direct object role, i.e. **p-pat-or-no-theta** in (13).

(13)

$$
\begin{bmatrix}
\text{trans/obl-trans/ditrans-sem} \sqsubseteq \text{trans/obl-trans/ditrans-sem} \\
\text{IND} = \boxed{0}\ \ \text{eve} \\
\text{PRED} = \ \text{and} \\
\text{ARG1} = \boxed{\text{verb-formula}} \\
\text{ARG2} = \begin{bmatrix}
\textbf{binary-formula} \\
\text{IND} = \boxed{0} \\
\text{PRED} = \ \text{and} \\
\text{ARG1} = \boxed{\text{p-agt-or-no-theta}} \\
\text{ARG2} = \begin{bmatrix}
\textbf{formula} \\
\text{IND} = \boxed{0} \\
\text{PRED} = \ \text{and} \\
\text{ARG1} = \boxed{\text{p-pat-or-no-theta}}
\end{bmatrix}
\end{bmatrix}
\end{bmatrix}
$$

Transitives with a subcategorized oblique/indirect object as well as ditransitives encode a prepositional role in addition to the proto-agent and proto-patient roles, as indicated in (14). The index of all thematic formulae is equal to the eventuality argument variable of the verbal predicate; this ensures that the individuals which instantiate these thematic formulae are appropriately understood as participants of the eventuality described by the verb.

(14)

$$
\begin{bmatrix}
\text{obl-trans/ditrans-sem} \sqsubseteq \text{trans/obl-trans/ditrans-sem} \\
\text{IND} = \boxed{0}\ \ \text{eve} \\
\text{PRED} = \ \text{and} \\
\text{ARG1} = \begin{bmatrix}
\textbf{verb-formula} \\
\text{IND} = \boxed{0} \\
\text{PRED} = \ \text{logical-pred} \\
\text{ARG1} = \boxed{0}
\end{bmatrix} \\
\text{ARG2} = \begin{bmatrix}
\textbf{binary-formula} \\
\text{IND} = \boxed{0} \\
\text{PRED} = \ \text{and} \\
\text{ARG1} = \begin{bmatrix}
\textbf{p-agt-formula} \\
\text{IND} = \boxed{0} \\
\text{PRED} = \ \text{p-agt} \\
\text{ARG1} = \boxed{0} \\
\text{ARG2} = \ \text{obj}
\end{bmatrix} \\
\text{ARG2} = \begin{bmatrix}
\textbf{binary-formula} \\
\text{IND} = \boxed{0} \\
\text{PRED} = \ \text{and} \\
\text{ARG1} = \begin{bmatrix}
\textbf{p-pat-formula} \\
\text{IND} = \boxed{0} \\
\text{PRED} = \ \text{p-pat} \\
\text{ARG1} = \boxed{0} \\
\text{ARG2} = \ \text{obj}
\end{bmatrix} \\
\text{ARG2} = \begin{bmatrix}
\textbf{prep-formula} \\
\text{IND} = \boxed{0} \\
\text{PRED} = \ \text{string} \\
\text{ARG1} = \boxed{0} \\
\text{ARG2} = \ \text{obj}
\end{bmatrix}
\end{bmatrix}
\end{bmatrix}
\end{bmatrix}
$$

Transitives which take a clausal complement have semantic type **trans-xcomp/comp-sem**, as shown in (15) where the innermost formula encodes the semantic of the clausal complement.

(15)

$$
\begin{bmatrix}
\text{trans-xcomp/comp-sem} \sqsubset \text{trans/obl-trans/ditrans-sem} \\
\text{IND} = \boxed{0} \ \text{eve} \\
\text{PRED} = \text{and} \\
\text{ARG1} = \boxed{\text{verb-formula}} \\
\text{ARG2} =
\begin{bmatrix}
\text{binary-formula} \\
\text{IND} = \boxed{0} \\
\text{PRED} = \text{and} \\
\text{ARG1} = \boxed{\text{p-agt-or-no-theta}} \\
\text{ARG2} =
\begin{bmatrix}
\text{binary-formula} \\
\text{IND} = \boxed{0} \\
\text{PRED} = \text{and} \\
\text{ARG1} = \boxed{\text{p-pat-or-no-theta}} \\
\text{ARG2} = \boxed{\text{formula}}
\end{bmatrix}
\end{bmatrix}
\end{bmatrix}
$$

They can be further classified as to whether the subject or object argument is thematic or non-thematic. Those which have a non-thematic object (viz. object raising verbs, e.g. *Bill believes Mary to have left*) have semantic type **no-theta-obj-trans-xcomp/comp-sem**:

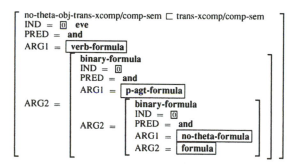

$$
\begin{bmatrix}
\text{no-theta-obj-trans-xcomp/comp-sem} \sqsubset \text{trans-xcomp/comp-sem} \\
\text{IND} = \boxed{0} \ \text{eve} \\
\text{PRED} = \text{and} \\
\text{ARG1} = \boxed{\text{verb-formula}} \\
\text{ARG2} =
\begin{bmatrix}
\text{binary-formula} \\
\text{IND} = \boxed{0} \\
\text{PRED} = \text{and} \\
\text{ARG1} = \boxed{\text{p-agt-formula}} \\
\text{ARG2} =
\begin{bmatrix}
\text{binary-formula} \\
\text{IND} = \boxed{0} \\
\text{PRED} = \text{and} \\
\text{ARG1} = \boxed{\text{no-theta-formula}} \\
\text{ARG2} = \boxed{\text{formula}}
\end{bmatrix}
\end{bmatrix}
\end{bmatrix}
$$

Those which have a thematic object have semantic type **p-pat-obj-trans-xcomp/comp-sem** (cf. (17)) and can be further classified according to whether the subject is thematic or pleonastic (see (16)):

(16) a   Thematic Subject:
           p-agt-subj-p-pat-obj-trans-xcomp/comp-sem, e.g.
           John persuaded Mary that the car was worth buying
           Bill persuades Mary to leave
      b   Pleonastic Subject:
           pleonastic-subj-trans-xcomp/comp-sem, e.g.
           It bothers Bill that Mary left
           It bothers Bill to leave.

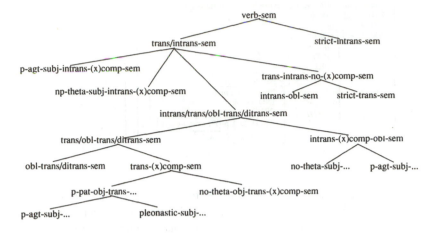

Figure 11.6: Verb semantic types

(17)

$$
\begin{bmatrix}
\text{p-pat-obj-trans-xcomp/comp-sem} \sqsubset \text{trans-xcomp/comp-sem} \\
\text{IND} = \boxed{0} \ \ \textbf{eve} \\
\text{PRED} = \ \textbf{and} \\
\text{ARG1} = \boxed{\textbf{verb-formula}} \\
\text{ARG2} = \begin{bmatrix}
\textbf{binary-formula} \\
\text{IND} = \boxed{0} \\
\text{PRED} = \ \textbf{and} \\
\text{ARG1} = \boxed{\textbf{p-agt-or-no-theta}} \\
\text{ARG2} = \begin{bmatrix}
\textbf{binary-formula} \\
\text{IND} = \boxed{0} \\
\text{PRED} = \ \textbf{and} \\
\text{ARG1} = \boxed{\textbf{p-pat-formula}} \\
\text{ARG2} = \boxed{\textbf{formula}}
\end{bmatrix}
\end{bmatrix}
\end{bmatrix}
$$

Here, our discussion of verb semantics comes to a close. A summary of the types described is given in the lattice fragment in Figure 11.6.

11.3   Verb Syntax

Insofar as all verbs minimally take a subject argument, the category type for all members of the verb class can be regarded as a subtype of **complex-cat**:

$$
\begin{bmatrix}
\text{verb-cat} \sqsubset \text{complex-cat} \\
\text{RESULT} = \ \textbf{cat} \\
\text{DIRECTION} = \ \textbf{direction} \\
\text{ACTIVE} = \boxed{\textbf{sign}}
\end{bmatrix}
$$

The top-most partition of verbal category types is established according to whether there is one subcategorized argument (i.e. active sign) or more. The first choice defines the category type of strict intransitive verbs shown in (18).

(18)

$$
\begin{bmatrix}
\text{strict-intrans-cat} \sqsubset \text{verb-cat} \\
\text{RESULT} = \boxed{\textbf{sent-cat}} \\
\text{DIRECTION} = \ \textbf{forward} \\
\text{ACTIVE} = \boxed{\textbf{np-sign}}
\end{bmatrix}
$$

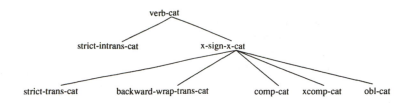

Figure 11.7: Subtypes of **verb-cat**

Verbs which subcategorize for more than one argument have category of type **x-sign-x-cat**. As shown in Figure 11.7, these can be further classified according to whether the outermost subcategorized sign is a direct object (**strict-trans-cat**), a prepositional object (**obl-cat**), a predicative complement (**xcomp-cat**), or a sentential complement (**comp-cat**). A further classificatory parameter is obtained taking into account presence of a direct object for verbs whose active sign is a prepositional, sentential or predicative complement (**backward-wrap-trans-cat**).

Verbs whose outermost subcategorized argument is a direct object NP — i.e. an active noun phrase which is assigned accusative case and either a proto-patient or non-thematic role (see below) — correspond to strict transitives:

$$
\begin{bmatrix}
\text{strict-trans-cat} \sqsubseteq \text{x-sign-x-cat} \\
\text{RESULT} = \boxed{\textbf{strict-intrans-cat}} \\
\text{DIRECTION} = \textbf{backward} \\
\text{ACTIVE} = \begin{bmatrix}
\textbf{dir-obj-np-sign} \\
\text{ORTH} = \underline{\textbf{orth}} \\
\text{CAT} = \begin{bmatrix}
\textbf{np-cat} \\
\text{CAT-TYPE} = \textbf{np} \\
\text{M-FEATS} = \begin{bmatrix} \textbf{nominal-m-feats} \\ \text{CASE} = \textbf{acc} \end{bmatrix}
\end{bmatrix} \\
\text{SEM} = \boxed{\textbf{p-pat-or-no-theta}}
\end{bmatrix}
\end{bmatrix}
$$

Verbs taking a direct object and either an oblique, sentential or predicative complement have category type **backward-wrap-trans-cat**. As indicated in (20), the direction attribute relative to the direct object NP is specified to be of type **backward-wrap**. Such a specification allows the direct object NP to be satisfied through the 'backward-wrapping' rule (cf. Figure 11.2). The oblique/clausal complement is the outermost subcategorized sign according to Dowty's *obliqueness hierarchy* (Dowty, 1982a, b), although it is the direct object which follows the verb (see (19)):

(19)   a   Bill gave a book to Mary
       b   Mary persuaded Bill that John is right
       c   Mary persuaded Bill to leave

This encoding is motivated with respect to a variety of linguistic generalizations concerning control of predicative complements, binding of pronouns and reflexives, morphosyntactic functionality and parameters which govern the distribution of relative clauses across languages — see Pollard and Sag (1987, pp. 117–121) and references therein. For example, the subcategorization order imposed by the obliqueness hierarchy makes it possible to provide a generalized treatment of subject and object control for verbs which take a predicative complement (see discussion of category types for control verbs below).

(20)
$$
\begin{bmatrix}
\text{backward-wrap-trans-cat} \sqsubset \text{x-sign-x-cat} \\[2pt]
\text{RESULT} = \begin{bmatrix}
\text{complex-cat} \\
\text{RESULT} = \boxed{\text{strict-intrans-cat}} \\
\text{DIRECTION} = \boxed{\text{backward-wrap}} \\
\text{ACTIVE} = \boxed{\text{dir-obj-np-sign}}
\end{bmatrix} \\
\text{DIRECTION} = \text{direction} \\
\text{ACTIVE} = \boxed{\text{sign}}
\end{bmatrix}
$$

Verbs whose outermost subcategorized complement is a sentential sign have category of type **comp-cat**:

$$
\begin{bmatrix}
\text{comp-cat} \sqsubset \text{x-sign-x-cat} \\
\text{RESULT} = \boxed{\text{complex-cat}} \\
\text{DIRECTION} = \text{forward} \\
\text{ACTIVE} = \begin{bmatrix}
\text{sign} \\
\text{ORTH} = \text{orth} \\
\text{CAT} = \boxed{\text{sent-cat}} \\
\text{SEM} = \text{sem}
\end{bmatrix}
\end{bmatrix}
$$

Various subtypes of **comp-cat** can be defined according to whether the subcategorized sentence is

- in base form with complementizer *that*, e.g. (21a)
- a *wh*-sentence, e.g. (21b)
- finite with or without complementizer *that*, e.g. (21c)
- infinitive preceded by a preposition, e.g. (21d)

(21)   a   She desires that he leave
             They petitioned the government that the law be reconsidered
        b   He wondered whether she would come
             He asked Bill whether she would come
        c   He wished (that) she had called
             It bothers Bill that Mary sleeps
             Bill tells John that Mary sleeps
        d   They would prefer for John to do it

The subtypes of **comp-cat** shown below characterize the first three of these subcategorization patterns.

(22)

$$
\begin{bmatrix}
\text{sbase-comp-cat} \sqsubset \text{comp-cat} \\
\text{RESULT} = \boxed{\text{complex-cat}} \\
\text{DIRECTION} = \text{forward} \\
\text{ACTIVE} = \begin{bmatrix}
\text{sign} \\
\text{ORTH} = \text{orth} \\
\text{CAT} = \begin{bmatrix}
\text{sent-cat} \\
\text{M-FEATS} = \begin{bmatrix}
\text{sent-m-feats} \\
\text{VFORM} = \text{base} \\
\text{COMP-FORM} = \text{that-comp}
\end{bmatrix}
\end{bmatrix}
\end{bmatrix}
\end{bmatrix}
$$

$$
\begin{bmatrix}
\text{swh-comp-cat} \sqsubset \text{comp-cat} \\
\text{RESULT} = \boxed{\text{complex-cat}} \\
\text{DIRECTION} = \text{forward} \\
\text{ACTIVE} = \begin{bmatrix}
\text{sign} \\
\text{ORTH} = \text{orth} \\
\text{CAT} = \begin{bmatrix}
\text{sent-cat} \\
\text{M-FEATS} = \begin{bmatrix}
\text{sent-m-feats} \\
\text{VFORM} = \text{fin} \\
\text{COMP-FORM} = \text{wh-comp}
\end{bmatrix}
\end{bmatrix}
\end{bmatrix}
\end{bmatrix}
$$

$$
\begin{bmatrix}
\text{sfin-comp-cat} \sqsubset \text{comp-cat} \\
\text{RESULT} = \boxed{\text{complex-cat}} \\
\text{DIRECTION} = \text{forward} \\
\text{ACTIVE} = \begin{bmatrix}
\text{sign} \\
\text{ORTH} = \text{orth} \\
\text{CAT} = \begin{bmatrix}
\text{sent-cat} \\
\text{M-FEATS} = \begin{bmatrix}
\text{sent-m-feats} \\
\text{VFORM} = \text{fin} \\
\text{COMP-FORM} = \text{no-or-that-comp}
\end{bmatrix}
\end{bmatrix}
\end{bmatrix}
\end{bmatrix}
$$

Each subtype in turn can be further subdivided according to whether the verb it characterizes is transitive (e.g. *He asked Bill whether she would come*) or intransitive (*He wondered whether she would come*). The two types **trans-comp-cat** and **intrans-comp-cat** below define these two possibilities.

(23)

$$
\begin{bmatrix}
\text{trans-comp-cat} \sqsubset \text{comp-cat, backward-wrap-trans-cat} \\
\text{RESULT} = \begin{bmatrix}
\text{complex-cat} \\
\text{RESULT} = \boxed{\text{strict-intrans-cat}} \\
\text{DIRECTION} = \text{backward-wrap} \\
\text{ACTIVE} = \boxed{\text{dir-obj-np-sign}}
\end{bmatrix} \\
\text{DIRECTION} = \text{forward} \\
\text{ACTIVE} = \begin{bmatrix}
\text{sign} \\
\text{ORTH} = \text{orth} \\
\text{CAT} = \boxed{\text{sent-cat}} \\
\text{SEM} = \text{sem}
\end{bmatrix}
\end{bmatrix}
$$

$$
\begin{bmatrix}
\text{intrans-comp-cat} \sqsubset \text{comp-cat} \\
\text{RESULT} = \boxed{\text{strict-intrans-cat}} \\
\text{DIRECTION} = \text{forward} \\
\text{ACTIVE} = \begin{bmatrix}
\text{sign} \\
\text{ORTH} = \text{orth} \\
\text{CAT} = \boxed{\text{sent-cat}} \\
\text{SEM} = \text{sem}
\end{bmatrix}
\end{bmatrix}
$$

Types for transitive and intransitive verbs which subcategorize for a sentential complement which is finite, in base form or a *wh*-question, are defined by intersecting the constraints of each of the types in (22) with those in (23). The category of verbs which take a non-finite sentential complement (c.f. (21d)) is

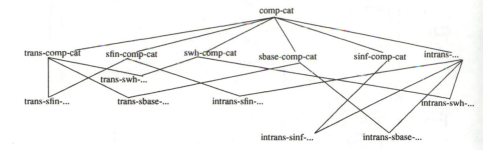

Figure 11.8: Subtypes of **comp-cat**

simply defined as a subtype of **intrans-comp-cat** (cf. **intrans-sfin-comp-cat**) since there seem to be no transitive verbs which exhibit this subcategorization pattern. A summary of category types which inherit from **comp-cat** is given in the lattice fragment in Figure 11.8.

Verbs whose outermost active sign is a predicative complement — i.e. a functor sign — have category type **xcomp-cat**.

$$
\begin{bmatrix}
\text{xcomp-cat} \sqsubseteq \text{x-sign-x-cat} \\
\text{RESULT} = \boxed{\text{complex-cat}} \\
\text{DIRECTION} = \text{forward} \\
\text{ACTIVE} = \begin{bmatrix} \text{sign} \\ \text{CAT} = \boxed{\text{complex-cat}} \end{bmatrix}
\end{bmatrix}
$$

These can be distinguished as to whether the predicative complement is controlled (e.g. *John wants to leave*) or can have arbitrary reference (*It won't hurt to remind him*); the types **control-cat** and **intrans-vpinf-cat** below express these two possibilities.

$$
\begin{bmatrix}
\text{control-cat} \sqsubseteq \text{xcomp-cat} \\
\text{RESULT} = \begin{bmatrix} \text{complex-cat} \\ \text{ACTIVE} = \begin{bmatrix} \text{sign} \\ \text{SEM} = \begin{bmatrix} \text{binary-formula} \\ \text{ARG2} = \boxed{0} \ \text{sem} \end{bmatrix} \end{bmatrix} \end{bmatrix} \\
\text{ACTIVE} = \begin{bmatrix} \text{sign} \\ \text{CAT} = \begin{bmatrix} \text{strict-intrans-cat} \\ \text{ACTIVE} = \begin{bmatrix} \text{sign} \\ \text{SEM} = \begin{bmatrix} \text{binary-formula} \\ \text{ARG2} = \boxed{0} \end{bmatrix} \end{bmatrix} \end{bmatrix} \end{bmatrix}
\end{bmatrix}
$$

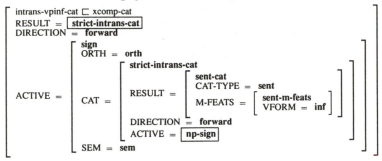

The term 'control' here is used with reference to both equi and raising verbs, e.g. *John wants to leave, John seems to be sad*. No special category types which express the equi-raising distinction are necessary since the contrast is represented semantically: with equi verbs the controlling NP is thematic (i.e. its thematic relation is **p-agt**, **p-pat** or **prep**), while with raising verbs the controlling NP is non-thematic (its thematic relation is of type **no-theta**). Control is encoded by equating the individual argument variable of the subcategorized NP which immediately precedes the predicative sign with the individual argument variable associated with the subject of the predicative sign. This encoding provides a specification of both subject and object control (see Figure 11.9).

As in the case of verbs taking sentential complements, verbs which subcategorize for a predicative complement can be classified taking into account presence of a direct object and morphosyntactic as well as categorial properties of the clausal complement. The types **intrans-control-cat** and **trans-control-cat** in (24) provide a categorial characterization of transitive and intransitive control verbs.

$$
(24) \quad
\begin{bmatrix}
\text{intrans-control-cat} \sqsubseteq \text{control-cat} \\[4pt]
\text{RESULT} =
\begin{bmatrix}
\text{strict-intrans-cat} \\
\text{ACTIVE} =
\begin{bmatrix}
\text{np-sign} \\
\text{SEM} =
\begin{bmatrix}
\text{theta-formula} \\
\text{ARG2} = \boxed{1} \ \text{dummy-or-obj}
\end{bmatrix}
\end{bmatrix}
\end{bmatrix} \\[4pt]
\text{DIRECTION} = \text{forward} \\[4pt]
\text{ACTIVE} =
\begin{bmatrix}
\text{sign} \\
\text{CAT} =
\begin{bmatrix}
\text{strict-intrans-cat} \\
\text{ACTIVE} =
\begin{bmatrix}
\text{np-sign} \\
\text{SEM} =
\begin{bmatrix}
\text{theta-formula} \\
\text{ARG2} = \boxed{1}
\end{bmatrix}
\end{bmatrix}
\end{bmatrix}
\end{bmatrix}
$$

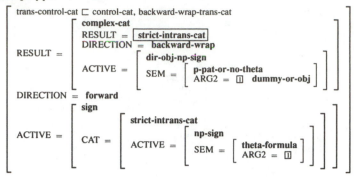

According to the constraints inherited from **control-cat**, the controlling NP is the one which immediately precedes the predicative complement in either case. Because of the subcategorization order imposed by the obliqueness hierarchy (i.e. the subject is the innermost complement, a predicative argument the outermost and the direct object stands in between), it follows that the controlling NP corresponds to the subject with intransitive control verbs and to the object with transitive control verbs. The data in (25) provide strong empirical evidence in favour of this characterization of control patterns.

(25)   a   Jon wants to leave
             Bill loves drinking
             Brad did not know what to say to her
             Mary feels better
        b   Mary persuaded Bill to leave
             I tried to shame her into voting in the election
             Mary believes John to be intelligent
             He hates people asking him for money
             I want this letter (to be) opened right now!
             I want the letter ready by tomorrow

A full classification of control verbs is obtained by intersecting the types **intrans-control-cat** and **trans-control-cat** with the category types **vpinf-control-cat, vping-control-cat, vpwh-control-cat, adj-control-cat** which characterize control verbs whose predicative complement is a plain infinitive VP, a gerundive VP, a *wh*-infinitive VP or an adjectival phrase — see (25a,b) for illustrative examples. The lattice fragment in Figure 11.9 illustrates the resulting hierarchy of control verb types.

Verbs which subcategorize for a prepositional complement have category type **obl-cat**. In the hierarchy for verb categories, this type is used to define the category of ditransitives (*John sent Bill a postcard*) as well as that of transitives taking an oblique object (*Mary attributes her success to hard work*). As shown in (26), these two verb types are categorially differentiated with respect to the

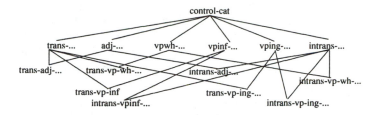

Figure 11.9: Subtypes of **control-cat**

case feature associated with the prepositional argument and the direction attribute relative to the direct object. The prepositional object of ditransitives occurs adjacent to the verb and receives objective case (**acc**). The assignment of objective case is motivated by the fact that the prepositional role of ditransitive has in some regards the syntactic functionality of a direct object, e.g it is amenable to passivization (*Bill was given a book*). By contrast, the oblique argument NP of a transitive (e.g. *attribute*) is case-marked by a preposition (**p-case**) and follows the direct object. Inheritance from **backward-wrap-trans-cat** makes it possible to capture the surface ordering of object complements without changing the subcategorization pattern imposed by the obliqueness hierarchy — i.e. the assignment of the direction feature **backward-wrap** to the direct object will induce application of the 'backward-wrapping' rule (see Figure 11.2).

(26)

$$
\begin{bmatrix}
\text{obl-cat} \sqsubseteq \text{x-sign-x-cat} \\
\text{RESULT} = \boxed{\text{complex-cat}} \\
\text{DIRECTION} = \text{backward} \\
\text{ACTIVE} = \begin{bmatrix}
\text{prep-np-sign} \\
\text{ORTH} = \text{orth} \\
\text{CAT} = \boxed{\text{np-cat}} \\
\text{SEM} = \boxed{\text{prep-formula}}
\end{bmatrix}
\end{bmatrix}
$$

$$
\begin{bmatrix}
\text{obl-trans-cat} \sqsubseteq \text{obl-cat, backward-wrap-trans-cat} \\
\text{ACTIVE} = \begin{bmatrix}
\text{prep-np-sign} \\
\text{CAT} = \begin{bmatrix}
\text{np-cat} \\
\text{M-FEATS} = \begin{bmatrix}
\text{nominal-m-feats} \\
\text{CASE} = \text{p-case}
\end{bmatrix}
\end{bmatrix}
\end{bmatrix}
\end{bmatrix}
$$

$$
\begin{bmatrix}
\text{ditrans-cat} \sqsubseteq \text{obl-cat} \\
\text{RESULT} = \text{strict-trans-cat} \\
\text{ACTIVE} = \begin{bmatrix}
\text{prep-np-sign} \\
\text{CAT} = \begin{bmatrix}
\text{np-cat} \\
\text{M-FEATS} = \begin{bmatrix}
\text{nominal-m-feats} \\
\text{CASE} = \text{acc}
\end{bmatrix}
\end{bmatrix}
\end{bmatrix}
\end{bmatrix}
$$

11.4 Verb Signs

Verb signs are formed by integrating the semantic and category types described in the previous two sections, and adding orthographic information. The integration of syntactic and semantic information is carried out by coindexing the semantics of subcategorized arguments in the category types with the argument roles in the semantic types. For example, the type for strict intransitive signs is defined by setting the semantic value of the active sign in **strict-intrans-cat** equal to the second argument formula of **strict-intrans-sem**:

$$
\begin{bmatrix}
\text{strict-intrans-sign} \sqsubseteq \text{verb-sign} \\[4pt]
\text{CAT} =
\begin{bmatrix}
\text{strict-intrans-cat} \\[4pt]
\text{ACTIVE} =
\begin{bmatrix}
\text{np-sign} \\
\text{SEM} = \boxed{0}\ \boxed{\text{p-agt-formula}}
\end{bmatrix}
\end{bmatrix} \\[16pt]
\text{SEM} =
\begin{bmatrix}
\text{strict-intrans-sem} \\
\text{ARG2} = \boxed{0}
\end{bmatrix}
\end{bmatrix}
$$

With respect to the subset of English verbs considered here, there are two additional ways of relating semantic and category types according to whether a verb subcategorizes for two or three arguments:

(27)
$$
\begin{bmatrix}
\text{2-complements-verb-sign} \sqsubseteq \text{verb-sign} \\[4pt]
\text{CAT} =
\begin{bmatrix}
\text{complex-cat} \\[4pt]
\text{RESULT} =
\begin{bmatrix}
\text{complex-cat} \\
\text{ACTIVE} =
\begin{bmatrix}
\text{sign} \\
\text{SEM} = \boxed{0}
\end{bmatrix}
\end{bmatrix} \\[10pt]
\text{ACTIVE} =
\begin{bmatrix}
\text{sign} \\
\text{SEM} = \boxed{1}\ \text{sem}
\end{bmatrix}
\end{bmatrix} \\[20pt]
\text{SEM} =
\begin{bmatrix}
\text{verb-sem} \\
\text{IND} = \boxed{2}\ \text{eve} \\
\text{PRED} = \text{and} \\
\text{ARG1} = \boxed{\text{verb-formula}} \\[4pt]
\text{ARG2} =
\begin{bmatrix}
\text{binary-formula} \\
\text{ARG1} = \boxed{0}\ \boxed{\text{p-agt-or-no-theta}} \\
\text{ARG2} = \boxed{1}
\end{bmatrix}
\end{bmatrix}
\end{bmatrix}
$$

$$
\begin{bmatrix}
\text{3-complements-verb-sign} \sqsubseteq \text{verb-sign} \\[4pt]
\text{CAT} =
\begin{bmatrix}
\text{complex-cat} \\[4pt]
\text{RESULT} =
\begin{bmatrix}
\text{complex-cat} \\
\text{RESULT} =
\begin{bmatrix}
\text{complex-cat} \\
\text{ACTIVE} =
\begin{bmatrix}
\text{sign} \\
\text{SEM} = \boxed{0}
\end{bmatrix}
\end{bmatrix} \\[10pt]
\text{ACTIVE} =
\begin{bmatrix}
\text{sign} \\
\text{SEM} = \boxed{2}\ \text{sem}
\end{bmatrix}
\end{bmatrix} \\[10pt]
\text{ACTIVE} =
\begin{bmatrix}
\text{sign} \\
\text{SEM} = \boxed{3}\ \text{sem}
\end{bmatrix}
\end{bmatrix} \\[20pt]
\text{SEM} =
\begin{bmatrix}
\text{intrans/trans/obl-trans/ditrans-sem} \\
\text{ARG1} = \boxed{\text{verb-formula}} \\[4pt]
\text{ARG2} =
\begin{bmatrix}
\text{binary-formula} \\
\text{ARG1} = \boxed{0}\ \boxed{\text{p-agt-or-no-theta}} \\[4pt]
\text{ARG2} =
\begin{bmatrix}
\text{binary-formula} \\
\text{ARG1} = \boxed{2} \\
\text{ARG2} = \boxed{3}
\end{bmatrix}
\end{bmatrix}
\end{bmatrix}
\end{bmatrix}
$$

Specific verbs types are defined by either adding constraints to the category and/or semantic attributes of the two types in (27), or merging them with other types. For example, a strict transitive is defined as a **2-complements-verb-sign** whose category and semantics are of type **strict-trans-cat** and **strict-cat-sem** respectively:

$$
\begin{bmatrix}
\text{strict-trans-sign} \sqsubseteq \text{2-complements-verb-sign} \\
\text{ORTH} = \textbf{orth} \\
\text{CAT} = \boxed{\textbf{strict-trans-cat}} \\
\text{SEM} = \boxed{\textbf{strict-trans-sem}}
\end{bmatrix}
$$

By contrast, control verbs which take two arguments (a subject and predicative phrase) are defined as the meet of **2-complements-verb-sign** and **control-verb-sign** which defines verbs whose category is of type **control-cat**:

$$
\begin{bmatrix}
\text{control-verb-sign} \sqsubseteq \text{verb-sign} \\
\text{CAT} = \boxed{\textbf{control-cat}} \\
\text{SEM} = \boxed{\textbf{verb-sem}}
\end{bmatrix}
$$

$$
\begin{bmatrix}
\text{subj-control-intrans-sign} \sqsubseteq \text{control-verb-sign, 2-complements-verb-sign}
\end{bmatrix}
$$

Subtypes for the class of control verbs with type **subj-control-intrans-sign** are defined according to whether the subject is thematic or not. Those which have a thematic subject correspond to subject equi verbs, e.g. *Jon wants to leave, Bill loves drinking, Brad did not know what to say to her*, and have semantics of type **p-agt-subj-intrans-xcomp/comp-sem**:

$$
\begin{bmatrix}
\text{subj-equi-intrans-sign} \sqsubseteq \text{subj-control-intrans-sign} \\
\text{SEM} = \boxed{\textbf{p-agt-subj-intrans-xcomp/comp-sem}}
\end{bmatrix}
$$

Those which have a non-thematic subject belong to the class of subject raising verbs, e.g. *John seems to sleep, Bill seems sad*, and have semantics of type **no-theta-subj-intrans-xcomp/comp-sem**.

$$
\begin{bmatrix}
\text{subj-raising-intrans-sign} \sqsubseteq \text{subj-control-intrans-sign} \\
\text{SEM} = \boxed{\textbf{no-theta-subj-intrans-xcomp/comp-sem}}
\end{bmatrix}
$$

A further classification of subject equi and raising intransitives is derived by taking into account morphosyntactic and categorial features of the predicative complement (see description of category types for control verbs in section 11.3, and the list of types for verb signs at the end of this section).

Other verbs whose argument and subcategorization structures are characterized by the type **2-complements-verb-sign** include intransitives which take a sentential complement or oblique object. Intransitives which subcategorize for a sentential complement — e.g. *He wished she had called, He wondered whether she would come, They would prefer for John to do it, She desires that you come at once, It seems that Mary sleeps* — inherit also from **comp-verb-sign** which define the class of verb signs with category type **comp-cat**:

$$
\begin{bmatrix}
\text{comp-verb-sign} \sqsubseteq \text{verb-sign} \\
\text{CAT} = \boxed{\textbf{comp-cat}}
\end{bmatrix}
$$

$$
\begin{bmatrix}
\text{comp-intrans-sign} \sqsubseteq \text{2-complements-verb-sign, comp-verb-sign} \\
\text{CAT} = \begin{bmatrix} \textbf{comp-cat} \\ \text{RESULT} = \boxed{\textbf{strict-intrans-cat}} \end{bmatrix}
\end{bmatrix}
$$

As in the case of control intransitives, various subtypes of **comp-intrans-sign** can be obtained according to whether the subject is thematic or non-thematic (i.e. pleonastic), taking into account morphosyntactic features of the sentential complement (see description of category types for verbs taking sentential complements in section 11.3, and the list of types for verb signs at the end of this section).

Intransitives which subcategorize for an oblique object (type **obl-intrans-sign**, e.g. *Bill talks to Mary*) inherit from **2-complements-verb-sign** and **obl-sign** which characterize verb signs with category type **obl-cat**; semantics is of type *intrans-obl-sem* and result category is **strict-intrans-cat**:

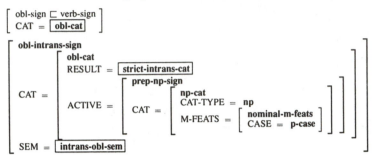

Verbs which take three arguments inherit the appropriate coindexing relations between their subcategorization and predicate-argument structures from the type **3-complements-verb-sign** shown above. In most cases, their subcategorization frame consists of a subject argument and either

- an oblique object followed by a clausal complement, e.g. *John promised (to) Mary that Bill will come*,
- a direct object followed or preceded by a prepositional object, e.g. *John gave a book to Mary, John gave Mary a book*, or
- a direct object followed by a clausal complement, e.g. *John persuaded Mary to leave.*

Those which take a prepositional object inherit also from **obl-sign**:

$$\left[\ \text{obl-xcomp/comp-intrans/obl-trans/ditrans-sign} \sqsubset \text{obl-sign, 3-complements-verb-sign} \ \right]$$

Verbs of this type include intransitive as well as transitive and ditransitive verbs. The intransitive ones inherit from **obl-xcomp/comp-intrans-sign** shown in (28) where **sign** instantiates a clausal complement.

(28)

$$\begin{bmatrix} \text{obl-xcomp/comp-intrans-sign} \sqsubset \text{obl-xcomp/comp-intrans/obl-trans/ditrans-sign} \\ \text{CAT} = \begin{bmatrix} \text{obl-cat} \\ \text{RESULT} = \begin{bmatrix} \text{complex-cat} \\ \text{RESULT} = \boxed{\text{strict-intrans-cat}} \\ \text{DIRECTION} = \textbf{forward} \\ \text{ACTIVE} = \boxed{\text{sign}} \end{bmatrix} \\ \text{DIRECTION} = \textbf{backward} \\ \text{ACTIVE} = \boxed{\text{prep-np-sign}} \end{bmatrix} \end{bmatrix}$$

Verbs of this type can be further classified according to whether the clausal complement is predicative or sentential, taking into account thematic properties of the subject:

- thematic subject with predicative complement, e.g.
  John promised (to) Mary to read a book
- non-thematic subject with predicative complement, e.g.
  John seems to me to have solved the problem
- thematic subject with sentential complement, e.g.
  John promised (to) Mary that Bill sleeps
- pleonastic subject with sentential complement, e.g.
  It seems to Bill that John sleeps

Where a predicative complement occurs, subject control is involved; the type **subj-control-obl-intrans-vpinf-sign** provides a specification for intransitives of this kind which subcategorize for an infinitive VP through reference to the type **intrans-vpinf-control-cat** in the result category.

$$
\begin{bmatrix}
\text{subj-control-obl-intrans-vpinf-sign} \sqsubseteq \text{obl-xcomp/comp-intrans-sign} \\
\text{CAT} = \begin{bmatrix}
\textbf{obl-cat} \\
\text{RESULT} = \boxed{\textbf{intrans-vpinf-control-cat}} \\
\text{DIRECTION} = \textbf{backward} \\
\text{ACTIVE} = \boxed{\textbf{prep-np-sign}}
\end{bmatrix}
\end{bmatrix}
$$

Further specifications concerning thematic properties of the subject argument provide subtypes of **subj-control-obl-intrans-vpinf-sign** for equi verbs and raising intransitives which subcategorize for an oblique object (e.g. *John promised (to) Mary to read a book, John seems to me to have solved the problem*). The equi type inherits also from **p-agt-subj-obl-xcomp/comp-intrans-sign**, a subtype of **obl-xcomp/comp-intrans-sign** which encodes a thematic subject:

$$
\begin{bmatrix}
\text{subj-raising-obl-intrans-vpinf-sign} \sqsubseteq \text{subj-control-obl-intrans-vpinf-sign} \\
\text{SEM} = \boxed{\textbf{no-theta-subj-intrans-xcomp/comp-obl-sem}}
\end{bmatrix}
$$

$$
\begin{bmatrix}
\text{p-agt-subj-obl-xcomp/comp-intrans-sign} \sqsubseteq \text{obl-xcomp/comp-intrans-sign} \\
\text{SEM} = \boxed{\textbf{p-agt-subj-intrans-xcomp/comp-obl-sem}}
\end{bmatrix}
$$

$$
\begin{bmatrix}
\text{subj-equi-obl-intrans-vpinf-sign} \sqsubseteq \begin{array}{l} \text{p-agt-subj-obl-xcomp/comp-intrans-sign,} \\ \text{subj-control-obl-intrans-vpinf-sign} \end{array}
\end{bmatrix}
$$

Intransitive verbs which take a sentential and oblique complement are defined as subtypes of either **obl-xcomp/comp-intrans-sign** or **p-agt-subj-obl-xcomp/comp-intrans-sign** according to whether the subject is thematic or pleonastic (see (29)):

(29) a Thematic Subject: **obl-comp-intrans-Sfin-sign**, e.g.
          John promised (to) Mary that Bill sleeps
      b Pleonastic Subject: **extrap-obl-comp-intrans-Sfin-sign**, e.g.
          It seems to Bill that John sleeps

$$
\left[
\begin{array}{l}
\text{obl-comp-intrans-sfin-sign} \sqsubseteq \text{p-agt-subj-obl-xcomp/comp-intrans-sign} \\
\text{CAT} = \left[
\begin{array}{l}
\text{obl-cat} \\
\text{RESULT} = \left[
\begin{array}{l}
\text{sfin-comp-cat} \\
\text{ACTIVE} = \left[
\begin{array}{l}
\text{np-sign} \\
\text{SEM} = \boxed{\text{p-agt-formula}}
\end{array}
\right]
\end{array}
\right]
\end{array}
\right]
\end{array}
\right]
$$

$$
\left[
\begin{array}{l}
\text{extrap-obl-comp-intrans-sfin-sign} \sqsubseteq \text{obl-xcomp/comp-intrans-sign} \\
\text{CAT} = \left[
\begin{array}{l}
\text{obl-cat} \\
\text{RESULT} = \left[
\begin{array}{l}
\text{sfin-comp-cat} \\
\text{ACTIVE} = \left[
\begin{array}{l}
\text{dummy-np-sign} \\
\text{SEM} = \boxed{\text{dummy-theta-formula}}
\end{array}
\right]
\end{array}
\right]
\end{array}
\right]
\end{array}
\right]
$$

Both ditransitives (*Mary sends Bill a postcard*) and transitive verbs which take a clausal complement or oblique object (*Mary persuaded Bill to leave, Mary attributes her success to hard work*) inherit from **obl-xcomp/comp-intrans/obl-trans/ditrans-sign** where the constraints conveyed by the two types **obl-sign** and **3-complements-verb-sign** are merged.

$$
\left[\ \text{obl-xcomp/comp-intrans/obl-trans/ditrans-sign} \sqsubseteq \text{obl-sign, 3-complements-verb-sign}\ \right]
$$

Ditransitives — as well as transitives which subcategorize for oblique object, see (30) — have semantics of type **obl-trans/ditrans-sem**:

$$
\left[
\begin{array}{l}
\text{ditrans-sign} \sqsubseteq \text{obl-xcomp/comp-intrans/obl-trans/ditrans-sign} \\
\text{CAT} = \boxed{\text{ditrans-cat}} \\
\text{SEM} = \boxed{\text{obl-trans/ditrans-sem}}
\end{array}
\right]
$$

Transitives which take an oblique object (**obl-trans-sign**) or clausal complement inherit also from **trans-xcomp/comp/obl-sign** which has category type **backward-wrap-trans-cat**. As discussed in sections 11.1 and 11.3, such a category specification allows the direct object to be the first argument to combine with the verb through 'backward-wrapping' even though the oblique/clausal complement is the outermost subcategorized sign according to Dowty's obliqueness hierarchy.

(30)
$$
\left[
\begin{array}{l}
\text{trans-xcomp/comp/obl-sign} \sqsubseteq \text{3-complements-verb-sign} \\
\text{CAT} = \boxed{\text{backward-wrap-trans-cat}} \\
\text{SEM} = \boxed{\text{intrans/trans/obl-trans/ditrans-sem}}
\end{array}
\right]
$$

$$
\left[
\begin{array}{l}
\text{obl-trans-sign} \sqsubseteq \\
\text{obl-xcomp/comp-intrans/obl-trans/ditrans-sign, trans-xcomp/comp/obl-sign} \\
\text{SEM} = \boxed{\text{obl-trans/ditrans-sem}}
\end{array}
\right]
$$

Transitives which subcategorize for a clausal complement can be classified according to whether the clausal complement is predicative or sentential, taking into account thematic properties of the subject and direct object arguments. Those which take a predicative complement inherit from both **trans-xcomp/comp/obl-sign** and **control-verb-sign**:

$$
\left[\ \text{control-trans-sign} \sqsubseteq \text{trans-xcomp/comp/obl-sign, control-verb-sign}\ \right]
$$

They are further classified according to whether the object is thematic or non-thematic:

(31)   a   Thematic Object: **equi-trans-sign**, e.g.
Mary persuades Bill to read a book
I tried to shame her into voting in the election

        b   Non-Thematic Object: **raising-trans-sign**, e.g.
Mary believes John to be intelligent
He hates people asking him for money

$$
\begin{bmatrix}
\text{equi-trans-sign} \sqsubseteq \text{control-trans-sign} \\
\text{SEM} = \boxed{\textbf{p-pat-obj-trans-xcomp/comp-sem}}
\end{bmatrix}
$$

$$
\begin{bmatrix}
\text{raising-trans-sign} \sqsubseteq \text{control-trans-sign} \\
\text{SEM} = \boxed{\textbf{no-theta-obj-trans-xcomp/comp-sem}}
\end{bmatrix}
$$

A first classification of transitive equi verbs is made according to whether the subject is pleonastic or thematic:

(32)   a   Pleonastic Subject: **extrap-equi-trans-vpinf-sign**, e.g.
It pleases Bill to read a good book

        b   Thematic Subject: **p-agt-subj-equi-trans-sign**, e.g.
Mary persuaded Bill to read a book

$$
\begin{bmatrix}
\text{extrap-equi-trans-vpinf-sign} \sqsubseteq \text{equi-trans-sign} \\
\text{CAT} = \begin{bmatrix}
\textbf{trans-vpinf-control-cat} \\
\text{RESULT} = \begin{bmatrix}
\textbf{complex-cat} \\
\text{RESULT} = \begin{bmatrix}
\textbf{strict-intrans-cat} \\
\text{ACTIVE} = \boxed{\textbf{dummy-np-sign}}
\end{bmatrix}
\end{bmatrix}
\end{bmatrix} \\
\text{SEM} = \boxed{\textbf{pleonastic-subj-trans-xcomp/comp-sem}}
\end{bmatrix}
$$

$$
\begin{bmatrix}
\text{p-agt-subj-equi-trans-sign} \sqsubseteq \text{control-trans-sign} \\
\text{SEM} = \boxed{\textbf{p-agt-subj-p-pat-obj-trans-xcomp/comp-sem}}
\end{bmatrix}
$$

Various subtypes of equi and raising transitives can be defined according to morphosyntactic and categorial features of the clausal complement (see description of category types for control verbs in section 11.3, and the list of types for verb signs below).

Transitives which subcategorize for a (finite) sentential complement inherit both from **comp-verb-sign** and **trans-xcomp/comp/obl-sign**:

$$
\begin{bmatrix}
\text{comp-trans-sign} \sqsubseteq \text{comp-verb-sign, trans-xcomp/comp/obl-sign} \\
\text{CAT} = \boxed{\textbf{sfin-comp-cat}}
\end{bmatrix}
$$

Two subtypes can be distinguished according to whether the subject is thematic or pleonastic:

(33)   a   Thematic Subject: **reg-comp-trans-sign**, e.g.
Bill told John that Mary sleeps

b   Pleonastic Subject: **extrap-comp-trans-sign**, e.g.
            It bothers Bill that Mary sleeps

$$\left[\begin{array}{l} \text{reg-comp-trans-sign} \sqsubset \text{comp-trans-sign} \\ \text{SEM} = \boxed{\text{p-agt-subj-p-pat-obj-trans-xcomp/comp-sem}} \end{array} \right]$$

$$\left[\begin{array}{l} \text{extrap-comp-trans-sign} \sqsubset \text{comp-trans-sign} \\ \text{SEM} = \boxed{\text{pleonastic-subj-trans-xcomp/comp-sem}} \end{array} \right]$$

To conclude the description of verb signs, here follows a list of all types defined along with illustrative examples.

- **strict-intrans-sign**, e.g. *John sleeps*
- **strict-trans-sign**, e.g. *John reads a book*
- **subj-equi-intrans-vpinf-sign**, e.g. *John wants to sleep*
- **subj-equi-intrans-vping-sign**, e.g. *John loves sleeping*
- **subj-equi-intrans-adj-sign**, e.g. *John feels sad*
- **subj-raising-intrans-vpinf-sign**, e.g. *John seems to sleep*
- **subj-raising-intrans-adj-sign**, e.g. *John seems sad*
- **pleonastic-subj-intrans-vpinf-sign**, e.g. *It hurts to feel sad*
- **equi-trans-vpinf-sign**, e.g. *John persuaded Mary to sleep*
- **equi-trans-vping-sign**, e.g. *John hates people asking him for money*
- **equi-trans-adj-sign**, e.g. *John found Mary sad*
- **raising-trans-vpinf-sign**, e.g. *John believes Mary to sleep*
- **raising-trans-vping-sign**, e.g. *John hates Mary sleeping*
- **raising-trans-adj-sign**, e.g. *John wants the book ready*
- **extrap-equi-trans-vpinf-sign**, e.g. *It pleases Mary to read a good book*
- **reg-comp-intrans-sfin-sign**, e.g. *John thinks (that) Mary sleeps*
- **reg-comp-intrans-swh-sign**, e.g. *Mary wonders whether John sleeps*
- **reg-comp-intrans-sinf-sign**, e.g. *Mary prefers for John to sleep*
- **reg-comp-intrans-sbase-sign**, e.g. *Mary desires that John sleep*
- **extrap-comp-intrans-sign**, e.g. *It seems that Mary sleeps*
- **extrap-comp-trans-sign**, e.g. *It bothers Bill that Mary sleeps*
- **reg-comp-trans-sign**, e.g. *Bill told John that Mary sleeps*
- **obl-intrans-sign**, e.g. *John talks to Bill*
- **ditrans-sign**, e.g. *Mary sends Bill a postcard*
- **obl-trans-sign**, e.g. *Mary attributes her success to hard work*
- **subj-equi-obl-intrans-vpinf-sign**, e.g. *John promised Mary to mow the lawn*
- **subj-raising-obl-intrans-vpinf-sign**, e.g. *John seems to Mary to sleep*
- **obl-comp-intrans-sfin-sign**, e.g. *John promises Mary that Bill will not come*
- **extrap-obl-comp-intrans-Sfin-sign**, e.g. *It seems to Bill that John sleeps*
- **subj-equi-intrans-vpwh-sign**, e.g. *Brad did not know what to say to her*

11.5   Lexical Defaults

The verb types described in section 11.4 have been used in conjunction with templates encoding word-sense specific information semi-automatically derived from Machine-Readable Dictionaries (MRDs) to develop verb lexicons for English (Sanfilippo and Poznanski, 1992). This practice allows the creation of large scale lexical components for NLP systems in a time- and cost-effective manner. Needless to say, currently available MRDs fall short of providing ideal lexical databases, as they are essentially meant for production of printed dictionaries. Consequently, it is generally impossible to recover the same piece of information across relevant entries in an exhaustive manner. This means that some of the features left underspecified in the declaration of verb types will inappropriately remain uninstantiated in a significative number of LKB entries. This inadequacy can be efficiently redressed by allowing feature specification through default inheritance.

In the ACQUILEX LKB, default inheritance is enforced by letting individual entries inherit from previously defined 'psorts' (Copestake, this volume). As for types, psorts can be hierarchically arranged. For example, the psort *defaults-obl-trans-sign* below provides a specification of default inheritance for both transitives taking an oblique object (**obl-trans-sign**) and ditransitives (**ditrans-sign**) with reference to morphosyntactic sentential features.

(34)
$$
\begin{bmatrix}
\text{obl-xcomp/comp-intrans/obl-trans/ditrans-sign} \\
\text{CAT RESULT RESULT RESULT M-FEATS} \\
= \begin{bmatrix}
\begin{bmatrix}
\text{sent-m-feats} \\
\text{REG-MORPH} = \text{true} \\
\text{VFORM} = \text{base} \\
\text{COMP-FORM} = \text{no-comp} \\
\text{DIATHESES} = \begin{bmatrix}
\text{ditrans/trans-obl-diatheses} \\
\text{PRT-ALT} = \text{no-info} \\
\text{TRANS-ALT} = \text{no-info} \\
\text{OBL-ALT} = \text{no-info}
\end{bmatrix}
\end{bmatrix}
\end{bmatrix}
\end{bmatrix}
$$

Psort `defaults-ditrans-obl-trans-sign`

The definition of specific psorts for the two verb types involve (non-default) inheritance from the psort in (34), as shown below where the path equation in the definition of `defaults-ditrans-sign` introduces a default specification relative to the 'dative movement' alternation.

```
defaults-obl-trans-sign
    <> <= defaults-ditrans-obl-trans-sign <>.

defaults-ditrans-sign
    <> <= defaults-ditrans-obl-trans-sign <>
    <cat:result:result:result:m-feats:diatheses:dat-movt>
        = ("to_1" "for_1").
```

Psorts so defined can then be integrated with templates encoding word specific information derived through access to MRD sources, e.g.

```
bounce L_1_2
OBL-TRANS-SIGN
<> < defaults-obl-trans-sign <>
<cat:result:result:result:m-feats:diatheses:trans-alt> = "caus-inch"
<cat:result:result:result:m-feats:diatheses:obl-alt> = CUM-PATH
<sem:ind> = DYN-EVE
<cat:result:result:active:sem:pred> = P-AGT-CAUSE
<cat:result:active:sem:pred> = P-PAT-MOVE-MANNER
<sense-id:dictionary> = "LDOCE"
<sense-id:ldb-entry-no> = "3767"
<sense-id: sense-no> = "2".
```

This integration will provide an appropriate lexical instantiation for whichever morphosyntactic sentential feature was left underspecified in the derivation of the template.

11.6   Conclusion

Current research in Natural Language Processing has shown that inheritance systems based on typed unification offer computationally efficient and formally adequate tools for large scale representation of lexical knowledge. In keeping with these developments, we have described a type system for English verbs which is based on a network of information structures related by inheritance links defined in the representation language of the ACQUILEX LKB. These information structures provide an efficient and detailed characterization of syntactic and semantic properties of verb forms in a format which can be tested for appropriateness in a parsing context and can be adjusted to suit several grammatical frameworks. The system integrates specifications for the inheritance of lexical defaults and provides effective means for semiautomatic construction of large lexicons from MRD sources.

Acknowledgements

In developing the study described in this chapter, I have benefitted from discussions with Ted Briscoe, John Carroll, Ann Copestake and Valeria de Paiva.

12   Defaults in Lexical Representation

ANN COPESTAKE

Abstract

In this chapter we discuss how the typed feature structure formalism described in the previous chapters is augmented with a default inheritance system. We first introduce our use of defaults informally and illustrate the sort of taxonomic data that motivated the design of our system. We then discuss some of the formal issues involved in introducing defaults into the representation language.

12.1   Taxonomies, Lexical Semantics and Default Inheritance

Our approach to default inheritance in the LKB has been largely motivated by consideration of the taxonomies which may be extracted automatically from MRDs, although the default inheritance mechanism can be used for other purposes, as discussed by Sanfilippo (this volume). In this section we introduce this concept of taxonomy, which is discussed in more detail by Vossen and Copestake (this volume). The notion of taxonomy that has been used in work on MRDs such as that by Amsler (1981), Chodorow *et al.* (1985) and Guthrie *et al.* (1990) is essentially an informal and intuitive one: a taxonomy is the network which results from connecting headwords with the genus terms in their definitions but the concept of genus term is not formally defined; however for noun definitions, which are all we will consider here, it is in general taken to be the syntactic head of the defining noun phrase (exceptions to this are discussed by Vossen and Copestake). For example, the LDOCE definition of one sense of *paraffin* is:

> **paraffin 1**   an oil made from petroleum, coal, etc., burnt for heat and in lamps for light

and here the genus term is taken to be a particular sense of *oil*. In most cases the relationship between a word sense and the genus term of its definition seems to be a hyponymy or IS_A relationship (again, see Vossen and Copestake for exceptions). In good lexicographic practice:

> The defining noun ... should pinpoint that property of a thing that is viewed by most speakers as being essential to it. (Landau, 1984)

223

Nevertheless the notion of taxonomy arrived at in this way is broader than the classical notion of taxonomies exemplified by biological classification; taxonomies extracted from dictionaries do not just include natural kind terms, and sister terms are not necessarily mutually exclusive (for example *stallion, palomino, palfrey* and *gee-gee* all come under *horse 1* in a taxonomy extracted from LDOCE).

A procedure for semi-automatic creation of sense-disambiguated taxonomies was described in Copestake (1990b). This operates in a top-down fashion; starting from a given, disambiguated word sense all the entries in which this is used as the genus term are found, and the program then recurses on the word sense corresponding to each of these entries, terminating on word senses which are never used as genus terms. A series of heuristics are used to disambiguate the genus terms in the definitions, the decision being confirmed by the user in the more critical cases. So starting from *liquid*² *1*, *oil*¹ *1* is one of the (large number of) entries found; this in turn is the genus term in entries such as *paraffin 1*. If *paraffin 1* is not used as a genus term in any entries, the process will bottom out at this point, and *paraffin 1* will be a leaf node in the taxonomy.

We use such taxonomies to structure the LKB in order to allow the inheritance of lexical semantic information. Some of this information is relatively simple; we represent information about physical state, for example, which could be used in a parser which incorporates selectional restrictions or preferences. By allowing such information to be inherited down a hierarchy of lexical entries derived from the taxonomy we achieve both economy of representation and efficiency in acquisition. Thus because the lexical entry derived from *liquid*² *1* has the property of being in the liquid state associated with it, this information will be inherited by default by the lexical entries for all the word senses found under *liquid*² *1* in the taxonomy, including *paraffin 1*.

However the approach to lexical semantics which we are currently pursuing requires the representation of a much richer range of attributes. For example, the treatment of logical metonymy adopted in Briscoe *et al.* (1990) following Pustejovsky (1989, 1991) allows the coercion of sentences such as:

John enjoyed the autobiography.

into the equivalent of:

John enjoyed reading the autobiography.

(in an informationally impoverished context). This is done by associating information about the default purpose of entities with the relevant lexical entry; Pustejovsky refers to this as the telic role and describes it as part of the qualia structure of nominals. A partial lexical entry for *autobiography* which specifies the telic role as reading is shown in Figure 12.1.

The definition of the relevant sense of *autobiography* in LDOCE is:

autobiography   a book written by oneself about one's own life

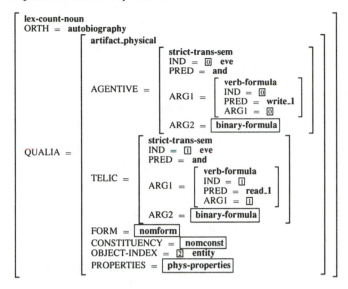

Figure 12.1: Lexical entry for autobiography

If an inheritance link is created on the basis of the taxonomic relationship and if the predicate for the telic role of *book* in the relevant sense is *read*, then this will be inherited by *autobiography*, allowing the lexical entry shown in Figure 12.1 to be produced without having to specify the telic role directly. However, this information is clearly defeasible; consider the definitions of *dictionary* and *lexicon* in LDOCE:

> **dictionary 1**   a book that gives a list of words in alphabetical order with their pronunciations and meanings
>
> **lexicon**   a dictionary esp. of an ancient language

Although a dictionary is a book, the purpose of a dictionary is to be referred to rather than read. We thus wish to allow entries lower in the taxonomy to override the inherited information; although *dictionary* is under *book*[1] *1* in the hierarchy, the inheritance of the telic role must be cancelled by more specific information about the purpose of dictionaries. This modified value should be inherited by *lexicon*.

It is not always appropriate to construct inheritance links of this form between the genus sense and the sense being defined. For example, consider the following definition:

> **rocket 1**   a tube-shaped case packed with gunpowder ...

The appropriate sense of *case* here is presumably:

> **case[2] 3**   a box or container for holding or protecting something

However, to state that *rocket* inherited from *case*[2] *3* would probably be a mistake, since its lexical semantic properties are quite different; for example, *case*, like other container denoting words, can be used to mean either the physical object or the stuff contained:

> John smashed open the case.
> Oddbins sells 3000 cases (of wine) a year.

This is clearly not true of *rocket*. It is intuitively plausible to claim the definition of *rocket 1* does not express an IS_A relationship, but intuitions on the question of what should be taken as an IS_A relationship vary widely.

We assume as a working hypothesis that the IS_A taxonomic relationships which license inheritance of lexical semantic properties between word senses correspond to the cases where the definitions can be taken as asserting that a subset relationship exists between the extensions of the defined word sense and the genus word sense. For example:

$$\text{autobiography ISA book}^1\ 1 \equiv [\![\text{autobiography}]\!] \subseteq [\![\text{book}^1\ 1]\!]$$

Thus we are assuming that the subset relationship is (usually) entailed by the semantics of the sort of dictionary definitions which we have been considering, although we are certainly not claiming that this is all that there is to their semantics. Traditional dictionaries follow the principle of substitutability; that is, that the word sense being defined (the definiendum) can be replaced by the definition when it occurs in a sentence with a result which is equivalent in meaning. Thus in the ideal dictionary definition the extension of the definition and the definiendum would be identical. This ideal is clearly rarely, if ever, attainable; however, this principle, plus that of pinpointing essential properties in the defining noun, lead to a characteristic pattern for definitions where the modifiers are intersective and specialise the meaning of the genus term to approximate to that of the definiendum. In the case of definitions such as that for *autobiography*, the modifiers of the genus term are intersective; a *book written by oneself* is a *book*. In contrast, a *case packed with gunpowder* is no longer a *case*, but such definition structures are relatively rare. (We can take this assumption about the inheritance relationship to cover mass terms and plurals as well as singular count nouns, given a suitable semantics, such as that developed in Copestake (1990a) (after Krifka, 1987, where singular, plural and mass entities have the same model-theoretic status.)

If we assume that lexical semantic properties are at least consistent with real world properties, the subset relationship supports the inheritance behaviour which we have just outlined. It is clear that properties which necessarily hold of some set of entities also hold for any subset of those entities and thus inheritance of necessary properties is justified. Lexical semantic properties are not usually necessary real world properties under our account, but the inheritance behaviour described does follow from the 'Penguin Principle', that properties which hold by default of some set of entities also hold by default for any subset of those entities, but that more specific information about the default behaviour of the subset will override the inherited behaviour. The Penguin Principle is frequently taken as a desirable property of a non-monotonic logic; see Morreau (this volume), for example. However, in representing the lexicon we do not wish to implement a non-monotonic logic directly, because we do not need the full power of such a formalism, but to use a default inheritance mechanism for lexical semantic information which is consistent with these observations. This mechanism is described in the rest of this paper.

12.2   Default Inheritance in the LRL

Default inheritance in the LRL is defined as a relationship between typed feature structures. As described in Copestake *et al.* (this volume) feature structures in the LRL may be specified as inheriting information from one or more other (well-formed) feature structures which we refer to in this context as *psorts*. Psorts may correspond to (parts of) lexical entries or be specially defined.

Non-default inheritance is implemented by unification of the feature structure with a copy of the relevant part of the psort. The default inheritance mechanism is similar except that default unification rather than ordinary unification is involved. The effect of default unification is that incompatible values for attributes are ignored, rather than causing unification failure. Non-default inheritance can be seen as producing a feature structure which is the minimal satisfier of the union of the set of local descriptions given in the attribute value language, with the set of descriptions of which the psort is the minimal satisfier. Default inheritance, in contrast, produces a feature structure which is the minimal satisfier of the union of the set of local descriptions with non-conflicting descriptions from the psort. (Deciding how to define the non-conflicting descriptions is a somewhat complex problem; default unification is discussed in detail in sections 12.3 and 12.4.)

Since psorts may themselves inherit information, default inheritance (notated by <, 'inherits from') in effect operates over a hierarchy of psorts, and the ordering on the psort hierarchy gives us an ordering on defaults (cycles in the inheritance ordering are prohibited). However, once information is incorporated into a feature structure no distinction between inherited and non-inherited information is maintained and a psort will be fully expanded before it is used; inheritance thus operates top-down.

So, for example, assume that the following is part of the lexical entry for book_L_1_1 (i.e. book_L_1_1 is the name of the psort, where the code L_1_1 refers to the sense number in the machine readable dictionary).

$$
\text{book\_L\_1\_1} \quad
\begin{bmatrix}
\text{lex-noun-sign} \\
\text{QUALIA} =
\begin{bmatrix}
\text{artifact\_physical} \\
\text{TELIC} =
\begin{bmatrix}
\text{verb-sem} \\
\text{PRED} = \text{read\_L\_1\_1}
\end{bmatrix} \\
\text{PHYSICAL-STATE} = \text{solid\_a}
\end{bmatrix}
\end{bmatrix}
$$

This feature structure shows part of the qualia structure mentioned earlier. The following path specifications make the lexical entries defined inherit their qualia structure from book_L_1_1:

```
autobiography_L_0_0   < QUALIA > < book_L_1_1 < QUALIA >.
dictionary_L_0_1      < QUALIA > < book_L_1_1 < QUALIA >
                      < QUALIA : TELIC >
                           <= refer_to_L_0_2 < SEM >.
lexicon_L_0_0         < QUALIA > < dictionary_L_0_1 < QUALIA >.
```

autobiography_L_0_1 thus has the same values as book_L_1_1 for both TELIC and PHYSICAL-STATE as shown in Figure 12.1. The entry dictionary_L_0_1 will inherit the value **solid_a** for the feature PHYSICAL-STATE but the value of the TELIC role, which is non-default inherited from refer_to_L_0_2, overrides that which would be inherited from book_L_1_ 1 (**read_L_1_1**). The entry lexicon_L_0_0 inherits its value for the telic role from dictionary_L_0_1 rather than from book_L_1_1.

$$
\text{lexicon\_L\_0\_0} \quad
\begin{bmatrix}
\text{lex-noun-sign} \\
\text{QUALIA} =
\begin{bmatrix}
\text{artifact\_physical} \\
\text{TELIC} =
\begin{bmatrix}
\text{verb-sem} \\
\text{PRED} = \text{refer\_to\_L\_0\_2}
\end{bmatrix} \\
\text{PHYSICAL-STATE} = \text{solid\_a}
\end{bmatrix}
\end{bmatrix}
$$

Our variant of default unification is restricted by the type system so that a feature structure will not inherit any information from a feature structure of incompatible type, unless it unifies fully with that feature structure. This implies that default inheritance has no effect in a description in which the non-defeasible information leads to a type t_1 being given to a feature structure if the psort is of type t_2 such that t_1 and t_2 are incompatible. Such a description is flagged as an error and thus the default inheritance ordering will reflect the order on the type hierarchy. The typing system restricts default inheritance essentially to the specification (or specialisation) of values for features which are defined by the type system.

Multiple default inheritance is allowed but is restricted to the case where the information from the parent psorts does not conflict. This is enforced by unifying all (fully expanded) immediate parent psorts before default unifying the result with the daughter psort. The type restriction on default inheritance means that all the psorts must have compatible types and the type of the daughter must be the meet of those types.

Although introducing psorts as well as types may seem unnecessarily complex, given that the type mechanism allows inheritance, there seem to be compelling reasons for doing so for this application, where we wish to use taxonomic information extracted from MRDs to structure the lexicon. The type hierarchy is not a suitable way for representing taxonomic inheritance for several reasons. Perhaps the most important is that taxonomically inherited information is defeasible, but typing and defaults are incompatible notions. Types are used to enforce an organisation on the lexicon; if the typing scheme can be overridden then none of the advantages of a typed system over a straight inheritance system hold. Error checking and classification, which are important properties of the type system for our application, as discussed in Copestake *et al.* (this volume), both require that information associated with types is non-defeasible. Furthermore the type system is taken to be complete, and various conditions are imposed on it, such as the greatest lower bound condition (see de Paiva, this volume), which ensure that deterministic classification is possible. Taxonomies extracted from dictionaries will not be complete in this sense, and will not meet these conditions. We want to be able to classify lexical entries into defined categories such as creature, person, animal, artifact and so on. If these are set up as types **creature, person, animal** etc, classification is possible based on the assumption of completeness of the type system; thus we in effect state that all **creature**s are either **person**s or **animal**s. But we would not expect to be able to use the finer-grained, automatically acquired information in this way; we will never extract all possible categories of *horse* for example. (Cf. Brachman *et al.*'s, 1985, distinction between terminological and assertional knowledge.)

In implementational terms, using the type hierarchy to provide the fine-grain of inheritance possible with taxonomic information would be very difficult. A type scheme should be relatively static; any alterations may affect a large amount of data and checking that the scheme as a whole is still consistent is a non-trivial process. Because the inheritance hierarchies are derived from taxonomies and thus are derived semi-automatically from MRDs, they will contain errors and it is important that these can be corrected easily.

In practice, deciding whether to make use of the type mechanism or the psort mechanism has been relatively straightforward. If we wish to define a feature which is particular to some group of lexical entries we have to introduce a type; if we wish to specify the value of a feature, especially if the information might be defeasible, we use a psort. For the lexical semantics of nouns the psort will usually correspond to a lexical entry, but it could be formed by combining lexical entries, using unification or generalisation, or by applying lexical rules. Psorts can also be specified purely for default inheritance (see Sanfilippo, this volume).

Several of the decisions involved in designing the default inheritance system were thus influenced by the application. The condition that the default inheritance ordering reflects the type ordering was partly motivated by the desire to be able to provide a QUALIA type for lexical entries on the basis of taxonomic data alone. (However, it also seems intuitively reasonable as a way of restricting default inheritance; it would be difficult to make any substantive claims about the appropriateness of the type system to capture some linguistic generalisation if default inheritance could be used to transform feature structures in a way which was not governed by the type system.)

Since we have to cope with errors in extraction of information from MRDs, and with the lexicographers' original mistakes, we adopted the conservative condition that information inherited from multiple parents has to be consistent. This is discussed in more detail below. However, our consistency condition seems to be met fairly naturally by the data. Taxonomies extracted from MRDs are in general tree-structured (once sense-disambiguation has been performed); there do not tend to be many examples of genuine conjunction in the genus term, for example. Multiple inheritance is mainly needed for cross-classification; artifacts, for example, may be defined principally in terms of their form or in terms of their function, but here different sets of features are specified, corresponding to different parts of the qualia structure, so the information is consistent (see Vossen and Copestake, this volume).

12.3   Default Unification of Untyped Feature Structures

Default unification is defined so that when a non-default feature structure is unified with a default feature structure only values in the default structure which do not conflict with values in the non-default structure are incorporated. In our case the default feature structure will be the feature structure associated with the psort and the non-default feature structure will be that associated with the inheritor. (The resulting feature structure may later be treated as the default in another default unification operation.) We will use $A \stackrel{<}{\sqcap} B$ to indicate default unification where A is non-default. In this section we consider the definition of default unification for untyped feature structures. This is discussed in detail in Carpenter (this volume); here we wish to extend that discussion slightly in order to illustrate the varieties of default unification which have been proposed and to describe our own variant. Typed feature structures are considered in the following section. (The notation used for the non-default operations on feature structures is as defined in de Paiva, this volume.)

We would like default unification to have the following properties:

1. $A \stackrel{<}{\sqcap} B \sqsubseteq A$

    Default unification adds information monotonically to the non-default. Clearly it should not be possible to remove non-default information, and all definitions of default unification of which we are aware do meet this criterion.

2. if $A \sqcap B \neq \bot$ then $A \sqcap B = A \stackrel{<}{\sqcap} B$

    Default unification behaves like ordinary unification in the cases where ordinary unification would succeed.

    Intuitively ordinary unification should correspond to the case where the default feature structure is totally compatible with the non-default structure.

3. $A \mathbin{\hat{\sqcap}} B \neq \bot$

Default unification never fails.

This is a property which could be taken as definitional for default unification. However, as we will see later, some versions of default unification drop this condition (or put preconditions on default unification such that it cannot be applied to some pairs of feature structures) in order to meet the other requirements.

4. Default unification returns a single result, deterministically.

It seems desirable not to introduce non-determinism into the system. Multiple results are awkward from the point of view of both implementation and usability.

It is in general necessary that default unification be implementable with reasonable efficiency, and it is highly desirable that it give results which are intuitively plausible to users.

The examples of default unification given in section 12.2 are unproblematic. However, there are cases where there are conflicts between parts of the default information because of reentrancy in the default or in the non-default feature structure, as in the following examples:

$$\begin{bmatrix} F = \boxed{1} \\ G = \boxed{1} \end{bmatrix} \mathbin{\hat{\sqcap}} \begin{bmatrix} F = a \\ G = b \end{bmatrix}$$

$$\begin{bmatrix} F = a \\ G = \top \end{bmatrix} \mathbin{\hat{\sqcap}} \begin{bmatrix} F = \boxed{1}\ b \\ G = \boxed{1} \end{bmatrix}$$

As shown in section 12.3.2 the various definitions of default unification that have been proposed are not in agreement about the result of default unification for such examples. The difficulty in defining default unification is to exclude the possibility of the result depending on the order in which individual parts of the default feature structure are unified with the non-default feature structure. All the definitions which we will discuss here exclude such order dependence, but they do so in different ways.

12.3.1 Definitions of Default Unification

In many ways we regard Carpenter's definition of skeptical default unification (this volume) as the ideal; it meets all the conditions enumerated above and has a definition which can be simply paraphrased as 'incorporate the maximal consistent information from the default'. Unfortunately it appears that it cannot be implemented efficiently (Carpenter, personal communication; see also below).

In order to compare Carpenter's definition with some of the other varieties of default unification which have been proposed, we will formalise them all in terms of successively unifying pieces of information carried by the default into the non-default feature structure while taking account of possible conflicts (cf. Russell *et al.*, this volume). A critical notion here is that of 'pieces of information'; we can define a general notion of decomposition of a feature structure *Decomp(F)* into component pieces of information. This must meet the following criterion (if default unification is to have the property of being equivalent to ordinary unification in the cases where that would succeed):

$$\sqcap(Decomp(F)) = F$$

F is equal to the unification of all the information in its decomposition.

We first consider the case where decomposition is into the minimal atomic units of information (Carpenter, this volume). We repeat Carpenter's definition of atomic feature structures here for convenience:

Definition 1 (Atomic Feature Structure)   *A feature structure is* atomic *if it is of one of the following two forms:*

- (Path Value)
  the feature structure contains a single path assigned to an atomic value.
- (Path Sharing)
  the feature structure contains only a pair of (possibly identical) paths which are shared.

The function *At* when applied to a feature structure F gives the set of atomic units:

$$At(F) = \{F' \sqsubseteq F \mid F' \text{ atomic}\}$$

Carpenter shows that *At* meets our criterion for the decomposition function (i.e. $\sqcap(At(F)) = F$).

We can thus give a definition of default unification in terms of incorporation of atomic feature structures which is equivalent to Carpenter's skeptical default unification:

Definition 2 (Skeptical Default Unification)
$F_1 \mathrel{\hat{\sqcap}} F_2 = F_1 \sqcap \sqcap \{F \in At(F_2) \mid F_1 \sqcap F \neq \perp \text{ and there is no } F' \text{ such that } F_2 \sqsubseteq F' \text{ and } F' \sqcap F_1 \neq \perp \text{ and } F' \sqcap F_1 \sqcap F = \perp\}$

The intuitive basis for this definition is to consider successively adding the minimal (atomic) units of information from the default into the non-default. In the cases where there are conflicts, such as the examples just given, this would give different results depending on the order in which the atomic feature structures were added in. To produce the equivalent of credulous default unification we would do the addition once for each possible ordering of default atomic feature structures (and remove duplicates). The definition above is equivalent to skeptical default unification because only information which is consistent with all possible orderings is added. It is thus obvious that the complexity of the algorithm as described is unacceptable (worse than exponential), since checking for all possible F' would involve creating the unification of each member of the power-set of $At(F_2)$. (An illustration of the type of feature structure which exhibits this worst case behaviour is shown in example 5, below.)

The option taken by Russell *et al.* (1991, this volume) is to keep the tractable (near-linear) behaviour of ordinary unification by defining default unification in such a way that it fails under the circumstances where there are conflicts in the default information. In terms of our definition above we can split $At(F)$ into $PE(F)$, the set of path equivalence specifications, and $PV(F)$ the set of path value specifications. If the reentrant part of the default unifies with the non-default, and the reentrant part of the non-default unifies with the default, no conflicts can arise in the default information. Thus Russell *et al.* have:

Definition 3 (Russell *et al.* Default Unification)

$$F_1 \stackrel{<}{\sqcap} F_2 = \bot \; \textit{if} \sqcap \mathrm{PE}(F_2) \sqcap F_1 = \bot$$
$$\textit{or} \; \sqcap \mathrm{PE}(F_1) \sqcap F_2 = \bot$$
$$= F_1 \sqcap \sqcap \{F \in At(F_2) \mid F_1 \sqcap F \neq \bot\} \; \textit{otherwise}$$

The LKB's current default unification algorithm also makes use of a distinction between reentrant and non-reentrant atomic feature structures. The definition used is:

Definition 4 (LRL Current)

$F_1 \stackrel{<}{\sqcap} F_2 = F_1 \sqcap \sqcap \{F \in At(F_2) \mid F_1 \sqcap F \neq \bot \; \textit{and for all conflicting } F' \textit{ such that}$
$F_2 \sqsubseteq F' \textit{ and } F' \sqcap F_1 \neq \bot \textit{ and } F' \sqcap F_1 \sqcap F = \bot, F \textit{ 'takes precedence over' } F'\}$
Where F takes precedence over F' iff F is a specification of path equivalence ($F \in \mathrm{PE}(F_1)$) and F' contains at least one path value specification.

Thus we introduce a precedence order between path equivalence and path value specifications. This was actually done because the linguists involved in designing the LRL expressed a preference for a behaviour where reentrancy took precedence over values; for our application in particular this seems desirable because reentrancy is usually set up manually (see, e.g. Sanfilippo, this volume), whereas values are more likely to be acquired automatically. (However, in our use of the LKB so far, this means that reentrancy tends to be set up in the type system, and is thus, in effect, non-default. This is considered further below.)

This approach to default unification can, in practice, be implemented considerably more efficiently than Carpenter's, although its worst case behaviour is still worse than exponential. Initially the reentrant parts of the default feature structure can be unified individually with the non-default, and it is only necessary to consider conflicts that arise in the reentrant set. Thus the exponential term involves only the path equivalence specifications, and since typically there are many fewer path equivalence specifications than path value specifications the implementation is not unreasonably slow. (Furthermore this is the worst case behaviour; it is usually possible to split $PE(F)$ into sets which are guaranteed not to interact.) The procedure then reduces to one of default unifying a tree-structured feature structure with a non-default reentrant structure. There are still possible conflicts of the type in example 3 below (which would cause unification failure by Russell *et al.*'s definition). However, it is possible to allow for these with a linear algorithm by storing the original non-default value in the feature structure representation at reentrant points as unification proceeds, and reverting to it if a conflict arises. In effect, what we are relying on is that if the non-default feature structure is the only reentrant one, all conflicts are localised.

However, this definition still seems unsatisfactory, even though it meets all the criteria we enumerated at the beginning of this section. The worst case complexity is exponential, the implementation is awkward and the behaviour can be obscure. A better compromise for our current use of default unification seems to be to specify that inheritance of information about reentrancy is non-defeasible, and that default unification fails in the case where the non-default feature structure and the reentrant part of the default feature structure do not unify.

Definition 5 (LRL Proposed)
$F_1 \stackrel{<}{\sqcap} F_2 = F_3 \sqcap \bigsqcap \{F \mid F \in PV(F_2) \text{ and there is no } F' \in PV(F_2) \text{ such that }$
$F' \sqcap F_3 \neq \bot \text{ and } F' \sqcap F_3 \sqcap F = \bot \}$
where $F_3 = F_1 \sqcap \bigsqcap PE(F_2)$

Such a definition, where default unification involves filling in values, and expanding, rather than modifying, existing feature structure skeletons, is relatively simple to understand.[1] In practice changing the definition seems unlikely to cause any significant problems with our use of the LKB, because reentrancy tends to be specified in the type system, and is then of course not defeasible.

Bouma's (1990a,b) treatment of default unification can also be described in terms of addition of pieces of information from the default structure to the non-default structure. However, we will not attempt to reformalise it in these terms here, since the mechanism by which conflicts are excluded is complex and Bouma's definition is lengthy. Instead we will give examples of the behaviour of Bouma's approach below, which illustrate that it does not conform to all of our original criteria.

12.3.2   *Examples of Default Unification*

The following examples illustrate the differences in behaviour between the definitions that have been proposed by Bouma (1990a,b), Carpenter (this volume),

---

[1] It also avoids the rather complex behaviour of Carpenter's definition with respect to the difference between specified and unspecified paths (see Carpenter, this volume). However, we will not discuss that further here, since default unification of typed feature structures, as actually used in the LKB, avoids the problem in any case.

Calder (1991), Russell *et al.* (1991, this volume) and ourselves.[2] As Carpenter notes, his definition of credulous default unification is equivalent to Calder's definition of priority union. We have limited these examples to the cases where the default and non-default structures have the same features, since we are ultimately interested in default unification in a strictly typed system.

$$(1) \quad \begin{bmatrix} F = a \\ G = \top \end{bmatrix} \stackrel{\leq}{\sqcap} \begin{bmatrix} F = b \\ G = c \end{bmatrix} = \begin{bmatrix} F = a \\ G = c \end{bmatrix}$$

This is the simplest case of default unification; the conflicting information in the default is ignored, but the non-conflicting information is incorporated. (Although we are discussing untyped feature structures, we use $\top$ to indicate an unspecified value.)

$$(2) \quad \begin{bmatrix} F = \boxed{1} \\ G = \boxed{1} \end{bmatrix} \stackrel{\leq}{\sqcap} \begin{bmatrix} F = a \\ G = \top \end{bmatrix} = \begin{bmatrix} F = \boxed{1} \\ G = \boxed{1} \end{bmatrix} \quad \text{Bouma}$$

$$= \begin{bmatrix} F = \boxed{1} \ a \\ G = \boxed{1} \end{bmatrix} \quad \text{other definitions}$$

We include this example to illustrate that Bouma's definition of default unification does not meet our second criterion, since it gives a different result from ordinary unification. This arises because in Bouma's approach any pieces of information in the default which potentially conflict with each other are excluded, and Bouma's algorithm treats the values of F and G as being in potential conflict. (In practice this behaviour is presumably not apparent, since Bouma proposes that ordinary unification is attempted before default unification.)

$$(3) \quad \begin{bmatrix} F = \boxed{1} \\ G = \boxed{1} \end{bmatrix} \stackrel{\leq}{\sqcap} \begin{bmatrix} F = a \\ G = b \end{bmatrix} = \left(\begin{bmatrix} F = \boxed{1} \ a \\ G = \boxed{1} \end{bmatrix} \cdot \begin{bmatrix} F = \boxed{1} \ b \\ G = \boxed{1} \end{bmatrix} \right) \quad \begin{array}{l} \text{Calder} \\ \text{Carpenter} \\ \text{(credulous)} \end{array}$$

$$= \begin{bmatrix} F = \boxed{1} \\ G = \boxed{1} \end{bmatrix} \quad \begin{array}{l} \text{Bouma} \\ \text{Carpenter} \\ \text{(skeptical)} \\ \text{LRL} \end{array}$$

$$= \bot \quad \text{Russell } et \ al.$$

Here the presence of reentrancy in the non-default means that the two default values are in conflict. A credulous definition will return multiple values; skeptical definitions return only that information which is common to all the credulous results.

---

[2] Since the first version of this paper was written I have become aware of another version of default unification described by van den Berg and Prüst (1991). In their paper a general notion of maximal incorporation of information is described which is apparently equivalent to Carpenter's. However the specific application to feature structures uses a process of normalisation similar to that of Bouma (see below), which results in reentrant structures being treated as equivalent to the non-reentrant case, where the paths terminate in distinct identical values.

$$\begin{bmatrix} F = a \\ G = \top \end{bmatrix} \stackrel{<}{\sqcap} \begin{bmatrix} F = \boxed{1} \ b \\ G = \boxed{1} \end{bmatrix} = \left(\begin{bmatrix} F = \boxed{1} \ a \\ G = \boxed{1} \end{bmatrix} \cdot \begin{bmatrix} F = a \\ G = b \end{bmatrix} \right) \quad \text{Calder}$$
Carpenter
(credulous)

$$= \begin{bmatrix} F = a \\ G = \top \end{bmatrix} \quad \text{Carpenter (skeptical)}$$

(4)

$$= \begin{bmatrix} F = \boxed{1} \ a \\ G = \boxed{1} \end{bmatrix} \quad \text{LRL}$$

$$= \begin{bmatrix} F = a \\ G = b \end{bmatrix} \quad \text{Bouma}$$

$$= \bot \quad \text{Russell } et \ al.$$

In example 3 there is no basis for deciding which of the conflicting information in the default structure should be incorporated. However, in example 4 we would claim that there is a basis for distinguishing between the two pieces of default information which could be potentially incorporated but which are in conflict with each other, since one involves a path equivalence specification and the other a path value specification;

< F > = < G >
< G > = b

As described above, in the LRL we made a decision to prefer specifications of equivalence to specifications of values. Bouma's result arises because he normalises default structures in a way which gives

< F > = b
< G > = b

for the default structure in example 4, whereas Carpenter's decomposition function *At* would give:

< F > = b
< G > = b
< F > = < G >

Bouma's normalisation function thus does not meet our criterion for the decomposition function, since the result of reunifying the pieces would be:

$$\begin{bmatrix} F = b \\ G = b \end{bmatrix}$$

Bouma justifies this on the basis that this structure has equivalent behaviour with respect to unification to the original default structure. This is a reasonable position to take if feature structure values are defined to be extensional (see Carpenter, 1990, 1992), but it does not seem natural for an intensional treatment, such as adopted in the LRL, nor does it extend naturally to the default unification of typed feature structures, where atomic values are not necessarily maximally specific.

(5)

$$
\begin{bmatrix} F = \top \\ G = a \\ H = b \\ J = \top \end{bmatrix} \sqcap \begin{bmatrix} F = \square \\ G = \square \\ H = \square \\ J = \square \end{bmatrix}
\begin{array}{ll}
= (4\ \text{possibilities}) & \text{Calder} \\
& \text{Carpenter} \\
& \text{(credulous)} \\[4pt]
= \begin{bmatrix} F = \top \\ G = a \\ H = b \\ J = \top \end{bmatrix} & \begin{array}{l}\text{Carpenter}\\ \text{(skeptical)}\\ \text{LRL (current)}\end{array} \\[16pt]
= \begin{bmatrix} F = \square \\ G = a \\ H = b \\ J = \square \end{bmatrix} & \text{Bouma} \\[16pt]
= \bot & \begin{array}{l}\text{Russell } et\ al.\\ \text{LRL (proposed)}\end{array}
\end{array}
$$

Here the conflict in the default information is entirely between specifications of reentrancy. This example illustrates why default unification involving maximal incorporation of information has exponential complexity; the atomic feature structure $< F > = < J >$ conflicts only with a particular combination of the other atomic feature structures from the default.

12.4 Default Unification of Typed Feature Structures

Consideration of typed feature structures further increases the possible definitions of default unification. We have not attempted to even approximate to a definition which corresponds to incorporating the maximal amount of information carried by the types in a feature structure, although Carpenter's definition could be extended in this way. There are two main reasons for this; first, as mentioned earlier, we wish to constrain default inheritance by using the type system. Furthermore maximal incorporation of typed information can give results which are quite unintuitive. Consider the following type system:

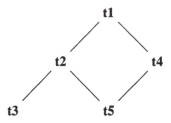

We assume the atomic types **true** and **false** to be subtypes of **bool** and that the constraints on the other types are:

$$
C(t1) = \begin{bmatrix} t1 \\ F_1 = \mathbf{bool} \end{bmatrix} \quad
C(t2) = \begin{bmatrix} t2 \\ F_1 = \mathbf{bool} \\ F_2 = \mathbf{bool} \end{bmatrix} \quad
C(t3) = \begin{bmatrix} t3 \\ F_1 = \mathbf{false} \\ F_2 = \mathbf{true} \end{bmatrix}
$$

$$
C(t4) = \begin{bmatrix} t4 \\ F_1 = \mathbf{bool} \\ F_3 = \mathbf{bool} \end{bmatrix} \quad
C(t5) = \begin{bmatrix} t5 \\ F_1 = \mathbf{true} \\ F_2 = \mathbf{bool} \\ F_3 = \mathbf{true} \end{bmatrix}
$$

We then have the following result for a definition of default unification based on unification of the non-default structure with the maximally informative possible feature structures which subsume the default and generalisation of the results:

$$
\begin{bmatrix} t4 \\ F_1 = \textbf{bool} \\ F_3 = \textbf{bool} \end{bmatrix} \stackrel{<}{\sqcap} \begin{bmatrix} t3 \\ F_1 = \textbf{bool} \\ F_2 = \textbf{true} \end{bmatrix} = \begin{bmatrix} t5 \\ F_1 = \textbf{true} \\ F_2 = \textbf{true} \\ F_3 = \textbf{true} \end{bmatrix}
$$

$$
\begin{bmatrix} t4 \\ F_1 = \textbf{bool} \\ F_3 = \textbf{bool} \end{bmatrix} \stackrel{<}{\sqcap} \begin{bmatrix} t3 \\ F_1 = \textbf{false} \\ F_2 = \textbf{true} \end{bmatrix} = \begin{bmatrix} t4 \\ F_1 = \textbf{bool} \\ F_3 = \textbf{bool} \end{bmatrix}
$$

These results seem unintuitive; adopting this approach leads to a situation where working out the results of default unification involves considering the interaction of the information ordering given by the type system with that of the feature structure system.

Thus we have chosen instead to use a definition in which the type system constrains default inheritance. In both the examples above, since $t3$ and $t4$ are incompatible types, our treatment of default unification would simply return the non-default feature structure. In general information which is carried by any feature structure which is part of the default is incorporated if it is fully compatible with the non-default (i.e. unifies with the relevant part), but is only ever partially incorporated (i.e. default unified) if its type is the same as, or more general than, the non-default.

We can formalise this in terms of a decomposition function (TypeDecomp) which differs from the atomic decomposition function in that it does not split up the feature structures completely. Only parts of the feature structure which are fully type compatible with the non-default structure are split; TypeDecomp is thus defined relative to the non-default structure. In what follows we assume that reentrancy is regarded as non-defeasible.

Definition 6   *If $F_1 = \langle Q_1, q_0, \delta_1, \alpha_1 \rangle$ and $F_2 = \langle Q_2, q_0', \delta_2, \alpha_2 \rangle$ where F_1 contains no path equivalence specifications then we define the decomposition of F_1 with respect to F_2, TypeDecomp(F_1, F_2), as follows:*
If $\alpha_2(q_0') \sqsubseteq \alpha_1(q_0)$ then TypeDecomp(F_1, F_2) is the set of all feature structures, $F_n = \langle Q_n, q_0'', \delta_n, \alpha_n \rangle$, such that:

- $\alpha_n(q_0'') = \alpha_1(q_0)$
- *If F_1 is non-atomic (i.e. $\text{Feat}_0(F_1)$ is non-empty), then $\delta_n(q_0'', f)$ for $f \in \text{Feat}_0(F_1)$ is a member of TypeDecomp($\delta_1(q_0, f), \delta_2(q_0', f)$) (where because of the type compatability condition $\delta_2(q_0', f)$ must be defined) and $\delta_n(q_0'', f')$ for all $f' \neq f$ is undefined*

If $\alpha_2(q_0') \not\sqsubseteq \alpha_1(q_0)$ then TypeDecomp(F_1, F_2) = $\{F_1\}$.

Note that the members of TypeDecomp(F_1, F_2) are not necessarily well-formed feature structures by this definition.

We can then define typed default unification as follows:

Definition 7 $F_1 \stackrel{\leq}{\sqcap} F_2 = F_3 \sqcap \prod \{F \mid F \in D(F_2)$ *and there is no* $F' \in D(F_2)$
such that $F' \sqcap F_3 \neq \perp$ *and* $F' \sqcap F_3 \sqcap F = \perp\}$
where $F_3 = F_1 \sqcap \prod PE(F_2)$ *and* $D(F_2)$ *is* TypeDecomp($\sqcap PV(F_2), F_1$).

For example, given:

$$F_1 = \begin{bmatrix} t1 \\ F = \begin{bmatrix} t2 \\ G = t5 \\ H = \top \end{bmatrix} \\ J = \begin{bmatrix} t3 \\ G = t5 \\ H = \top \end{bmatrix} \end{bmatrix} \; ; F_2 = \begin{bmatrix} t1 \\ F = \begin{bmatrix} t2 \\ G = t6 \\ H = t7 \end{bmatrix} \\ J = \begin{bmatrix} t4 \\ G = t6 \\ H = t7 \end{bmatrix} \end{bmatrix} \; ; t5 \sqcap t6 = \perp \text{ and } t3 \not\sqsubseteq t4$$

then:

$$F_1 \stackrel{\leq}{\sqcap} F_2 = \begin{bmatrix} t1 \\ F = \begin{bmatrix} t2 \\ G = t5 \\ H = t7 \end{bmatrix} \\ J = \begin{bmatrix} t3 \\ G = t5 \\ H = \top \end{bmatrix} \end{bmatrix}$$

since TypeDecomp($\sqcap PV(F_2), F_1$) =

$$\left\{ \begin{bmatrix} t1 \\ F = \begin{bmatrix} t2 \\ G = t6 \end{bmatrix} \end{bmatrix} \cdot \begin{bmatrix} t1 \\ F = \begin{bmatrix} t2 \\ H = t7 \end{bmatrix} \end{bmatrix} \cdot \begin{bmatrix} t1 \\ J = \begin{bmatrix} t4 \\ G = t6 \\ H = t7 \end{bmatrix} \end{bmatrix} \right\}$$

12.5   Inheritance Hierarchies and Multiple Inheritance

One way of allowing inheritance to operate over a hierarchy would be to modify
the definition of default unification, to order the information units in a way which
corresponded to the inheritance hierarchy (compare the way in which we defined preference of path equivalence specifications to path value specifications).
Clearly this is not any more computationally feasible than the formulation of
default unification which we gave originally. Conflicts can arise, not just from
reentrancy, but also from multiple inheritance conflicts of the 'Nixon Diamond'
type, where there is no ordering between defaults to allow resolution. Again
we could produce variant definitions; if reentrancy is regarded as non-defeasible
for example, all the reentrant atomic feature structures could be unified first
and if that succeeded the non-reentrant structures could be considered in groups
according to their priority. Essentially definitions along these lines give a skeptical, 'bottom-up', inheritance scheme.

We did not attempt to implement such a scheme in the LKB. We define
inheritance to operate top-down over whole feature structures; that is, a psort
will be fully expanded with inherited information before it is used for default
inheritance. As Carpenter explains this can give different results from a bottom-
up definition, since default unification is non-associative. The particular example
that Carpenter uses does not have non-associative behaviour under our definition
of default unification, but there are other cases which have non-associative
behaviour under both definitions. Consider an example lexical entry file:

```
A    < F > = < G > .

B    < F > = true
     < G > = true
     <> < A <>.

C    < F > = false
     <> < B <>.
```

We have the following results (assuming a typing scheme such that F and G are appropriate features for all lexical entries with value **bool**):

(6)

$$\begin{bmatrix} F = \boxed{1}\ \text{false} \\ G = \boxed{1} \end{bmatrix} \quad \text{LKB default unification, top-down}$$

$$\begin{bmatrix} F = \text{false} \\ G = \text{true} \end{bmatrix} \quad \text{LKB default unification, bottom-up}$$

$$\begin{bmatrix} F = \text{false} \\ G = \text{boolean} \end{bmatrix} \quad \text{Carpenter's skeptical default unification, top-down}$$

$$\begin{bmatrix} F = \text{false} \\ G = \text{true} \end{bmatrix} \quad \text{Carpenter's skeptical default unification, bottom-up}$$

If we view default inheritance in terms of individual units of information being asserted at various points in an inheritance hierarchy, top-down inheritance can thus result in information which is asserted at a higher level being preferred over information asserted at the lower level.

However, we want default inheritance to be a relationship between coherent parts of fully formed lexical entries. Thus we believe that the top-down behaviour is justifiable. It is also far more efficient than bottom-up inheritance would be, for this application, since the expanded psort can be cached. And again in practice, the top-down, bottom-up distinctions in behaviour arise with very low frequency.

Our decision to restrict multiple default inheritance to the cases where the information inherited is consistent was determined by our use of semi-automatically acquired data. A fundamental point is that we cannot decide on an appropriate way of resolving conflicts in multiple inheritance without knowing what type of conflicts actually arise. Given that automatic extraction of information from MRDs is inevitably error prone, and that lexicographers' definitions are frequently not mutually consistent, we expected that most conflicts would be due to errors in the extraction process, or to inadequate definitions. Thus disallowing multiple inheritance conflicts seemed reasonable as an initial position. This at least gives the user the option of manually editing the lexical entries in order to get the desired behaviour, whereas any approach which did not signal the presence of conflicts would not.

12.6   Specification of Information and Default Inheritance

Our restriction on multiple default inheritance has not significantly limited the utility of the LKB for our application so far. However, a less frequently discussed issue has arisen which seems to have general relevance for default inheritance systems, and non-monotonic logics which attempt to capture the 'Penguin Principle'. It arises because we may wish to override inherited information not by giving a conflicting value for the attribute, but by giving a value which is less specified or only partially conflicts.

As an illustrative example, if substance is a psort of type **physical**:

```
substance
<> = physical
< INDIVIDUATED > = false
< ANIMATE > = false.
```

we can override the value for individuated for a more specific psort by specifying [individuated = true]. However, suppose we want to create the lexical entry for *cake* and that *cake* should inherit information from *substance*. In this case we might want to override the information that [individuated = false] without specifying a new value, in order to allow both for mass and count usages of *cake*. But if we specify

```
cake
<> = physical
<> < substance <>
< INDIVIDUATED > = bool.
```

default unification gives:

$$
cake \qquad \begin{bmatrix} \textbf{physical} \\ \text{INDIVIDUATED} = \textbf{false} \\ \text{ANIMATE} = \textbf{false} \end{bmatrix}
$$

Clearly we cannot simply claim that the lexical entry:

```
cake
<> = physical
<> < substance <>.
```

should give [individuated = false] whereas

```
cake
<> = physical
< INDIVIDUATED > = bool
<> < substance <>.
```

should give [individuated = bool] if the type entry was

```
physical (top)
< INDIVIDUATED > = bool
< ANIMATE > = bool.
```

since the expansion of the non-default feature structure would result in the same thing in both cases.

A problem which seems to be related arises when constructing entries automatically. For example:[3]

---

[3] These definitions are taken from the *Italian Garzanti Dictionary* (Schiannini, 1984); my thanks to

> **cacio**   latte di vacca, pecora o capra cagliato, salto e seccato in forma;
> formaggio
>
> **marzolino**   cacio fatto con latte di pecora o di bufala

Schematically the LKB entries can be represented as:

```
cacio
< MILK-SOURCE > = (cow sheep goat).
```

```
marzolino
<> < cacio <>
< MILK-SOURCE > = (sheep buffalo).
```

where disjunction is indicated by bracketing a list of types. But (default) unification results in a feature structure for *marzolino* of:

```
[ MILK-SOURCE = (sheep) ]
```

whereas the desired result seems obviously to be:

```
[ MILK-SOURCE = (sheep buffalo) ]
```

These sort of examples appear plausible in general default reasoning, and the same problems can arise in any system if conflicts are necessary to block inheritance. For example, the following seem reasonable statements:

> Usually Quakers are pacifists.
> Nominal Quakers (i.e. people who are technically members of the Society of Friends but who are not now active members) may or may not be pacifists.
> Nixon is a nominal Quaker.

Intuitively we should be able to make some inferences about Nixon by virtue of the fact that he is technically a Quaker (even if only that his name is on some list), but even though we would not expect most other properties of Quakers to hold, we have no grounds for stating conflicting values for these properties for the class of nominal Quakers. Thus given the information above we should only conclude by default:

> Nixon may or may not be a pacifist.

We might also expect information about current political conviction to be able to set the property of pacifism without there being any conflict, thus allowing one possible way of avoiding the Nixon Diamond.

Intuitively it seems that both in this context and in that of dictionary definitions a statement about a class or an individual entity with respect to some property (e.g. type of milk used, pacifism) should be taken to be *maximally specific*, in that it obeys Grice's first sub-maxim of Quantity and is 'the strongest, or most informative, that can be made in the situation' (Levinson, 1983). The most

Elisabetta Marinai and Simonetta Montemagni for bringing them to my attention.

informative default statements about some properties of some classes may have to be weaker than valid statements about their superclasses, if defaults have a probabilistic interpretation in even the very loose sense that:

Usually Xs are Ys.

has a paraphrase:

If all that is known about something is that it is an X (and all inferences from this) then if you assume that it is a Y you will be right significantly more than half of the time.

There must be some subclass Z of X for which neither of the following statements is true:

Usually Zs are Ys.
Usually Zs are not Ys.

(It may be that this is not a situation that arises frequently with natural classes and natural properties in a taxonomic setting. However, if this is the case, it implies that natural classes have extra semantic properties besides that of being a subset of the superclass.)

There thus seem to be good technical reasons for wanting to allow this inference pattern in a representation language, and some intuitive justification for its validity. But given a non-monotonic logic which represents statements such as 'Usually Quakers are pacifists' as:

$$Q > P$$

where one can conclude this from:

$$Q \Rightarrow P$$

we cannot represent the statement about nominal Quakers simply as:

$$N > (P \vee \neg P)$$

and expect the desired effect to arise, since this will be true for any N and P, not just nominal Quakerism and pacificism.

The application of the default to the N has to be explicitly blocked. In a non-monotonic logic such as that of Delgrande (1988), this can be done by asserting the negation of the individual default statements $N > P$ and $N > \neg P$. Since this logic adopts the Penguin Principle this prevents application of the default $Q > P$. We would claim that this captures the intuition that the disjunct is maximally informative. Thus we actually need to state:

$\neg(N > P)$ (It is not the case that nominal Quakers are usually pacifists)
$\neg(N > \neg P)$ (It is not the case that nominal Quakers are usually not pacifists)

In general, for disjunctive statements, such as:

> Marzolino is usually made from sheep or buffalo milk.

uttered in a context where maximal informativeness can be assumed, we have to assert the negation of the individual default statements:

$$M > (S \vee B)$$
$$\neg(M > S)$$
$$\neg(M > B)$$

(where $\neg(B \wedge S)$). This will prevent the application of a default such as $C > S$ where $M \Rightarrow C$.

In terms of the LRL we can achieve an equivalent effect by using equality rather than subsumption constraints in our description of a feature structure. Take the earlier example:

```
cake
<> = physical
<> < substance <>
< INDIVIDUATED > = bool.
```

The path specification `<individuated>` = `bool` in effect constrains the feature structure so that the value for the path `<individuated>` must be subsumed by **bool**. In general for path π and value t, the constraint on the final feature structure, $F = \langle Q, q_0, \delta, \theta \rangle$, is:

$$\delta(\pi, q_0) \sqsubseteq C(t)$$

(where C(t) is the constraint on type t). To implement the intuitive idea that we have maximal information, we simply use an equality constraint (or more precisely a constraint that the only variance is alphabetic) rather than a subsumption constraint on the value of the path. That is, the constraint on F is:

$$\delta(\pi, q_0) \sim C(t) \text{ where } F \sim F' \equiv F \subseteq F' \text{ and } F' \subseteq F$$

Thus if equality up to alphabetic variance is represented by ==[4] in the path notation we have:

```
cake
<> = physical
<> < substance <>
< INDIVIDUATED > == bool.
```

12.7   Conclusion

In this paper we have attempted both to define the LRL's default component and to illustrate how default inheritance can be used to structure the lexicon on a

---

[4] In an earlier version of the LRL this was used to represent non-default inheritance, for which we now use <=.

lexical semantic dimension. Our use of taxonomic data from MRDs means that this structuring can be achieved automatically, and we have discussed the justification for this on the basis of the semantics of the dictionary entries. We have tried to show some parallels between default inheritance of semantic information in the lexicon and non-monotonic logic descriptions of reasoning with real world knowledge. However, we have not formalised the default mechanism in these terms, since we see lexical semantics as concerned with knowledge about word meaning that has a direct linguistic effect and which therefore must be represented in a way which is integrated with the syntactic representation. We attempt to achieve this by using typed feature structures as the basis of the representation language and by defining default inheritance of lexical semantic information to be compatible with inheritance seen as a more general reasoning mechanism.

Acknowledgements

I am grateful to Bob Carpenter for his advice about default inheritance and default unification, and to Gerald Gazdar and Ted Briscoe for their comments on this chapter. Errors, however, are the responsibility of the author.

13 Untangling Definition Structure into Knowledge Representation

PIEK VOSSEN AND ANN COPESTAKE

13.1 Introduction

Traditionally it is assumed that dictionary definitions exhibit a classical structure in terms of a *genus* and discriminating *differentiae*. The genus is assumed to correspond with the syntactic kernel of the definition and the differentiae with its modifiers, as in the following examples (taken, as are all the examples in this paper, from the *Longman Dictionary of Contemporary English*, (LDOCE); Procter, 1978):

Sense	Definition	Structure
moussaka	a	Determiner
	Greek	Pre-modifier
	dish	Syntactic kernel
	made from meat and aubergines	Post-modifier
	often with cheese on top	Post-modifier
cocktail 1	a	Determiner
	mixed	Pre-modifier
	alcoholic	Pre-modifier
	drink	Syntactic kernel

Once this structure is explicit and once the correct sense of each word in the definition has been determined (*dish*[1] 1 is a vessel, *dish*[1] 2 is cooked food[1]) it is possible to trace the entry word/genus relations in dictionaries by recursively looking up the genus in the same source:

> **moussaka**   a Greek dish made from meat and aubergines, often with cheese on top
>
> **dish**[1] **2**   (an amount of) cooked food of one kind
>
> **food**   an eatable substance
>
> **substance 1**   a material
>
> **material**[2] **1**   anything from which something is or may be made
>
> **anything**[1] **1**   any one thing; something

---

[1] We use a superscript to denote a specific homonym in the source dictionary if different homonyms are distinguished and a following numeral to specify the sense division within the entry.

246

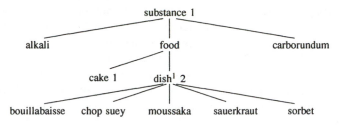

Figure 13.1: A portion of the substance taxonomy extracted from LDOCE

thing 1   any material object
object[1] **1**   a thing

Following these kernels we get a classificational chain which can be used to gather the information expressed by the modifiers or differentiae, which can then be inherited by default; thus for *moussaka* we not only can infer that it is 'Greek', 'made from meat and aubergines', and 'often has cheese on top', but also via *dish*[1] 2 that it is 'cooked', via *food* that it is 'eatable', and via *substance* that it is 'material'. The more general terms at the top of the chains are of limited use; the definitions become very vague and at some point circularity is inevitable.

By constructing many such chains we can in principle form a taxonomy of word senses. (Alternatively we can form a taxonomy by a top-down procedure in which we start from a general sense such as *substance 1*, find the senses in which it is the genus, and recursively apply the procedure to those senses.) Thus under *substance 1* we also have *alkali*, *carborundum* and *food*, for example; under *food* we find many senses such as *cake 1* as well as *dish*[1] 2 (see Figure 13.1). The inherited information that is appropriate for *moussaka* will also apply to *sorbet*, *sauerkraut*, *chop suey*, *bouillabaisse* and all the other senses which are defined as *dish*[1] 2.

In the ACQUILEX project this information is being extracted from the definitions of nouns in several monolingual Machine Readable Dictionaries (MRDs) of English, Dutch, Italian and Spanish, in order to build a common multilingual knowledge base (LKB) usable in various Natural Language Processing (NLP) tasks. For this purpose programs have been developed which automatically make the structure of the definitions explicit and which indicate the sense of the defining words (Vossen, 1990a; Copestake, 1990b; Ageno *et al.*, 1992; Montemagni and Vanderwende, 1992). The taxonomies based on the kernel information from these analyses form the hierarchical skeleton of the knowledge base, via which information extracted from the modifiers or added manually can be inherited. From this perspective the fact that a word is under *dish*[1] 2, *food*, *substance 1* etc. in the taxonomy is not so important, but what is important is that we can infer from this that it is 'eatable', 'concrete', 'cooked', etc. By formally expressing detailed semantic information for senses such as *food* and combining this with an inheritance device, which exploits the taxonomy chains, it is possible to derive massive semantic data on words usable in all kinds of applications. There will be some lexical information that we wish to represent which cannot be automatically acquired from the differentia of the dictionary definitions, but even if we have to manually associate information with some of the higher nodes in the hierarchy, inheritance of that information by the lower nodes gives us a cost-effective way of creating a large lexicon semi-automatically.

There are a number of phenomena in dictionary definitions, however, which make building taxonomies out of them more complex. Not only are we dealing with an enormous amount of data (LDOCE, being a relatively small dictionary, has about 37,500 noun-senses interrelated via about 5,000 genus terms, constituting about 45,000 relations), but the taxonomies are more like tangled hierarchies than the neat tree structures in which the classical definition structure would result (Amsler, 1980). Many definitions have a structure that results in a semantic effect different from that of the classical one where the relationship between the defined term and the genus term is hyponymic. Inheritance via their kernels is either not straightforward or simply not sufficient to predict essential semantic features of words. In this paper we will give an overview of the major complications we have encountered so far while examining the definitions of LDOCE and other dictionaries and the work done to untangle their structure in terms of a well-defined lexical representation language, the LRL, described in the previous papers in this volume.

In the next section our use of the LRL will be described and in the successive sections several complications will be discussed together with possible solutions (or suggestions for solutions): synonymy relations, definitions with complex kernels, coordination of genus terms, relatedness of senses, and variation in classification.

13.2   The Representation of Hyponymy Relations

In order to generate the taxonomic part of the LKB entries automatically from the dictionary definitions we need to know:

1. The genus word.
2. The sense of the genus word used in that definition.
3. Whether the relationship between the entry sense and the genus sense is one of straightforward hyponymy (in other words an IS_A relationship, as defined by Copestake, this volume.)

Techniques for extracting this information semi-automatically are discussed by Vossen (1990a) and Copestake (1990b). If the relationship is one of hyponymy, then the lexical entry for the word sense will specify that its lexical semantic structure is inherited from the lexical semantics of the feature structure which represents the genus sense lexical entry. We refer to this as a *psort*. In order for a complete LKB entry to be produced a lexical entry for the psort parent is also necessary.

The use of the LKB's default inheritance mechanism in representing the relatively straightforward taxonomic links, which we can extract from definitions such as those given as examples so far, was outlined by Copestake (this volume). The lexical entries for *moussaka, dish*[1] *2, food* and *substance 1* are shown below.

```
substance L_0_1
lex-count-noun
< QUALIA > = physical.


food L_0_1+2
lex-noun-sign
< QUALIA > = comestible
< QUALIA : TELIC > <= eat_L_0_1+2 < SEM >
< QUALIA > < substance_L_0_1 < QUALIA >.


dish L_1_2
lex-count-noun
< QUALIA > = c_artifact
< QUALIA : AGENTIVE > <= cook_L_2_1 < SEM >
< QUALIA > < food_L_0_1+2 < QUALIA >.


moussaka L_0_0
lex-uncount-noun
< QUALIA > < dish_L_1_2 < QUALIA >.
```

(The LKB entry for *food* shown has been produced by combining two LDOCE senses.) The expanded lexical entry for *moussaka* is shown in Figure 13.2. There are five top-level attributes: ORTH gives the orthography, CAT the syntactic information, SEM the formal argument structure and SENSE-ID the information about how the dictionary from which the lexical entry was derived; QUALIA introduces the lexical semantic structure. In this figure, and subsequent examples of feature structures in this paper, the less relevant parts of the lexical entry are not shown completely; this is indicated by a box round the type. We will omit the CAT, SEM and SENSE-ID features in subsequent diagrams, since we are concentrating on the lexical semantic representation. As explained by Copestake, the default inheritance mechanism allows the lexical semantic type of moussaka to be inferred, non-defeasibly, from the default inheritance specification.

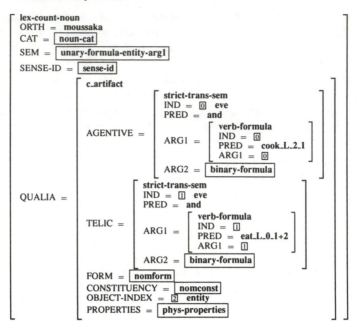

Figure 13.2: Expanded lexical entry for moussaka

Our representation of lexical semantic information is based on Pustejovsky's (1989, 1991) notion of qualia structure.[2] The four qualia are represented as separate parts of the feature structure, indicated by the features TELIC, AGENTIVE, CONSTITUENCY and FORMAL. The telic role indicates the purpose of an entity, and the agentive role its origin or way in which it was created. Both of these may have values which correspond to the semantics of the relevant verb. Thus the telic role for *moussaka* corresponds to the semantics for *eat* (in an appropriate sense) and the agentive role to *cook*. Some features will only be appropriate for particular types of lexical entry; for example, only **artifact**s have an agentive role which corresponds to a verb. The formal role of an entity gives information about its physical form, and constituency its component parts. As will be seen in later examples, the division of the lexical semantics into the four qualia allows for differential inheritance of attributes. (Some of our lexical entries also have a fifth attribute PROPERTIES, which is used for information which does not seem to fit naturally into our current concept of qualia.)

Our goal is a representation that accounts for the lexical semantics of nouns in a way that interacts appropriately with their syntactic and formal semantic

---

[2] For ease of exposition we make use of a version of the lexical semantic type system which is somewhat simpler than the 'relativised qualia structure', adopted for the ACQUILEX project as a whole.

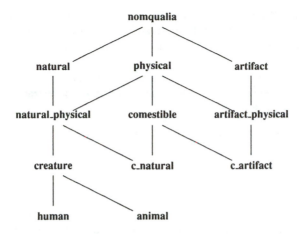

Figure 13.3: A fragment of the lexical semantic type hierarchy

representation. The following papers give detailed accounts of the treatment of particular phenomena within this framework: Briscoe *et al.* (1990) describe how an earlier version of the LKB can be used in the representation of logical metonymy (Pustejovsky, 1989, 1991), Copestake and Briscoe (1991) discuss how the lexical rule mechanism can be used in conjunction with the lexical semantic representation to provide an account of sense extensions and some aspects of derivational morphology, Copestake (1992a) concerns the representation of group nouns.

A fragment of the type hierarchy used for the lexical entries in the current paper is shown in Figure 13.3. As mentioned above the type of a lexical entry can be determined from the default inheritance specification and thus the primary use of the taxonomic relationship in the LKB is in determining the appropriate semantic type for the lexical entry. This in turn determines which features are appropriate; the secondary use of the hierarchical relationship is that default values for some of those features may be provided.

As discussed in Copestake (this volume) the hierarchical structure of the lexicon is based on the assumption that dictionary definitions exhibit a classical structure in terms of a genus and discriminating differentiae which respectively correspond with the syntactic kernel of the definition and its modifiers. However, many definitions have a structure that results in a different semantic effect which cannot be described in terms of such a hyponymy relation. If we derive inappropriate hierarchical relationships in the LKB from such definitions a variety of problems may arise:

1. The lexical semantic type specified for the entry may be incorrect. (This may be detected automatically if other information derived from

the definition leads to the assignment of a conflicting feature structure.)

2. The type may be correct, but the default information may be inappropriate. This will cause problems if the correct information cannot be derived in other ways.

3. The type may be correct but very underspecified. This will lead to a less useful lexical entry unless other information is extracted which further specifies the type.

In the following sections we discuss some of the definition structures which cause problems.

13.3   Synonymy Relations

In some cases the definitions do not exhibit the classical structure because they lack modifiers that distinguish them from other words with the same genus:

> **bobby**   *infml BrE* a policeman
>
> **bull**[1] **3**   *sl, esp. AmE* a policeman
>
> **cop**[2]   *infml* policeman
>
> **copper**[4]   *infml* a policeman
>
> **flatfoot**   *sl* a policeman
>
> **peeler**[2]   *BrE old sl* a policeman
>
> **pig**[1] **4**   *derog sl* policeman

It is rather unintuitive to say that all these words refer to specific kinds of *policeman*. The referent of such a word is not different from the referent of the word *policeman*, so that the lack of modifiers is in a sense justifiable. The differences from *policeman* are in respect of register indicated by the various labels in their definitions such as 'infml' and 'sl' (slang). In terms of semantic features, therefore, they cannot be seen as being strictly subsumed by *policeman* and it would be more appropriate to analyse them as 'cognitive synonyms' (Cruse, 1986) with specific values for the feature REGISTER. This makes them different from the following examples, in which the words do refer to more specific concepts:

> **constable 1**   a policeman of the lowest rank
>
> **outrider**   a policeman riding on a motor cycle ...
>
> **policewoman 1**   a female policeman
>
> **ranger 2b**   a policeman who rides through country areas to see that the law is kept

If the LKB is regarded as a traditional NLP lexicon (i.e. as a means of providing information about individual word senses, where the way in which information becomes associated with lexical entries is unimportant) then this distinction is irrelevant. None of the three problems enumerated at the end of the previous section will arise. From this viewpoint, treating *cop*[2] as inheriting all its lexical semantic information from *policeman*, but specifying the value of REGISTER as **informal**,[3] gives a correct lexical entry and so is an adequate representation.

```
cop L_2_0
< QUALIA > < policeman_L_0_0 < QUALIA >
< REGISTER > = informal.
```

although it would perhaps be slightly more perspicuous to make use of non-default inheritance (notated by $<=$[4]):

```
cop L_2_0
< QUALIA > <= policeman_L_0_0 < QUALIA >
< REGISTER > = informal.
```

When we consider the structured lexicon as a whole, this LKB representation is inadequate because it does not explicitly constrain the semantics of *cop*[2] to be identical to those of *policeman*, since further information might be specified in the entry for *cop*[2]. (The non-default inheritance relationship can be seen as a constraint that the parent structure subsumes the daughter structure.) Thus the relationship between these lexical entries cannot be distinguished from examples in which the referents differ but the restriction cannot be adequately represented or is not seen as significant. For example, the extra information about *ranger 2b*, 'rides through country areas to see that the law is kept', would not be represented in the current LKB type system, and thus the difference in the relationship between *policeman* and *ranger 2b* and that between *policeman* and *cop*[2] would not be expressed. However the constraint that the feature structure representing the lexical semantics of *cop*[2] is identical to that of *policeman* can be straightforwardly captured in the LRL (equality of information content between feature structures being defined in terms of mutual subsumption; see Copestake, this volume).

We have thus extended the syntax of the LKB to allow equality between feature structures to be specified by ==, resulting in the following lexical entries:

```
cop L_2_0
< QUALIA > == policeman_L_0_0 < QUALIA >
< REGISTER > = informal.

ranger_L_0_2_b
< QUALIA > < policeman_L_0_0 < QUALIA > .
```

---

[3] We do not mean to suggest that register can really be represented so simplistically, but the complexities are unimportant here.

[4] Earlier versions of the LKB used == to indicate non-default inheritance.

13.4   Complex Kernels

Consider the following examples, where although all the words defined have the same syntactic kernel *part* they form a very heterogeneous group:

> **magazine 3**   the part of a gun or weapon of that type...
>
> **bastion 1**   a part of the wall of a castle or fort...
>
> **morning 1**   the first part of the day...
>
> **cathode**   the part of an electrical instrument...
>
> **collar**[1] **1**   the part of a shirt, dress or coat...
>
> **root**[1] **1**   the part of a plant that...
>
> **artillery 2**   the part of the army trained to use such weapons
>
> **proscenium 2**   the part of a stage that...

On purely syntactic grounds *part* is the kernel of all these definitions (it must be in agreement with the main verb when the structure as a whole is subject), but there is little that the entry words have in common; even very general properties such as animacy, concreteness and collectiveness cannot be predicted on the basis of the information we get from *part* alone. We cannot assign any semantic type other than the most general. Although all these word senses stand in an IS_A relationship to *part*, *part* by itself is semantically very unrestrictive; everything except *everything* can be described as a part of something! But *part* is being used as a relational noun in these definitions and thus the heads of the of-complements of *part* seem to be more informative. We will use *complex kernel* to refer to the syntactic kernel plus of-complements in definitions of this sort and *relator* to refer to the syntactic kernel.

From an inventory of all words that frequently occur in this kind of structure, and do not frequently occur without such of-complementation, four different classes of relations have been found in total (relators are underlined; the head of the complement is italicised):

1.   TYPE/KIND

> **cheddar**   a type of firm smooth usu. yellowish *cheese*
>
> **limestone**   a type of *rock* containing material from bones ...

2.   QUANTITY/MASS

> **meal**[1] **1**   an amount of *food* eaten at one time
>
> **whisky 2**   an amount of *this* [whisky 1] drunk in one glass
>
> **band**[1] **1**   a thin flat narrow piece of *material* ...
>
> **waste**[1] **1**   an unused or useless stretch of *land*

3.   MEMBER/GROUP

> **policeman**   a member of a *police force*

band³ **2**   a group of *musicians* ...

4.   COMPONENT/WHOLE

cockpit   the part of a *plane or racing car* ...

circulatory system   the system of *blood, blood vessels, and heart* ...

dolmen   a group of upright *stones* supporting a large flat piece of stone, built in ancient times in Britain and France

TYPE/KIND can be regarded as the explicit version of the ordinary hyponymy or IS_A relation and can be represented in the same way as related 'implicit' definitions, allowing inheritance of lexical semantic properties. Thus we would treat the definition of *cheddar* above as being equivalent to:

cheddar   firm smooth usu. yellowish *cheese*

and ignore the relator *type*.⁵ However, the other three classes do not allow for inheritance in the same, relatively straightforward way.

These sort of definitions have been discussed previously, in Guthrie *et al.* (1990) and Klavans and Wacholder (1990), for example. Several authors have proposed that multiple link types be distinguished to deal with the varieties of complex kernels. For example, Guthrie *et al.* suggest that a HAS_MEMBER link is necessary as well as an IS_A link. However, since a semantics for these proposed links is not provided it is impossible to evaluate these claims. Even regarded as a notational device we think that creating new types of link for each potentially different case should be avoided, since it seems likely to result in the imposition of a structure on the entries which is not really there, because it complicates the concept of genus term as accepted by lexicographers. Our approach is to attempt to provide a more linguistically motivated account of complex kernels, as they appear in definitions, and from this to determine their behaviour in terms of the LKB.

In order to discuss the effect of complex kernels we will assume that there are three basic semantic classes of nouns; ordinary individuals, groups and uncountable masses. In definitions with complex kernels a conversion or shift

---

⁵ The semantic effect of *kind* and *type* in dictionary definitions is unclear and difficult to establish, because the lexicographers' use is uneven; for most cases where *kind* and *type* are used apparently parallel definitions may be found where they are omitted; for example:

slate¹ **1**   heavy rock formed from mud by pressure ...

It is well-known that all nouns can have either a type or a token reading, but it is possible that *kind* and *type* in a definition indicate that the type usage is especially salient. For examples which derive from place names, or other proper names, such as *cheddar* and *Stilton*, the type usage might be intuitively said to be 'primary', but, as Nunberg (1978) shows, attempting to make such a distinction linguistically is unrevealing. Our lexical representations are appropriate for token usages; type usages are derivable from them and not stored individually, so from this viewpoint ignoring the use of *type* and *kind* in definitions seems justified.

between these classes frequently occurs. One difference between *band*[1] *1* and *material*, for instance, is that the former is a countable individualised object and the latter is an uncountable mass. The effect of *piece* is that it individuates *material*, shifting the type from an uncountable mass to a countable individual. In this particular case the shape of the resultant individual is specified ('thin flat narrow'). The 'portioning' sense extension, exemplified by whisky, is a special case of individuation, as discussed below.

The MEMBER/GROUP class of definitions shift between individual and group denoting nouns. We distinguish between these cases and the COMPONENT/WHOLE examples where there is not necessarily any shift of semantic class. Even though a dolmen is described as being made up of individual stones it is not a group noun, in contrast to *band*[3] *2*. This distinction is discussed further below.

Particular kernel structures tend to indicate different classes of relationship. Their effects are summarised in Figure 13.4. We consider the LKB representation of each of these classes in turn. This will lead to a refinement of the informal definition of the categories of relationship given above.

The treatment of these constructions in dictionary definitions is ultimately dependent on their general linguistic treatment. In principle our treatment of a complex kernel should be to construct an appropriate representation for it, just as we would if parsing the phrase, and then to use this as the psort from which to inherit information (by default). However, since we are interested in characterising the constructions which are used relatively frequently in definition kernels, and their usual semantic effect there, we can regard the definition language as a specialised sublanguage and ignore many of the complexities which would be involved in a full treatment of the various partitive and pseudo-partitive constructions involved. Furthermore, since we are considering the construction of the appropriate LKB entries, what we are interested in specifically is how these constructions affect the lexical semantic qualia structure. The LKB representations can be more explicitly justified on the basis of a general theory of the formal semantics of mass nouns and plurals, but here we will present examples of the representations and attempt to describe them informally.

13.4.1   *Quantity/Mass*

Consider the following definitions:

> **meal**[1] **1**   an amount of food eaten at one time
> **whisky 2**   an amount of this [whisky 1] drunk in one glass
> **band**[1] **1**   a thin flat narrow piece of material
> **waste**[1] **1**   an unused or useless stretch of land

Definitions of this form can be regarded as producing an individual from a mass denoting genus term by describing the way in which the entity is to be

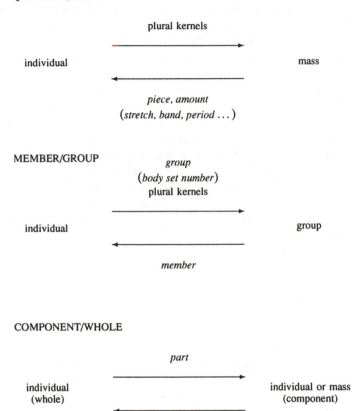

Figure 13.4: The more significant definition structures which cause shifts in semantic class

individuated; in the case of concrete nouns this may involve specifying its physical shape to some extent (e.g. *band*), or its quantity (e.g. *glass*) or merely indicating that there is some limit to physical extent without saying what that limit is (e.g. *piece, amount*).

Thus if we assume that the lexical semantics of nouns is defined in terms of qualia structure as described in the previous sections, we can regard the lexical entry as inheriting all its qualia from the genus term except those which refer to physical form. The FORM feature can be regarded as being specified by the syntactic kernel; for *amount* all that can be specified is that there is some individuation, for *piece* we might want to assume physical separation, for *band* the FORM role could be more completely instantiated. Of course the other qualia (TELIC, ORIGIN, CONSTITUENCY) may also have to be further instantiated, possibly even overriding the inherited information, but this is no different from the normal cases of hyponymy. We can motivate this because it appears that mass nouns can be taken as referring distributively, in the context of dictionary definitions, thus a 'piece of material' will always be 'material' and all the properties of 'material' should apply. There has been considerable discussion of whether this property can be taken to hold of mass nouns in general (see, for example, Bunt 1985, Pelletier and Schubert, 1986), but the sort of examples which have been claimed as exceptions to this (e.g. 'are electrons gold?', 'is a chair leg furniture?') do not arise in dictionary definitions in our experience. Figure 13.5 shows an LKB entry for *meal*[1] *1* and the instantiated feature structure that results.

The example of *whisky 2* is clearly a special case in that the individual and the mass reading are senses of the same headword. This is an example of the 'portioning' sense extension (see Copestake and Briscoe, 1991); in general most food denoting nouns can also be used to denote a portion of that food, and in the case of drinks the extended sense is frequently lexicalised. The portioning lexical rule is shown in Figure 13.6. Lexical rules are feature structures which represent the relationship between a pair of lexical entries. Although there is no inherent directionality in lexical rules, we refer to input and output entries, which are designated by the features 1 and 0 respectively. In this particular case the lexical rule transforms the syntactic type of the lexical entry from mass to count, but preserves the qualia structure with the exception of the feature FORM. The effects of the lexical rule on the qualia structure thus correspond to the inheritance behaviour described above. Since we allow for the possibility that a lexicalised example of sense extension may override the information predicted, treating *whisky 2* as formed by sense extension from *whisky 1* is precisely equivalent to the inheritance treatment given above (see Figure 13.7).

The other possibility that we will consider under the QUANTITY/MASS heading is the use of count denoting kernels in the definition of a mass denoting sense. This is usually indicated by a syntactically plural kernel, which may or may not be complex. For example:

```
meal L_1_1
lex-count-noun
< QUALIA > < food_L_0_1+2 < QUALIA >
< QUALIA : FORM : RELATIVE > = portion.
```

$$
\begin{bmatrix}
\textbf{lex-count-noun} \\
\text{ORTH} = \textbf{meal} \\
\text{QUALIA} =
\begin{bmatrix}
\textbf{comestible} \\
\text{AGENTIVE} = \textbf{nomagent} \\
\text{TELIC} =
\begin{bmatrix}
\textbf{strict-trans-sem} \\
\text{IND} = \boxed{0}\ \textbf{eve} \\
\text{PRED} = \textbf{and} \\
\text{ARG1} =
\begin{bmatrix}
\textbf{verb-formula} \\
\text{IND} = \boxed{0} \\
\text{PRED} = \textbf{eat\_L\_0\_1+2} \\
\text{ARG1} = \boxed{0}
\end{bmatrix} \\
\text{ARG2} = \boxed{\textbf{binary-formula}}
\end{bmatrix} \\
\text{FORM} =
\begin{bmatrix}
\textbf{nomform} \\
\text{RELATIVE} = \textbf{portion}
\end{bmatrix} \\
\text{CONSTITUENCY} = \boxed{\textbf{nomconst}} \\
\text{OBJECT-INDEX} = \boxed{1}\ \textbf{entity} \\
\text{PROPERTIES} = \boxed{\textbf{phys-properties}}
\end{bmatrix}
\end{bmatrix}
$$

Figure 13.5: Lexical entry and expanded feature structure for *meal*[1] *1*

$$
\begin{bmatrix}
\textbf{lexical-rule} \\
1 =
\begin{bmatrix}
\textbf{lex-uncount-noun} \\
\text{ORTH} = \boxed{0} \\
\text{QUALIA} =
\begin{bmatrix}
\textbf{comestible} \\
\text{AGENTIVE} = \boxed{1} \\
\text{TELIC} = \boxed{2} \\
\text{FORM} =
\begin{bmatrix}
\textbf{nomform} \\
\text{RELATIVE} = \textbf{mass}
\end{bmatrix} \\
\text{CONSTITUENCY} = \boxed{3} \\
\text{OBJECT-INDEX} = \boxed{6}\ \textbf{entity} \\
\text{PROPERTIES} = \boxed{5}
\end{bmatrix}
\end{bmatrix} \\
0 =
\begin{bmatrix}
\textbf{lex-count-noun} \\
\text{ORTH} = \boxed{0}\ \textbf{orth} \\
\text{QUALIA} =
\begin{bmatrix}
\textbf{comestible} \\
\text{AGENTIVE} = \boxed{1}\ \textbf{nomagent} \\
\text{TELIC} = \boxed{2}\ \boxed{\textbf{verb-sem}} \\
\text{FORM} =
\begin{bmatrix}
\textbf{nomform} \\
\text{RELATIVE} = \textbf{portion}
\end{bmatrix} \\
\text{CONSTITUENCY} = \boxed{3}\ \boxed{\textbf{nomconst}} \\
\text{OBJECT-INDEX} = \boxed{4}\ \textbf{entity} \\
\text{PROPERTIES} = \boxed{5}\ \boxed{\textbf{phys-properties}}
\end{bmatrix}
\end{bmatrix}
\end{bmatrix}
$$

Figure 13.6: Lexical rule for portioning

$$
\begin{bmatrix}
\textbf{lex-uncount-noun} \\
\text{ORTH} = \textbf{whisky} \\
\text{QUALIA} = \begin{bmatrix}
\textbf{comestible} \\
\text{AGENTIVE} = \textbf{nomagent} \\
\text{TELIC} = \boxed{\textbf{verb-sem}} \\
\text{FORM} = \begin{bmatrix} \textbf{nomform} \\ \text{RELATIVE} = \textbf{form} \end{bmatrix} \\
\text{CONSTITUENCY} = \boxed{\textbf{nomconst}} \\
\text{OBJECT-INDEX} = \boxed{1}\ \textbf{entity} \\
\text{PROPERTIES} = \begin{bmatrix} \textbf{phys-properties} \\ \text{STATE} = \textbf{liquid\_a} \end{bmatrix}
\end{bmatrix}
\end{bmatrix}
$$

whisky 1

$$
\begin{bmatrix}
\textbf{lex-count-noun} \\
\text{ORTH} = \textbf{whisky} \\
\text{QUALIA} = \begin{bmatrix}
\textbf{comestible} \\
\text{AGENTIVE} = \textbf{nomagent} \\
\text{TELIC} = \boxed{\textbf{verb-sem}} \\
\text{FORM} = \begin{bmatrix} \textbf{nomform} \\ \text{RELATIVE} = \textbf{portion} \end{bmatrix} \\
\text{CONSTITUENCY} = \boxed{\textbf{nomconst}} \\
\text{OBJECT-INDEX} = \boxed{1}\ \textbf{entity} \\
\text{PROPERTIES} = \begin{bmatrix} \textbf{phys-properties} \\ \text{STATE} = \textbf{liquid\_a} \end{bmatrix}
\end{bmatrix}
\end{bmatrix}
$$

whisky 2

Figure 13.7: Lexical entries for whisky

```
down L_0_1
lex-uncount-noun
< QUALIA > < ( feather_L_1_1 + plural ) < QUALIA >
< QUALIA : FORM : RELATIVE > = mass.
```

$$
\begin{bmatrix}
\textbf{lex-uncount-noun} \\
\text{ORTH} = \textbf{down} \\
\text{QUALIA} = \begin{bmatrix}
\textbf{physical} \\
\text{AGENTIVE} = \textbf{nomagent} \\
\text{TELIC} = \boxed{\textbf{verb-sem}} \\
\text{FORM} = \begin{bmatrix} \textbf{nomform} \\ \text{RELATIVE} = \textbf{mass} \end{bmatrix} \\
\text{CONSTITUENCY} = \begin{bmatrix} \textbf{nomconst} \\ \text{PARTICLES} = \textbf{feather\_L\_1\_1} \end{bmatrix} \\
\text{OBJECT-INDEX} = \boxed{0}\ \textbf{entity} \\
\text{PROPERTIES} = \boxed{\textbf{phys-properties}}
\end{bmatrix}
\end{bmatrix}
$$

Figure 13.8: LKB entry for *down* [6] *1*, showing inheritance of qualia structure from *feathers*

haulm [U] the stems of crops like peas, beans, potatoes etc., left after gathering

darning 2 [U] clothes that need to be or are being darned

down[6] **1** [U] fine soft feathers

gravel 2a [U] small bits of stone-like material in the bladder

Such definitions correspond to cases where something is regarded as individuated with respect to one predicate (e.g. *feather* [1] *1*) but not with respect to the sense being defined (*down* [6] *1*). (This will only apply to mass nouns where there is some obvious granularity; most are defined in terms of other (potentially) mass nouns such as *material* or *substance*.)

Again inheritance from the genus term will involve the TELIC, ORIGIN and CONSTITUENCY qualia, but the FORM will be specified as unindividuated with respect to the sense being defined (although we also represent the potential for individuation with respect to the genus term in order to make the appropriate inferences about distributivity of reference possible). We can motivate this difference from the normal hyponymy relation, since we are in effect claiming that properties are inherited from the plural entity (i.e. *feathers*). See Figure 13.4.1.

13.4.2   Member/Group

In this category we first consider definitions where a group is defined in terms of its members. Examples are:

band[3] **2**   a group of musicians

We would not, however, regard the following as indicating a member/group relation but rather as a component/whole:

> **dolmen** a group of upright stones supporting a large flat piece of stone, built in ancient times in Britain and France

The distinction we draw is based on whether the noun being defined is a group noun according to the following tests:

1. Singular or plural pronouns can be used:
    The band played well tonight. Its / their tour has sold out.
    The dolmen is on a mountain. It's / *they're very eroded.
2. Either singular or plural agreement with the verb is possible:
    The band play / plays well.
    The dolmen has / *have fallen down.
3. Individual members can be referred to by using 'one of' etc:
    One of the band bit the head off a live chicken.
    *One of the dolmen fell down.

There is clearly a semantic, as well as a syntactic, distinction between group and non-group nouns; when a group noun is used the individual components of the entity denoted are sufficiently obvious that it can be referred to as though it were a plural term. Therefore there has to be a difference in the LKB's semantic representation of group and non-group nouns and we cannot give a uniform treatment for all definitions with the relator *group*.[6]

Although most group nouns denote groups with human (or sometimes animal) members, there are a few exceptions, such as *fleet* and *convoy*. It is therefore necessary to represent the type of the individuals which comprise group denoting nouns, and we do this as part of the constituent role of the qualia structure; see Figure 13.9, for example.

In general usage it is arguably not possible to assume that a group as a whole has a property even if all its members have that property, and the property is one which could hold for the group as a whole. For example:

> All the members of the committee are against the poll tax.

does not necessarily entail that:

> The committee is against the poll tax.[7]

However, such examples are exceptional, and in the special case of dictionary definitions if a group is defined in terms of its members it can be taken to inherit

---

[6] In the majority of cases in LDOCE where *group* is used as the relator in a definition, the sense being defined is a group noun according to the criteria used here. However many such examples have not been marked by the appropriate LDOCE grammar codes and therefore automatically distinguishing the group nouns is not straightforward.

[7] It is not clear that such problematic examples are intrinsically connected with group denoting nouns. There are examples of non-substitutivity involving individuals which seem similar (see Landman, 1989).

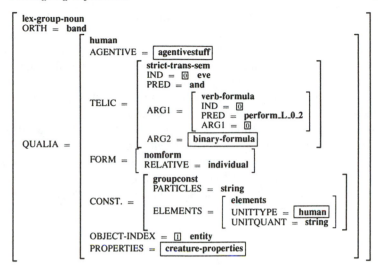

Figure 13.9: Lexical entry for *band*³ 2

appropriate properties from them. (We have not found any counter-examples to this in LDOCE so far.) So the TELIC role of *band*³ 2 is inherited from *musician*, for example. The LKB entry for *band*³ 2 is shown in Figure 13.9.

The other half of this category of definitions are those in which an individual is defined in terms of the group of which it is a member. For example:

policeman   a member of a police force

committeeman   a member of a committee

In general the appropriate type can be obtained from examination of the ELE-MENTS feature of the CONSTITUENCY part of the qualia of the group denoting psort, if this has been fully specified. Since the use of complex kernels of the form 'a member of X' is in LDOCE almost entirely restricted to human denoting definitions, we can in fact normally assume that the lexical semantic type is **human**, even if the elements of the group have not been derived.

In contrast with the mass noun case, group nouns do not refer distributively, so we would not expect to be able to make any logically valid inheritance about the members of a group based on information specified for the group as a whole. Even when predicates which normally refer distributively are applied to a group, it is not possible to conclude that they apply to individual members. The sentence

The committee voted for Major.

does not entail that each member of the committee voted for Major. However, again dictionary definitions are a special case, since a noun would not be defined in terms of its group membership if it denoted an atypical member of the group (or if it was defined as such the atypicality would be explicitly marked or indicated). Thus inheriting the TELIC role from the group genus will normally give an appropriate result, since the function of an individual, regarded as the member of a group, will normally be the same as the function of the group as a whole, although possibly more specialised. Inheriting the agentive role is more problematic, since it is likely to refer to the group collectively.

To summarise, our treatment of group denoting nouns defined in terms of their members, and of individuals defined in terms of the group of which they form a part, is based on two assumptions. The first is that there are limitations to the lexicalisation of group formations in English; the second is that in the context of dictionary definitions we can take distributive predicates as being true of members of groups by default.

13.4.3 Component/Whole

Thus at least some aspects of the lexical semantics of senses with definitions in the MEMBER/GROUP and QUANTITY/MASS categories can be predicted relatively straightforwardly. But in the the COMPONENT/WHOLE relation very little can be predicted about the entry word. Individuals often consist of many different components which can belong to different types and it is not predictable in general how the semantics of the whole relate to the semantics of the components:

> **juice**[1] **1**   the liquid part of fruit, vegetables and meat
>
> **flesh 3**   the soft part of a fruit or vegetable, which can be eaten
>
> **organ 1**   a part of an animal or plant that has a special purpose
>
> **sleeve 1**   a part of a garment for covering (part of) an arm
>
> **albumen 1**   the white or colourless part of an egg
>
> **backwater 1**   a part of a river, usu. a branch,...
>
> **base 9**   the main part or substance of a mixture

In all these examples the entry word is related to the of-complement via *part*. Only in those cases, however, where the complement is a uniform homogeneous entity can the semantics of the defined word sense be predicted e.g. *part of a river*. A *part* of *fruit*, *vegetable* or *meat* is not necessarily *liquid* and *mass* (*juice* and *flesh*), and *part of an animal or plant* (*organ*) can also be *mass* and *liquid* instead of a countable individualised thing. There are a few generalisations; a part of some physical entity will also be a physical entity, part of some time period will also be a time period etc., but this is only adequate to predict semantic type in extremely broad terms.

The reverse situation also occurs when an entry is described as a complex WHOLE of components:

batter²   a mixture of flour, eggs and milk...

mortar²   a mixture of lime, sand and water...

block and tackle   an arrangement of wheels and ropes...

assembly line   an arrangement of workers and machines...

waterworks 1   buildings, pipes and supplies of water...

post chaise   a carriage and horses...

goulash   meat and vegetables cooked together with paprika...

bust¹ **1**   the human head, shoulders and chest...

Either a relator is used to indicate the WHOLE (*mixture*, *arrangement*) or a coordination is used from which the complex WHOLE has to be inferred. In either case, however, there is no way to infer the lexical semantic type of the WHOLE from the composition, at least without extensive knowledge and inference.

Thus it does not seem possible to produce a uniform semantics for constituency that usefully predicts the lexical semantics of the word sense defined. There is no primitive 'PART-OF' link in the LKB, since this would have no function other than recording an under-analysed pattern in the dictionary definition, which is clearly inappropriate. It is clear that for some classes of definitions a predictive relationship can be established — parts of the body — for example, but progress depends on a better automatic analysis of the dictionary definitions.

One starting point would be to allow not only genus terms to be used as psorts but also particular differentiae. In case of *juice*¹ *1*, for example, the differentiae *liquid* contains more information about the relevant type than *part*. The lexical semantics of *juice* could then be inferred from the unification of the qualia of *part* and *liquid*, since *liquid* is an intersective modifier. These should be compatible, since the lexical semantics for *part* will be very general. In other cases inheritance of particular parts of the qualia structure would be more appropriate. The problem then is to decide which differentiae can have such status and how to specify the amalgamation of the psorts. Using this approach we could start off with a very restrictive set of possibilities (e.g. only using psorts derived from material denoting adjectives such as *liquid*, *glass* or function denoting derivation pairs such as *cover-covering*, *contain-container*) and then study ways to extend it.

Complex WHOLEs are often more covertly and implicitly coded. The following example contains a simple genus (although coordinated), but the concept as a whole is still complex as follows from the differentiae:

> **charlotte**   cooked apple or other fruit covered with very fine pieces of bread (crumbs), baked and eaten as food

Apparently the fruit is too recognisable for *charlotte* to be defined as a dish, although the crumbs are probably as essential to charlotte as the fruit is. There are many cases of definitions in which something is 'added' to the genus. For inheritance, however, these cases are usually not too problematic, since the salience of the genus in the concept also implies that most properties of the genus (in this case *apple* or *fruit* in an extended mass sense) can be inherited, and those that cannot are explicitly expressed in the differentiae (*cooked*, *baked* and *covered*, which have implications for the AGENTIVE and CONSTITUENCY roles).

The COMPONENT/WHOLE definitions form a relatively small proportion of the total number of noun definitions (estimated at around 3.5% on the basis of frequency of the relators *part*, *mixture* and so on, and of conjunction with *and*). However, senses may be defined in this way which have many descendants in the taxonomy, *organ 1*, for example. If no semantics is provided for *organ 1* then no semantics will be inherited by those LKB entries which have *organ 1* as a direct or indirect psort parent. Thus for the time being we will have to provide semantics for such entries by hand; however, this is clearly reasonably cost-effective, since all the descendants will inherit those properties.

We have not discussed the problems of automatically distinguishing between the different classes of complex kernels in order to provide the correct representation. Clearly this is not straightforward, and a range of information has to be used. For example MEMBER-GROUP relationships can often be differentiated from COMPONENT-WHOLE relationships in LDOCE, by checking for the codes for group nouns (grammar codes and box codes). Our current approach is based on combining such heuristics and hand-checking the more important entries, specifically those from which other entries inherit information.

13.5   Coordination of Genus Terms

Many entries (about 20% of all noun senses) have definitions in which genus terms are coordinated, in some cases in combination with complex kernels:

> **staging 2**   movable boards and frames for standing on
>
> **breeder**   an animal, bird or fish that produces young
>
> **borer**   a person, tool or insect that makes round holes

In some previous work (e.g. Chodorow *et al.*, 1985) coordinated genus terms are interpreted as each being parents of the word being defined in the taxonomic structure, which is one way in which a tangled hierarchy results. This is clearly inappropriate if the taxonomic structure is viewed as allowing inheritance; in the LKB it would mean that each coordination is interpreted as the unification of the parents' feature structures. This is only appropriate for strict logical conjunction, which is rare in definition kernels. If we look at the distribution of coordination as shown in Table 13.1 we see that three elements are mainly used (*or*, *and* and *etc.*) and that most cases of coordination are disjunctive with *or*.

Table 13.1: Distribution of coordination in LDOCE noun-senses

3573 senses with non-complex genus terms are coordinated
(12% of all noun-senses)

2898 senses with *or* (1908 different types)
326 senses with *and* (307 different types)
349 senses with *etc.* (335 different types)

2801 senses with complex genus terms are also coordinated
(7.5% of all noun-senses)

1819 senses with *or*
501 senses with *and*
481 senses with *etc.*

Table 13.2: Most frequent coordinated genus terms in LDOCE

person or thing	126	word or phrase	16
act or state	90	act or condition	15
act or action	75	act or practice	14
quality or state	54	person or machine	14
state or quality	50	art or practice	12
act or result	23	action or state	10
person or animal	22	girl or woman	10
act or sound	18	state or condition	10

The number of different pairs of genus terms is very high, each pair having a rather low frequency. Of the 2898 non-complex genus terms coordinated with 'or' there are 1908 different pairs. Those with 10 or more occurrences are shown in Table 13.2.

No coordinations with *etc.* have a frequency greater than 3 ("newspaper, magazine, etc." and "letters, parcels, etc.") and none with *and* occur more than 4 times ("copper and coin", "study and practice").

As far as the interpretation of the coordinations is concerned two major classes can be distinguished: either the coordinated elements are alternatives between which a choice has to be made (e.g. "albino: an animal or plant..."), or the entry word is a complex WHOLE of which they are components or constituents, as seen in the previous section. There are also examples where *and* is used with a temporal meaning which can also be regarded as describing the elements of a complex event denoting whole:

montage 3   the choosing, cutting and combining together of separate
photographic material...

Composites are always coordinated with *and*, but coordination with *and* does not necessarily result in a composite as is illustrated by the following examples, where *and* seems to be used to indicate non-exclusive alternatives:

growing pains 1   aches and pains in the limbs...

glamour 1   charm and beauty with a romantic power of attraction

wealth   money and possessions

However, most alternatives are indicated by the use of *or* or *etc.* Examination of the definitions suggests that a distinction can be usefully made between *close* and *distant* alternatives. Close alternatives share many features and will probably be found in the same section of the taxonomy:

allegory 1   a story, poem, painting, etc., in which...

tribulation   trouble, grief, worry, suffering, etc.

albino 2   an animal or plant that lacks the typical colouring

breeder   an animal, bird or fish that produces young

A special case of close alternatives is *level alternatives* in which a superordinate word is coordinated with a subordinate:

acorn   the fruit or nut of the oak tree...

bearer 5   a fruit-producing tree or plant

In these examples the entry word is related to its genus but also directly to the genus of the genus:

nut[1] **1**   a dry fruit with a seed...

tree[1] **1**   a type of tall plant...

Distant alternatives (coordinator is always 'or') share few features and will be found in quite separate parts of the taxonomy.

threat 2   a person, thing or idea regarded as a possible danger

stationer   a person or shop that sells stationery

non-starter   a person or idea without any chance of success

borer   a person, tool or insect that makes round holes

legend 5   a famous person or act, esp. in a particular area of activity

performer   a person (or thing) that performs (2), esp an actor, musician etc.

Both close and distant alternatives could in principle be represented by use of a disjunctive feature structure. However, our LRL does not permit disjunction of arbitrary feature structures. If it were allowed, the computational problems could be considerable, since inheritance from a disjunctive feature structure would tend to yield a feature structure with more complex disjunction. The operation which we use instead is that of generalisation, ⊔, the opposite of unification, which yields a single, non-disjunctive feature structure, containing only the information common to both feature structures. For example, the lexical entry for *albino 2* would be:

```
albino L_0_2
lex-count-noun
< QUALIA > < ( animal_L_1_1+2 < QUALIA >
              \/ plant_L_2_1 < QUALIA > ) <> .
```

The generalisation of two level alternatives will result in a psort which is equivalent to the higher of the two, except in the case where some inherited values were overridden by the lower alternative, since if $F_1 \sqsubseteq F_2$ then $F_1 \sqcup F_2 = F_2$.

For the close alternatives the decision not to allow disjunction in the LKB does not seem unduly restrictive. A reasonably specific psort can be produced by generalisation, and this allows quite well for the use of *etc.*, which disjunction would not (as *etc.* presumably indicates that some members of a class are being enumerated). On the whole we expect that if the type system is set up in a way which accords with the lexicographer's intuitions about classes, generalisation will tend to give a reasonably specific and appropriate result.

Distant alternatives are more problematic because the results of generalisation will be very uninformative. The feature structure resulting from analysing 'person, tool or insect' in the definition of *borer* above, for example, will be of type **physical**, the most general type for concrete nouns. This seems to be a case where the disjunction would be preferable because it would carry so much more information. One alternative would be to split the entries into different senses. However, it is quite noticeable that many distant alternatives arise in definitions of derived nominals. In cases such as *borer* the LDOCE lexicographers seem to have used the genus terms more loosely than usual to indicate the prototypical agents or instruments of an action. If taken strictly, this definition and a considerable proportion of the other LDOCE definitions of derived nominals seem over-restrictive; here worms and molluscs are excluded, which seems inappropriate. Our proposed representation of derived nominals in the LKB involves the use of default inheritance from the result of the application of a regular morphological rule to the verb, and thus the bulk of the information in the lexical entry would not be derived from the genus term. In those cases such as *borer*, which are formed by subject nominalisation (Bauer, 1983), information about the lexical semantic type of the derived nominal will be derived from the selectional restriction on the subject of the verb. Hence using the (relatively) uninformative generalisation as a psort is a better option than taking the probably over-restrictive disjunction.

Thus our common strategy for both close and distant alternatives is to take the generalisation of the psorts involved. Although this might lead to an under-specified type for the lexical entry in the case of those distant alternatives where there is no connection with a verb entry, at least it is possible to detect such entries, and to make use of other strategies (possibly even user intervention) in order to further refine them.

13.6   Relatedness of Senses

Taxonomies are built out of links between word senses. In some cases, however, this is an over-simplification. Words used as genus terms often have more than one sense of which several may apply in the definition in which they have been used. In some cases, discussed in Copestake (1990b) and Vossen (1990b), the lexicographer has made a distinction between closely related senses which are best treated as generating a single lexical entry in the LKB, since it is difficult to disambiguate the use of the genus term manually (and impossible automatically), and the resulting lexical entries would in any case not be distinguishable, at least with our current type system and approach to lexical semantics. For these cases we generate a single psort for the merged sense from which other entries can inherit. However, there are other cases where this is not possible.

For example, *cake* and *stone* have separate senses in which they are countable (grammar code 'C') and uncountable (grammar code 'U').

Headword	Sense	Code	Definition
cake	1	U	a food made by baking ...
	2	C	a piece of this food
stone	1	C	a piece of rock, esp. ...
	2	U	solid mineral material

In the following entries where either *cake* or *stone* is the genus word the un-countable and countable uses have been merged into one sense, and both senses of *cake* or *stone* apply.

Headword	Sense	Code	Definition
gâteau		U; C	a specially attractive type of cream cake
seedcake		C; U	(a) sweet cake containing...
tortilla		C; U	(a) thin round flat cake made...
diamond		C; U	a very hard, valuable, precious stone, ...
onyx		C; U	a (type of) precious stone ...
opal		C; U	a (type of) precious stone which ...

In other examples, however, only one sense is applicable:

Headword	Sense	Code	Definition
bun	1	C	a small round sweet cake
shortbread		U	a thin hard kind of sweet cake ...
pebble	1	C	a small roundish smooth stone ...
portland stone		U	a type of yellowish-white stone...

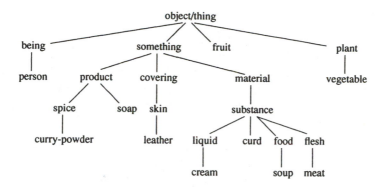

Figure 13.10: Partial taxonomy showing variations in classification

Thus it would not be appropriate to merge the senses of *cake* and *stone*.

Where such polysemy is regular it can be handled by formulating sense extension rules. In these particular cases the portioning rule mentioned in section 13.4.1 would be applicable; this captures the fact that mass nouns denoting some kinds of substance, in particular foodstuffs, can also refer to portions of that substance. Assuming that it is possible to detect that the rule is applicable to the lexical entries generated for these definitions, the relationship between the senses can be derived straightforwardly. However, recognition of merged senses is complicated in practice by the kind reading which makes it possible for any mass nouns to be used as count nouns (e.g. 'Portland stone is a limestone' is equivalent to 'Portland stone is a type of limestone'); the lexicographers sometimes give count grammar codes as an option in order to mark this usage when it is especially frequent (e.g. *fabric*). (Since the kind reading is always possible, a lexical or grammar rule would be used to allow for this in a complete system; it is not necessary or desirable to give distinct kind senses in the LKB.)

13.7 Variation in Classification

Given the set of features that make up a definition, lexicographers make different choices to select one feature to be represented as the genus and the other features as the differentiae. This choice affects the structure of the taxonomy that will come out and with it the process of inheritance. In a systematic hierarchy one would expect that, for example, all substances are also interrelated with the word *substance*. From the partial taxonomy shown in Figure 13.10, which is based on the definitions in LDOCE, it can be seen that this is not always the case. Words such as *soap* and all *spices* are defined as *product*, which is in no way related to *substance*. The feature structure inherited via *substance* has to be derived in some other way for these words. Similar things can be said for edible objects and substances which are not found as subordinates of *food*: *fruit*, *vegetable*, *cream, meat.* In the case of *curd* the level of *food* is completely bypassed and it is directly classified as *substance.* These different classifications seem to be triggered by either primarily taking a more functional perspective (*food, covering, product*) and specifying the constitutional properties in the differentiae (*soup* is 'liquid food') or by primarily taking a more constitutional perspective (*substance*) and specifying the functional properties as additional.

This variation in classification (Vossen, 1990b, 1991) can be described in terms of:

1. a different priming of features: given a set of features that are essential for the meaning of a word, a lexicographer can make a different choice in selecting one feature as the genus and the other features as the differentiae.

2. a different abstraction of features: given a set of features a lexicographer can always choose to classify the sense at a more abstract level and to specify the extra discriminating features as differentiae.

In the following examples two features, 'covering' and 'material', seem to compete for the status of genus:

armour   strong protective covering on fighting vehicles,...

blanket   a thick, esp. woollen covering...

carpet   heavy woven often woollen material for covering floors or stairs

daub   (a) soft sticky material for covering surfaces like walls

These sort of examples illustrate the inadequacies of taxonomies when taken in isolation. The type system is intended to allow a more consistent classification; all the examples above would share the type **artifact-physical,** for example. But in order to represent such entries multiple inheritance in the LKB may be desirable. For example, we could specify that *soup* inherited from two psorts *liquid* and *food.* The type system separates features which describe function (the TELIC role in the qualia structure) from those describing form (the FORMAL role). Although some information about physical form is inherited from psorts such as those for *food*, which primarily denote function, and thus conflicts are potentially possible, no such clear cases have yet actually arisen where this would happen. The more serious difficulty with dealing with such definitions is the extraction of the extra information. Currently we do not attempt to represent such definitions by multiple inheritance because the issues of automatically extracting a secondary genus term are far from straightforward.

In the following examples different abstraction levels are chosen for the genus terms. In the case of *curd* and *cream 1* the edibility is explicitly expressed in the differentiae, whereas it would be inherited for *cream 3* and *cheese* from *food*:

curd   the thick soft almost solid substance that separates from milk when it becomes sour, eaten as food or used for making cheese

cream 1   the thick fatty slightly yellowish liquid that separates from and rises to the top of milk when left to stand, and is eaten as food,...

cream 3   food made of or containing a sweet soft smooth substance, like this

cheese   soft or firm solid food made from pressed and sometimes ripened milk solids

A possible interpretation of this difference could be that edibility is less significant for *curd* and *cream 1*. Arguably the distinction could be captured, to some extent, in the LKB by giving different features different weights according to the way they are represented in a particular definition. However no mechanism is provided in the LRL for capturing such a distinction. Weighting features differentially does have some utility in creating links between LKB entries derived from different dictionaries semi-automatically (for which see Copestake *et al.*, 1992) but it is not clear how it would be used in the final representation.

13.8   Conclusion

Our experiences with these problematic definitions in the LKB have lead us to augment its syntax to allow specification of equality, subsumption and generalisation, which were part of the underlying LRL but not accessible to the user. This allows us to represent many cases of coordination and also to represent synonymy more elegantly. In contrast, treatment of complex kernels has lead us to consider the semantics of the linguistic constructions involved and the likely implications for inheritance in the particular case of dictionary definitions. However, we do not yet have a good treatment of COMPONENT/WHOLE relationships. It appears that in these cases and some others it is not possible to determine the semantic type from the definitions without some fairly complex inference. For example:

loaf[1] 1   bread shaped and baked in one piece, usu. fairly large

Here we do not have a straightforward trigger in the genus phrase, such as *piece of*, which allows us to recognise that a type shift from an unindividuated substance to an individuated object has occurred. Instead the information is in the differentiae. The genus, which is *bread* in the mass sense, refers to the material which is the input of a process (baking and shaping) which results in an individuated homogeneous entity. In general there are a variety of nominal definitions where the genus term cannot be used to determine the type by itself, because of a temporal, change of state element in the definition. (The example of *charlotte*, given in section 13.4.3, also illustrates this effect.) Ultimately determining the semantic type for such entries will probably involve having a sufficiently detailed lexicon to recognise what the type shift involved might be (e.g. that the change of state induced by *shape* results in an individuated object) and using knowledge of the general domain (e.g. food) to characterise the most likely shifts.

In general we have discussed the classes of definitions which a combination of statistical investigations and our extensive experience of LDOCE suggest are the most important exceptions to the simple treatment of noun taxonomies described in Copestake (this volume). We have tried to show how the LKB representations suggested are consistent with the semantics of the definitions. Although the semantics of the constructions involved are, in general, complex and not well understood, we have found that we can make some simplifying assumptions and treat LDOCE definitions as a specialised sublanguage, which allows us to extend the process of semi-automatically constructing a lexicon containing detailed lexical semantic information to a large class of noun definitions.

Appendix A: A Bibliography of ACQUILEX Papers Connected with the LKB

Ageno, A., S. Cardoze, I. Castellon, M.A. Marti, G. Rigau, H. Rodriguez, M. Taule and M.F. Verdejo (1991) *An Environment for the Management and Extraction of Taxonomies from On-line Dictionaries.*
ESPRIT BRA-3030 ACQUILEX WP NO.20

Ageno, A., I. Castellon, M.A. Marti, G. Ribas, G. Rigau, H. Rodriguez, M. Taule and M.F. Verdejo (1991) *The Extraction of Semantic Information from MRDs.*
ESPRIT BRA-3030 ACQUILEX WP NO.28

Ageno, A., I. Castellon, M.A. Marti, G. Ribas, G. Rigau, H. Rodriguez, M. Taule and M.F. Verdejo (1991) *SEISD: User Manual. Guide to the Extraction and Conversion of Taxonomies.*
ESPRIT BRA-3030 ACQUILEX WP NO.30

Ageno, A., I. Castellon, M.A. Marti, G. Ribas, G. Rigau, H. Rodriguez, M. Taule and M.F. Verdejo (1992) *A semi-automatic process to create LKB entries.*
ESPRIT BRA-3030 ACQUILEX WP NO.38

Ageno, A., I. Castellon, M.A. Marti, G. Ribas, G. Rigau, H. Rodriguez, M. Taule and M.F. Verdejo (1992) *From LDB to LKB.*
ESPRIT BRA-3030 ACQUILEX WP NO.39

Ageno, A., I. Castellon, G. Rigau, H. Rodriguez, M.F. Verdejo, M.A. Marti and M. Taule (1992) 'SEISD: An Environment for Extraction of Semantic Information from On-Line Dictionaries', *Proceedings of the 3rd Conference on Applied Natural Language Processing (ANLP-92)*, Trento, Italy, pp. 253–255.

Briscoe, E. (1991) 'Lexical Issues in Natural Language Processing' in E. Klein and F. Veltman (eds.), *Natural Language and Speech*, Springer-Verlag, pp. 39–68.
ESPRIT BRA-3030 ACQUILEX WP NO.41

Briscoe, E., A. Copestake and B. Boguraev (1990) 'Enjoy the Paper: Lexical Semantics via Lexicology', *Proceedings of the 13th Coling*, Helsinki, pp. 42–47.
ESPRIT BRA-3030 ACQUILEX WP NO.11

Briscoe, E. and A. Copestake (1991) 'Sense Extensions as Lexical Rules', *Proceedings of the IJCAI Workshop on Computational Approaches to Non-Literal Language*, Sydney, Australia, pp. 12–20.
ESPRIT BRA-3030 ACQUILEX WP NO.22

Calzolari, N. (1991) 'Acquiring and Representing Semantic Information in a Lexical Knowledge Base', *Proceedings of the Proceedings of ACL SIGLEX Workshop on Lexical Semantics and Knowledge Representation*, Berkeley, California, pp. 188–198.
ESPRIT BRA-3030 ACQUILEX WP NO.16

Copestake, A. (1990) 'An approach to building the hierarchical element of a lexical knowledge base from a machine readable dictionary', *Proceedings of the Workshop on Inheritance in Natural Language Processing*, Tilburg, The Netherlands, pp. 19–29.

ESPRIT BRA-3030 ACQUILEX WP NO.8

Copestake, A. (1992) 'The ACQUILEX LKB: Representation Issues in Semi-automatic Acquisition of Large Lexicons', *Proceedings of the 3rd Conference on Applied Natural Language Processing (ANLP-92)*, Trento, Italy, pp. 88–96.

ESPRIT BRA-3030 ACQUILEX WP NO.36

Copestake, A. (1992) 'The Representation of Group Denoting Nouns in a Lexical Knowledge Base', *Proceedings of the Second Seminar on Computational Lexical Semantics*, Toulouse, France, pp. 106–118.

ESPRIT BRA-3030 ACQUILEX WP NO.37

Copestake, A. and E. Briscoe (1991) 'Lexical Operations in a Unification Based Framework', *Proceedings of the ACL SIGLEX Workshop on Lexical Semantics and Knowledge Representation*, Berkeley, California, pp. 88–101.

ESPRIT BRA-3030 ACQUILEX WP NO.21

Copestake, A., B. Jones, A. Sanfilippo, H. Rodriguez, P. Vossen, S. Montemagni and E. Marinai (1992) *Multilingual Lexical Representation*.

ESPRIT BRA-3030 ACQUILEX WP NO.43

Montemagni S. and L. Vanderwende (1992) 'String Patterns versus Structural Patterns for Extracting Semantic Information from Dictionaries', *Proceedings of the COLING '92*, Nantes, France.

ESPRIT BRA-3030 ACQUILEX WP NO.32

Montemagni, S. (1992) 'Specializing a Broad Coverage Grammar for the Analysis of Dictionary Definitions', *Proceedings of the 5th EURALEX*, Tampere, Finland.

ESPRIT BRA-3030 ACQUILEX WP NO.23

Östling, A. (1991) *Sense Extensions in the Italian Food Subset*.

ESPRIT BRA-3030 ACQUILEX WP NO.24

Sanfilippo, A. and V. Poznanski (1992) 'The Acquisition of Lexical Knowledge from Combined Machine-Readable Sources', *Proceedings of the 3rd Conference on Applied Natural Language Processing (ANLP-92)*, Trento, Italy, pp. 80–88.

ESPRIT BRA-3030 ACQUILEX WP NO.35

Sanfilippo, A., E. Briscoe, A. Copestake, M.A. Marti and A. Alonge (1992) 'Translation Equivalence and Lexicalization in the ACQUILEX LKB', *Proceedings of the 4th International Conference on Theoretical and Methodological Issues in Machine Translation (TMI-92)*, Montreal, Canada.

ESPRIT BRA-3030 ACQUILEX WP NO.42

Vossen, P. (1991) *Converting Data from a Lexical Database to a Knowledge Base*.

ESPRIT BRA-3030 ACQUILEX WP NO.27

Vossen, P. (1992) 'An Empirical Approach to Automatically Constructing a Knowledge Base from Dictionaries', *Proceedings of the 5th EURALEX*, Tampere, Finland.

Appendix B: The LKB Description Language Syntax

The description language which is used to define feature structures in the LKB is loosely based on the path notation used in PATR, with : used to separate features. However, in a notation for a typed system it must be possible to specify the types of non-terminal nodes in the feature structure; in the LKB this may be done either by making the type the value of the relevant path or by specifying the type in the path (as an optional value, before the feature). For example:

```
< lex-count-noun QUALIA :
        physical FORM : RELATIVE > = individuated
```

is equivalent to:

```
<> = lex-count-noun
< QUALIA > = physical
< QUALIA : FORM : RELATIVE > = individuated
```

Instead of specifying the empty path in a path value specification, the type name alone can be used:

```
lex-count-noun
< QUALIA > = physical
< QUALIA : FORM : RELATIVE > = individuated
```

A path can also be specified as having a value which has a particular relationship with a feature structure which is either some specified part of another named feature structure or some combination of such feature structures. (Ordinary path/value equations can be seen as a special case of this, where the feature structure is the constraint on the type.) The possible relationships are:

    == Equality
    <= Non-default inheritance (subsumption)
    < Default inheritance

Operators available to combine feature structures are:

    /\ Unification
    \/ Generalisation
    + Lexical rule application

The following examples are intended to illustrate the syntax:

```
down L_0_1
lex-uncount-noun
< QUALIA > < ( FEATHER_L_1_1 + plural ) < QUALIA >
```

```
< QUALIA : FORM : RELATIVE > = mass .
```
This lexical entry is defined as inheriting its qualia feature, by default, from the qualia of the result of applying the morphological rule, plural, to the lexical entry for a particular sense of *feather*.

```
albino L_0_2
lex-count-noun
< QUALIA > <= ( animal_L_1_1+2 < QUALIA >
              \/  plant_L_2_1 < QUALIA > ) < > .
```
The lexical entry for *albino* is described as inheriting its qualia from the generalisation of the qualia of the two other lexical entries.

BNF Description of the Syntax

The lexical entry description language consists of statements which allow relationships between feature structures to be represented.

```
Lexentry -> LexID PPath_spec⁺
LexID -> orth sense-id
PPath_spec -> EPath < FS | EPath <= FS | EPath == FS
           | EPath =* Typevalue | Path_spec | typename
FS -> psortname Epath | CFS Epath
CFS -> ( FS \/ FS ) | ( FS /\ FS )
           | ( CFS + rulename ) | ( psortname + rulename )
Path_spec -> EPath = Typevalue | Path = Path
Typevalue -> typename | ( typename⁺ )
Epath -> Path | <>
Path -> < Type_F_pair_list >
Type_F_pair_list -> Type_Feature_pair
           | Type_Feature_pair :  Type_F_pair_list
Type_Feature_pair -> [typename] feature
```
orth, sense-id, typename, psortname, rulename and feature are terminal symbols.

Lexical rules and translation links differ from lexical entries only in that the identifier is not split.

A rather more limited language is available for the definition of types.

```
Type specification ->
            typename Parents [Comment][Constraint] .
Comment -> " string "
Parents -> ( typename* )
Constraint -> Path_spec_list | Enumeration
Path_spec_list -> Path_spec*
Enumeration -> ( OR typename⁺ )
```
Enumeration is syntactic sugar for enumerated atomic types. For example:

```
state (Top) (OR solid liquid gas).
```

expands out into the equivalent of:

```
state (Top).
solid (state).
liquid (state).
gas (state).
```

Appendix C: Software Availability

LKB

A stand-alone version of the LKB software system, with demonstration type systems, lexicons and so on is available for distribution; contact the authors for further details.

The Sussex DATR Implementation

The Sussex implementation of DATR comprises a compiler written in Prolog, and a wide-ranging collection of DATR example files. The compiler takes a DATR theory and produces Prolog code for query evaluation relative to that theory. The code is readily customisable, and customisations for Poplog Prolog, CProlog, Arity Prolog, Prolog2, Quintus Prolog and Sicstus Prolog are provided. Source listings, documentation and many of the example files may also be found in "The DATR Papers, Volume 1" (Cognitive Science Research Report 139).

This implementation is provided 'as is', with no warranty or support, and for research purposes only. Copyright remains with the University of Sussex.

The Prolog source code and the example files for the DATR system are available on a 720K 3.5 inch MS-DOS disk for £12.00 (within the UK) or US $25 (outside the UK) from: **Technical Reports, School of Cognitive and Computing Sciences, University of Sussex, Brighton BN1 9QH, UK**. "The DATR Papers, Volume 1" (Cognitive Science Research Report 139) is also available for £6 (US $12) from the same address.

References

Abdulrad, H. and J-P. Pécuchet (1990) 'Solving word equations', in C. Kirchner (ed.), *Unification*, Academic Press, Orlando, Florida.

Aït-Kaci, H. (1984) *A Lattice Theoretic Approach to Computation Based on a Calculus of Partially Ordered Types Structures*, PhD thesis, University of Pennsylvania.

Aït-Kaci, H. (1986) 'An Algebraic Semantics Approach to the Effective Resolution of Type Equations', *Theoretical Computer Science*, vol. 45, 293–351.

Aït-Kaci, H. (1986) 'Solving type equations by graph rewriting', in J-P. Jouannaud (ed.), *Rewriting techniques and applications*, Lecture Notes in Computer Science, vol. 202, Springer-Verlag, Berlin, pp. 158–179.

Aït-Kaci, H. and A. Podelski (1991) 'Towards a meaning of LIFE', in J. Maluszynski and M. Wirsing (eds.), *Proceedings of the 3rd International Symposium on Programming Language Implementation and Logic Programming (PLILP-91)*, Lecture Notes in Computer Science, vol. 528, Springer-Verlag, Berlin, pp. 255–274.

Ageno, A., I. Castellon, G. Rigau, H. Rodriguez, M. F. Verdejo, M. A. Marti and M. Taule (1992) 'SEISD: An environment for extraction of semantic information from on-line dictionaries', *Proceedings of the 3rd Conference on Applied Natural Language Processing (ANLP-92)*, Trento, Italy, pp. 253–255.

Allen, J. H. and H. B. Greenough (1903) *New Latin Grammar*, Ginn and Company, Boston.

Allport, D. (1988a) 'Understanding RTA's', *Proceedings of the UK IT Conference 1988*, Swansea, Wales.

Allport, D. (1988b) 'The TIC: Parsing interesting text', *Proceedings of the 2nd ACL Conference on Applied Natural Language Processing (ANLP-88)*, Austin, Texas.

Amsler, R. A. (1980) *The Structure of the Merriam-Webster Pocket Dictionary*, PhD thesis, University of Texas, Austin.

Amsler, R. A. (1981) 'A taxonomy for English nouns and verbs', *Proceedings of the 19th Annual Meeting of the Association for Computational Linguistics (ACL)*, Stanford, California, pp. 133–138.

Anderson, S. R. (1988a) 'Inflection', in M. Hammond and M. Noonan (eds.), *Theoretical Morphology*, Academic Press, Orlando, Florida, pp. 23–43.

Anderson, S. R. (1988b) 'Morphological Theory', in F. J. Newmeyer (ed.), *Linguistics: The Cambridge Survey, vol. 1*, Cambridge University Press, Cambridge, pp. 146–91.

Andry, F., N. M. Fraser, S. McGlashan, S. Thornton and N. J. Youd (1992) 'Making DATR Work for Speech: Lexicon Compilation in SUNDIAL', *Computational Linguistics*, vol. 18.3, 245–267.

Aronoff, M. (1976) *Word Formation in Generative Grammar*, Linguistic Inquiry Monograph 1. MIT Press, Cambridge, Massachusettes.

Asher, N. and M. Morreau (1991) 'Commonsense entailment — A modal theory of nonmonotonic reasoning', *Proceedings of the 12th International Joint Conference on Artificial Intelligence (IJCAI-91)*, Sydney, Australia, pp. 387–392.

Bach, E. (1988) 'Categorial grammars as theories of language', in R. T. Oehrle, E. Bach and D. Wheeler (eds.), *Categorial Grammars and Natural Language Structures*, D. Reidel, Dordrecht and Boston, pp. 17–34.

Backofen, R., L. Euler and G. Görz (1990) 'Towards the integration of functions, relations and types in an AI programming language', *Proceedings of the 16th German Workshop on AI (GWAI-90)*, Springer-Verlag, Berlin

Bauer, L. (1983) *English Word-formation*, Cambridge University Press, Cambridge.

van den Berg, M. and H. Prüst (1991) 'Common denominators and default unification', *Proceedings of the Computational Linguistics in the Netherlands (CLIN), First Meeting*, Utrecht, The Netherlands, pp. 1–16.

Bird, S. (1990) *Prosodic morphology and constraint-based phonology*, Research Paper EUCCSRP-38, Centre for Cognitive Science, University of Edinburgh.

Boguraev, B. and E. J. Briscoe (1989) *Computational lexicography for natural language processing*, Longman, London.

Borgida, A., R. J. Brachman, D. L. McGuiness and L. A. Resnick (1989) 'CLASSIC: A structural data model for objects', *Proceedings of the 1989 ACM SIGMOD International Conference on Management of Data*, Portland, Oregon.

Bouma, G. (1990a) 'Defaults in unification grammar', *Proceedings of the 28th Annual Meeting of the Association for Computational Linguistics (ACL)*, Pittsburg, Pennsylvania, pp. 165–173.

Bouma, G. (1990b) 'Non-monotonic inheritance and unification', *Proceedings of the First International Workshop on Inheritance in Natural Language Processing*, Tilburg, The Netherlands, pp. 1–8.

Brachman, R. J. and J. G. Schmolze (1985) 'An overview of the KL-ONE knowledge representation language', *Cognitive Science*, vol. 9, 171–216.

Brachman, R. J., V. P. Gilbert and H. J. Levesque (1985) 'An essential hybrid reasoning system: Knowledge and symbol level accounts of Krypton', *Proceedings of the 9th International Joint Conference on Artificial Intelligence (IJCAI-85)*, Los Angeles, California, pp. 532–539.

Bresnan, J. (1982) *The Mental Representation of Grammatical Relations*, MIT Press, Cambridge, Massachusettes.

Bresnan, J. and J. Kanerva (1989) 'Locative inversion in Chichewa: A case study of factorization in grammar', *Linguistic Inquiry*, vol. 20, 1–50.

Briscoe, E. J. (1991) 'Lexical Issues in Natural language Processing', in E. Klein and F. Veltman (eds.), *Natural Language and Speech*, Springer-Verlag, Berlin, pp. 39–68.

Briscoe, E. J., A. Copestake and B. Boguraev (1990) 'Enjoy the paper: Lexical semantics via lexicology', *Proceedings of the 13th International Conference on Computational Linguistics (COLING-90)*, Helsinki, Finland, pp. 42–47.

Briscoe, E. J. and A. Copestake (1991) 'Sense extensions as lexical rules', *Proceedings of the IJCAI Workshop on Computational Approaches to Non-Literal Language*, Sydney, Australia, pp. 12–20.

Briscoe, E. J., A. Copestake and A. Lascarides (in press) 'Blocking', in P. St. Dizier and E. Viegas (eds.), *Computational Lexical Semantics*, Cambridge University Press, Cambridge.

Bunt, H. (1985) *Mass Terms and Model-theoretic semantics*, Cambridge Studies in Linguistics 42, Cambridge University Press, Cambridge.

Cahill, L. J. and R. Evans (1990) 'An application of DATR: The TIC lexicon', *Proceedings of the 9th European Conference on Artificial Intelligence (ECAI-90)*, Stockholm, Sweden, pp. 120–125.

Calder, J. (1987) 'Typed unification for natural language processing', in E. Klein and J. van Benthem (eds.), *Categories, Polymorphism and Unification*, Centre for Cognitive Science, University of Edinburgh, pp. 65–72.

Calder, J. (1989) 'Paradigmatic morphology', *Proceedings of the 4th Conference of the European Chapter of the Association for Computational Linguistics (EACL)*, Manchester, England, pp. 58–65.

Calder, J. (1991) *Some notes on Priority Union*, Paper presented at the ACQUILEX Workshop on Default Inheritance in the Lexicon, Cambridge, England.

Cardelli, L. and P. Wegner (1985) 'On understanding types, data abstraction, and polymorphism', *ACM Computing Surveys*, vol. 17.4, 471–522.

Carlson, G. (1984) 'On the role of thematic roles in linguistic theory', *Linguistics*, vol. 22, 259–279.

Carpenter, R. (1989) *PROP: A Prolog implementation of PATR-II*, Technical Report LCL-89-3, Laboratory for Computational Linguistics, Carnegie Mellon University.

Carpenter, R. (1990) 'Typed feature structures: Inheritance, (in)equality and extensionality', *Proceedings of the First International Workshop on Inheritance in Natural Language Processing*, Tilburg, The Netherlands, pp. 9–18.

Carpenter, R. (1991) 'The generative power of categorial grammars and Head-Driven Phrase Structure Grammar with lexical rules', *Computational Linguistics*, vol. 17.3, 301–313.

Carpenter, R. (1992) *The Logic of Typed Feature Structures*, Tracts in Theoretical Computer Science. Cambridge University Press, Cambridge.

Carpenter, R., C. Pollard and A. Franz (1991) 'The specification and implementation of constraint-based unification grammars', *Proceedings of the 2nd International Workshop on Parsing Technologies*, Cancun, Mexico, pp. 143–154.

Carroll, J. and C. Grover (1989) 'The derivation of a large computational lexicon for English from LDOCE', in B. Boguraev and E. J. Briscoe (eds.), *Computational lexicography for natural language processing*, Longman, London, pp. 117–134.

Chodorow, M. S., R. J. Byrd and G. E. Heidorn (1985) 'Extracting semantic hierarchies from a large on-line dictionary', *Proceedings of the 23rd Annual Meeting of the Association for Computational Linguistics (ACL)*, University of Chicago, pp. 299–304.

Chomsky, N. (1970) 'Remarks on Nominalization', in R. Jacobs and P. Rosenbaum (eds.), *Readings in English Transformational Grammar*, Ginn, Waltham, Mass..

Cook, W., W. Hill and P. Canning (1990) 'Inheritance is not subtyping', *Proceedings of the SIGACT-SIGPLAN — Symposium on Principles of Programming Languages (POPL)*, San Francisco, California.

Copestake, A. (1990a) *Some Notes on Mass Terms and Plurals*, Technical Report 190, Computer Laboratory, University of Cambridge, England.

Copestake, A. (1990b) 'An approach to building the hierarchical element of a lexical knowledge base from a machine readable dictionary', *Proceedings of the First International Workshop on Inheritance in Natural Language Processing*, Tilburg, The Netherlands, pp. 19–29.

Copestake, A. (1992a) 'The representation of group denoting nouns in a lexical knowledge base', *Proceedings of the Second Seminar on Computational Lexical Semantics*, Toulouse, France, pp. 106–118.

Copestake, A. (1992b) 'The ACQUILEX LKB: Representation issues in semi-automatic acquisition of large lexicons', *Proceedings of the 3rd Conference on Applied Natural Language Processing (ANLP-92)*, Trento, Italy, pp. 88–96.

Copestake, A. and E. J. Briscoe (1991) 'Lexical operations in a unification based framework', *Proceedings of the ACL SIGLEX Workshop on Lexical Semantics and Knowledge Representation*, Berkeley, California, pp. 88–101.

Copestake, A., B. Jones, A. Sanfilippo, H. Rodriguez, P. Vossen, S. Montemagni and E. Marinai (1992) *Multilingual Lexical Representation*, ACQUILEX Working Paper no. 043, University of Cambridge.

Cruse, D. A. (1986) *Lexical Semantics*, Cambridge University Press, Cambridge.

Daelemans, W., K. de Smedt and G. Gazdar (1992) 'Inheritance in natural language processing', *Computational Linguistics*, vol. 18.2, 205–218.

Davey, B. A. and H. Priestley (1990) *Introduction to Lattices and Order*, Cambridge Mathematical Textbooks, Cambridge University Press, Cambridge.

Dawar, A. and K. Vijay-Shanker (1989) 'A three-valued interpretation of negation in feature structures descriptions', *Proceedings of the 27th Annual Meeting of the Association for Computational Linguistics (ACL)*, Vancouver, Canada, pp. 18–24.

Delgrande, J. P. (1988) 'An approach to default reasoning based on a first-order conditional logic: Revised report', *Artificial Intelligence*, vol. 36, 63–90.

Dershowitz, N. and D. A. Plaisted (1988) 'Equational programming', in J. E. Hayes, D. Michie and J. Richards (eds.), *Machine Intelligence 11*, Clarendon Press, Oxford, pp. 21–56.

Dik, S. C. (1978) *Stepwise Lexical Decomposition*, Peter de Ridder Press, Lisse, The Netherlands.

Dörre, J. and A. Eisele (1989) 'Determining consistency of feature terms with distributed disjunctions', in D. Metzing (ed.), *Proceedings of GWAI-89 (15th German Workshop on AI, Berlin)*, Springer-Verlag, Berlin, pp. 270–279.

Dörre, J. and A. Eisele (1991) *A comprehensive unification-based grammar formalism*, Technical Report Deliverable R3.1.B, DYANA, Centre for Cognitive Science, Edinburgh.

Dowty, D. (1982a) 'More on the categorial analysis of grammatical relations', *Proceedings of the Harvard Conference on Grammatical Relations: Subjects and Other Subjects*, Bloomington, Indiana.

Dowty, D. (1982b) 'Grammatical relations and Montague grammar', in P. Jacobson and G. K. Pullum (eds.), *The Nature of Syntactic Representation*, D. Reidel, Dordrecht, The Netherlands, pp. 79–130.

Dowty, D. (1989) 'On the semantic content of the notion 'Thematic Role'', in G. Chierchia, B. Partee and R. Turner (eds.), *Property Theory, Type Theory and Natural Language Semantics*, D. Reidel, Dordrecht, The Netherlands, pp. 69–129.

Dowty, D. (1991) 'Thematic proto-roles and argument selection', *Language*, vol. 67, 547–619.

Emele, M. (1991) 'Unification with lazy non-redundant copying', *Proceedings of the 29th Annual Meeting of the Association for Computational Linguistics (ACL)*, Berkeley, California, pp. 323–330.

Emele, M. and R. Zajac (1990a) 'A fixed-point semantics for feature type systems', *Proceedings of the 2nd Workshop on Conditional and Typed Rewriting Systems – CTRS-90*, Montreal, Canada.

Estival, D. (1990) ELU *User Manual*, Technical Report 1, ISSCO, Geneva, Switzerland.

Evans, R. (1987) 'Towards a formal specification of defaults in GPSG', in E. Klein and J. van Benthem (eds.), *Categories, Polymorphism and Unification*, University of Edinburgh, pp. 73–93.

Evans, R. (1990) 'An introduction to the Sussex Prolog DATR Implementation', in R. Evans and G. Gazdar (eds.), *The DATR Papers*, Cognitive Science Research Paper

CSRP 139, School of Cognitive and Computing Sciences, University of Sussex, pp. 63–72.

Evans, R. and G. Gazdar (1989a) 'Inference in DATR', *Proceedings of the 4th Conference of the European Chapter of the Association for Computational Linguistics (EACL)*, Manchester, England, pp. 66–71.

Evans, R. and G. Gazdar (1989b) 'The semantics of DATR', in A. G. Cohn (ed.), *Proceedings of the Seventh Conference of the Society for the Study of Artificial Intelligence and Simulation of Behavior (AISB)*, Pitman/Morgan Kaufmann, London, pp. 79–87.

Evans, R. and G. Gazdar (1990) *The DATR Papers. Cognitive Science Research Paper CSRP 139*, School of Cognitive and Computing Sciences, University of Sussex.

Evans, R., R. Gaizauskas and A. F. Hartley (1990) *POETIC — The Portable Extendable Traffic Information Collator*, OECD Workshop on Knowledge-Based Expert Systems in Transportation, Espoo, Finland.

Flickinger, D. (1987) *Lexical Rules in the Hierarchical Lexicon*, PhD thesis, Stanford University.

Flickinger, D. and J. Nerbonne (1992) 'Inheritance and complementation: A case study of *easy* adjectives and related nouns', *Computational Linguistics*, vol. 18.3, 269–310.

Flickinger, D., C. Pollard and T. Wasow (1985) 'Structure sharing in lexical representation', *Proceedings of the 23rd Annual Meeting of the Association for Computational Linguistics (ACL)*, University of Chicago, pp. 262–268.

Franz, A. (1990) *A Parser for HPSG*, Technical Report LCL-90-3, Laboratory for Computational Linguistics, Carnegie Mellon University.

Fraser, N. and R. Hudson (1992) 'Inheritance in word grammar', *Computational Linguistics*, vol. 18.2, 133–158.

Gabbay, D. (1985) 'Theoretical foundations for nonmonotonic reasoning in expert systems', in K. Apt (ed.), *Logics and Models of Concurrent Systems*, Springer-Verlag, Berlin, pp. 439–457.

Gazdar, G. (1987) 'Linguistic applications of default inheritance mechanisms', in P. Whitelock, H. Somers, P. Bennett, R. Johnson and M. McGee Wood (eds.), *Linguistic Theory and Computer Applications*, Academic Press, London, pp. 37–68.

Gazdar, G. (1990) 'An introduction to DATR', in R. Evans and G. Gazdar (eds.), *The DATR Papers. Cognitive Science Research Paper CSRP 139*, School of Cognitive and Computing Sciences, University of Sussex, pp. 1–14.

Gazdar, G., E. Klein, G. Pullum and I. Sag (1985) *Generalized Phrase Structure Grammar*, Basil Blackwell, Oxford.

Gazdar, G., E. Klein, G. Pullum, R. Carpenter, T. Hukari and R. Levine (1988) 'Category structures', *Computational Linguistics*, vol. 14, 1–19.

Gibbon, D. (1989) **PCS-DATR:** *A DATR Implementation in* **PC Scheme**, English/Linguistics Interim Report No. 3, University of Bielefeld.

Goguen, J. A. and J. Meseguer (1987) *Unifying Functional, Object-Oriented and Relational Programming with Logical Semantics*, CSLI Report CLSI-87-93, Stanford University.

Grimshaw, J. (1990) *Argument Structure*, MIT Press, Cambridge, Massachusetts.

Gunther, C. and D. Scott (1991) 'Semantic domains', in J. van Leeuwen (ed.), *Handbook of Theoretical Computer Science*, Elsevier Science Publishers, pp. 634–674.

Guthrie, L., B. M. Slator, Y. Wilks and R. Bruce (1990) 'Is there content in empty heads?', *Proceedings of the 13th International Conference on Computational Linguistics (COLING-90)*, Helsinki, Finland, pp. 138–143.

Hardy, S. (1982) *The POPLOG Programming Environment*, Cognitive Studies Research Paper No. CSRP82-06, University of Sussex.

Hobbs, J., W. Croft, T. Davies, D. Edwards and K. Laws (1987) 'Commonsense metaphysics and lexical semantics', *Computational Linguistics,* vol. 13, 241–250.

Hoeksema, J. (1985) *Categorial Morphology,* Garland, New York.

Huet, G. (1976) *Résolution d'équations dans les langages d'ordre 1, 2, . . . , ω,* PhD thesis, Université de Paris VII, September 1976.

Jackendoff, R. (1990) *Semantic Structures,* MIT Press, Cambridge, Massachusetts.

Johnson, M. (1988) *Attribute Value Logic and the Theory of Grammar,* Center for the Study of Language and Information, Stanford, California.

Johnson, R. and M. Rosner (1989) 'A rich environment for experimentation with unification grammars', *Proceedings of the 4th Conference of the European Chapter of the Association for Computational Linguistics (EACL),* Manchester, England, pp. 182–189.

Kaplan, R. (1987) 'Three seductions of computational psycholinguistics', in P. Whitelock, H. Somers, P. Bennett, R. Johnson, and M. McGee Wood (eds.), *Linguistic Theory and Computer Applications,* Academic Press, London, pp. 149–188.

Kaplan, R. and J. Bresnan (1982) 'Lexical-functional grammar: A formal system for grammatical representation', in J. Bresnan (ed.), *The Mental Representation of Grammatical Relations,* MIT Press, Cambridge, Massachusetts, pp. 173–281.

Karttunen, L. (1984) 'Features and values', *Proceedings of the 10th International Conference on Computational Linguistics (COLING-84),* Stanford, California, pp. 28–33.

Karttunen, L. (1986) 'D-PATR: A development environment for unification-based grammars', *Proceedings of the 11th International Conference on Computational Linguistics (COLING-86),* Bonn, Germany, pp. 74–80.

Karttunen, L. (1986) *D-PATR: A development environment for unification-based grammars,* Technical Report CSLI-86-61, Center for the Study of Language and Information, Stanford University.

Kasper, R. T. and W. C. Rounds (1986) 'A logical semantics for feature structures', *Proceedings of the 24th Annual Conference of the Association for Computational Linguistics,* Columbia University, pp. 235–242.

Kasper, R. T. and W. C. Rounds (1990) 'The logic of unification in grammar', *Linguistics and Philosophy,* vol. 13.1, 35–58.

Kathol, A. (1991) *Verbal and adjectival passives in German,* MIT Working Papers in Linguistics, vol. 14, MIT Press, Cambridge, Massachusetts.

Kay, M. (1984) 'Functional unification grammar: A formalism for machine translation', *Proceedings of the 10th International Conference on Computational Linguistics (COLING-84),* Stanford, California, pp. 75–78.

Kay, M. (1985) 'Parsing in functional unification grammar', in D. Dowty and L. Karttunen (eds.), *Natural Language Parsing,* Cambridge University Press, Cambridge, pp. 251–278.

Keene, S. (1989) *Object-Oriented Programming in Common Lisp,* Addison-Wesley, Reading, Massachusetts.

Kilbury, J., P. Naerger, and I. Renz (1991) 'DATR as a lexical component for PATR', *Proceedings of the 6th Conference of the European Chapter of the Association for Computational Linguistics (EACL),* Berlin.

Klavans, J. L. and N. Wacholder (1990) 'From dictionary to knowledge base via taxonomy', *Proceedings of the 6th annual Conference of the Waterloo Centre for the New OED and Text Retrieval,* Waterloo, Canada.

Klop, J. W. (1991) 'Term rewriting systems', in S. Abramsky, D. Gabbay and T. Maibaum (eds.), *Handbook of Logic in Computer Science,* vol. 1, Oxford University Press, Oxford.

Konolige, K. (1988) 'On the relation between default and autoepistemic logic', *Artificial Intelligence,* vol. 35, 343–382.

Koskenniemi, K. (1983) 'Two-level model for morphological analysis', *Proceedings of the Eighth International Joint Conference on Artificial Intelligence (IJCAI-83),* Karlsruhe, Germany, pp. 683–685.

Krieger, H.-U. (1991) *Eliminating complex non-reversible functions in derivational morphology,* Technical Report xx, Deutsches Forschungsinstitut für Künstliche Intelligenz, Saarbrücken, Germany.

Krifka, M. (1987) 'Nominal reference and temporal constitution: Towards a semantics of quantity', *Proceedings of the 6th Amsterdam Colloquium,* University of Amsterdam, pp. 153–173.

Landau, S. I. (1984) *Dictionaries: The Art and Craft of Lexicography,* Scribner, New York.

Landman, F. (1989) 'Groups I + II', *Linguistics and Philosophy,* vol. 12 (5,6), 559–606, 723–744.

Lécluse, C., P. Richard and F. Velez (1988) 'O₂, an object-oriented data model', *Proceedings of the ACM SIGMOD Conference,* Chicago, Illinois.

Levin, B. (1988, in press) 'Approaches to lexical semantic representation', in D. Walker, A. Zampolli and N. Calzolari (eds.), *Automating the Lexicon: Research and Practice in a Multilingual Environment,* Cambridge University Press, Cambridge.

Levin, B. (1992) *Towards a Lexical Organization of English Verbs,* University of Chicago Press, Chicago.

Levinson, S. C. (1983) *Pragmatics,* Cambridge University Press, Cambridge.

Makinson, D. (1989) 'A general theory of cumulative inference', in Reinfrank, de Kleer, Ginsberg and Sandewall (eds.), *Nonmonotonic Reasoning,* Lecture Notes in Artificial Intelligence, vol. 346, Springer-Verlag, Berlin.

Matthews, P. H. (1972) *Inflectional Morphology: A Theoretical Study Based on Aspects of Latin Verb Conjugation,* Cambridge University Press, Cambridge.

Matthews, P. H. (1974) *Morphology,* Cambridge University Press, Cambridge.

McCarthy, J. (1980) 'Circumscription — a form of nonmonotonic reasoning', *Artificial Intelligence,* vol. 13 (1,2), 27–40.

McCarthy, J. (1986) 'Applications of circumscription to formalizing common-sense knowledge', *Artificial Intelligence,* vol. 28, 89–116.

Mellish, C. M. (1988) 'Implementing systemic classification by unification', *Computational Linguistics,* vol. 14.1, 40–51.

Moens, M., J. Calder, E. Klein, M. Reape and H. Zeevat (1989) 'Expressing generalizations in unification-based grammar formalisms', *Proceedings of the 4th Conference of the European Chapter of the Association for Computational Linguistics (EACL),* Manchester, England, pp. 66–71.

Montemagni, S. and L. Vanderwende (1992) 'String patterns versus structural patterns for extracting semantic information from dictionaries', *Proceedings of the 15th International Conference on Computational Linguistics (COLING-92),* Nantes, France, pp. 546–552.

Moore, R. (1985) 'Semantical considerations on nonmonotonic logic', *Artificial Intelligence,* vol. 25, 75–94.

Moortgat, M., T. Hoekstra and H. van der Hulst (1980) *Lexical Grammar,* Foris, Dordrecht, The Netherlands.

Moshier, M. D. (1988) *Extensions to Unification Grammar for the Description of Programming Languages,* PhD thesis, University of Michigan.

Moshier, M. D. and W. C. Rounds (1987) 'A logic for partially specified data structures', *Proceedings of the 14th ACM Symposium on the Principles of Programming Languages*, Munich, Germany, pp. 156–167.

Nunberg, G. (1978) *The Pragmatics of Reference*, PhD thesis, University of California, reproduced by the Indiana University Linguistics Club.

Nunberg, G. and A. Zaenen (1992) 'Systematic polysemy in lexicology and lexicography', *Proceedings of the Euralex*, Tampere, Finland.

Östling, A. (1991) *Sense Extensions in the Italian Food Subset*, ACQUILEX Working Paper no. 024, University of Pisa.

Parsons, T. (1980) 'Modifiers and quantifiers in natural language', *Canadian Journal of Philosophy*, vol. VI, 29–60.

Parsons, T. (1990) *Events in the Semantics of English: A Study in Subatomic Semantics*, MIT Press, Cambridge, Massachusetts.

Pelletier, F. J., and L. K. Schubert (1986) 'Mass Expressions', in D. Gabbay and F. Guenthner (eds.), *Handbook of Philosophical Logic, Vol. 4*, Reidel, Dordrecht, The Netherlands.

Pereira, F. C. N. and S. M. Shieber (1984) 'The semantics of grammar formalisms seen as computer languages', *Proceedings of the 10th International Conference on Computational Linguistics (COLING-84)*, Stanford, California, pp. 123–129.

Pollard, C. (1984) *Generalized Phrase Structure Grammars, Head Grammars, and Natural Language*, Unpublished PhD Dissertation, Stanford University.

Pollard, C. and I. Sag (1987) *An Information-Based Approach to Syntax and Semantics: Volume 1 Fundamentals*, CSLI Lecture Notes 13, Stanford, California.

Pollard, C. J. and M. D. Moshier (1990) 'Unifying partial descriptions of sets' in P. Hanson (ed.) *Information, Language and Cognition*, vol. 1 of *Vancouver Studies in Cognitive Science*. University of British Columbia Press, Vancouver, Canada.

Procter, P. (ed.) (1978) *Longman Dictionary of Contemporary English*, Longman, London.

Pustejovsky, J. (1989) 'Current issues in computational lexical semantics', *Proceedings of the 4th Conference of the European Chapter of the Association for Computational Linguistics (EACL)*, Manchester, England, pp. xvii–xxv.

Pustejovsky, J. (1991) 'The Generative Lexicon', *Computational Linguistics*, vol. 17.4, 409–441.

Reape, M. (1991) *An introduction to the semantics of unification-based grammar formalisms*, Technical Report R3.2.A, DYANA, University of Edinburgh.

Reiter, R. (1980) 'A logic for default reasoning', *Artificial Intelligence*, vol. 13, 81–132.

Ritchie, G. D., S. G. Pulman, A. W. Black and G. Russell (1987) 'A computational framework for lexical description', *Computational Linguistics*, vol. 13.3,4), 290–307.

Rounds, W. C. and R. T. Kasper (1986) 'A complete logical calculus for record structures representing linguistic information', *Proceedings of the 1st Annual IEEE Symposium on Logic in Computer Science*, Cambridge, Massachusetts, pp. 38–43.

Russell, G., J. Carroll and S. Warwick (1990) 'Multiple inheritance in a unification-based lexicon', *Proceedings of the First International Workshop on Inheritance in Natural Language Processing*, Tilburg, The Netherlands, pp. 93–103.

Russell, G., J. Carroll and S. Warwick (1991) 'Multiple default inheritance in a unification-based lexicon', *Proceedings of the 29th Annual Meeting of the Association for Computational Linguistics (ACL)*, Berkeley, California, pp. 215–221.

Sadock, J. (1985) 'Autolexical syntax: A proposal for the treatment of noun incorporation and similar phenomena', *Natural Language and Linguistic Theory*, vol. 3, 379–439.

Sag, I. and C. Pollard (1987) *Head-driven phrase structure: An informal synopsis*, Technical Report CSLI-87-89, Center for the Study of Language and Information, Stanford University.

Sanfilippo, A. (1990) *Grammatical Relations, Thematic Roles and Verb Semantics*, PhD thesis. Centre for Cognitive Science, University of Edinburgh.

Sanfilippo, A. and V. Poznanski (1992) 'The acquisition of lexical knowledge from combined machine-readable sources', *Proceedings of the 3rd Conference on Applied Natural Language Processing (ANLP-92)*, Trento, Italy, pp. 80–88.

Sanfilippo, A., E. J. Briscoe, A. Copestake, M. A. Marti and A. Alonge (1992) 'Translation equivalence and lexicalization in the ACQUILEX LKB', *Proceedings of the 4th International Conference on Theoretical and Methodological Issues in Machine Translation (TMI-92)*, Montreal, Canada.

Schiannini, D. (1984) *Il Nuovo Dizionario Italiano Garzanti*, Garzanti, Italy.

Schmolze, J. G. and T. A. Lipkis (1983) 'Classification in the KL-ONE knowledge representation system', *Proceedings of the Eighth International Joint Conference on Artificial Intelligence (IJCAI-83)*, Karlsruhe, Germany, pp. 330–332.

Selman, B. and H. J. Levesque (1989) 'The tractability of path-based inheritance', *Proceedings of the Eleventh International Joint Conference on Artificial Intelligence (IJCAI-89)*, Detroit, Michigan, pp. 1140–1145.

Shieber, S. M., H. Uszkoreit, F. C. N. Pereira, J. Robinson and M. Tyson (1983) *The formalism and implementation of PATR-II*, Research on Interactive Acquisition and Use of Knowledge, SRI Final Report, no. 1894. SRI International, Menlo Park, California.

Shieber, S. M. (1986) *An Introduction to Unification-Based Approaches to Grammar*, CSLI Lecture Notes 4, Stanford, California.

de Smedt, K. (1984) 'Using object-oriented knowledge representation techniques in morphology and syntax programming', in T. O'Shea (ed.), *Proceedings of the 6th European Conference on Artificial Intelligence (ECAI-84)*, Elsevier, Amsterdam, pp. 181–184.

Smolka, G. (1988) *A feature logic with subsorts*, LILOG-REPORT 33, IBM – Deutschland GmbH, Stuttgart, Germany.

Smolka, G. (1989) *Feature constraint logics for unification grammars*, IWBS Report 93, IBM – Deutschland GmbH, Stuttgart, Germany. To appear in *Journal of Logic Programming*.

Smolka, G. and H. Aït-Kaci (1988) 'Inheritance hierarchies: Semantics and unification', *Journal of Symbolic Computation*, vol. 7, 343–370.

Steedman, M. (1985) 'Dependency and coordination in the grammar of Dutch and English', *Language*, vol. 61, 523–568.

Steele Jr., G. L. (1990) *Common Lisp*, Digital Press, Bedford, Massachusetts, second edition.

Tennison, B. (1975) *Sheaf Theory*, London Mathematical Society Lecture Notes, vol. 20, Cambridge University Press, Cambridge.

Toman, J. (1983) *Wortsyntax: Eine Diskussion ausgewählter Probleme deutscher Wortbildung*, Niemeyer, Tübingen, Germany.

Touretzky, D. S. (1986) *The Mathematics of Inheritance Systems*, Pitman/Morgan Kaufmann, London; Los Altos, California.

Touretzky, D. S., J. F. Horty and R. M. Thomason (1987) 'A clash of intuitions: The current state of nonmonotonic multiple inheritance systems', *Proceedings of the Tenth International Joint Conference on Artificial Intelligence (IJCAI-87)*, Milan, Italy, pp. 476–482.

Trost, H. (1990) 'The application of two-level morphology to non-concatenative German morphology', *Proceedings of the 13th International Conference on Computational Linguistics (COLING-90)*, Helsinki, Finland, pp. 371–376.

Truszczyński, M. (1991) 'Modal interpretations of default logic', *Proceedings of the 12th International Joint Conference on Artificial Intelligence (IJCAI-91)*, Sydney, Australia, pp. 393–398.

Veltman, F. (1991) *Defaults in Update Semantics*, ITLI prepublication series LP-91-02, University of Amsterdam, The Netherlands.

Vossen, P. (1990a) *A Parser-Grammar for the Meaning Descriptions of LDOCE*, Links Project Technical Report 300-169-007, University of Amsterdam.

Vossen, P. (1990b) 'The end of the chain: Where does stepwise lexical decomposition lead us eventually?', *Proceedings of the 4th Functional Grammar Conference*, Kopenhagen, Denmark.

Vossen, P. (1991) *Comparing noun-taxonomies cross-linguistically*, ACQUILEX Working Paper no. 014, University of Amsterdam.

Zaenen, A. (1993) 'Unaccusativity in Dutch: Integrating syntax and lexical semantics', in J. Pustejovsky (ed.), *Semantics and the Lexicon*, Kluwer Academic, Dordrecht.

Zajac, R. (1990) *Semantics of typed feature structures*, Presented at the *International Workshop on Constraint Based Formalisms for Natural Language Generation*, Bad Teinach, Germany, November 1990.

Zeevat, H., E. Klein and J. Calder (1987) 'An Introduction to Unification Categorial Grammar', in N. Haddock, E. Klein and G. Morrill (eds.), *Categorial Grammar, Unification Grammar, and Parsing: Working Papers in Cognitive Science*, vol. 1, Centre for Cognitive Science, University of Edinburgh, pp. 195–222.

Zwicky, A. M. (1985) 'How to describe inflection', *Proceedings of the 11th Annual Meeting of the Berkeley Linguistics Society*, Berkeley, California, pp. 372–86.

Zwicky, A. M. (1990) 'Inflectional morphology as a (sub)component of grammar', in W. U. Dressler, H. C. Luschützky, O. E. Pfeiffer and J. R. Rennison (eds.), *Contemporary Morphology*, Mouton de Gruyter, Berlin, pp. 217–236.

Author index

Subject Index